HISTORY

OF THE

WAR IN THE PENINSULA

AND IN THE

SOUTH OF FRANCE

FROM THE YEAR 1807 TO THE YEAR 1814

VOLUME IV

HISTORY

OF THE

WAR IN THE PENINSULA

AND IN THE

SOUTH OF FRANCE,

FROM THE YEAR 1807 TO THE YEAR 1814.

BY

W. F. P. NAPIER, C.B.

COLONEL H. P. FORTY-THIRD REGIMENT, MEMBER OF THE ROYAL SWEDISH ACADEMY OF MILITARY SCIENCES.

VOL. IV.

CONSTABLE · LONDON

This edition first published in Great Britain 1993
by Constable and Company Limited
3 The Lanchesters, 162 Fulham Palace Road
London W6 9ER

Originally published in London in 1834
by Thomas and William Boone

ISBN 0 09 471870 9

Printed in Great Britain by
St Edmundsbury Press Ltd
Bury St Edmunds, Suffolk

TABLE OF CONTENTS.

BOOK XIII.

CHAP. I.

CHAP. II.

CHAP. III.

CHAP. IV.

CHAP. V.

CHAP. VI.

BOOK XIV.

CHAP. I.

CHAP. II.

CHAP. III.

CHAP. IV.

BOOK XV.

CHAP. I.

CHAP. II.

CHAP. III.

CHAP. IV.

CHAP. V.

BOOK XVI.

CHAP. I.

APPENDIX.

LIST OF PLATES.

ERRATA.

Page 3, line 23, *for* "armies" *read* "parties."
. . 35, . . 9, *for* "prisoners" *read* "provisions."

NOTICE.

In addition to the manuscript authorities used for the former volumes, several memoirs, journals, and notes of officers employed in the different operations have been consulted for this volume. Amongst others, the Journal of general Harvey of the Portuguese service, and some original papers supplied by sir Howard Douglas.

HISTORY

OF THE

PENINSULAR WAR.

BOOK XIII.

CHAPTER I.

CHAP. I. 1810.

While marshal Beresford followed Soult towards Llerena lord Wellington recommenced the siege of Badajos, but the relation of that operation must be delayed until the transactions which occurred in Spain, during Massena's invasion of Portugal, have been noticed, for it is not by following one stream of action that a just idea of this war can be obtained. Many of lord Wellington's proceedings might be called rash, and others timid, and slow, if taken separately; yet, when viewed as parts of a great plan for delivering the whole Peninsula, they will be found discreet or daring, as the circumstances warranted: nor is there any portion of his campaigns, that requires this wide-based consideration, more than his early sieges; which, being instituted contrary to the rules of art, and unsuccessful, or, when successful, attended with a mournful slaughter, have given occasion for questioning his great military qualities, which were however, then most signally displayed.

BOOK XIII.

1810.

OPERATIONS IN SPAIN.

In the northern provinces the events were of little interest. Gallicia after the failure of Renovales' expedition and the shipwreck that followed, became torpid; the junta disregarded general Walker's exhortations, and, although he furnished vast supplies, the army, nominally twenty thousand strong, mustered only six thousand in the field: there was no cavalry, and the infantry kept close in the mountains about Villa Franca, while a weak French division occupied the rich plains of Leon. General Mahi having refused to combine his operations with those of the Anglo-Portuguese army, was thought to be disaffected, and at the desire of the British authorities had been removed to make way for the duke of Albuquerque: he was however immediately appointed to the command of Murcia, by Blake, in defiance of the remonstrances of Mr. Wellesley, for Blake disregarded the English influence.

See Vol. III p. 404.

Official abstract of general Walker's despatches

Official abstract of Mr. Wellesley's despatches MSS.

When Albuquerque died, Gallicia fell to Castaños, and while that officer was co-operating with Beresford in Estremadura, Santo-cildes assumed the command. Meanwhile Caffarelli's reserve having joined the army of the north, Santona was fortified, and Bessieres, as I have before observed, assembled seven thousand men at Zamora to invade Gallicia.

See Vol. III pp. 312, 407, and 475.

In the Asturias, Bonet, although harassed, on the side of Potes, by the Guerillas from the mountains of Liebaña; and on the coast by the English frigates, remained at Oviedo, and maintained his communications by the left with the troops in Leon.

In November 1810 he defeated a considerable body of insurgents, and in February 1811 the Spanish general St. Pol retired before him with the regular forces, from the Xalon to the Navia; but this retreat caused such discontent in Gallicia that St. Pol advanced again on the 19th March, and was again driven back. Bonet then dispersed the Partidas, and was ready to aid Bessieres' invasion of Gallicia; and although the arrival of the allied forces on the Coa in pursuit of Massena stopped that enterprise, he made an incursion along the coast, seized the Spanish stores of English arms and clothing, and then returned to Oviedo. The war was, indeed, so little formidable to the French, that in May Santander was evacuated, and all the cavalry in Castile and Leon joined Massena for the battle of Fuentes Onoro, and yet the Gallician and Asturian regular armies gained no advantage during their absence.

Mr Stuart's Papers, MSS.

The Partidas, who had re-assembled after their defeat by Bonet, were more active. Porlier, Campillo, Longa, Amor, and Merino cut off small French armies in the Montaña, in the Rioja, in Biscay, and in the Baston de Laredo; they were not, indeed, dangerous in action, nor was it very difficult to destroy them by combined movements, but these combinations were hard to effect, from the little accord amongst the French generals, and thus they easily maintained their posts at Espinosa de Monteres, Medina, and Villarcayo. Campillo was the most powerful after Porlier. His principal haunts were in the valleys of Mena and Caranza; but he was in communication with Barbara, Honejas, and Curillas, petty chiefs of Biscay, with whom he concerted attacks upon couriers and weak

Intercepted letter of general Barthelemy to general Drouet, 1810. MSS.

BOOK XIII. 1810. detachments: and he sometimes divided his band into small parties, with which he overran the valleys of Gurieso, Soba, Carrado, and Jorrando, partly to raise contributions, partly to gather recruits, whom he forced to join him. His chief aim was, however, to intercept the despatches going from Bilbao to Santander, and for this purpose he used to infest Liendo between Ovira and Laredo, which he was enabled the more safely to do, because general Barthelemy, the governor of the Montaña, was forced to watch more earnestly towards the hilly district of Liebana, between Leon and the Asturias. This district was Porlier's strong-hold, and that chief, under whom Campillo himself would at times act, used to cross the Deba and penetrate into the valleys of Cabuerniego, Rio Nauza, Cieza, and Buelna, and he obliged the people to fly to the mountains with their effects whenever the French approached: nevertheless the mass were tired of this guerilla system and tractable enough, except in Liebana.

To beat Campillo once or twice would have been sufficient to ruin him, but to ruin Porlier required great combinations. It was necessary to seize Espinosa, not that of Monteres, but a village in the mountains of Liebana, from whence the valleys all projected as from a point, and whence the troops could consequently act towards Potes with
1811. success. General Barthelemy proposed this plan to Drouet, then with the 9th corps on the Upper Douro, whom he desired to co-operate from the side of Leon, while Bonet did the same from the side of the Asturias: but though partially adopted, the execution was not effectually followed up, the districts of Liebana and Santander continued to

be disturbed, and the chain of Partidas was prolonged through Biscay and the Rioja, to Navarre.

1811. May.

In this last province Mina had on the 22d of May defeated at the Puerto de Arlaban, near Vittoria, twelve hundred men who were escorting a convoy of prisoners and treasure to France; his success was complete, but alloyed by the death of two hundred of the prisoners, unfortunately killed during the tumult; and it was stained by the murder of six Spanish ladies, who, for being attached to French officers, were in cold blood executed after the fight. Massena, whose baggage was captured, was to have travelled with this escort, but disliking the manner of the march, he remained in Vittoria until a better opportunity, and so escaped.

MrStuart's Papers, MSS.

These partizan operations, combined with the descents on the coast, the aspect of the war in Estremadura, and the unprotected state of Castile, which was now menaced by Santo-cildes, were rendered more important by another event to be noticed hereafter: Bessieres therefore resolved to contract his position in the north; and first causing Reille and Caffarelli to scour Biscay and the Rioja, he ordered Bonet to abandon the Asturias. On the 14th of June that general, having dismantled the coast-batteries, sent his sick and baggage by sea to St. Ander and marched into Leon, where Santo-cildes, who had now increased the Gallician field army to thirteen thousand men, was menacing Astorga, which place the French evacuated after blowing up some of the works. Serras and Bonet then united on the Esla, and being supported by three thousand men from Rio Seco, skirmished at the Ponte de Orvigo on the 23d, but had the

BOOK XIII. 1811. June.

worst, and general Valletaux was killed on their side: and as lord Wellington's operations in Estremadura soon drew the French armies towards that quarter Santo-cildes held his ground at Astorga until August. Meanwhile two thousand French were thrown into Santona, and general Rognet coming, from the side of Burgos, with a division of the young guard, made a fruitless incursion against the Partidas of Liebana.

This system of warfare was necessarily harassing to the French divisions actually engaged, but it was evident that neither the Asturias nor Gallicia could be reckoned as good auxiliaries to lord Wellington. Gallicia with its lordly junta, regular army, fortified towns, rugged fastnesses, numerous population, and constant supplies from England, was of less weight in the contest than five thousand Portuguese militia conducted by Trant and Wilson. The irregular warfare was now also beginning to produce its usual effects; the tree though grafted in patriotism bore strange fruit. In Biscay, which had been longest accustomed to the presence of the invaders, the armed peasantry were often found fighting in the ranks of the enemy, and on one occasion did of themselves attack the boats of the Amelia frigate to save French military stores! Turning now to the other line of invasion, we shall find the contest fiercer, indeed, and more honourable to the Spaniards, but the result still more unfavourable to their cause.

Appendix. No. I. Section 1.

OPERATIONS IN THE EASTERN PROVINCES.

It will be remembered that Suchet, after the fall

1811. June.

of Mequinenza, was ordered to besiege Tortoza while Macdonald marched against Taragona. Massena was then concentrating his army for the invasion of Portugal, and it was the emperor's intention that Suchet should, after taking Tortoza, march with half of the third corps to support the prince of Esling. But the reduction of Tortoza proved a more tedious task than Napoleon anticipated, and as the course of events had now given the French armies of Catalonia and Aragon a common object, it will be well to compare their situation and resources with those of their adversary.

Suchet was completely master of Aragon, and not more by the force of his arms, than by the influence of his administration; the province was fertile, and so tranquil in the interior, that his magazines were all filled, and his convoys travelled under the care of Spanish commissaries and conductors. Mina was however in Navarre on his rear, and he communicated on the right bank of the Ebro with the Partidas in the mountains of Moncayo and Albaracin; and these last were occasionally backed by the Empecinado, Duran, and others whose strong-holds were in the Guadalaxara, and who from thence infested Cuença and the vicinity of Madrid. From Albaracin, Villa Campa continued the chain of partizan warfare and connected it with the Valencian army, which had also a line of operation towards Cuença. Mina, who communicated with the English vessels in the bay of Biscay, received his supplies from Coruña; and the others, in like manner, corresponded with Valencia, from whence the English consul Tupper suc-

BOOK XIII. 1811. June.

coured them with arms, money, and ammunition. Thus a line was drawn quite across the Peninsula which it was in vain for the enemy to break, as the retreat was secure at both ends, and the excitement to renewed efforts constant.

On the other flank of Suchet's position the high valleys of the Pyrenees were swarming with small bands, forming a link between Mina and a division of the Catalonian army stationed about the Seu d'Urgel, which was a fortified castle, closing the passage leading from the plain of that name to the Cerdaña: this division in conjunction with Rovira, and other partizans, extended the irregular warfare on the side of Olot and Castelfollit to the Ampurdan; and the whole depended upon Taragona, which itself was supported by the English fleet in the Mediterranean. Aragon may therefore be considered as an invested fortress, which the Spaniards thought to reduce by famine, by assault, and by exciting the population against the garrison; but Suchet baffled them; he had made such judicious arrangements that his convoys were secure in the interior, and all the important points on the frontier circle were fortified, and connected, with Zaragoza, by chains of minor ports radiating from that common centre. Lerida, Mequinenza, and the plain of Urgel in Catalonia, the fort of Morella in Valencia, were his; and by fortifying Teruel and Alcanitz he had secured the chief passages leading through the mountains to the latter kingdom: he could thus, at will, invade either Catalonia or Valencia, and from Mequinenza he could, by water, transport the stores necessary to besiege Tortoza. Nor were these advantages the result of aught but his uncommon talents for war, a consideration which rendered them doubly formidable.

The situation of the French in Catalonia was different. Macdonald, who had assumed the command at the moment when Napoleon wished him to co-operate with Suchet, was inexperienced in the peculiar warfare of the province, and unprepared to execute any extended plan of operations. His troops were about Gerona and Hostalrich, which were in fact the bounds of the French conquest at this period; for Barcelona was a military point beyond their field systόm, and only to be maintained by expeditions; and the country was so exhausted of provisions in the interior, that the army itself could only be fed by land-convoys from France, or by such coasters as, eluding the vigilance of the English cruizers, could reach Rosas, St. Filieu, and Palamos. Barcelona like the horse-leech continually cried for more, and as the inhabitants as well as the garrison depended on the convoys, the latter were enormous, reference being had to the limited means of the French general, and the difficulty of moving; for, although the distance between Hostalrich and Barcelona was only forty miles, the road, as far as Granollers, was a succession of defiles, and crossed by several rivers, of which the Congosta and the Tordera were considerable obstacles; and the nature of the soil was clayey and heavy, especially in the defiles of the Trenta Pasos.

These things rendered it difficult for Macdonald to operate in regular warfare from his base of Gerona, and as the stores for the siege of Taragona were to come from France, until they arrived he

BOOK XIII. 1810. July.

could only make sudden incursions with light baggage, trusting to the resources still to be found in the open country, or to be gathered in the mountains by detachments which would have to fight for every morsel. This then was the condition of the French armies, that starting from separate bases, they had to operate on lines meeting at Tortoza. It remains to shew the situation of the Catalan general.

After the battle of Margalef, Henry O'Donnel reunited his scattered forces, and being of a stern unyielding disposition, not only repressed the discontent occasioned by that defeat, but forced the reluctant Miguelettes to swell his ranks and to submit to discipline. Being assisted with money and arms by the British agents, and having free communication by sea with Gibraltar, Cadiz, and Minorca, he was soon enabled to reorganize his army, to collect vast magazines at Taragona, and to strengthen that place by new works. In July his force again amounted to twenty-two thousand men exclusive of the Partidas, and of the Somatenes, who were useful to aid in a pursuit, to break up roads, and to cut off straggling soldiers. Of this number one division under Campo Verde, was, as I have before said, in the higher valleys, having a detachment at Olot, and being supported by the fortified castles of Seu D'Urgel, Cardona, Solsona, and Berga. A second division was on the Llobregat, watching the garrison of Barcelona, and having detachments in Montserrat, Igualada, and Manresa to communicate with Campo Verde. The third division, the reserve and the cavalry were on the hills about Taragona, and that place and Tortoza had large garrisons.

CHAP. I.

1810. July.

By this disposition, O'Donnel occupied Falcet, the Col de Balaguer, and the Col del Alba, which were the passages leading to Tortoza; the Col de Ribas and Momblanch, which commanded the roads to Lerida; San Coloma de Queralt and Igualada, through which his connection with Campo-Verde was maintained; and thus the two French armies were separated not only by the great spinal ridges descending from the Pyrenees, but by the position of the Spaniards, who held all the passes, and could at will concentrate and attack either Suchet or Macdonald. But the Catalonian system was now also connected with Valencia, where, exclusive of irregulars, there were about fifteen thousand men under General Bassecour. That officer had in June occupied Cuença, yet having many quarrels with his officers he could do nothing, and was driven from thence by troops from Madrid: he returned to Valencia, but the disputes continued and extended to the junta or congress of Valencia, three members of which were by the general imprisoned. Nevertheless, as all parties were now sensible that Valencia should be defended at Tortoza, Bassecour prepared to march to its succour by the coast road where he had several fortified posts. Thus, while Suchet and Macdonald were combining to crush O'Donnel, the latter was combining with Bassecour, to press upon Suchet; and there was always the English maritime force at hand to aid the attacks or to facilitate the escape of the Spaniards.

General Doyle's Correspondence, MSS. Colonel Green's do. MSS.

Official Abstracts of Mr. Wellesley's Despatches, MSS. Mr. Stuart's Papers, MSS.

In the above exposition I have called the native armies by the names of their provinces, but in December 1810 the whole military force being reorganized by the regency the armies were designated by numbers. Thus the Catalonian forces,

BOOK XIII. 1810. July.

formerly called *the army of the right*, was now called the *first army*. The Valencians, together with Villa Campa's division, and the partidas of the Empecinado and Duran, were called the *second army*. The Murcian force was called the *third army*. The troops at Cadiz, at Algesiras, and in the Conde Niebla were called the *fourth army*. The remnants of Romana's old Gallician division which had escaped the slaughter on the Gebora formed the *fifth army*. The new-raised troops of Gallicia and those of the Asturias were called the *sixth army*. And the partidas of the north, that is to say, Mina's, Longa's, Campillo's, Porlier's, and other smaller bands formed the *seventh army*.

Such was the state of affairs when Napoleon's order to besiege Tortoza arrived. Suchet was ready to execute it. More than fifty battering guns selected from those at Lerida were already equipped, and his depots were established at Mequinenza, Caspe, and Alcanitz. All the fortified posts were provisioned; twelve thousand men under general Musnier, intended for the security of Aragon, were disposed at Huesca and other minor points on the left bank of the Ebro, and at Daroca, Teruel, and Calatayud on the right bank; and while these arrangements were being executed, the troops destined for the siege had assembled at Lerida and Alcanitz, under generals Habert and Laval, their provisions being drawn from the newly conquered district of Urgel.

From Mequinenza, which was the principal depot, there was water-carriage, but as the Ebro was crossed at several points by rocky bars, some of which were only passable in full water, the communication was too uncertain to depend upon, and

Suchet therefore set workmen to reopen an old road thirty miles in length, which had been made by the duke of Orleans during the war of the succession. This road pierced the mountains on the right bank of the Ebro, passed through Batea and other places to Mora, and from thence by Pinel to Tortoza, running through a celebrated defile called indifferently the *Trincheras* and the *Passage of Arms*. When these preliminary arrangements were made general Habert assembled his division at Belpuig near Lerida, and after making a feint as if to go towards Barcelona, suddenly turned to his right, and penetrating through the district of Garriga, reached Garcia on the left bank of the Lower Ebro the 5th of July. Laval at the same time quitted Alcanitz, made a feint towards Valencia by Morella, and then turning to his left, came so unexpectedly upon Tortoza by the right bank of the Ebro, that he surprized some of the outposts on the 2d, and then encamped before the bridge-head. The 4th he extended his line to Amposta, seized the ferry-boat of the great road from Barcelona to Valencia, and posted Boussard's cuirassiers, with a battalion of infantry and six guns, at Uldecona, on the Cenia river, to observe Bassecour's Valencians.

See plans, No. 1 & 3.

During these operations Suchet fixed his own quarters at Mora, and as the new road was not finished, he occupied Miravet, Pinel, and the Trincheras, on its intended line; and having placed flying bridges, with covering works, on the Ebro, at Mora and Xerta, made those places his depôt of siege. He likewise seized the craft on the river, established posts at Rapita, near the mouth of the Ebro, and at Amposta, and made a fruitless attempt

BOOK XIII. 1810. July.

to burn the boat bridge of Tortoza, with fire vessels. Following Napoleon's order, Macdonald should at this time have been before Taragona; but on the 9th, Suchet learned, from a spy, that the seventh corps was still at Gerona, and he thus found himself exposed alone to the combined efforts of the Catalans and Valencians. This made him repent of having moved from Aragon so soon, yet thinking it would be bad to retire, he resolved to blockade Tortoza; hoping to resist both O'Donnel and Bassecour until Macdonald could advance.

The Spaniards who knew his situation, sallied on the right bank the 6th and 8th, and on the 10th his outposts on the left bank were driven in at Tivisa by a division from Falcet, which, the next day, fell on his works at Mora, but was repulsed; and the 12th, general Paris pushed back the Spanish line, while Habert took post in force at Tivisa, by which he covered the roads to Xerta and Mora. O'Donoghue, who commanded Bassecour's advanced guard, now menaced Morella, but general Montmarie being detached to its succour, drove him away.

The 30th, O'Donnel having brought up fresh troops to Falcet, made a feint with ten thousand men against Tivisa, and then suddenly entered Tortoza, from whence at mid-day, on the 3d of August, he passed the bridge and fell with the bayonet on Laval's entrenchments. The French gave way at first, but soon rallied, and the Spaniards fearing for their communications regained the town in disorder, having lost two hundred prisoners besides killed and wounded.

This operation had been concerted with general Caro, who having superseded O'Donoghue, was now marching with the Valencians by the coast-road towards Uldecona: Suchet therefore, judging that the intention of the Spaniards was to force him away from the Lower Ebro, before Macdonald could pass the Llobregat, resolved first to strike a sudden blow at the Valencians, and then turn upon the Catalans. In this view he contracted his quarters on the Ebro, and united at Uldecona, on the 13th, eleven battalions with eight hundred horsemen. Caro was then in a strong position covering the two great routes to Valencia, but when the French, after driving in his advanced guard from Vinaros, came up, his Valencians would not stand a battle, and being followed beyond Peniscola separated and retreated in disorder by different roads. Whereupon Suchet returned to Mora, and there found an officer of Macdonald's army, who brought information that the seventh corps was at last in the plains of Reus, and its communications with the third corps open.

1810. August.

OPERATIONS OF THE SEVENTH CORPS.

When Macdonald succeeded Augereau he found the troops in a state of insubordination, accustomed to plunder, and excited to ferocity by the cruelty of the Catalans, and by the conduct of his predecessor; they were without magazines or regular subsistence, and lived by exactions: hence the people, driven to desperation, were more like wild beasts than men, and the war was repulsive to him in all its features. It was one of shifts and devices, and he better understood methodical movements; it was one of plunder, and he was a severe disciplinarian; it was full of cruelty on all sides, and he was of a humane and just disposition. Being re-

1810. June.

Vacani.

Victoires et Conquêtes des François.

BOOK XIII. 1810. June.

solved to introduce regular habits, Macdonald severely rebuked the troops for their bad discipline and cruelty, and endeavoured to soothe the Catalans, but neither could be brought to soften in their enmity; the mutual injuries sustained, were too horrible and too recent to be forgiven. The soldiers, drawn from different countries, and therefore not bound by any common national feeling, were irritated against a general, who made them pay for wanton damages, and punished them for plundering; and the Catalans attributing his conduct to fear, because he could not entirely restrain the violence of his men, still fled from the villages, and still massacred his stragglers with unrelenting barbarity.

Vacani.

While establishing his system it was impossible for Macdonald to take the field, because, without magazines, no army can be kept in due discipline; wherefore he remained about Gerona, drawing with great labour and pains his provisions from France, and storing up the overplus for his future operations. On the 10th of June however the wants of Barcelona became so serious, that leaving his baggage under a strong guard at Gerona, and his recruits and cavalry at Figueras, he marched with ten thousand men and a convoy, to its relief, by the way of the Trenta Pasos, Cardedieu, and Granollers. The road was heavy, the defiles narrow, the rivers swelled, and the manner of march rather too pompous for the nature of the war, for Macdonald took post in order of battle on each side of the defiles, while the engineers repaired the ways: in every thing adhered to his resolution of restoring a sound system; but while imitating the Jugurthine Metellus, he forgot that he had not Romans, but a mixed and ferocious multitude under his command, and he lost more by wasting of time, than he gained by enforcing an irksome discipline. Thus when he had reached Barcelona, his own provisions were expended, his convoy furnished only a slender supply for the city, and the next day he was forced to return with the empty carts in all haste to Gerona, where he resumed his former plan of action, and demolished the forts beyond that city.

In July he collected another convoy and prepared to march in the same order as before, for his intent was to form magazines in Barcelona sufficient for that city and his own supply, during the siege of Taragona; but meanwhile Suchet was unable to commence the siege of Tortoza, in default of the co-operation of the seventh corps; and Henry O'Donnel having gained time to re-organize his army and to re-establish his authority was now ready to interrupt the French marshal's march, proposing, if he failed, to raise a fresh insurrection in the Ampurdan, and thus give further occupation on that side. He had transferred a part of his forces to Caldas, Santa Coloma, and Bruñolas, taking nearly the same positions that Blake had occupied during the siege of Gerona; but the French detachments soon obliged him to concentrate again behind the defiles of the Congosta, where he hoped to stop the passage of the convoy; Macdonald, however, entered Hostalrich on the 16th, forced the Trenta Pasos on the 17th, and although his troops had only fifty rounds of ammunition he drove three thousand men from the pass of Garriga on the 18th, reached Barcelona that night, delivered his convoy, and returned immediately.

Vacani.

The French soldiers now became sickly from the

BOOK XIII. 1810. August.

hardships of a march rendered oppressive by the severity of their discipline, and many also deserted; yet others, who had before gone off, returned to their colours, reinforcements arrived from France, and the emperor's orders to take the field were becoming so pressing, that Macdonald, giving Baraguay d'Hilliers the command of the Ampurdan, marched on the 8th of August with a third convoy for Barcelona, resolved at last to co-operate with Suchet. Instructed by experience he however moved this time with less formality, and having reached Barcelona the 11th, deposited his convoy, appointed Maurice Mathieu governor of that city, and on the 15th forced the pass of Ordal, and reached Villa Franca with about sixteen thousand men under arms. O'Donnel, still smarting from the affair at Tortoza, retired before him to Taragona without fighting, but directed Campo Verde to leave a body of troops under general Martinez in the mountains about Olot, and to move himself through Montserrat to the district of Garriga, which lies between Lerida and Tortoza; meanwhile the seventh corps passed by Braffin and Valls into the plain of Reus, and as we have seen opened the communication with Suchet, but to how little purpose shall be shewn in the next chapter.

CHAPTER II.

CHAP. II. 1810. August.

As the Spanish general knew that the French could at Reus find provisions for only a few days, he withdrew his division from Falcet, and while Campo Verde, coming into the Garriga, occupied the passes behind them, and other troops were placed in the defiles between Valls and Villafranca, he held the main body of his army concentrated at Taragona, ready to fall upon Macdonald whenever he should move. This done, he became extremely elated, for like all Spaniards he imagined that to surround an enemy was the perfection of military operations. Macdonald cared little for the vicinity of the Catalan troops, but he had not yet formed sufficient magazines at Barcelona to commence the siege of Taragona, nor could he, as O'Donnel had foreseen, procure more than a few days supply about Reus, he therefore relinquished all idea of a siege and proposed to aid Suchet in the operation against Tortoza, if the latter would feed the seventh corps; and pending Suchet's decision he resolved to remove to Lerida.

The 25th of August leaving seven hundred sick men in Reus, he made a feint against the Col de Balaguer, but soon changing his direction marched upon Momblanch and the Col de Ribas: his rear-guard, composed of Italian troops, being overtaken near Alcover, offered battle at the bridge of Goy, but this the Spaniards declined, and they also neglected to secure the heights on each

BOOK XIII. 1810. Sept.

side, which the Italians immediately turned to account and so made their way to Pixamoxons. They were pursued immediately, and Sarsfield coming from the Lerida side disputed the passage of Pixamoxons; but Macdonald, keeping the troops from Taragona in check with a rear-guard, again sent his Italians up the hills on the flanks while he pushed his French troops against the front of the enemy, and so succeeded; for the Italians quickly carried the heights, the rear-guard was very slightly pressed, the front was unopposed, and in two hours, the army reached Momblanch, whence after a short halt, it descended into the plains of Urgel.

Suchet being informed of this march came from Mora to confer with Macdonald, and they agreed that the seventh corps should have for its subsistence the magazines of Monzon and the plains of Urgel, which had not yet delivered its contributions. In return Macdonald lent the Neapolitan division to guard Suchet's convoys down the Ebro, and promised that the divisions of Severoli and Souham should cover the operations of the third corps, during the siege of Tortoza, by drawing the attention of the Catalan generals to the side of Cardona.

The seventh corps was now quartered about Tarega, Cervera, Guisona, and Agramunt, and Severola was detached with four thousand men over the Segre to enforce the requisitions about Talarn. He drove four hundred Swiss from the bridge of Tremp, and executed his mission, but with such violence that the people, becoming furious, assassinated the stragglers, and laid so many successful schemes of murder, that Macdonald was forced reluctantly to renew the executions and burnings of his predecessors. Indeed, to feed an

Vacani.

army forcibly when all things are paid for, will, in a poor and mountainous country, create soreness, because the things taken cannot easily be replaced; but with requisitions severity is absolutely necessary. In rich plains the inhabitants can afford to supply the troops and will do so, to avoid being plundered; but mountaineers having scarcely any thing besides food, and little of that, are immediately rendered desperate and must be treated as enemies or left in quiet. 1810. Sept.

While Severoli was ravaging Tremp and Talarn, general Eugenio marched with another Italian detachment towards Castelfollit, which had a French garrison, and Macdonald removed his own quarters to Cervera. Meanwhile O'Donnel, having replaced his division at Falcet to observe Suchet, distributed his other forces on the line of communication through San Coloma de Querault, Igualada, Montserrat, and Cardona; he thus cut off all connection between Macdonald and the Ampurdan, and enabled Campo Verde closely to follow the operations of the seventh corps, and that general seeing the French army separated, fell first upon the head-quarters at Cervera, but being unsuccessful, marched against Eugenio, and was by him also repulsed near Castelfollit. Eugenio, distinguished alike by his valour and ferocity, then returned with his booty to Agramunt, and afterwards invading Pons, spoiled and ravaged all that district without hindrance. The provisions obtained, were heaped up in Lerida and Balaguer; but while Macdonald was thus acting in the plain of Urgel, O'Donnel formed and executed the most skilful plan which had yet graced the Spanish arms.

We have seen that Baraguay d'Hilliers was left

BOOK XIII. 1810. Sept.

with eighteen or twenty thousand men in the Ampurdan, but these troops were necessarily scattered: seven hundred were at Palamos, San Filieu, and other small ports along the coast; twelve hundred, under general Swartz, were quartered in Abispal, one short march from Gerona, and two hundred were at Calonjé, connecting Abispal with Palamos; the rest were in Figueras, Rosas, Olot, Castelfollit, Gerona, and Hostalrich, and several thousand were in hospital. O'Donnel having exact knowledge of all this, left a small garrison in Taragona, placed the baron d'Errolles at Montserrat, colonel Georget at Igualada, and Obispo at Martorel, while with six thousand infantry and four hundred cavalry he marched himself through the mountains, by San Culgat to Mattaro on the sea-coast: then crossing the Tordera below Hostalrich, he moved rapidly by Vidreras to Llagostera which he reached the 12th of September. His arrival was unknown to Macdonald, or Maurice Mathieu, or Baraguay d'Hilliers, for though many reports of his intentions were afloat, most of them spread by himself, no person divined his real object: by some he was said to be gone against a French corps, which, from the side of Navarre, had entered the Cerdaña; by others that he was concentrating at Manresa, and many concluded that he was still in Taragona.

Having thus happily attained his first object, O'Donnel proceeded in his plan with a vigour of execution equal to the conception. Leaving Campo Verde with a reserve in the valley of Aro, he sent detachments to fall on Calonjé and the posts along the coast, the operations there being seconded by two English frigates; and while this was in progress, O'Donnel himself on the 14th marched violently down from Casa de Silva upon Abispal. Swartz, always unfortunate, had his infantry and some cavalry under arms in an entrenched camp, and accepted battle; but after losing two hundred men and seeing no retreat, yielded, and all the French troops along the coast were likewise forced to surrender. The prisoners and spoil were immediately embarked on board the English vessels and sent to Taragona.

Until this moment Baraguay d'Hilliers was quite ignorant of O'Donnel's arrival, and the whole Ampurdan was thrown into confusion; for the Somatenes, rising in all parts, cut off the communications with Macdonald, whose posts on the side of Calaf and Cervera were at the same time harassed by Errolles and Obispo: nevertheless, although a rumour of Swartz's disaster reached him, Macdonald would not credit it, and continued in the plain of Urgel. Baraguay d'Hilliers was therefore unable to do more than protect his own convoys from France, and would have been in a dangerous position if O'Donnel's activity had continued; but that general having been severely wounded, the Spanish efforts relaxed, and Napoleon, whose eyes were every where, sent general Conroux, in the latter end of October, with a convoy and reinforcement of troops from Perpignan to Gerona. O'Donnel, troubled by his wound, then embarked; and Campo Verde, who succeeded to the command, immediately sent a part of the army to Taragona, left Rovira, and Claros, and Manso, to nourish the insurrection in the Ampurdan, and took post himself at Manresa, from thence he at first menaced Macdonald's posts at Calaf; but his real object was to break up that road,

BOOK XIII. 1810. October.

which he effected, and then passed suddenly through Berga and Cardona to Puigcerda, and drove the French detachment, which had come from Navarre to ravage the fertile district of Cerdaña, under the guns of Fort Louis.

This excursion attracted Macdonald's attention, he was now fully apprized of Swartz's misfortune, and he hoped to repair it by crushing Campo Verde, taking Cardona, and dispersing the local junta of Upper Catalonia, which had assembled in Solsona; wherefore, on the 18th, he put his troops in motion, and the 19th, passing the mountains of Portellas, entered Solsona; but the junta and the inhabitants escaped to Cardona and Berja, and up the valleys of Oleana and Urgel. Macdonald immediately sent columns in all directions to collect provisions and to chase the Spanish detachments, and this obliged Campo Verde to abandon the Cerdaña, which was immediately foraged by the troops from Fort Louis. It only remained to sieze Çardona, and on the 21st the French marched against that place; but Campo Verde, by a rapid movement, arrived before them, and was in order of battle with a considerable force when Macdonald came up.

COMBAT OF CARDONA.

This town stands at the foot of a rugged hill, which is joined by a hog's-back ridge to the great mountain spine, dividing Eastern from Western Catalonia. The Cardona river washed the walls, a castle of strength crowned the height above, and though the works of the place were weak, the Spanish army, covering all the side of the hill between the town and the castle, presented such an imposing spectacle, that the French general resolved to avoid a serious action. But the French and Italians marched in separate columns, and the latter under Eugenio, who arrived first, attacked contrary to orders; yet he soon found his hands too full, and thus, against his will, Macdonald was obliged also to engage to bring Eugenio off. Yet neither was he able to resist Campo Verde, who drove all down the mountain, and followed them briskly as they retreated to Solsona.

Macdonald lost many men in this fight, and on the 26th returned to Guisona. It was now more than two months since he had left the Ampurdan, and during that time he had struck no useful blow against the Spaniards, nor had he, in any serious manner, aided Suchet's operations; for the Catalans continually harassed that general's convoys, from the left of the Ebro, while the seventh corps, besides suffering severely from assassinations, had been repulsed at Cardona, had excited the people of the plain of Urgel to a state of rabid insurrection, and had lost its own communications with the Ampurdan. In that district the brigade of Swartz had been destroyed, the ports of Filieu and Palamos taken, and the Catalans were every where become more powerful and elated than before: Barcelona also was again in distress, and a convoy from Perpignan destined for its relief dared not pass Hostalrich. Macdonald therefore resolved to return to Gerona by the road of Manreza, Moya, and Granollers, and having communicated his intention to Suchet, and placed his baggage in Lerida, commenced his march the 4th of November.

Campo Verde getting intelligence of this design,

took post to fight near Calaf, yet when the French approached, his heart failed, and he permitted them to pass. The French general therefore reached Manreza the 7th, and immediately despatched parties towards Vich and other places to mislead the Spaniards, while with his main body he marched by Moya and the Gariga pass to Granollers, where he expected to meet Baraguay d'Hilliers with the convoy from Barcelona; but being disappointed in this, he returned by the Trenta Pasos to Gerona the 10th, and sent his convalescents to Figueras.

The vicinity of Gerona was now quite exhausted, and fresh convoys from France were required to feed the troops, while the posts in the Ampurdan were re-established and the district re-organized. Macdonald's muster-rolls presented a force of fifty-one thousand men, of which ten thousand were in hospital, six thousand in Barcelona, and several thousand distributed along the coast and on the lines of communication, leaving somewhat more than thirty thousand disposable for field-operations. Of this number, fourteen thousand were placed under Baraguay d'Hilliers to maintain the Ampurdan, and when the convoys arrived from France the French marshal marched, with the remaining sixteen thousand, for the fourth time, to the succour of Barcelona. His divisions were commanded by Souham and Pino, for Severoli had been recalled to Italy to organize fresh reinforcements; but following his former plan, this march also was made in one solid body, and as the defiles had been cut up by the Spaniards, and the bridge over the Tordera broken, Macdonald set his troops to labour, and in six hours opened fresh ways over the hills on the right and left of the Trenta Pasos, and so, without opposition, reached the more open country about Granollers and Moncada. The Spaniards then retired by their own left to Tarasa and Caldas, but Macdonald continued to move on in a solid body upon Barcelona; for as he was resolved not to expose himself to a dangerous attack, so he avoided all enterprise. Thus, on the 23d, he would not permit Pino to improve a favourable opportunity of crushing the Catalans in his front, and on the 24th, after delivering his convoy and sending the carts back to Belgarde, instead of pursuing Campo Verde to Tarasa, as all the generals advised, he marched towards the Llobregat; and as Souham and Pino remained discontented at Barcelona, their divisions were given to Frere and Fontanes. Vacani.

Macdonald moved, on the 27th, towards Taragona, but without any design to undertake the siege; for though the road by Ordal and Villa Franca was broad and good, he carried no artillery or wheel-carriages: the Spaniards, seeing this, judged he would again go to Lerida, and posted their main body about Montserrat and Igualada; but he disregarded them, and after beating Sarsfield from Arbos and Vendril, turned towards the pass of Massarbones, which leads through the range of hills separating Villa Franca from the district of Valls. The Catalans had broken up both that and the pass of Christina leading to the Gaya, yet the French general again made new ways, and on the 30th spread his troops over the Paneda or plain of Taragona: thus shewing of how little use it is to destroy roads as a defence, unless men are also prepared to fight.

Instead of occupying Reus as before, Macdonald

BOOK XIII. 1811. January.

now took a position about Momblanch, having his rear towards Lerida, but leaving all the passes leading from Taragona to the Ebro open for the Spaniards; so that Suchet derived no benefit from the presence of the seventh corps, nor could the latter feed itself, nor yet in any manner hinder the Catalans from succouring Tortoza. For Campo Verde, coming from Montserrat and Igualada, was encamped above the defiles between the French position and Taragona, principally at Lilla, on the road from Valls; and O'Donnel, who still directed the general movements, although his wound would not suffer him to appear in the field, sent parties into the Gariga behind Macdonald's right flank to interrupt his foraging parties, and to harass Suchet's communications by the Ebro.

From the strong heights at Lilla, the Catalans defied the French soldiers, calling upon them to come up and fight, and they would have done so if Macdonald would have suffered them, but after ten days of inactivity he divided his troops into many columns, and in concert with Abbé's brigade of the third corps, which marched from Xerta, endeavoured to inclose and destroy the detachments in the Gariga; the Spaniards however disappeared in the mountains and the French army only gained some mules and four thousand sheep and oxen. With this spoil they united again on the left bank of the Ebro, and were immediately disposed on a line extending from Vinebre, which is opposite to Flix, to Masos, which is opposite to Mora, and from thence to Garcia and Gniestar. Suchet was thus enabled to concentrate his troops about Tortoza and the siege of that place was immediately commenced.

CHAP. II.

1810. Sept.

The operations of the third corps during the five months it had been dependent upon the slow movements of the seventh corps shall now be related.

Suchet, by resigning the plain of Urgel and the magazines at Monzon, for Macdonald's subsistence, in September, had deprived himself of all the resources of the left bank of the Ebro from Mequinenza to Tortoza, and the country about the latter place was barren; hence he was obliged to send for his provisions to Zaragoza, Teruel, and other places more than one hundred miles from his camp; and meanwhile the difficulty of getting his battering train and ammunition down the river from Mequinenza was increased because of the numerous bars and weirs which impeded the navigation when the waters were low: moreover Macdonald, by going to Cardona, exposed the convoys to attacks from the left bank, by the Spanish troops which being stationed between Taragona, Momblanch, and Falcet, were always on the watch. Considering these things Suchet had, while the seventh corps was yet at Lerida, and the waters accidentally high, employed the Neapolitan brigade of the seventh corps to escort twenty-six pieces of artillery down the river. This convoy reached Xerta the 5th of September, and the Neapolitans were then sent to Guardia; general Habert was placed at Tivisa; Mas de Mora was occupied by a reserve, and the Spaniards again took post at Falcet. At this time general Laval died, and his division was given to general Harispe, a person distinguished throughout the war by his ability, courage, and humanity.

Meanwhile the Valencian army had again con-

BOOK XIII. 1810. Sept.

centrated to disturb the blockade of Tortoza, wherefore Suchet strengthened Boussard's detachment at Uldecona, and gave the command to general Musnier, who was replaced at Zaragoza by general Paris. At the same time colonel Kliski was sent to command the detachments on the side of Montalvan, Teruel, Daroca, and Calatayud, where a partizan warfare was continued with undiminished activity by Villa Campa, who had contrived to open secret communications, and to excite some commotions even in Zaragoza. On the 7th of August he had beaten a French foraging detachment near Cuevas, and recaptured six thousand sheep, and at Andorra had taken both convoy and escort. On the side of Navarre also, Mina coming down into the Cinco Villas destroyed some detachments, and impeded the foraging parties. Thus the third corps also began to suffer privations, and no progress was made towards the conquest of Catalonia.

In September, however, Villa Campa, having increased his forces, advanced so near Suchet that general Habert attacked and drove him over the frontier in dispersion, and recaptured all the sheep before lost, and Suchet then brought down the remainder of the battering train, and the stores for the siege; but as the waters of the Ebro were low, the new road was used for the convoys, which thus came slowly and with many interruptions and considerable loss; especially on the 17th of September, when a whole Neapolitan battalion suffered itself to be taken without firing a shot.

In this manner affairs dragged on until the 28th of October; but then Macdonald (O'Donnel having meantime captured Swartz and raised the Ampurdan) returned to Gerona, whereby Suchet's hopes of commencing the siege were again baffled. And, as it was at this moment that the assembling of the Cortez gave a new vigour to the resistance in Spain and the regency's plan of sending secret juntas, to organize and regulate the proceedings of the partidas, was put in execution, the activity of those bands became proportioned to the hopes excited, and the supplies and promises thus conveyed to them. One of those secret juntas composed of clergy and military men having property or influence in Aragon, endeavoured to renew the insurrection formerly excited by Blake in that province, and for this purpose sent their emissaries into all quarters, and combined their operations with Mina. They, also, diligently followed a plan of secretly drawing off the provisions from Aragon, with a view to starve the French, and general Carbajal, one of the junta, joining Villa Campa, assumed the supreme command on that side; while captain Codrington, at the desire of Bassecour, carried a Valencian detachment by sea to Peniscola to fall on the left flank of Suchet, if he should attempt to penetrate by the coast road to Valencia. Thus, at the moment when Macdonald returned to the Ampurdan, the Aragonese became unquiet, the partidas from Navarre and the district of Montalvan and Calatayud, closed in on Suchet's communications, the Valencians came up on the one side, towards Uldecona, and on the other Garcia Navarro moving from Taragona with a division again assumed the position of Falcet.

To check this tide of hostility the French general resolved first to crush the insurrection project, and for this purpose detached seven battalions and four hundred cavalry against Carbajal. Chlopiski, who

BOOK XIII. 1810. Nov.

commanded them, defeated the Spaniards the 31st at Alventoza on the route to Valencia, taking some guns and ammunition. Nevertheless Villa Campa rallied his men in a few days on the mountain of Fuente Santa, where he was joined by Carbajal, and having received fresh succours renewed the project of raising the Aragonese. But Chlopiski again defeated him the 12th of November, and the Spaniards fled in confusion towards the river Libras, where the bridge breaking many were drowned. The French lost more than a hundred men in this sharp attack, and Chlopiski then returned to the blockade, leaving Kliski with twelve hundred men to watch Villa Campa's further movements.

The Ebro having now risen sufficiently, the remainder of the battering train and stores were embarked at Mequinenza, and on the 3d dropt down the stream; but the craft outstripped the escort, and the convoy being assailed from the left bank, lost two boats; the others grounded on the right bank, and were there defended by the cannoneers, until the escort came up on the one side, and on the other, general Abbé, who had been sent from Guardia to their succour. The waters, however, suddenly subsided, and the convoy was still in danger until Suchet reinforced Abbé, who was thus enabled to keep the Spaniards at bay, while Habert, with fifteen hundred men, made a diversion by attacking the camp at Falcet. On the 7th the waters again rose and the boats with little loss reached Xerta on the 9th, and thus all things were ready to commence the siege, but the seventh corps still kept aloof.

Suchet was now exceedingly perplexed; for the provisions he had with so much pains collected, from the most distant parts of Aragon, were rapidly wasting; forage was every day becoming scarcer, and the plain of Urgel, was by agreement given over to the seventh corps, which thus became a burthen instead of an aid to the third corps. The latter had been, since the beginning of the year, ordered to supply itself entirely from the resources of Aragon without any help from France; and the difficulty of so doing may be judged of by the fact, that in six months they had consumed above a hundred and twenty thousand sheep and twelve hundred bullocks.

To obviate the embarrasments thus accumulating, the French general called the notables and heads of the clergy in Aragon to his head-quarters, and with their assistance reorganized the whole system of internal administration, in such a manner, that, giving his confidence to the natives, removing many absurd restrictions of their industry and trade, and leaving the municipal power and police entirely in their hands, he drew forth the resources of the provinces in greater abundance than before. And yet with less discontent, being well served and obeyed, both in matters of administration and police, by the Aragonese, whose feelings he was careful to soothe, shewing himself in all things, an able governor, as well as a great commander.

Macdonald was now in march from Barcelona towards Taragona, and Suchet to aid this operation attacked the Spanish troops at Falcet. General Habert fell on their camp in front the 19th, and to cut off the retreat, two detachments were ordered to turn it by the right and left; but Habert's assault was so brisk, that before the flanking corps could take their stations the Catalans fled, leaving

BOOK XIII. 1810. Nov.

their general Garcia Navarro and three hundred men in the hands of the victors. But while Suchet obtained this success on the side of Falcet, the Valencian general Bassecour, thinking that the main body of the French would be detained by Navarro on the left bank of the Ebro, formed the design of surprising general Musnier at Uldecona. To aid this operation, a flotilla from the harbour of Peniscola, attacked Rapita, and other small posts occupied by the French, on the coast between the Cenia and the Ebro; and at the same time the governor of Tortoza menaced Amposta and the stations at the mouth of the Ebro.

Bassecour moved against Uldecona in three columns, one of which, following the coast-road towards Alcanar, turned the French left, while another passing behind the mountains took post at Las Ventallas, in rear of Musnier's position, to cut him off from Tortoza. The main body went straight against his front, and in the night of the 26th the Spanish cavalry fell upon the French camp outside the town; but the guards, undismayed, opened a fire which checked the attack, until the troops came out of the town and formed in order of battle.

At daylight the Spanish army was perceived covering the hills in front; and those in rear also, for the detachment at Ventallas was in sight; the French were thus surrounded and the action immediately commenced; but the Valencians were defeated with the loss of sixteen hundred men, and the detachment in the rear seeing the result made off to the mountains again. Bassecour then withdrew in some order behind the Cenia, where in the night Musnier surprised him, and at the same time sent the cuirassiers by the route of Vinaros to

Suchet's Memoirs.

CHAP. II.

1810. Nov.

cut off his retreat, which was made with such haste and disorder that the French cavalry falling in with the fugitives near Benicarlo, killed or took nine hundred. Bassecour saved himself in Peniscola, and thither also the flotilla, having failed at Rapita, returned.

Official Abstract of Mr. Wellesley's Despatch. MSS.

Suchet having thus cleared his rear, sent his prisoners to France by Jaca, and directed a convoy of prisoners, newly collected at Mequinenza, to fall down the Ebro to the magazines at Mora: fearing however that the current might again carry the boats faster than the escort, he directed the latter to proceed first, and sent general Abbé to Flix to meet the vessels. The Spaniards in the Garriga observing this disposition, placed an ambuscade near Mequinenza, and attacked the craft before they could come up with the escort; the boats were then run ashore on the right side, and seventy men from Mequinenza came down the left bank to their aid, which saved the convoy, but the succouring detachment was cut to pieces. Soon after this the seventh corps having scoured the Garriga took post on the left bank of the Ebro, and enabled the third corps to commence the long delayed siege.

CHAPTER III.

BOOK XIII.

1810. Dec.

TORTOZA, with a population of ten thousand souls and a garrison of from eight to nine thousand regular troops, was justly considered the principal bulwark of both Catalonia and Valencia, but it was under the command of general Lilli, Conde d'Alacha, a feeble man, whose only claim was, that he had shewn less incapacity than others before the battle of Tudela in 1808. However, so confident were the Spaniards in the strength of the place that the French attack was considerably advanced ere any interruption was contemplated, and had any well considered project for its relief been framed, it could not have been executed, because jealousy and discord raged amongst the Spanish chiefs. Campo Verde was anxious to succeed O'Donnel in command of the Catalonian army, Bassecourt held unceasing dispute with his own officers, and with the members of the junta or congress of Valencia; and Villa Campa repelled the interference both of Carbajal and Bassecour.

At this critical time therefore every thing was stagnant, except the English vessels which blockaded Rosas, Barcelona, and the mouths of the Ebro, or from certain head-lands observed and pounced upon the enemy's convoys creeping along from port to port: they had thrown provisions, ammunition, and stores of all kinds into Taragona and Tortoza, and were generally successful, yet at times met with disasters. Thus captain Rogers of the Kent, having with him the Ajax, Cambrian, Sparrow-hawk, and Minstrel, disembarked six hundred men and two field-pieces under captain Fane at Palamos, where they destroyed a convoy intended for Barcelona; but as the seamen were re-embarking in a disorderly manner, the French fell upon them and took or killed two hundred, captain Fane being amongst the prisoners. CHAP. III. 1810. Dec.

The Catalan army was thirty thousand strong, including garrisons, and in a better state than it had hitherto been; the Valencians, although discouraged by the defeat at Uldecona, were still numerous, and all things tended to confirm the Spaniards in the confident expectation that whether succoured or unsuccoured the place would not fall. But O'Donnel, who had been created Conde de' Bispal was so disabled by wounds, that he resigned the command soon after the siege commenced, and Campo Verde was by the voice of the people raised in his stead; for it was their nature always to believe that the man who made most noise was the fittest person to head them, and in this instance, as in most others, they were greatly mistaken. Official Abstract of Mr. Wellesley's despatches MSS.

Tortoza, situated on the left of the Ebro, communicated with the right bank by a bridge of boats, which was the only Spanish bridge on that river, from Zaragoza to the sea; and below and above the place there was a plain, but so narrowed by the juttings of the mountains at the point where the town was built, that while part of the houses stood close to the water on flat ground, the other part stood on the bluff rocky points shot from the hills above, and thus appeared to tie the mountains, the river, and the plains together. Vacani. Rogniat. Suchet.

BOOK XIII. 1810. Dec.

Five of these shoots were taken into the defence, either by the ramparts or by outworks. That on the south of the town was crowned by the fort of Orleans, and on the north another was occupied by a fort called the Tenaxas. To the east a horn-work was raised on a third shoot, which being prolonged, and rising suddenly again between the suburbs and the city, furnished the site of a castle or citadel: the other two, and the deep ravines between them were defended by the ramparts of the place, which were extremely irregular, and strong from their situation, rather than their construction.

There were four fronts.

1°. *The northern defending the suburb.* Although this front was built on the plain, it was so imbedded between the Ebro, the horn-work, the citadel, and the Tenaxas, that it could not even be approached without first taking the latter fort.

2°. *The eastern. Extending from the horn-work to the bastion of San Pico.* Here the deep ravines and the rocky nature of the ground, which was also overlooked by the citadel and flanked by the horn-work, rendered any attack very difficult.

3°. *The south eastern. From the bastion of San Pico to the bastion of Santa Cruz.* This front, protected by a deep narrow ravine, was again covered by the fort of Orleans, which was itself covered by a second ravine.

4°. *The southern. From the Santa Cruz to the Ebro.* The ground of approach here was flat, the soil easy to work in, and the fort of Orleans not sufficiently advanced to flank it with any dangerous effect; wherefore against this front Suchet resolved to conduct his attack.

The Rocquetta, a rising ground opposite the bridge-head on the right bank of the Ebro, was fortified and occupied by three regiments, but the other troops were collected at Xerta; and the 15th, before day-break, Suchet crossed the Ebro by his own bridge at that point, with eight battalions, the sappers, and two squadrons of hussars. He marched between the mountains and the river upon the fort of Tenaxas, while general Habert, with two regiments and three hundred hussars, moved from the side of Perillo, and attacked a detachment of the garrison which was encamped on the Col d'Alba eastward of the city. When Suchet's column arrived in sight of the works, the head took ground, but the rear, under general Harispe, filed off to the left, across the rugged shoots from the hills, and swept round the place, leaving in every ravine and on every ridge a detachment, until the half circle ended on the Ebro, below Tortoza. The investment was then perfected on the left bank by the troops from Rocquetta; and during this movement Habert, having seized the Col d'Alba, entered the line of investment, driving before him six hundred men, who hardly escaped being cut off from the place by the march of Harispe. The communication across the water was then established by three, and afterwards by four flying bridges, placed above and below the town; a matter of some difficulty and importance, because all the artillery and stores had to come from Rocquetta, across the water, which was there two hundred yards wide, and in certain winds very rough.

Suchet. Official extract of Mr. Wellesley's despatches MSS.

The camps of investment were now secured, and meanwhile Macdonald, sending the greatest part of his cavalry, for which he could find no forage, back

BOOK XIII. 1810. Dec.

to Lerida by the road of Lardecans, marched, from Mas de Mora, across the hills to Perillo, to cover the siege. His patroles discovered a Spanish division in a position resting upon the fort of Felipe de Balaguer, yet he would not attack them, and thinking he could not remain for want of provisions, returned on the 19th to Gniestar; but this retrograde movement was like to have exposed the investing troops to a disaster, for as the seventh corps retired, a second Spanish division coming from Reus reinforced the first. However, Macdonald, seeing this, placed Frere's division of six thousand infantry and a regiment of cavalry at Suchet's disposal, on condition that the latter should feed them, which he could well do. These troops were immediately stationed behind the investing force, on the road of Amposta, by which the Spaniards from Taragona could most easily approach; and the remainder of the seventh corps encamped at Gniestar, a strong position covering the siege on the side of Falcet, only fifteen miles distant from Tortoza. In this situation it could be more easily fed from Lerida, and could with greater facility send detachments up the Ebro, to protect the convoy of the third corps coming from Mequinenza.

Wimphen's Memoir.

The Catalan army was now divided, part being kept on the Llobregat, under general Caro, part under general Yranzo at Momblanch, and part, under Campo Verde, on the hills watching Frere's covering division. O'Donnel had before directed two convoys upon Tortoza, but the rapidity with which the investment had been effected prevented them from entering the place; and while he was endeavouring to arrange with Bassecour and Campo Verde a general plan of succour, his wounds forced

Explanatory Sketch
OF THE
SIEGE OF TORTOZA,
1811.

London: Published by T. & W. BOONE.

him to embark for Valencia, when the command, of right, belonged to Yranzo, but the people, as I have before said, insisted upon having Campo Verde.

SIEGE OF TORTOZA.

The half bastion of San Pedro, which was situated in the plain, and close to the river, was the first object of the French attack, and to prevent the fire of Fort Orleans from incommoding the trenches, the line of approach was traced in a slanting direction, refusing the right, and pushing forward the left; and to protect its flanks on the one side, Fort Orleans was masked by a false attack, while, on the other side of the Ebro, trenches were opened against the bridge-head, and brought down close to the water.

The 19th the posts of the besieged were all driven in, and an unfinished Spanish work, commenced on the heights in advance of Fort Orleans, was taken possession of. In the night, a flying sap was commenced upon an extent of three hundred and sixty yards, and at a distance of only one hundred and sixty from the fort; but in the following night, the true attack was undertaken in the plain, during a storm of wind which, together with the negligence of the Spaniards, who had placed no guards in front of their covered way, enabled the besiegers to begin this work at only one hundred and fifty yards from the half bastion of San Pedro. This parallel was above five hundred yards long, extending from the false attack against Fort Orleans, down to the bank of the river; two communications were also

1810. Dec.

begun, and on the left bank ground was broken against the bridge-head.

The 21st, at day-break, the Spaniards, perceiving the works, commenced a heavy fire, and soon after made a sally; but they were overwhelmed by musketry from the false attack of Fort Orleans, and from the trenches on the right bank of the Ebro.

In the night of the 21st, the communication in the plain was extended to fourteen hundred yards, nine batteries were commenced, and bags of earth were placed along the edge of the trenches, whence chosen men shot down the Spanish artillery men.

On the 23rd, a night sally, made from the bridge-head, was repulsed; and on the 24th, the second parallel of the true attack was commenced.

In the night of the 25th, at eleven o'clock and at one o'clock, separate sallies were again made, but both were repulsed, and the works were advanced to within twenty-five yards of the pallisades; a tenth battery was also commenced, and when day broke the Spanish gunners quailed under the aim of the chosen marksmen.

In the night of the 26th, the besieged fell upon the head of the sap, which they overturned, and killed the sappers, but were finally repulsed by the reserve, and the approach was immediately pushed forward to the place of arms. Thus, on the seventh night of open trenches, the besiegers were lodged in the covered way, before a shot had been fired from either breaching or counter batteries; a remarkable instance of activity and boldness, and a signal proof that the defence was ill-conducted.

The night of the 27th, the works were enlarged as much as the fire of the place which was untouched would permit; but the Spaniards seeing the besiegers' batteries ready to open, made a general sally through the eastern gates, against the false attack at Fort Orleans; and through the southern gates against the works in the plain. General Habert drove them back with slaughter from the former point, but at the latter they beat the French from the covered way, and arriving at the second parallel, burnt the gabions and did much damage ere the reserves could repulse them.

The night of the 28th, the batteries were armed with forty-five pieces, of which seventeen were placed on the right bank, to take the Spanish works at the main attack in reverse and to break the bridge. At day-break all these guns opened, and with success, against the demi-bastion, on the left bank of the river; but the fire from the castle, the bridge-head, the horn-work, and the quay, overpowered the French guns on the right bank, and although the bridge was injured, it was not rendered impassable.

On the 30th, the Spanish fire was in turn overpowered by the besiegers, the bridge was then broken, and in the following night an attempt was made to pass the ditch at the true attack; but two guns which were still untouched and flanked the point of attack, defeated this effort.

In the morning of the 31st, the Spaniards abandoned the bridge-head, and the French batteries on the right bank dismounted the two guns which had defended the half bastion of San Pedro. The besiegers then effected the passage of the ditch without difficulty, and attached the miner to the scarp.

In the night of the 31st, the miner worked into the wall, and the batteries opened a breach in the

BOOK XIII. 1811. January.

curtain, where a lodgement was established in preparation for an assault. At ten o'clock in the morning the besieged, alarmed at the progress of the attack, displayed the white flag. The negotiations for a surrender were, however, prolonged until evening by the governor, without any result, and the miner resumed his work in the night.

At seven o'clock on the 1st of January, two practicable breaches besides that in the curtain were opened by the artillery, and the mine was ready to explode, when three white flags were seen to wave from different parts of the fortress; nevertheless the disposition of the garrison was mistrusted, and Suchet demanded as a preliminary the immediate possession of one of the forts,—a necessary precaution, for disputes arose amongst the besieged, and general Lilli intimated to Suchet, that his own authority was scarcely recognised.

In this critical moment, the French general gave proof that his talents were not those of a mere soldier, for suddenly riding up to the gates with a considerable staff, and escorted only by a company of grenadiers, he informed the Spanish officer on guard, that hostilities had ceased, and then, leaving his grenadiers on the spot, desired to be conducted to the governor who was in the citadel. Lilli still wavering, was upon the point of renewing the defence, in compliance with the desires of the officers about him, when the French general thus came suddenly into his presence, and, although the appearance of the Spanish guards was threatening, assumed an imperious tone, spoke largely of the impatience of the French army, and even menaced the garrison with military execution if any further delay occurred; during this extraordinary scene general Habert brought in the grenadiers from the gate, and the governor then signing a short capitulation, gave over the citadel to the French.

When this event was known in the city, the Spanish troops assembled, and Alacha, in the presence of Suchet ordered them to lay down their arms. Four hundred French and about fourteen hundred Spaniards had fallen during the siege; and many thousand prisoners, nine standards, one hundred pieces of artillery, ten thousand muskets, and immense magazines, enhanced the value of the conquest, which by some was attributed to general Lilli's treachery, by others to his imbecility, and it would seem that there was reason for both charges.

The fall of Tortoza, besides opening the western passage into Catalonia, and cutting off the communication between that province and Valencia, reduced the Spanish army to twenty thousand men, including the garrisons of the towns which still remained in their possession. Campo Verde immediately retired from Falcet to Momblanch, and Suchet, always prompt to make one success the prelude to another, endeavoured in the first moment of consternation and surprise to get possession of the forts of Peniscola and of Felipe de Balaguer: nor was he deceived with respect to the last, for that place, in which were five guns and a hundred men, was taken on the 9th by Habert; but at Peniscola his summons was disregarded and his detachment returned.

Meanwhile Macdonald leaving the Neapolitan brigade still on the Ebro, passed by Falcet to Reus, where he encamped the 11th, as if to invest Taragona; but without any real intention to do so, for

BOOK XIII. 1811. January.

his cavalry and field artillery were left at Lerida and Tortoza, and his actual force did not exceed twelve thousand men. Campo Verde, who had retreated before him, then posted Sarsfield with six thousand men at Valls, from whence he made incursions against Macdonald's foragers, and also surprised at Tarega, on the other side of the mountains, a regiment of Italian dragoons, which would have been destroyed but for the succour of a neighbouring post.

On the 14th Macdonald having marched towards Valls, Sarsfield retired to Pla, and was pursued by general Eugenio with two thousand Italian infantry. This officer being of a headstrong intractable disposition, pushed into the plain of Pla, contrary to his orders, and was nearing that town, when a strong body of cavalry poured out of it; and on each side the Spanish infantry were seen descending the hill in order of battle. Eugenio, instead of retiring, attacked the first that entered the plain, but he fell mortally wounded, and his men retreated fighting: meanwhile the firing being heard at Valls Palombini marched to his assistance, but was himself beaten and thrown into confusion, and Sarsfield at the head of the Spanish horse was preparing to complete the victory, when the French colonel Delort bringing up some squadrons charged with great fury, and so brought off the Italians; yet Delort himself was desperately wounded, and the whole loss was not less than six hundred men.

Vacani. Victoires et Conquêtes. General Doyle's despatches MSS.

Macdonald would not suffer his main body to stir, and Vacani asserts that it was only by entreaty, that Palombini obtained permission to succour Eugenio, which was certainly a great error, for so hot and eager was Sarsfield in the pursuit, that he was come within two miles of Valls, and being on open ground might have been crushed in turn. He, however, returned unmolested to the pass of Cabra, leaving his cavalry as before in Pla, whence through bye-roads they communicated with Taragona.

A few days after this fight Sarsfield came out again in order of battle, and at the same time Campo Verde appeared with a division on the hills in rear of Valls. Macdonald was thus surrounded, but Palombini's brigade sufficed to send Campo Verde back to Taragona, and Sarsfield refused battle; then the French marshal, who had resolved to go to Lerida, but wished to move without fighting, broke up from Valls in the night, and, with great order and silence, passed by the road of Fuencalde, between the defiles of Cabra and Ribas, and though both were occupied by the Spaniards, they did not discover his movements until the next day. From thence he marched by Momblanch, upon Lerida, where he arrived the 19th, and three days afterwards spread his troops over the plains of Urgel, to collect provisions, money, and transport, and to watch the defiles of the mountains.

On the other hand the Catalan general, who had received stores and arms both from England and Cadiz, renewed the equipment of his troops, and called out all the Miguelettes and Somatenes, of the hills round the plain of Urgel, to replace the loss sustained by the fall of Tortoza. These new levies were united at Santa Coloma de Querault under Sarsfield, while the regular army assembled at Igualada and Villafranca, by which the Spaniards holding a close and concentrated position

BOOK XIII. — 1811. February.

themselves, cut off Macdonald equally from Barcelona and the Ampurdan; and this latter district was continually harassed by Errolles, Rovira, and the brigade of Martinez, which still kept the mountains behind Olot, Vich, and the Cerdaña.

Meanwhile Suchet being called by the exigences of his government to Zaragoza, carried one division there, and distributed another under Musnier at Teruel, Molina, Alcanitz, and Morella: he also withdrew his troops from Cambril, which Habert had surprised on the 7th of February, but he left that general, with a division, in command of Tortoza, having two thousand men at Perillo to connect the city with San Felipe de Balaguer. Thus all things seemed to favour the Spanish side, and give importance to their success, against Eugenio; for they did not fail to attribute both Suchet's and Macdonald's retreats, to fear occasioned by the skirmish with that general; and with some shew of reason as regarded the latter, seeing that his night march had all the appearance of a flight.

Macdonald, while gathering provisions at Lerida, and stores and guns at Tortoza, also repaired the works of Balaguer near Lerida, to serve as a pivot for the troops employed to forage the country watered by the Noguera, Cinca, and Legre rivers. However Sarsfield and Campo Verde kept about Cervera and Calaf, watching for an opportunity to fall on the French detachments, and meanwhile the organization of the province went on.

Appendix, No. I. Section 2.

It may appear extraordinary that the war could have been continued by either side under such difficulties, but the resources were still great. A patriotic junta had been formed in Catalonia to procure provisions, and although the English orders in council interfered with the trade of neutral vessels bringing grain, bread could be bought at the rate of 12lbs. to the dollar, while with lord Wellington's army in Castile it often cost half a dollar a pound. When the French foraging parties came out from Barcelona, their march could be always traced by the swarms of boats, loaded with people and provisions, which shooting out from the coast-towns, would hover, for a while, under the protection of the English vessels, and then return when the danger was over: and the enemy did never meddle with these boats lest they should remove the cover to their own supplies. Suchet however armed Rapita, and other small places, at the mouth of the Ebro, with a view to afford shelter to certain craft, which he kept to watch for provision-vessels, sailing from Valencia for Taragona, and to aid French vessels engaged in a like course coming from France.

To feed Barcelona, Maurice Mathieu at times occupied the head-lands from St. Filieu, to Blanes, with troops, and thus small convoys crept along shore; a fleet loaded with provisions and powder, escorted by three frigates, entered it in February, and a continual stream of supply was also kept up by sailing-boats and other small vessels, which could not be easily detected amidst the numerous craft belonging to the people along the coast. And besides these channels, as the claims of hunger are paramount to all others, it was necessary, for the sake of the inhabitants, to permit provision sometimes to reach Barcelona by land; the Spanish generals winked at it, and Milans and Lacy, have even been charged with permitting corn to pass into that city for private profit, as well as

BOOK XIII.

1811. March.

from consideration for the citizens. By these, and like expedients, the war was sustained.

No important event occurred after the skirmish in which Eugenio fell, until the 3d of March, when the Spaniards having observed that the garrison of Tortoza was weakened by the detachment at Perillo, endeavoured to cut the latter off, intending if successful to assault Tortoza itself. At the same time they also attacked the fort of San Filippe, but failed, and the French at Perillo effected their retreat although with considerable loss. This attempt was however followed by a more important effort. On the 19th of March, Campo Verde having assembled eight thousand men at Molinos del Rey, four thousand at Guisols, and three thousand at Igualada, prepared to surprise the city and forts of Barcelona, for he had, as he thought, corrupted the town-major of Monjuic. Trusting to this treason, he first sent eight hundred chosen grenadiers in the night by the hills of Hospitalette, to enter that place, and they descended into the ditch in expectation of having the gate opened; but Maurice Mathieu, apprized of the plan, had prepared every thing to receive this unfortunate column, which was in an instant overwhelmed with fire.

Official Abstract of Mr. Wellesley's Despatches. MSS.

Napoleon now changed the system of the war. All that part of Catalonia west of the Upper Llobregat, and from Igualada by Ordal to the sea, including the district of Tortoza, was placed under Suchet's government, and seventeen thousand of Macdonald's troops were united to the third corps, which was thus augmented to forty-two thousand men, and took the title of the "*Army of Aragon.*" It was destined to besiege Taragona, while Macdonald, whose force was thus reduced to twenty-seven thousand under arms, including fifteen thousand in garrison and in the Ampurdan, was restricted to the upper part of Catalonia. His orders were to attack Cardona, Berga, Seu d'Urgel, and Montserrat, and to war down Martinez, Manso, Rovira, and other chiefs, who kept in the mountains between Olot and the Cerdaña: and a division of five thousand men, chiefly composed of national guards, was also ordered to assemble at Mont Louis, for the purpose of acting in the Cerdaña, and on the rear of the partizans in the high valleys. By these means the line of operations for the invasion of Catalonia was altered from France to Aragon, the difficulties were lessened, the seventh corps reduced in numbers, became, instead of the principal, the secondary army; and Macdonald's formal method was thus exchanged for the lively vigorous talent of Suchet. But the delay already caused in the siege of Tortoza, could never be compensated; Suchet had been kept on the Ebro, when he should have been on the Guadalaviar, and this enabled the Murcians to keep the fourth corps in Grenada, when it should have been on the Tagus aiding Massena.

CHAPTER IV.

BOOK XIII.

1811. March.

WHEN the troops of the seventh corps were incorporated with the army of Aragon, the preparations for the siege of Taragona, were pushed forward with Suchet's usual activity; but previous to touching upon that subject it is necessary to notice the guerilla warfare, which Villa Campa, and others, had carried on against Aragon during the siege of Tortoza. This warfare was stimulated by the appointment of the secret juntas, and by the supplies which England furnished, especially along the northern coast, from Coruña to Bilbao, where experience had also produced a better application of them than heretofore. The movements of the English squadrons, in that sea, being from the same cause better combined with the operations of the Partidas, rendered the latter more formidable, and they became more harassing to the enemy as they acquired something of the consistency of regular troops in their organization, although irregular in their mode of operations: for it must not be supposed, that because the guerilla system was in itself unequal to the deliverance of the country, and was necessarily accompanied with great evils, that as an auxiliary it was altogether useless. The interruption of the French correspondence was, as I have already said, tantamount to a diminution on their side of thirty thousand regular troops, without reckoning those who were necessarily

CHAP. IV.

1811. March.

employed to watch and pursue the Partidas; this estimate may even be considered too low, and it is certain that the moral effect produced over Europe by the struggle thus maintained, was very considerable.

Nevertheless the same number of men under a good discipline would have been more efficacious, less onerous to the country people, and less subversive of social order. When the regular army is completed, all that remains in a country may be turned to advantage as irregulars, yet they are to be valued as their degree of organization approaches that of the regular troops: thus militia are better than armed bodies of peasantry, and these last, if directed by regular officers, better than sudden insurrections of villagers. But the Spanish armies were never completed, never well organized; and when they were dispersed, which happened nearly as often as they took the field, the war must have ceased in Spain, had it not been kept alive by the Partidas, and it is there we find their moral value. Again, when the British armies kept the field, the Partidas harassed the enemy's communications, and this constituted their military value; yet it is certain that they never much exceeded thirty thousand in number; and they could not have long existed in any numbers without the supplies of England, unless a spirit of order and providence, very different from any thing witnessed during the war, had arisen in Spain. How absurd then to reverse the order of the resources possessed by an invaded country, to confound the moral with the military means, to place the irregular resistance of the peasants first, and that of the soldiers last in the scale of physical defence.

Appendix, No. I. Section 2.

BOOK XIII. 1811. March.

That many of the Partida chiefs became less active, after they received regular rank, is undeniable; but this was not so much a consequence of the change of denomination, as of the inveterate abuses which oppressed the vigour of the regular armies, and by which the Partidas were necessarily affected when they became a constituent part of those armies; many persons of weight have indeed ascribed entirely to this cause, the acknowledged diminution of their general activity at one period. It seems, however, more probable that a life of toil and danger, repeated defeats, the scarcity of plunder, and the discontent of the people at the exactions of the chiefs, had in reality abated the desire to continue the struggle; inactivity was rather the sign of subjection than the result of an injudicious interference by the government. But it is time to support this reasoning by facts.

During the siege of Tortoza, the concentration of the third and seventh corps exposed Aragon and Catalonia to desultory enterprises at a moment when the Partidas, rendered more numerous and powerful by the secret juntas, were also more ardent, from the assembly of the Cortez, by which the people's importance in the struggle seemed at last to be acknowledged. Hence no better test of their real influence on the general operations can be found than their exploits during that period, when two French armies were fixed as it were to one spot, the supplies from France nearly cut off by natural difficulties, the district immediately around Tortoza completely sterile, Catalonia generally exhausted, and a project to create a fictitious scarcity in the fertile parts of Aragon diligently and in some sort successfully pursued by the secret juntas. The number of French foraging parties, and the distances to which they were sent were then greatly increased, and the facility of cutting them off proportionably augmented. Now the several operations of Villa Campa during the blockade have been already related, but, although sometimes successful, the results were mostly adverse to the Spaniards; and when that chief, after the siege was actually commenced, came down, on the 19th December 1810, towards the side of Daroca, his cavalry was surprised by colonel Kliski, who captured or killed one hundred and fifty in the village of Blancas. The Spanish chief then retired, but being soon after joined by the Empecinado from Cuença, he returned in January to the frontier of Aragon, and took post between Molina and Albaracin.

At this period Tortoza had surrendered, and Musnier's division was spread along the western part of Aragon, wherefore Suchet immediately detached general Paris with one column from Zaragoza, and general Abbé with another from Teruel, to chase these two Partidas. Paris fell in with the Empecinado near Molina, and the latter then joined Villa Campa, but the French general forced both from their mountain position near Frias, where he was joined by Abbé; and they continued the pursuit for several days, but finding that the fugitives took different routes, again separated; Paris followed Villa Campa, and Abbé pursued the Empecinado through Cuenca, from whence Carbajal and the secret junta immediately fled. Paris failing to overtake Villa Campa, entered Beleta, Cobeta, and Paralejos, all three containing manufactories for arms, which he destroyed, and then returned; and the whole expedi-

BOOK XIII. 1811. April.

tion lasted only twelve days, yet the smaller Partidas, in Aragon, had taken advantage of it to cut off a detachment of fifty men near Fuentes: and this was followed up on the side of Navarre by Mina, who entered the Cinco Villas in April, and cut to pieces one hundred and fifty *gens d'armes* near Sadava. However Chlopiski pursued him also so closely, that he obliged his band to disperse near Coseda in Navarre.

During this time the Valencians had been plunged in disputes, Bassecour was displaced, and Coupigny appointed in his stead. The notables, indeed, raised a sum of money for recruits, but Coupigny would not take the command, because the Murcian army was not also given to him; and that army, although numerous, was in a very neglected state, and unable to undertake any service. However, when Tortoza fell, the Valencians were frightened, and set about their own defence. They repaired and garrisoned the fort of Oropesa, and some smaller posts on the coast, along which runs the only artillery-road to their capital: they commenced fortifying Murviedro, or rather the rock of Saguntum overhanging it, and they sent fifteen hundred men into the hills about Cantavieja. These last were dispersed on the 5th of April by a column from Teruel; and on the 11th another body having attempted to surprise Uldecona, which was weakly guarded, were also defeated and sabred by the French cavalry.

These different events, especially the destruction of the gun-manufactories, repressed the activity of the partizans, and Suchet was enabled to go to Lerida, in the latter end of March, to receive the soldiers to be drafted from the seventh corps: Macdonald himself could not, however, regain Barcelona without an escort, and hence seven thousand men marched with him on the 29th of the month, not by Igualada, which was occupied in force by Sarsfield, but by the circuitous way of Manresa; for neither Macdonald nor Suchet wished to engage in desultory actions with the forces destined for the siege. Nevertheless Sarsfield, getting intelligence of the march, passed by Calaf with his own and Eroles' troops, and waited on Macdonald's flanks and rear near the Cardenera river, while a detachment, barricading the bridge of Manresa, opposed him in front. This bridge was indeed carried, but the town being abandoned, the Italian soldiers wantonly set fire to it in the night; an act which was immediately revenged, for the flames being seen to a great distance, so enraged the Catalans, that in the morning all the armed men in the district, whether regulars, Miguelettes, or Somatenes, were assembled on the neighbouring hills, and fell with infinite fury upon Macdonald's rear, as it passed out from the ruins of the burning city. The head of the French column was then pushing for the bridge of Villamara, over the Llobregat, which was two leagues distant; and as the country between the rivers was one vast mountain, Sarsfield, seeing that the French rear stood firm to receive the attack of the Somatenes, while the front still advanced, thought to place his division between, by moving along the heights which skirted the road. Macdonald, however, concentrated his troops, gained the second bridge, and passed the Llobregat, but with great difficulty and with the loss of four hundred men, for his march was continually under Sarsfield's fire, and some of his troops were even cut off from the bridge, and obliged to cross by a

BOOK XIII.

1811. April.

ford higher up. During the night, however, he collected his scattered men, and moved upon Sabadel, whence he pushed on alone for Barcelona, and on the 3d of April, Harispe, who commanded the escort, recommenced the march, and passing by Villa Franca, Christina, Cabra, and Momblanch, returned to Lerida the 10th.

The invasion of Catalonia was now divided into three parts, each assigned to a distinct army.

1°. Suchet, with that of Aragon, was to take Taragona and subdue the lower part of the province.

2°. Macdonald, with that part of the seventh corps called the active army of Catalonia, was to break the long Spanish line extending from Taragona, through Montserrat to the Cerdaña, and the high mountains about Olot.

3°. Baraguay d'Hilliers, having his head-quarters at Gerona, was to hold the Ampurdan with the troops before assigned to his charge, and to cooperate, as occasion might offer, with Macdonald, under whose orders he still remained; and the division of five thousand men before mentioned as having been collected near Mount Louis, at the entrance of the French Cerdaña, was to act on the rear of the Spaniards in the mountains, while the others attacked them in front. Nor did the success appear doubtful, for the hopes and means of the province were both sinking. The great losses of men sustained at Tortoza and in the different combats; the reputation of Suchet; the failure of the attempts to surprise Barcelona, Perillo, and San Filippe de Balaguer; the incapacity of Campo Verde, which was now generally felt, and the consequent desertion of the Miguelettes, would probably have rendered certain the French plans, if at the very moment of execution they had not been marred by Rovira, who surprised the great fortress of Figueras, the key of the Pyrenees on that side of Catalonia. This, the boldest and most important stroke made by a Partida chief, during the whole war, merits a particular detail.

CHAP. IV.

1811. April.

SURPRISE OF FERNANDO DE FIGUERAS.

The governor of the place, general Guillot, enforced no military discipline, his guards were weak, he permitted the soldiers to use the pallisades for fuel, and often detached the greatest part of the garrison to make incursions to a distance from the place; in all things disregarding the rules of service. The town, which is situated below the hill, upon which the great fortress of Fernando stands, was momentarily occupied by the Italian general Peyri, with about six hundred men, who were destined to join Macdonald, and who trusting to the strength of the fortress above, were in no manner on their guard. And the garrison above was still more negligent; for Guillot had on the 9th of April sent out his best men to disperse some Somatenes assembled in the neighbouring hills, and this detachment having returned at night fatigued, and being to go out again the next day, slept while the gates were confided to convalescents, or men unfit for duty: thus the ramparts were entirely unguarded. Now there were in the fort two Catalan brothers named Palopos, and a man called Juan, employed as under-storekeepers, who being gained by Rovira had, such was the negligence of discipline, obtained from the head of their department

Vacani. Official Abstract of Mr. Wellesley's Despatches. MSS. General Campbell's MSS. General Doyle's MSS. Capt. Codrington's MSS. Mr. Stuart's Papers. MSS.

BOOK XIII.

1811. April.

the keys of the magazines, and also that of a postern under one of the gates.

Rovira, having arranged his plan, came down from the mountain of St. Lorens de Muga in the night of the 9th, and secretly reached the covered way with seven hundred chosen men of his own Partida. General Martinez followed in support with about three thousand Miguelettes, and the Catalan brothers, having previously arranged the signals, opened the postern, and admitted Rovira, who immediately disarmed the guard and set wide the gates for the reserve; and although some shots were fired, which alarmed the garrison, Martinez came up so quickly that no effectual resistance could be made. Thirty or forty men were killed or wounded, the magazines were seized, the governor and sixteen hundred soldiers and camp-followers were taken in their quarters, and thus in an hour Rovira mastered one of the strongest fortresses in Europe: three cannon-shot were then fired as a signal to the Somatenes in the surrounding mountains, that the place was taken, and that they were to bring in provisions as rapidly as possible. Meanwhile general Peyri alarmed by the noise in the fortress and guessing at the cause, had collected the troops, baggage, sick men, and stores in the town below, and sent notice to Gerona, but he made no attempt to retake the place, and at daylight retired to Bascara. For having mounted the hills during the night, to observe how matters went, he thought nothing could be done, an opinion condemned by some as a great error; and indeed it appears probable that during the confusion of the first surprise, a brisk attempt by six hundred fresh men might have recovered the fortress. At Bascara five hundred men detached from Gerona, on the spur of the occasion, met him with orders to re-invest the place, and Baraguay d'Hilliers promised to follow with all his forces without any delay. Then Peyri, although troubled by the fears of his troops, many of whom were only national guards, returned to Figueras, and driving the Spaniards out of the town took post in front of the fort above; but he could not prevent Martinez from receiving some assistance in men and provisions from the Somatenes. The news of Rovira's exploit spread with inconceivable rapidity throughout the Peninsula, extending its exhilarating influence, even to the Anglo-Portuguese army, then not much given to credit or admire the exploits of the Spaniards, but Baraguay d'Hilliers with great promptness assembled his dispersed troops, and on the 13th invested the fort with six thousand infantry and five hundred cavalry; and this so quickly that the Spaniard had not time, or, more probably neglected, to remove, sixteen thousand muskets which were in the place.

Martinez remained governor, but Rovira was again in the mountains, and all Catalonia, animated by the Promothean touch of this Partida chief, seemed to be moving at once upon Figueras. Campo Verde came up to Vich, intending first to relieve Figueras, and then in concert with the English and Spanish vessels to blockade Rosas by land and sea. Rovira himself collected a convoy of provisions near Olot. Captain Bullen with the Cambrian and Volontaire frigates, taking advantage of the French troops having been withdrawn from Gerona, drove out the small garrison from San Filieu and Palamos, destroyed the batteries, and

BOOK XIII. 1811. April.

made sail to join captain Codrington at Rosas. A Spanish frigate, with a fleet of coasting-vessels loaded with supplies, anchored at Palamos; and Francisco Milans, after beating a small French detachment near Arens de Mar, invested Hostalrich; Juan Claros hovered about Gerona, and Eroles and Manso coming from Montserrat reduced Olot and Castelfollit. Sarsfield however remained in the Seu d'Urgel, and directed the mountaineers to establish themselves at Balaguer, but they were driven away again with great loss by a detachment from the garrison of Lerida.

On the 3d of May, Rovira having brought his convoy up to Besalu, Campo Verde, who had arranged that captain Codrington should make a diversion by an attack on Rosas, drew Milans from Hostalrich, and having thus united eleven thousand men marched in several columns from Avionet and Villa Fan against the town, hoping to draw Baraguay d'Hilliers to that side; and to beat him, while Rovira, forcing a small camp near Llers, at the opposite quarter, should introduce the convoy and its escort into the fortress. The circuit of investment was wide, and very difficult, and therefore slightly furnished of men; but it was strengthened by some works, and when the Spanish columns first advanced, the French general reinforced the camp near Llers, and then hastened with four thousand men against Campo Verde, who was already in the valley of Figueras, and only opposed by one battalion. Baraguay d'Hilliers immediately fell on the right flank of the Spaniards and defeated them; the French cavalry, which had been before driven in from the front, rallied and completed the victory, and the

Spaniards retreated with a loss of fifteen hundred including prisoners. This affair was exceedingly ill-managed by Campo Verde, who was so sure of success that he kept the sheep of the convoy too far behind, to enter, although the way was open for some time, hence the succour was confined to a few artillery-men, some tobacco, and medicines. Meanwhile the English ships landed some men at Rosas, but neither did this produce any serious effect, and the attempt to relieve Figueras having thus generally failed, that place was left to its own resources which were few; for the French with an unaccountable negligence had always kept a scanty supply of provisions and stores there. Martinez, who had now above four thousand men, was therefore obliged to practise the most rigorous economy in the distribution of food, and in bearing such privations the peninsular race are unrivalled.

Macdonald was so concerned for the loss of Figueras, that, setting aside all his own plans, he earnestly adjured Suchet to suspend the siege of Taragona, and restore him the troops of the seventh corps: Maurice Mathieu also wrote from Barcelona in a like strain, thinking that the possession of Upper Catalonia depended upon one powerful effort to recover the lost fortress. But Suchet, who had no immediate interest in that part of the province, whose hopes of obtaining a marshal's staff rested on the taking of Taragona, and whose preparations were all made for that siege, Suchet I say, whose judgement was unclouded, and whose military talent was of a high order, refused to move a step towards Figueras, or even to delay, for one moment, his march against Taragona.

He said that "his battalions being scattered, in

BOOK XIII. 1811. April.

search of supplies, he could not reunite them, and reach Figueras under twenty-five days; during that time the enemy, unless prevented by Baraguay d'Hilliers, could gather in provisions, receive reinforcements, and secure the fortress. A simple blockade might be established by the nearest troops, and to accumulate great numbers on such a sterile spot would not forward the recapture, but would create infinite difficulties with respect to subsistence. It was probable Napoleon had already received information of the disaster, and given orders for the remedy; and it was by no means reasonable to renounce the attack on Taragona, the only remaining bulwark of Catalonia, at the very moment of execution, because of the loss of a fort; it was in Taragona, the greatest part of the forces of Catalonia would be shut up, and it was only in such a situation that they could be made prisoners; at Lerida, Mequinenza, and Tortoza, eighteen thousand men and eight hundred officers had been captured, and if ten or twelve thousand more could be taken in Taragona, the strength of Catalonia would be entirely broken. If the Spaniards failed in revictualling Figueras, that place, by occupying their attention, would become more hurtful than useful to them; because Campo Verde might, and most probably would, march to its succour, and thus weaken Taragona, which was a reason for hastening rather than suspending the investment of the latter; wherefore he resolved, notwithstanding the separation of his battalions and the incomplete state of his preparations, to move down immediately and commence the siege." A wise determination and alone sufficient to justify his reputation as a general.

Macdonald was now fain to send all the troops

he could safely draw together, to reinforce Baraguay d'Hilliers. In June, when a detachment from Toulon, and some frontier guards had arrived at Figueras, the united forces amounting to fifteen thousand men, he took the command in person and established a rigorous blockade, working day and night, to construct works of circumvallation and contravallation; his lines six miles in length, crowning the tops of the mountains and sinking into the deepest valleys, proved what prodigious labours even small armies are capable of. Thus with incessant wakefulness Macdonald recovered the place; but this was at a late period in the year, and when Suchet's operations had quite changed the aspect of affairs.

When Tortoza fell, that general's moveable columns traversing the borders of Castile, the eastern districts of Valencia, a portion of Navarre, and all the lower province of Catalonia, protected the collection of supplies, and suppressed the smaller bands which swarmed in those parts; hence, when the siege of Taragona was confided to the third corps, the magazines, at Lerida and Mora, were already full; and a battering train was formed at Tortoza, to which place the tools, platforms, and other materials, fabricated at Zaragosa were conveyed. Fifteen hundred draft horses, the greatest part of the artillery-men and engineers, and ten battalions of infantry were also collected in that town, and from thence shot and shells were continually forwarded to San Felippe de Balaguer. This was a fine application of Cæsar's maxim, that war should maintain itself, for all the money, the guns, provisions, and materials, collected for this siege, were

BOOK XIII. 1811. April.

the fruits of former victories; nothing was derived from France but the men. It is curious, however, that Suchet so little understood the nature and effects of the English system of finance, that he observes, in his memoirs, upon the ability with which the ministers, made Spain pay the expense of this war by never permitting English gold to go to the Peninsula; he was ignorant, that the paper money system had left them no English gold to send.

The want of forage in the district of Tortoza, and the advantage of the carriage-road by the Col de Balaguer, induced the French general to direct his artillery that way; but his provisions, and other stores, passed from Mora by Falcet and Momblanch to Reus, in which latter town he proposed to establish his stores for the siege, while Mora, the chief magazine, was supplied from Zaragoza, Caspe, and Mequinenza. Divers other arrangements, of which I shall now give the outline, contributed to the security of the communications, and enabled the army of Aragon to undertake the great enterprize for which it was destined.

1°. Detachments of gens-d'armes and of the frontier guards of France, descending the high valleys of Aragon, helped to maintain tranquillity on the left bank of the Ebro, and occupied the castles of Venasque and Jaca, which had been taken by Suchet in his previous campaign.

2°. The line of correspondence from France, instead of running as before through Guipuscoa and Navarre, by Pampeluna, was now directed by Pau, Oleron, and Jaca to Zaragoza; and in the latter city, and in the towns around it, four or five battalions, and a proportion of horsemen and artillery, were disposed, to watch the Partidas from Navarre and the Moncayo mountains.

3°. Four battalions with cavalry and guns, were posted at Daroca under general Paris, whose command extended from thence to the fort of Molina, which was armed and garrisoned.

4°. General Abbé was placed at Teruel with five battalions, three hundred cuirassiers, and two pieces of artillery, to watch Villa Campa, and the Valencian army which was again in the field.

5°. Alcanitz aud Morella were occupied by fourteen hundred men, whereby that short passage through the mountains from Aragon to Valencia was secured; and from thence the line to Caspe, and down the Ebro from Mequinenza to Tortoza, was protected by twelve hundred men; Tortoza itself was garrisoned by two battalions, the forts at the mouth of the Ebro were occupied, and four hundred men were placed in Rapita.

This line of defence from right to left was fourteen days march, but the number of fortified posts enabled the troops to move from point to point, without much danger; and thus the army of the great and rich province of Valencia, the division of Villa Campa, the Partidas of New Castile and Navarre, including Mina and the Empecinado, the most powerful of those independent chiefs, were all set at nought by twelve thousand French, although the latter had to defend a line of one hundred and fifty miles. Under cover of this feeble chain of defence, Suchet besieged a strong city which had a powerful garrison, an open harbour, a commanding squadron of ships, and a free communication, by sea, with Cadiz, Valencia, Gibraltar, and the Balearic

BOOK XIII. 1811. April.

islands. It is true that detachments from the army of the centre, acting on a large circuit round Madrid, sometimes dispersed, and chased the Partidas that threatened Suchet's line of defence, but at this period, from circumstances to be hereafter mentioned, that army was in a manner paralysed.

While the French general's posts were being established, he turned his attention to the arrangements for a permanent supply of food. The difficulty of procuring meat was become great, because he wisely refrained from using up the sheep and cattle of Aragon, lest the future supply of his army should be anticipated, and the minds of the people of that province alienated by the destruction of their breeding flocks; to avoid this, he engaged contractors to furnish him from France, and so completely had he pacified the Aragonese, through whose territories the flocks were brought, and with whose money they were paid for, that none of his contracts failed. But as these resources were not immediately available, the troops on the right bank of the Ebro made incursions after cattle beyond the frontiers of Aragon; and when Harispe returned from Barcelona, eight battalions marched upon a like service up the higher valleys of the Pyrenees.

It was in this state of affairs that Suchet received intelligence of the surprise of Figueras, which induced him to hasten the investment of Taragona. Meanwhile, fearing that Mina might penetrate to the higher valleys of Aragon, and in conjunction with the partidas of Upper Catalonia cut off all correspondence with France, he detached Chlopiski with four battalions and two hundred hussars to watch the movements of that chief only, and demanded of the emperor, that some troops from Pampeluna should occupy Sanguessa, while others, from the army of the north, should relieve the detachments of the army of Aragon, at Soria and Calatayud.

The battalions sent up the high valleys of Catalonia returned in the latter end of April. Suchet then reviewed his troops, issued a month's pay, and six day's provisions to each soldier, loaded many carriages and mules with flour, and, having first spread a report, that he was going to relieve Figueras, commenced his march to Taragona by the way of Momblanch. Some Miguelettes entrenched in the pass of Ribas, were dispersed by Harispe's division on the 1st of May, and the army descended the hills to Alcover; but four hundred men were left in Momblanch, where a post was fortified, to protect the line of communication with Lerida, and to prevent the Spanish partizans on that flank, from troubling the communication between Mora and Reus. The 2d the head-quarters were fixed at Reus, and the 3d the Spanish outposts were driven over the Francoli; meanwhile Habert, sending the artillery from Tortoza by the Col de Balaguer, moved himself with a large convoy from Mora by Falcet to Reus.

CHAPTER V.

BOOK XIII.

1811. May.

In Taragona, although a siege had been so long expected, there was a great scarcity of money and ammunition, and so many men had, as Suchet foresaw, been drawn off to succour Figueras, that the garrison, commanded by colonel Gonzalez, was not more than six thousand, including twelve hundred armed inhabitants and the seamen of the port. The town was encumbered with defensive works of all kinds, but most of them were ill-constructed, irregular, and without convenient places for making sallies.

Taragona itself was built upon rocks, steep on the north-east and south, but sinking gently on the south-west and west into low ground. A mole formed a harbour capable of receiving ships of the line, and beyond the mole there was a roadstead. The upper town was surrounded by ancient walls, crowning the rocks, and these walls were inclosed by a second rampart with irregular bastions which ran round the whole city. On the east, across the road to Barcelona, there was a chain of redoubts connected by curtains, with a ditch and covered way; and behind this line there was a rocky space called the Milagro, opening between the body of the place and the sea. The lower town, or suburb, was separated from the upper, by the inner ramparts of the latter, and was protected by three regular and some irregular bastions with a ditch; a square work, called Fort Royal, formed a species of citadel within, and the double town presented the figure of an irregular oblong, whose length lying parallel to the sea, was about twelve hundred yards.

On the east beyond the walls, a newly constructed line of defence was carried along the coast to the mouth of the Francoli, where it ended in a large redoubt, built to secure access to that river when the ancient aqueducts which furnished the city with water should be cut by the French. This line was strengthened by a second redoubt, called the Prince, half-way between that near the Francoli and the town; and it was supported by the mole which being armed with batteries, and nearly in a parallel direction, formed as it were a second sea-line.

The approach on the side of the Francoli river was of a level character, and exposed to the fire of the Olivo, a large outwork on the north, crowning a rocky table-land of an equal height with the upper town, but divided from it by a ravine nearly half-a-mile wide, across which the aqueducts of the place were carried. This Olivo was an irregular horn-work, four hundred yards long, with a ditch twenty-four feet deep and forty wide, but the covered way was not completed, and the gorge was only closed by a loopholed wall; neither was this defence quite finished, as the steepness of the rock, and the fire of the city appeared to render it secure. The bastion on the left of the Olivo, was cut off by a ditch and a rampart from the body of the work, and on the right also within the rampart there was a small redoubt of refuge, with a high cavalier or bank, on which three guns were placed

BOOK XIII. 1811. May.

that overlooked all the country round. The ordinary garrison of the Olivo was from twelve to fifteen hundred men, and it contained fifty out of three hundred pieces of artillery which served the defence of Taragona.

The nature of the soil combined with the peculiarities of the works, determined Suchet's line of attack. On the north and east side the ground was rocky, the fronts of defence wide, the approaches unfavourable for breaching batteries; and as all the guns and stores would have to be dragged over the hills on a great circuit, unless the Olivo was first taken, no difficulty could be avoided in an attack. Wherefore, on the side of the lower town the French resolved to approach, although the artificial defences were there accumulated, and the ground between the town and the Francoli river taken in reverse by the Olivo, which rendered it necessary first to reduce that outwork. But this part was chosen by the French, because the soil was deep and easily moved, their depôts and parks close at hand, the ground-plot of the works so salient that they could be easily embraced with fire, and because the attack would, it was supposed, cut off the garrison from fresh water, yet this last advantage was not realized.

On the 4th of May the French, passing the Francoli, drove in the outposts, took possession of two small detached redoubts, situated on the northern side, called the forts of Loretto, and invested the place. However the Spanish troops supported by the fire of the Olivo killed and wounded two hundred men, and the next day a fruitless attempt was made to retake the lost ground; at the same time the fleet under captain Codrington, consisting of three English ships of the line and three frigates, besides sloops and Spanish vessels of war, cannonaded the French right, and harassed their convoys, then coming by the coast-road from the Col de Balaguer. The investing troops whose posts were very close to the Olivo, were also greatly incommoded by the heavy fire from that outwork, yet the line was maintained and perfected.

Habert's division, forming the right wing, extended from the sea to the bridge of the Francoli; general Frere's division connected Habert with Harispe's, whose troops occupied the ground before the Olivo; the Italian division prolonged Harispe's left to the road of Barcelona which runs close to the sea on the east side of Taragona; three regiments were placed in reserve higher up on the Francoli, where a trestle bridge was cast, and the park, which was established on the right of that river, at the village of Canonja, contained sixty-six battering guns and mortars, each furnished with seven hundred rounds. There were also thirty-six field-pieces, two thousand artillery-men to serve the guns, seven hundred sappers and miners, fourteen hundred cavalry, and nearly fifteen thousand infantry. The head-quarters were fixed at the village of Constanti, a strong covering position, the depôt at Reus was secured by fortified convents, and the works at Mora were defended by several battalions. Other troops, placed at Falcet, guarded the communications, which were farther secured by the escorts belonging to the convoys; and the French had cut off the water of the aqueducts from the Olivo, but this water, whose source was ten or twelve miles off, was also necessary to the besiegers on that sterile land, and was

BOOK XIII. 1811. May.

again cut off by the Somatenes, which obliged the French to guard its whole course during the siege.

Meanwhile Campo Verde after his defeat at Figueras had sent Sarsfield and Eroles to their former posts near Valls, Momblanch, and Igualada, and embarking at Mattaro himself, with four thousand men, came on the 10th to Taragona, where the sudden appearance of the French had produced great consternation. Yet when Campo Verde arrived with this reinforcement, and when colonel Green, the English military agent, arrived on the 15th from Cadiz, in the Merope, bringing with him fifty thousand dollars and two transports laden with arms and stores, Spanish apathy again prevailed, and the necessary measures of defence were neglected. Beyond the walls, however, the French post at Momblanch was attacked by two thousand Miguelettes, and the Somatenes assembled in the vicinity of Reus.

Appendix, No. II. Section 1.

Suchet detached general Frere with four battalions to relieve the former place, where the attack had failed; the commandant of Reus also dispersed the Somatenes, and meanwhile Harispe pushed his patroles over the Gaya as far as Torre de Barra, where he found some wounded Spaniards. These men were within the protection of a convention, made by St. Cyr with Reding, by which the wounded men of both armies were to be left in the civil hospitals of the different towns, and mutually taken care of, without being made prisoners; and it is remarkable that this compact was scrupulously executed on both sides, while beyond those hospitals the utmost ferocity and a total disregard of civilized usages prevailed.

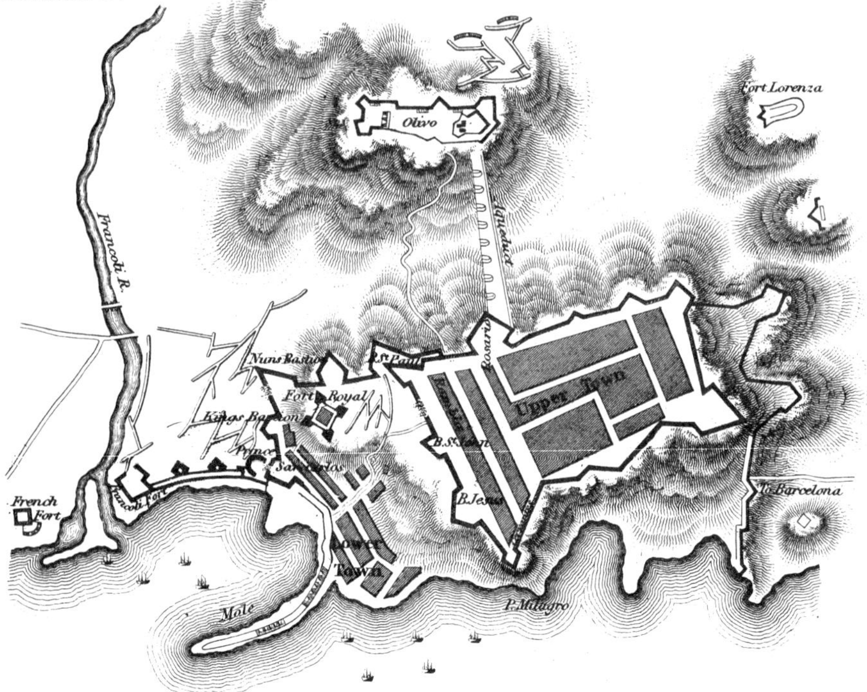

Explanatory Sketch OF THE SIEGE OF TARAGONA.

London Published by T. & W. BOONE.

Sarsfield's arrival near Momblanch threatened the communications between Reus and Mora, and at the same time a Valencian column, acting in concert with captain Adam of the Invincible, attacked the posts of Rapita and Amposta: the former was abandoned by the garrison, and the latter was surrounded by the Valencians, but a regiment sent from Tortoza, after disengaging Amposta, defeated the Valencians near Rapita; nevertheless Suchet, unwilling to lessen his already too small force, did not restore the latter post.

SIEGE OF TARAGONA.

The French general having resolved to attack the lower town, commenced his operations by constructing a fort and batteries, on the right of the Francoli, near the sea-shore, with a view to keep the English ships of war and the gun-boats at a distance from his projected trenches. These works commenced in the night of the 7th, were successfully continued towards the mouth of the river under the fire of the vessels; a trench, lined with musqueteers, was also carried from the left along the bank of the river to the bridge, but the Spaniards continually harassed the investing troops both from within and from without, and made some attempts against the camp; wherefore the brigade of general Salme, which was close to the Olivo, was obliged to entrench, and yet lost fifty or sixty men daily by the enemy's skirmishers.

On the night of the 13th, during a tempest, the French stormed two external entrenchments near the Olivo, and then turned them against the be-

BOOK XIII. 1811. May.

Appendix, No. II. Sect. 1.

sieged; the next morning a vigorous attempt to retake them was repulsed with a loss of one hundred men, and on the Francoli side, a sally supported by the shipping failed in consequence of the cowardice of some Spanish officers. On the same day, besides this attack on the side of the Francoli, the garrison came out from the Barcelona gate, and six hundred Somatenes from the Upper Gaya fell on the patroles of the Italian division, whereupon Palombini scoured the country on the 15th as far as Arbos.

The 18th a powerful sortie from the lower town was made by Gonzalez, who passed the bridge, and, aided by a fire from the place, from the Olivo, and from the fleet, pressed Habert's division hard; Suchet however came down with his reserve, pushed between the river and the Olivo, and menaced the Spanish line of retreat, which obliged Gonzalez to retire with loss. On the 20th three other sallies were made from the Olivo, and from the upper town, on the Barcelona side, but they were all in like manner repulsed; and that day Sarsfield took post with twelve hundred men on a high and rugged place near Alcover, thus menacing the depôt at Reus. The French general therefore detached two battalions of infantry and some cavalry, under general Broussard, to dislodge him, which was effected with the loss of a hundred French; but three days later he appeared before Momblanch, and was only driven away by the united brigades of Frere and Palombini, who marched against him. Divers attempts were also made upon the line of Falcet, especially at Grattallopes, where the Spanish colonel, Villamil, having attacked Morozinski, a Pole, the latter defended himself successfully, and with a bravery that has always distinguished the people of that heroic nation; a nation whose glory springs like an *ignis fatuus* from the corruption of European honour!

These repeated attacks having warned Suchet how difficult it would be to maintain, with his weak army, so great an extent of communication, he abandoned his post at Momblanch, and contented himself with preserving the lines of Falcet and of Felippe de Balaguer; a measure the more necessary, that the garrison of Taragona was now greatly augmented; for on the 16th, the Blake had sailed for Valencia to seek reinforcements, and Carlos O'Donnel, who had succeeded Bassecour, gave him above two thousand infantry and two hundred cannoneers, who were safely landed at Taragona on the 22d, two thousand stand of arms being, in return, delivered by captain Codrington to O'Donnel, to equip fresh levies. Above twelve thousand men were thus collected in the fortress, but all the richest citizens had removed with their families and effects to Villa Nueva de Sitjes, and the people were dispirited.

Suchet broke ground before the Olivo in the night of the 21st, and carried on his approaches from both ends of the Spanish entrenchments which he had seized on the night of the 13th. His engineers wished to reach a round hill, close to the works, on which they proposed to plant their first breaching battery, and they crowned it on the 22d, but with much loss, being obliged to carry the earth for the work, up the hill in baskets, and they were continually interrupted by sallies. Three counter-batteries were, however, completed and armed on the 27th with thirteen pieces, of which

BOOK XIII. 1811. May. Suchet.

six threw shells; but to effect this, the soldiers dragged the artillery over the rocks, under a heavy fire of grape, and the garrison making a vigorous sally, killed general Salme, when he opposed them with the reserves. The moment was dangerous to the French, but they were finally victorious, and the fire of the batteries having opened the same morning, was sustained until the evening of the 29th, when a breach being formed, the assault was ordered.

STORMING OF THE OLIVO.

Upon the success of this attack, Suchet thought, and with reason, that his chance of taking the town would depend, seeing that his army was too feeble to bear any serious check. Wherefore, having formed his columns of assault, he personally encouraged them, and at the same time directed the troops along the whole line of investment to advance simultaneously, and menace every part of the town. The night was dark, and the Spaniards were unexpectant of an attack, because none of their guns had yet been silenced; but the French, full of hope and resolution, were watching for the signal. When that was given, the troops on the Francoli, and those on the Barcelona side, made a sudden discharge of musketry, beat all their drums, and with loud shouts approached the town at those opposite quarters; the rampart of the place was instantly covered with fire from within and from without; the ships in the offing threw up rockets, and amidst the noise of four hundred guns the storming columns rushed upon the Olivo.

The principal force made for the breach; but a

second column, turning the fort, got between it and the town, at the moment when fifteen hundred men, sent to relieve the old garrison, were entering the gates. Some of the French instantly fell on their rear, which hurrying forward, gave an opportunity to the assailants to penetrate with them before the gates could be closed, and thirty sappers with hatchets having followed closely, endeavoured to break the door, while Papignay, their officer, attempted to climb over the wall; the Spaniards killed him and most of the sappers, but the other troops, planted their ladders to the right and left, and cutting through the pointed stakes above, entered the place and opened the gate.

Suchet. Vacani.

At the main attack the French boldly assailed the narrow breach, but the ditch was fifteen feet deep, the Spaniards firm, and the fire heavy, and they were giving way, when the historian, Vacani, followed by some of his countrymen, (it is a strange error to think the Italians have not a brave spirit!) cut down the paling which blocked the subterranean passage of the aqueduct, and thus got into the ditch and afterwards into the fort. Then the Spaniards were driven from the ramparts on all sides, back to the little works of refuge, before noticed, as being at each end of the Olivo, from whence they fired both musketry and guns; but the French and Italian reserves, followed by Harispe with a third column now entered the place, and with a terrible slaughter ended the contest. Twelve hundred men perished, some escaped, a thousand were taken, and amongst them their commander who had received ten wounds.

In the morning three thousand Spaniards came out of Taragona, yet retired without attacking, and

BOOK XIII. 1811. June.

Suchet demanded a suspension of arms to dispose of the dead; this was however treated with scorn and the heaps were burned, for the sterile rocks afforded no earth to bury them. Campo Verde now gave general Senens de Contreras the command of Taragona, and went himself to the field-army, which was about ten thousand strong, including some new levies made by the junta of Catalonia.

Suchet's investment having been precipitated by the fall of Figueras his stores were not all collected until the 1st of June, when trenches were opened to embrace the whole of the lower town including the fort of Francoli and its chain of connecting works running along the sea-shore, that is to say, 1°. The Nun's bastion and a half-moon called the King's, which formed, on the Spanish right, a sort of hornwork to the royal fort or citadel. 2°. The bastion of San Carlos and a half-moon called the Prince's, which stood on the left, in the retiring angle where the sea-line joined the body of the place, and served as a counter-guard to the bastion of San Carlos. 3°. The sea-line itself and the Francoli fort.

The 2d of June the besieged made a fruitless sally, and in the night of the 3d some advanced Spanish entrenchments were destroyed by the French. Sarsfield then entered Taragona with a detachment, and took the command of what was called the Port, which included the Mole, the works leading to the Francoli, and the suburb or lower town, Contreras still remaining governor of all, although reluctantly, for he expected no success.

In the night of the 4th the approaches were carried forward by the sap, the second parallel was commenced, and on the 6th the besiegers were within twenty yards of the Francoli fort, which had a wet ditch and was of regular construction. The breaching batteries which had been armed as the trenches proceeded, opened their fire against it on the 7th. The fresh masonry crumbled away rapidly, and at ten o'clock that night, the fort being entirely destroyed, three hundred chosen men in three columns, one of which forded the Francoli river, attacked the ruins, and the defenders retired fighting, towards the half-moon of the Prince. The assailants then made a disorderly attempt to enter with them, but were quickly repulsed with a loss of fifty men, yet the lodgement was under a heavy fire secured; and the next night a battery of six pieces was constructed there, with a view to silence the guns of the Mole, which together with that of the place, endeavoured to overwhelm the small space thus occupied, with shot.

In the nights of the 8th and 9th under terrible discharges from both the upper and lower town, the second parallel was prolonged to fort Francoli on the right, and on the left, carried to within seventy yards of the Nun's bastion.

The 11th Sarsfield making a sally, killed some men, and retarded the works; but before the 15th, three approaches by the sap were conducted against the Nun's bastion, where the besiegers crowned the glacis, and against the half-moon of the King and Prince. Fresh batteries were also constructed, whose fire embraced the whole front from the Prince to the Nun's bastion.

On the morning of the 16th fifty-four guns opened from the French batteries, and the Spaniards placing sand-bags along the parapets endeavoured

BOOK XIII. 1811. June.

by musketry to kill the gunners, who were much exposed, while all the cannon of the place which could be directed upon the trenches were employed to crush the batteries. Towards evening this fire had in a great degree mastered that of the besiegers, destroyed the centre of their second parallel, and silenced a battery on their right; but the loss and damage was great on both sides, for two consumption magazines exploded in the town and the Nun's bastion was breached. The engineers also observed that the ditch of the Prince was not carried round to the sea, and hence Suchet who feared a continuation of this murderous artillery battle, resolved to storm that point at once, hoping to enter by the defect in the ditch.

At nine o'clock two columns, supported by a reserve, issued from the trenches, and after a short resistance entered the work both by the gap of the ditch, and by escalade; the garrison fought well, and were put to the sword, a few only escaping along the quay, these were pursued by a party of the French, who passing a ditch, and drawbridge which cut off the road from the bastion of San Carlos, endeavoured to maintain themselves there, but being unsupported were mostly destroyed. The lodgement thus made was immediately secured and included in the trenches.

During the night of the 17th the old batteries were repaired and the construction of a new one, to breach the bastion of San Carlos, was begun upon the half-moon of the Prince; the saps and other approaches were also pushed forward, a lodgement was effected in the covered way of the Nun's bastion, and the third parallel was commenced; but on the right of the trenches, in advance of the Prince, the workmen came upon water which obliged them to desist at that point.

The 18th the third parallel was completed and the descent of the ditch at the Nun's bastion was commenced by an under-ground gallery; yet the fire from the upper town plunged into the trenches, and thirty-seven shells thrown very exactly into the lodgement on the counterscarp, obliged the besiegers to relinquish their operations there during the day. At this time also the gun-boats which hitherto had been of little service in the defence, were put under the direction of the British navy, and worked with more effect; yet it does not appear that the enemy ever suffered much injury from the vessels of war, beyond the interruption sometimes given to their convoys on the Col de Balaguer road.

During the nights of the 19th and 20th all the French works were advanced, and the morning of the 21st the new battery, in the Prince, being ready, opened its fire against San Carlos, and was followed by all the other batteries. The explosion of an expense magazine silenced the Prince's battery after a few rounds, the damage was however repaired, and at four o'clock in the evening nearly all the Spanish guns being overcome and the breaches enlarged, Suchet resolved to storm the lower town. But previous to describing this terrible event, it is necessary to notice the proceedings within and without the place, that a just idea of the actual state of affairs on both sides may be formed.

Macdonald had continued the blockade of Figueras with unceasing vigilance; and as the best of the Miguelettes were shut up there, and as the defeat

BOOK XIII. 1811. June.

of Campo Verde, on the 3d of May, had spread consternation throughout the province, the operations to relieve it were confined to such exertions as Rovira, Manso, and other chiefs could call forth. In like manner Francisco Milans was left in the Hostalrich district, and by his local popularity amongst the people of the coast between Palamos and Barcelona, was enabled to keep up an irregular force; but his object was to be made captain-general of the province, and his desire of popularity, or some other motive, led him to favour the towns of his district at the expense of the general cause. Mattaro and Villa Nueva de Sitjes trafficked in corn with Barcelona, and one of their secret convoys was detected at a later period passing the outposts with Milans' written authority. He put the men to death who permitted the convoy to pass, but he did not succeed in removing the suspicion of corruption from himself. This traffic was very advantageous for the French, and Maurice Mathieu being either unwilling to disturb it, or that having recently suffered in a skirmish at Mattaro, he feared to risk his troops, made no movement to aid the siege of Taragona, which it would appear, he might have done by taking possession of Villa Nueva de Sitjes.

Appendix, No. II. Section 4.

Such was the state of Eastern Catalonia, and in the western parts, the infantry of Sarsfield, and of Eroles, who had come down to the vicinity of Valls, and the cavalry under Caro, which was a thousand strong, formed, with the new levies ordered by the junta, an army of seven or eight thousand men. This force might have done much, if Campo Verde, a man of weak character, and led by others, had not continually changed his plans. At the opening of the siege, Sarsfield had acted, as we have seen, with some success on the side of Momblanch and Reus; but when he was sent into the lower town, the active army being reduced to Eroles' division, the cavalry could do no more than supply small detachments, to watch the different French convoys and posts. Campo Verde, however, fixed his quarters at Igualada, sent detachments to the Gaya and Villa Franca, and holding Villa Nueva de Sitjes as his post of communication with the fleet, demanded assistance from Murcia and Valencia, and formed a general plan for the succour of the place. But in Taragona his proceedings were viewed with dislike, and discord and negligence were rendering the courage of the garrison of no avail.

We have seen that captain Codrington landed two thousand five hundred Valencians on the 22d of May; besides that reinforcement, vessels loaded with powder and other stores, and additional mortars for the batteries, came from Carthagena and from Cadiz in the beginning of June. From Murcia also came reinforcements; but such was the perversity of some authorities and the want of arrangement in all, that the arms of these men were taken away from them before they sailed; and yet in Taragona there were already two thousand men without arms, a folly attributed by some to the Spanish authorities of Murcia, by others to colonel Roche, the English military agent. Nor did the confusion end here; for captain Codrington, when he sailed from Taragona to Peniscola in the latter end of May, supplied O'Donnel with arms for two thousand recruits, who were to replace the Valencians then embarked; and a few days afterwards he delivered so many more at the city

Appendix, No. II. Section 1.

BOOK XIII. 1811. June.

of Valencia, that Villa Campa and the Empecinado, whose troops, after their dispersion in April by Abbé and Paris, had remained inactive, were enabled again to take the field. Thus it appears that, while men were sent without arms from Valencia to Taragona, arms were being conveyed from the latter place to Valencia.

Appendix, No. II. Section 1.

The troops in Taragona had, by these different reinforcements, been augmented to near seventeen thousand men; however that number was never available at one time, for the Murcians were sent to Montserrat to be armed, and the losses during the operations, including those caused by sickness, had reduced the garrison at this period to less than twelve thousand. Several colonels of regiments, and many other officers, feigning sickness, or with open cowardice running away, had quitted the town, leaving their battalions to be commanded by captains; the general of artillery was incapablé, and Contreras himself, unknown to the inhabitants, unacquainted with the place or its resources, was vacillating and deceitful to those serving under him. He was very unwilling to undertake the defence, and he was at variance with Campo Verde outside, and jealous of Sarsfield inside. In the fleet also some disagreement occurred between captain Codrington and captain Bullen, and the commanders of the Diana and Prueba Spanish ships of war were accused of gross misconduct.

Report of Contreras.

Carlos O'Donnel and his brother the Conde de Abispal, at the desire of captain Codrington, had permitted Miranda to embark with four thousand of the best Valencian troops for Taragona, there to join in a grand sally; but they exacted from Codrington a pledge to bring those who survived back, for they would not suffer this their second aid in men to be shut up in the place when the object was effected. These troops landed the 12th at Taragona, yet the next day, at Campo Verde's order, Miranda, instead of making a sally as had been projected, carried them off by sea to Villa Nueva de Sitjes, and from thence marched to meet a detachment of horse coming from Villa Franca; and on the 15th two squadrons of cavalry issuing from Taragona by the Barcelona gate, passed the French line of investment, without difficulty, and also joined Miranda who then marched to unite with Campo Verde at Igualada.

This movement was in pursuance of a grand plan to succour the place; for the junta of Catalonia, having quitted Taragona after the fall of the Olivo, repaired with the archives to Montserrat, and as usual made their clamours for succour ring throughout the peninsula: they had received promises of cooperation from O'Donnel, from Villa Campa, and from the partizans, and Campo Verde proposed, that the English ships of war should keep between the Col de Balaguer and Taragona, to cannonade the French convoys on that route; that a detachment should take post at Ordal to watch the garrison of Barcelona, and that he with the remainder of his forces, which including Miranda's division amounted to ten thousand infantry and a thousand cavalry, should take some commanding position near Reus. In this situation he designed to send a detachment towards San Filippe de Balaguer to communicate with the fleet, and, avoiding any serious action, to operate by small corps against the French line of supply, and thus oblige them to raise the siege, or if they

BOOK XIII. 1811. June.

came out of their lines to fight them in strong positions.

Contreras treated this plan with contempt. He said it would cause the loss both of the place and the army; that the French would not raise the siege except for a general battle, and that within their lines the best mode of fighting them would be in concert with the garrison; wherefore he desired the general-in-chief to attack them in conjunction with himself, and the junta, who were at variance with Campo Verde, backed this proposal.

Neither of these plans, however, appear sound; for though it is certain, if the generals could have depended upon their troops, such was the reduced state of Suchet's force, and so extensive was his line of investment, that it would have been easy to break through; yet, unless the French were put entirely to the route, which was unlikely, no great advantage would have followed, because the communication was already open by sea. On the other hand Campo Verde's plan was only proposed on the 13th, and would have been too slow for the critical nature of the case. It would have been more in accord with that great maxim of war, which prescribes the *attack of an enemy's weakest point with the greatest possible numbers*, to have marched with his whole force upon Mora, or upon Reus, to beat the troops there, and destroy the depôts; and then seizing some strong posts on the hills close to the besieger's lines to have entrenched it and operated daily and hourly against their rear. If Campo Verde had destroyed either of these depôts the siege must have been raised; and if he was unable to beat two or three thousand infantry at those places, he could not hope, even with the assistance of the garrison, to destroy sixteen thousand of all arms in the entrenchments before Taragona. Suchet did not fear a battle on the Francoli river; but so tender was he of the depôts, that when Campo Verde sent an officer to raise the Somatenes about Mora, he called Abbé with three thousand infantry from Teruel, and that general who was active and experienced in the guerilla warfare, soon dispersed the Spanish levies, and took their chief with many others prisoners, after which he joined the besieging army.

Suchet required this reinforcement. He had lost a general, two hundred inferior officers, and above two thousand five hundred men during the siege, and had not more than twelve thousand infantry fit for duty; but colonel Villamil, a partizan of Campo Verde's, taking advantage of Abbé's absence, marched with a thousand men to attack Mora, and being beaten on the 16th was succeeded by Eroles, who came with his whole division to Falcet on the 20th, and captured a convoy of loaded mules, driving back the escort with some loss to Mora. The design was to tempt Suchet to send a strong detachment in pursuit of Eroles, in which case the latter was by a rapid march to rejoin Campo Verde near Alcover, when the whole army was to attack Suchet thus weakened. However the French general would not turn from his principal object, and his magazines at Reus were still so full that the loss of the convoy did not seriously affect him.

Such was the situation of affairs on the 21st of June, when the order to assault the lower town was given to an army, small in number, but full of vigour, and confident of success; while, in the

BOOK XIII. 1811. June. place there was confusion, folly, and cowardice. Contreras indeed acted a shameful part; for during captain Codrington's absence, Sarsfield had concerted with the navy, that in the case of the lower town being stormed, the ships should come to the mole and the garrison would retire there, rather than to the upper town; meanwhile Campo Verde recalled him to the active army, intending that general Velasco should replace him; but at three o'clock on the 21st, the breaches being then open, and the assault momentarily expected, Contreras commanded Sarsfield instantly to embark, falsely averring that such was the peremptory order of Campo Verde. Sarsfield remonstrated in vain, and a boat from the Cambrian frigate carried him and his personal staff and his effects on board that vessel; thus the command of the troops was left to an inefficient subordinate officer, the assault took place at that moment, and when Velasco arrived, he found only the dead bodies of those he was to have commanded. Contreras then assured captain Codrington and the junta, that Sarsfield had acted without his consent, and had in fact betrayed his post!

Appendix, No. II. Section 1.

STORMING OF THE LOWER TOWN.

This calamitous event happened in the evening of the 21st. Two breaches had been made in the bastions, and one in the fort Royal; they were not wide, and a few Spanish guns still answered the French fire; nevertheless the assault was ordered, and as some suppose, because Suchet had secret intelligence of Sarsfield's removal, and the consequent confusion in the garrison.

Rogniat. Vacani. Suchet. Captain Codrington's Papers, MSS.

Fifteen hundred grenadiers, destined for the attack, were assembled under Palombini in the trenches; a second column was formed to support the storming troops, and to repel any sally from the upper town; and while the arrangements were in progress, the French guns thundered incessantly, and the shouts of the infantry, impatient for the signal, were heard between the salvos, redoubling as the shattered walls gave way. At last Harispe's division began to menace the ramparts on the side of Barcelona, to distract the attention of the Spaniards, and then Suchet exhorting the soldiers to act vigorously, gave the signal and let them loose while it was still day. In an instant the breaches were crowned, and the assailants swarmed on the bastions, the ramparts, and the fort Royal; the Spaniards, without a leader, were thrown into confusion, and falling in heaps broke and fled towards the port, towards the mole, and towards the upper town, and a reserve stationed under the walls of the latter was overthrown with the same shock. Then some of the fugitives, running towards the mole, were saved by the English launches, others escaped into the upper town, a few were made prisoners, and the rest were slaughtered.

At eight o'clock the lower town was in the possession of the enemy. Fifteen hundred bodies, many of whom were inhabitants, lay stretched upon the place, and the mercantile magazines of the port being set on fire, the flames finished what the sword had begun. When the carnage ceased, the troops were rallied, working parties were set to labour; and ere the confusion in the upper town had subsided, the besiegers were again hidden in

BOOK XIII.

1811. June.

their trenches and burrowing forward to the walls of the upper town.

The front before them consisted of four bastions with curtains, but without a ditch. The bastion of St. Paul was opposite their left, that of St. John opposite their centre, that of Jesus opposite their right; but the bastion of Cervantes, which covered the principal landing place of the Milagro, although on the same front of defence, was somewhat retired and not included within the attack. A hollow piece of ground, serving as a trench, had enabled the French to establish their left in a side bastion of the wall, connecting the upper with the lower town; and their right was strongly protected by some houses lining the road, for between the two parts of the city there were four hundred yards of open garden-ground interspersed with single houses. A battery was constructed to play upon the landing places of the Milagro, two mortars which were on the hill of the fort Loretto, concurred in this object, and the light troops were pushed close up to the wall; but at daylight the ships of war passed the port delivering their broadsides in succession, Contreras then showed the heads of columns as if for a sally, and the French skirmishers retired; whereupon the Spanish general, contented with having thus cleared his front, re-entered the place.

The men saved from the mole, by the ships, were now relanded in the upper town, and the second reinforcement from Murcia arrived, but being like the first detachment without arms only added to the confusion and difficulties of the governor. Nevertheless as the loss of the French in the storming was about six hundred, and that of the Spaniards not more than two thousand, the besieged had still nine thousand fighting men; a number nearly equal to the whole infantry of Suchet's army; and hence Contreras, far from quailing beneath the blow, would not even receive a flag of truce by which the French general offered honourable conditions.

Suchet's position was becoming more embarrassing every moment; he had now delivered four assaults, his force was diminished nearly one-fifth of its original number, and the men's strength was spent with labouring on his prodigious works: his line of communication with Lerida was quite intercepted and that with Mora interrupted, and he had lost a large convoy of provisions together with the mules that carried it. The resolution of the besieged seemed in no manner abated, and their communication with the sea, although partially under the French fire, was still free; the sea itself was covered with ships of war, overwhelming reinforcements might arrive at any moment, and Campo Verde with ten thousand men was daily menacing his rear. The Valencian army, Villa Campa, the Empecinado, Duran who had defeated a French detachment near Mirando del Ebro, Mina who had just then taken the convoy with Massena's baggage at the Puerto de Arlaban, in fine all the Partidas of the mountains of Albaracin, Moncayo, and Navarre, were in motion, and menacing his position in Aragon. This rendered it dangerous for him to call to his aid any more troops from the right of the Ebro, and yet a single check might introduce despondency amongst the soldiers of the siege, composed as they were of different nations, and some but lately come under his command; indeed their labours and dangers were so incessant and wearing, that it is no

BOOK XIII. 1811. June.

small proof of the French general's talent, and the men's spirit, that the confidence of both was still unshaken.

On the 24th the crisis seemed at hand, intelligence arrived in the French camp, that the Spanish army was coming down the Gaya river to fight, at the same time the garrison got under arms, and an active interchange of signals took place between the town and the fleet. Suchet immediately placed a reserve to sustain the guards of his trenches, and marched with a part of his army to meet Campo Verde. That general, pressed by the remonstrances of Contreras and the junta, had at last relinquished his own plan, recalled Eroles, and united his army at Momblanch on the 22nd, and then moving by Villardoña, had descended the hills between the Gaya and the Francoli; he was now marching in two columns to deliver battle, having directed Contreras to make a sally at the same moment. But Miranda, who commanded his right wing, found, or pretended to find, some obstacles and halted, whereupon Campo Verde instantly relinquished the attack, and marched to Vendril before the French general could reach him.

The 25th he again promised Contreras to make a decisive attack, and for that purpose desired that three thousand men of the garrison should be sent to Vendril, and the remainder be held ready to cut their way through the enemy's lines during the action. He likewise assured him that four thousand English were coming by sea to aid in this project, and it is probable some great effort was really intended, for the breaching batteries had not yet opened their fire, and the wall of the place was consequently untouched; ten thousand infantry and a thousand cavalry under Campo Verde were within a few miles of the French camp on the Barcelona side; eight thousand men accustomed to fire were still under arms within the walls; and on the 26th colonel Skerrett appeared in the roadstead, not with four thousand, but with twelve hundred British soldiers, sent from Cadiz and from Gibraltar to succour Taragona.

The arrival of this force, the increase of shipping in the roadstead, and the promises of Campo Verde, raised the spirits of the garrison from the depression occasioned by the disappointment of the 27th; and they were still more elated when in the evening colonel Skerrett and his staff, accompanied by general Doyle, captain Codrington, and other officers of the navy, disembarked, and proceeded to examine the means of defence. But they were struck with consternation when they heard that the British commander, because his engineers affirmed that the wall would give way after a few salvos from the breaching batteries, had resolved to keep his troops on board the transports, idle spectators of the garrison's efforts, to defend the important place which he had been sent to succour.

Contreras' Report, Appendix, No. II, Section 1.

Contreras, thus disappointed on all sides, and without dependence on Campo Verde, resolved, if the French delayed the storm until the 29th, to make way by a sally on the Barcelona road, and so join the army in the field; meanwhile to stand the assault if fortune so willed it. And he had good reason for his resolution, for the ground in front of the walls was high and narrow; and although there was neither ditch nor covered way, a thick hedge of aloe trees, no small obstacle to troops, grew at the foot of the rampart, which was also cut

BOOK XIII.

1811. June.

off from the town, and from the side works, by an internal ditch and retrenchment. Behind the rampart the houses of the great street called the Rambla, were prepared for defence, furnishing a second line of resistance; and although the cuts on the flanks hindered the making of sallies in force, which at such a period was a good mode of defence, the reduced state of the French army gave reason to believe that eight thousand brave men could resist it effectually.

The 28th a general plan for breaking out on the Barcelona side, the cooperation of the fleet, and a combined attack of the Spanish army, was arranged; and Eroles embarked for the purpose of re-landing at Taragona, to take the leading of the troops destined to sally forth on the 29th. The French general had however completed his batteries on the night of the 27th, and in the morning of the 28th they opened with a crashing effect. One magazine blew up in the bastion of Cervantes; all the guns in that of San Paulo were dismounted; the wall fell away in huge fragments before the stroke of the batteries, and from the Olivo, and from all the old French trenches, the guns and mortars showered bullets and shells into the place. This fire was returned from many Spanish pieces, still in good condition, and the shoulders of the French batteries were beaten down; yet their gunners, eager for the last act of the siege, stood to their work uncovered, the musketry rattled round the ramparts, the men on both sides crowded to the front, and while opprobrious words and mutual defiance passed between them, the generals, almost within hearing of each other, exhorted the soldiers to fight with the vigour that the crisis demanded.

CHAP. V.

1811. June.

STORMING OF THE UPPER TOWN.

At five o'clock in the evening the French fire suddenly ceased, and fifteen hundred men led by general Habert passing out from the parallel, went at full speed up against the breach; twelve hundred under general Ficatier followed in support, general Montmarie led a brigade round the left, to the bastion of Rosario, with a view to break the gates there during the assault, and thus penetrating, to turn the interior defence of the Rambla. Harispe took post on the Barcelona road, to cut off the retreat of the garrison.

Suchet. Rogniat. Vacani. Codrington's papers.MSS.

The columns of attack had to pass over an open space of more than a hundred yards before they could reach the foot of the breach; and when within twenty yards of it, the hedge of aloes obliged them to turn to the right, and left, under a terrible fire of musketry and of grape, which the Spaniards, who were crowding on the breach with apparent desperation, poured unceasingly upon them. The destruction was great, the head of the French column got into confusion, gave back, and was beginning to fly, when the reserves rushed up, and a great many officers coming forward in a body, renewed the attack. At that moment one Bianchini, an Italian soldier, who had obtained leave to join the column as a volunteer, and whose white clothes, amidst the blue uniforms of the French, gave him a supernatural appearance, went forth alone from the ranks, and gliding silently and sternly up the breach, notwithstanding many wounds reached the top, and there fell dead. Then the multitude bounded forward with a shout, the first

BOOK XIII. 1811. June.

line of the Spaniards fled, and the ramparts were darkened by the following masses of the French.

Meanwhile Montmarie's sappers cut away the palisades at Rosario, and his light troops finding a rope hanging from the wall, mounted by it, at the moment when the assailants at the breach broke the Spanish reserves with one shock, and poured into the town like a devastating torrent. At the Rambla a momentary stand was indeed made, but the impulse of victory was too strong to be longer resisted, and a dreadful scene of slaughter and violence ensued. Citizens and soldiers, maddened with fear, rushed out in crowds by the Barcelona gate, while others, throwing themselves over the ramparts, made for the landing-places within the Milagro; but that way also had been intercepted by general Rogniat with his sappers, and then numbers throwing themselves down the steep rocks were dashed to pieces, while they who gained the shore were still exposed to the sword of the enemy. Those that went out by the Barcelona gate were met by Harispe's men, and some being killed, the rest, three thousand in number, were made prisoners. But within the town all was horror; fire had been set to many houses, Gonzales, fighting manfully, was killed, Contreras, wounded with the stroke of a bayonet, was only saved by a French officer; and though the hospitals were respected by the soldiers, in every other part their fury was unbounded. When the assault first commenced, the ship-launches had come close into the Milagro, and now saved some of the fugitives, but their guns swept the open space beyond, killing friends and enemies, as, mixed together, they rushed to the shore; and the French dragoons, passing through

CHAP. V.

1811. June.

the flaming streets at a trot, rode upon the fugitives, sabring those who had outstripped the infantry. In every quarter there was great rage and cruelty, and although most of the women and children had, during the siege, been removed from Taragona by the English shipping, and that the richest citizens had all gone to Sitjes, this assault was memorable as a day of blood. Only seven or eight hundred miserable creatures, principally soldiers, escaped on board the vessels; nine thousand, including the sick and wounded, were made prisoners; more than five thousand persons were slain, and a great part of the city was reduced to ashes.

CHAPTER VI.

BOOK XIII. 1811. June.

Suchet had lost in killed and wounded during the siege between four and five thousand men, yet scarcely had the necessary orders to efface the trenches, secure the prisoners, and establish order in the ruined city been given, than the French general was again in movement to disperse Campo Verde's force. In the night of the 29th Frere's division marched upon Villa Franca, Harispe's upon Villa Nueva, being followed by Suchet himself with Abbé's brigade and the heavy cavalry. Campo Verde then abandoned Vendril, and Harispe's column, although cannonaded by the English squadron, reached Villa Nueva, where a great multitude, military and others, were striving to embark in the vessels off the port. The light cavalry sabred some and made fifteen hundred prisoners, including the wounded men who had been carried there from Taragona during the siege; and Frere's column in a like manner dispersed the Spanish rear-guard at Vendril and Villa Franca. Campo Verde then fled with the main body to Igualada, and Suchet pushed on with the reserve to Barcelona, where he arranged with Maurice Mathieu a plan to prevent the Valencian division from re-embarking, or marching to aid the blockade of Figueras.

Distrust, confusion, and discord now prevailed amongst the Catalans. The people were enraged against Campo Verde, and the junta sent to Cadiz to demand the duke of Infantado as a chief. Milans, who had assembled some Miguelettes and Somatenes about Arens de Mar, openly proposed himself, and Sarsfield, whose division was the only one in any order, was at variance with Eroles. The country people desired to have the latter made captain-general, and a junta of general officers actually appointed him; yet he would not accept it while Campo Verde remained, and that general had already reached Agramunt, whence, overwhelmed with his misfortunes, he meant to fly towards Aragon. He was, however, persuaded to return to Cervera, and call a council of war, and then it was proposed to abandon Catalonia as a lost country, and embark the army; and this disgraceful resolution, although opposed by Sarsfield, Santa-Cruz, and even Campo Verde himself, was adopted by the council, and spread universal consternation. The junta remonstrated loudly, all the troops who were not Catalans deserted, making principally for the Segre and Cinça rivers, in hope to pass through Aragon into New Castile, and so regain their own provinces; every place was filled with grief and despair.

Appendix, No. II. Section 5.

In this conjuncture captain Codrington refused to embark any Catalans, but he had promised to take back the Valencians, and although the conditions of his agreement had been grossly violated by Campo Verde and Miranda, he performed his contract: yet even this was not arranged without a contest between him and Doyle, on the one side, and Miranda and Caro on the other. Meanwhile colonel Green, instead of remaining at the Spanish head-quarters, returned to Peniscola with all the money and arms under his controul; and the captain

Appendix, No. II. Section 2.

BOOK XIII.

1811. July.

Appendix, No. II. Section 3.

of the Prueba frigate, having under his command, several Spanish vessels of war loaded with wounded men, the archives of the municipality, ammunition, stores, and money, all belonging to Catalonia, set sail for Majorca under such suspicious circumstances, that captain Codrington thought it necessary to send a ship to fetch him back by force.

In the midst of these afflicting scenes Suchet brought up his troops to Barcelona, and Maurice Mathieu with a part of his garrison marching upon Mataro, dispersed a small body of men that Eroles had collected there; but the Valencian infantry to the number of two thousand four hundred escaped to Arens de Mar, and being received on board the English vessels were sent back to their own country. The cavalry, unwilling to part with their horses, would not embark, and menaced their general Caro, who fled from their fury; nevertheless Eroles rallied them, and having gathered some stores and money from the smaller depôts, marched inland. Campo Verde then embarked privately in the Diana to avoid the vengeance of the people, and general Lacy, who had arrived from Cadiz, took the command; yet he would have been disregarded, if Eroles had not set the example of obedience. Suchet however moved against him, and first scouring the valley of the Congosta and that of Vich, spread his columns in all directions, and opened a communication with Macdonald at Figueras. Lacy, thus pressed, collected the cavalry and a few scattered Catalonian battalions remaining about Solsona, Cardona, and Seu d'Urgel, and took refuge in the hills, while Eroles threw himself into Montserrat, where large magazines had been previously formed.

Suchet unable to find subsistence in the valleys,

resolved to attack this celebrated place, and for this purpose leaving Frere and Harispe at Vich and Moya, with orders to move at a given time upon Montserrat, returned himself with the reserve to Reus. Here he received despatches from Napoleon, who had created him a marshal, and had sent him orders to take Montserrat, to destroy the works of Taragona, with the exception of a citadel, and finally to march against Valencia. He therefore preserved the upper town of Taragona, ruined the rest of the works, carried the artillery to Tortoza, and marched against Montserrat on the 22d of July by the way of Momblanch and San Coloma to Igualada. At the same time Harispe and Frere moved by Manresa, and Maurice Mathieu entered Esparaguera with a part of the garrison of Barcelona.

TAKING OF MONTSERRAT.

This strong-hold was occupied by fourteen or fifteen hundred Miguelettes and Somatenes, inadequate as it proved to defend it against a great body of men such as Suchet was bringing up. But Eroles was daily raising recruits and adding works to the natural strength, and it would soon have been impregnable; for on all sides the approaches were through the midst of steeps and precipices, and high upon a natural platform, opening to the east, and overlooking the Llobregat, stood the convent of "*Nuestra Senōra de Montserrat,*" a great edifice, and once full of riches, but the wary monks had removed their valuables to Minorca early in the war. It was now well stored and armed, and above

BOOK XIII. 1811. July.

it huge peaks of stone shot up into the clouds so rude, so naked, so desolate, that, to use Suchet's expressive simile, "It was like the skeleton of a mountain."

There were three ways of ascending to this convent; one from Igualada which winded up on the north, from Casa Mansana, between a perpendicular rock and a precipice; this road which was the only one supposed practicable for an attack, was defended by two successive batteries, and by a retrenchment immediately in front of the convent itself. The other two ways were, a foot-path on the south leading to Colbato, and a narrow road crossing the Llobregat and running by Monistrol on the east, but both so crossed and barred by precipices as to be nearly inaccessible to troops.

Suchet disposed one brigade at Colbato to menace that front, and to intercept the retreat of the Spaniards; he then occupied the roads of Igualada and Monistrol with Harispe's and Frere's divisions, and directed Abbé's brigade to attack from the convent by the northern line. The 24th Abbé drove the Spaniards from Casa Mansana, and the 25th advanced up the mountain, flanked by some light troops, and supported by Suchet in person with the Barcelona troops, but exposed to the fire of the Somatenes, who had gathered round the peaks above. In a short time the first Spanish battery opened upon the head of the column as it turned an angle, but more light troops being sent out, they climbed the rough rocks, and getting above the battery shot down upon the gunners, while the leading companies of the column rushed forward, in front, and before a second discharge could be made, reached the foot of the battery beneath the line of fire. The Spaniards then threw down large stones upon the French until the fire of the light troops above, became so galling that the work was abandoned, the French however followed close, and the men above continued clambering along with that energy which the near prospect of success inspires; thus the Spaniards, unable to rally in time, were overtaken and bayoneted in the second battery, and the road was opened.

Abbé now re-formed his troops and marched on to assail the entrenchments of the convent, but as he advanced a sharp musketry was heard on the opposite quarter, and suddenly the Spanish garrison came flying out of the building pursued by French soldiers, who were supposed to be the brigade from Colbato; they however proved to be the light troops first sent out, to keep off the Somatenes from the right flank; for when the column advanced up the mountain, these men, about three hundred in number, had wandered too far to the right, and insensibly gaining ground up hill, had seized one or two of the hermitages with which the peaks are furnished; then growing more daring, they pressed on unopposed, until they gained the rock immediately overhanging the convent itself, and perceiving their advantage, with that intelligence which belongs only to veterans, immediately attacked the Spanish reserves. Their commanding position, the steep rocks, and narrow staircases, compensated for their inferiority of numbers, and in a little time they gained one of the doors, entered, and fought the defenders amongst the cloisters and galleries, with various turns of fortune, until the fugitives from the batteries, followed by Abbé, arrived, and then the whole garrison gave way and

BOOK XIII. 1811. July.

fled down the eastern precipices to the Llobregat, where from their knowledge of the country they easily avoided Harispe's men.

The loss of this place, which by Eroles and others was attributed to colonel Green's having carried off the money destined for strengthening it, was deeply felt from its military importance, and from the superstitious veneration in which it was held: several towns then offered their submission, many villages gave up their arms, and a general fear of Suchet's prowess began to spread all over Spain; but the Catalans, a fierce and constant race, were not yet conquered. The anarchy attendant upon the fall of Taragona and the after movements of Suchet had indeed been great; and as we have seen, most of the persons who might have aided to restore order, acted so as to increase the general confusion, and their bad example was followed by the authorities in other provinces who were most immediately connected with Catalonia: thus Cuesta, at this time governor of the Balearic isles, Bassecour who was at Cuenca, and Palacios, who had just been made captain-general of Valencia, did in no manner comport themselves as the occasion required. Cuesta who had neglected to send from Minorca the guns wanted in Catalonia, now entered into a negotiation to exchange the prisoners at Cabrera against those of Taragona, a praiseworthy thing, if, as Suchet asserts, it arose from humanity; and not an ill-judged measure in itself, because the Catalonian soldiers to be exchanged were the best in Spain, and the French prisoners were ruined in constitution by their hard captivity. But at this period of distress it was impolitic, and viewed with suspicion by the Catalonians, as tending to increase the French force. At the desire of Mr. Wellesley this exchange was, however, peremptorily forbidden by the regency, and Cuesta refused to receive any more prisoners at Cabrera, which while those already there were so tormented, was, from whatever motive arising, a meritorious act, and the last important one of his life, for he soon after died. The prisoners remained, therefore, a disgrace to Spain and to England; for if her envoy interfered to prevent their release, she was bound to insist, that thousands of men, whose prolonged captivity was the result of her interference, should not be exposed upon a barren rock, naked as they were born, and fighting for each other's miserable rations to prolong an existence inconceivably wretched.

Appendix, No. I. Section 4.

This untoward state of affairs in Catalonia was aggravated by the English, Spanish, and French privateers, who taking advantage of the times, plundered the people along the coast in concert; and they were all engaged in the smuggling of tobacco, the monopoly of which here as in other parts of Spain formed the principal resource of the revenue. Yet there were many considerable resources left to the Catalans. The chief towns had fallen, but the mountainous districts were not subdued and scarcely crossed by the French lines of invasion. The Somatenes were numerous, more experienced, and still ready to come forward, under a good general, if arms were provided for them, and the English squadron was always at hand to aid them: Admiral Keats brought three thousand muskets from Gibraltar, Sir E. Pellew, who had succeeded to the command of the Mediterranean fleet, was anxious to succour the province to the

Appendix, No. I. Ssction 4.

BOOK XIII.

1811. August.

full extent of his means, and Minorca was a great depôt of guns, stores, and even men. Lacy, Eroles, Rovira, and others, therefore, raised fresh levies; and while the blockade of Figueras continued to keep all Macdonald's army employed, the Spaniards seized the opportunity to operate partially on the side of Besalu and Bispal, and even in the French Cerdaña, which being unprotected, was invaded by Lacy.

Suchet, whose posts now extended from Lerida to Montserrat on one side, and on the other from Taragona to Mequinenza, foresaw that a new and troublesome Catalonian war was preparing; but he was obliged to return to Saragoza, partly to prepare for the invasion of Valencia, partly to restore tranquillity in Aragon, which had been disturbed by the passage of the seceders from Campo Verde's army. The Valencian cavalry also, when Eroles threw himself into Montserrat, had under the conduct of general Gasca endeavoured to push through Aragon towards Navarre; and although they were intercepted by general Reille, and followed closely by Chlopiski, they finally reached Valencia without much loss, and the rest of the fugitives gained the Moncayo mountains and afterwards joined Mina. That chief was then in a very low state; he had been defeated on the 14th at Sanguessa, by Chlopiski, and Reille, who using the reinforcements then pouring into Spain, had pursued and defeated him again at Estella on the 23d of July, at Sorlada on the 24th, and at Val de Baygory on the 25th; yet he finally escaped to Motrico on the Biscay coast, where he received fresh arms and stores from the English vessels; but he was again defeated by Caffarelli, and finally driven for refuge to the district of Leibana; here the soldiers flying from Taragona and Figueras joined him, and he soon reappeared more fierce and powerful than before.

CHAP. VI.

1811. August.

Meanwhile Villa Campa, whose division had been re-equipped from the supplies given by captain Codrington, concerted his operations with the partida chiefs Duran and Campillo; and their combined forces being eight thousand strong, having advanced from different quarters on the right bank of the Ebro, invested Calatayud, and sought to carry off grain, which was now very scarce. This delayed the invasion of Valencia, for Suchet would not undertake it until he had again secured the frontier of Aragon, and many of his battalions were then escorting the prisoners to France. But when they returned, he directed numerous columns against the partidas, and at the same time troops belonging to the army of the centre came down by the way of Medina Celi; whereupon the Spaniards retired to their fastnesses in the mountains of Soria on one side, and in those of Albaracin on the other.

Mr. Stuart's papers, MSS.

Four thousand of the Valencian army had meanwhile marched against Rapita and Amposta, for the former post was re-established after the fall of Taragona, but although Habert, marching out of Tortoza with seven or eight hundred men, defeated them with a considerable loss, the embarrassments of the third corps were not removed; for while these successes were obtained on the right of the Ebro the Catalans began to harass the posts between Lerida and Montserrat. On the 9th of August the Somatenes fell on some Italians placed in Monistrol, and were with difficulty repulsed; and a few days after, a convoy coming from Igualada to Montserrat, was attacked by fifteen hundred

BOOK XIII. 1811. August.

insurgents, and was unable to proceed until Palombini arrived with a battalion and dislodged the Catalans, but he lost more than a hundred of his own men in the action. Suchet finding from these events that he could not safely withdraw his main body from Catalonia until the fall of Figueras should let loose the army of the upper province, sent fresh troops to Montserrat, and ordered Palombini to move with his garrison to aid Macdonald in the blockade; that place had, however, surrendered before Palombini had passed Barcelona.

General Martinez, after making many vain efforts to break the line of blockade, and having used every edible substance, prepared, on the 16th of August, to make a final effort, in concert with Rovira who came down to Llers. An officer deserting from the garrison betrayed the project; and Rovira was beaten in the morning before the garrison sallied, nevertheless, in the night Martinez endeavoured to cut his way through the lines on the side of Rosas, but was driven back with a loss of four hundred men. Three days after, the place was given up and three thousand famished men were made prisoners. Thus ended the fourth great effort of the Catalonians. The success of the French was not without alloy, more than a fourth part of the blockading troops had died of a pestilent distemper; Macdonald himself was too ill to continue in the command, and the remainder of his army was so weakened, that no further active operations could be undertaken; Suchet was still occupied in Aragon, and Lacy thus obtained time and means to reorganize troops for a fifth effort.

The persons who had betrayed the place to Rovira were shot by Macdonald, and the commandant whose negligence had occasioned this misfortune was condemned to death; but Napoleon, who has been so foully misrepresented as a sanguinary tyrant, Napoleon, who had commuted the sentence of Dupont, now pardoned general Guillot; a clemency in both cases remarkable, seeing that the loss of an army by one, and of a great fortress by the other, not only tended directly and powerfully to the destruction of the emperor's projects, but were in themselves great crimes; and it is to be doubted if any other sovereign in Europe would have displayed such a merciful greatness of mind.

OBSERVATIONS.

1°. The emperor was discontented with Macdonald's operations, and that general seems to have mistaken both the nature of mountain warfare in general, and that of Catalonia in particular. The first requires a persevering activity in seizing such commanding posts on the flanks or rear of an adversary as will oblige him to fight on disadvantageous terms; and as the success greatly depends upon the rapidity and vigour of the troops, their spirit should be excited by continual enterprize, and nourished by commendation and rewards. Now Macdonald, if we may believe Vacani, an eye-witness, did neither gain the confidence of his soldiers, nor cherish their ardour; and while he exacted a more rigid discipline, than the composition of his troops and the nature of the war would bear, he let pass many important opportunities of crushing his enemies in the field. His intent was to reduce the ferocious and insubordinate disposition of his men, but the peculiar state of feeling with respect to the

BOOK XIII. 1811. August.

war on both sides, did not permit this, and hence his marches appeared rather as processions and ceremonies than warlike operations. He won no town, struck no important blow in the field, gave no turn to the public feeling, and lost a most important fortress, which, with infinite pains and trouble, he could scarcely regain.

The plans of all the French generals had been different. St. Cyr used to remain quiet, until the Spaniards gathered in such numbers that he could crush them in general battles; but then he lost all the fruit of his success by his inactivity afterwards. Augereau neither fought battles nor made excursions with skill, nor fulfilled the political hopes which he had excited. Macdonald was in constant movement, but he avoided battles; although in every previous important attack the Catalans had been beaten, whether in strong or in weak positions. Suchet alone combined skill, activity, and resolution, and the success which distinguished his operations is the best comment upon the proceedings of the others. It is in vain to allege that this last marshal was in a better condition for offensive operations, and that the emperor required of the seventh corps exertions which the extreme want of provisions prevented it from making. Napoleon might have been deceived as to the resources at first, and have thus put it upon enterprises beyond its means; but after two years' experience, after receiving the reports of all the generals employed there, and having the most exact information of all occurrences, it is impossible to imagine that so consummate a captain would have urged Macdonald to undertake impracticable operations; and the latter gave no convincing proof that his own views were sound.

Notwithstanding the continual complaints of St. Cyr, and other French writers, who have endeavoured to show that Napoleon was the only man who did not understand the nature of the war in Spain, and that the French armies were continually overmatched, it is certain that, after Baylen, the latter never lost a great battle except to the English; that they took every town they besieged, and never suffered any reverse from the Spaniards which cannot be distinctly traced to the executive officers. It would be silly to doubt the general merit of a man who in so many wars, and for many years, has maintained the noblest reputation, midst innumerable dangers, and many great political changes in his own country, but Macdonald's military talents do not seem to have been calculated for the irregular warfare of Catalonia.

2°. The surprise of Figueras has been designated as a misfortune to the Spaniards, because it shut up a large body of their best Miguelettes, who fell with the place; and because it drew off Campo Verde from Taragona at a critical period. Let us, however, contrast the advantages, and, apart from the vigour and enterprise displayed in the execution, no mean help to the cause at the time, it will be seen that the taking of that fortress was a great gain to the Catalans; for, first, it carried away Macdonald from Barcelona, and thus the fall of Montserrat was deferred, and great danger of failure incurred by Suchet at Taragona; a failure infallible, if his adversaries had behaved with either skill or courage. Secondly, it employed all the French army of Upper Catalonia, the national guards of the frontier, and even troops from Toulon, in a blockade, during which the sword and

BOOK XIII. 1811.

sickness destroyed more than four thousand men, and the remainder were so weakened as to be incapable of field service for a long time; meanwhile Lacy reorganized fresh forces, and revived the war, which he could never have done if the seventh corps had been disposable. Thirdly, seeing that Campo Verde was incapable of handling large masses, it is doubtful if he could have resisted or retarded for any time the investment of Taragona; but it is certain that the blockade of Figueras gave an opportunity to Catalonia, to recover the loss of Taragona; and it obliged Suchet, instead of Macdonald, to take Montserrat, which disseminated the former force, and retarded the invasion of Valencia. Wherefore Rovira's daring, in the surprise, and Martinez' resolution in the maintaining of Figueras, were as useful as they were glorious.

3°. The usual negligence, and slowness of the Spaniards, was apparent during this campaign; although resolution, perseverance, and talent were evinced by Suchet in all his operations, the success was in a great measure due to the faults of his opponents, and amongst those faults colonel Skerrett's conduct was prominent. It is true that captain Codrington and others agreed in the resolution not to land; that there was a heavy surf, and that the engineers predicted on the 27th that the wall would soon be beaten down; but the question should have been viewed in another light by colonel Skerrett. Taragona was the bulwark of the principality, the stay and hope of the war. It was the city of Spain whose importance was next to Cadiz, and before its walls the security or the ruin of Valencia as well as of Catalonia was to be found. Of the French scarcely fourteen thousand infantry were under arms, and those were exhausted with toil. The upper town, which was the body of the place, was still unbreached, it was only attacked upon one narrow front, and behind it the Rambla offered a second and a more powerful defence. There were, to use the governor's expression, within the walls "*eight thousand of the most warlike troops in Spain,*" and there was a succouring army without, equal in number to the whole infantry of the besiegers. Under these circumstances the stoutest assailants might have been repulsed, and a severe repulse would have been fatal to the French operations.

Captain Codrington asserts that in the skirmishes beyond the walls, the valour of the garrison was eminent; and he saw a poor ragged fellow endeavouring, such was his humanity and greatness of mind, to stifle the burning fuze of a shell with sand, that some women and children might have time to escape. Feeling and courage, the springs of moral force, were therefore not wanting, but the virtue of the people was diminished, and the spirit of the soldiery overlaid, by the bad conduct of their leaders. The rich citizens fled early to Villa Nueva, and they were followed by many superior officers of regiments; Contreras jealous of Sarsfield had obliged him, as we have seen, to quit his post at a critical moment, and then represented it to the garrison as a desertion; the Valencians were carried off after being one day in the place, and the Murcians came without arms; and all this confusion and mischief were so palpable, that the poor Spanish soldiers could anticipate nothing but failure if left to themselves, and it was precisely for this reason that the British should have been landed to restore confidence. And is there nothing to be

BOOK XIII. 1811.

allowed for the impetuous fury of an English column breaking out of the place at the moment of attack? Let it be remembered also, that in consequence of the arrival of a seventy-four, convoying the transports, such was the number of ships of war, that a thousand seamen and marines might have been added to the troops; and who can believe that three or four thousand French and Italians, the utmost that could be brought to bear in mass on one point, and that not an easy point, for the breach was narrow and scarcely practicable, would have carried the place against eight thousand Spaniards and two thousand British. But then the surf and the enemy's shot at the landing-place, and the opinion of general Doyle and of captain Codrington and of the engineers! The enemy's shot might have inflicted loss, but could not, especially at night, have stopped the disembarkation; and the opinion of the engineers, was a just report of the state of the walls, but in no manner touched the moral considerations.

When the Roman Pompey was adjured by his friends not to put to sea during a violent storm he replied, "*it is necessary to sail—it is not necessary to live.*" It was also necessary to save Taragona! Was no risk to be incurred for so great an object? Was an uncertain danger to be weighed against such a loss to Spain? Was the British intrepidity to be set at nought? Were British soldiers to be quiet spectators, while Spaniards stood up in a fight too dangerous for them to meddle with? Is that false but common doctrine, so degrading to soldiers, that brick-and-mortar sentiment, that the courage of the garrison is not to be taken into account, to be implicitly followed? What if the

Spaniards had been successful? The result was most painful! Taragona strongly fortified, having at different periods above fifteen thousand men thrown into it, with an open harbour and free communication by sea, was taken by less than twenty thousand French and Italian infantry, in the face of a succouring army, a British brigade, and a British fleet!

4°. The cruelty of the French general and the ferocity of his soldiers, have been dwelt upon by several writers, but Suchet has vindicated his own conduct, and it is therefore unnecessary here to enter into a close investigation of facts which have been distorted, or of reasoning which has been misapplied. That every barbarity, commonly attendant upon the storming of towns, was practised may be supposed; there is in the military institutions of Europe nothing calculated to arrest such atrocities. Soldiers of every nation look upon the devastation of a town taken by assault as their right, and it would be unjust to hold Suchet responsible for the violence of an army composed of men from different countries, exasperated by the obstinacy of the defence, and by a cruel warfare; in Spanish towns also the people generally formed a part of the garrison.

OPERATIONS IN VALENCIA AND MURCIA.

The transactions in the first of these provinces during the siege of Taragona have been already sufficiently noticed; and those in Murcia were of See Vol. III
little interest, for the defeat of Blake at Cullar in November 1810, and the fever which raged at

BOOK XIII. 1811.

Carthagena, together with the frequent change of commanders, and the neglect of the government had completely ruined the Murcian army. The number of men was indeed considerable, and the fourth French corps, weakened by drafts for the expedition to Estremadura, and menaced by the Barossa expedition, could not oppose more than five or six thousand men; yet the province had never been touched by an enemy, and the circumstances were all favorable for the organization and frequent trial of new troops.

In February 1811 colonel Roche, the military agent, described the whole army as " ready to disperse on the first appearance of an enemy," and in the following June he says that "after being left to themselves for three years, the Murcian troops were absolutely in a worse state than they were at the commencement of the revolution, that general Freire, although at the head of sixteen thousand infantry and three thousand cavalry, dared not attack the six thousand French before him, lest his men should disperse, and they thought as little of the general as he did of them; that indolence, lassitude, and egotism prevailed in all parts; that the establishment of the Cortes had proved but a slight stimulus to the enthusiasm, which was fast dying away, and that the most agreeable thing in the world at the moment to the Spaniards, would be to remain neuter, while England and France fought the battle and paid all the expense." The Murcian force was increased after Mahi's arrival to twenty-two thousand men, but remained inactive until August, when Blake assumed the command, and the events which followed will be treated of hereafter.

The petty warfare in the south of Grenada and Andalusia, deserves little notice, for during Blake's absence in Estremadura with the fourth army, it was principally confined to the Ronda, where the Serranos aided at times by the troops from Algesiras, and by succours from Gibraltar, were always in arms; yet even there, the extreme arrogance and folly of the Spanish generals, so vexed the Serranos, that they were hardly prevented from capitulating in form with the French, and while Soult continued at Llerena after the battle of Albuera. The Escopeteros and civic guards sufficed to keep the Partidas in check. Thus the blockade of the Isla remained undisturbed from without, and Cadiz itself, the seat of all intrigues and follies, was fed by English fleets and defended by English troops.

The narrative of the circle of secondary operations being now completed, and the fate of Spain proved to depend upon the British general alone, it will be proper in the next book to take a view of political affairs shewing how strongly they bore upon lord Wellington's decisions; and if such an interruption of the military story should be distasteful to any reader I would have him reflect, that war is not so much a series of battles, as a series of difficulties in the preparations to fight them with success.

BOOK XIV.

CHAPTER I.

POLITICAL SITUATION OF JOSEPH.

BOOK XIV.

1810.

Joseph's papers captured at Vittoria, MSS.

Appendix No. III. Section 1.

After the conquest of Andalusia, the intrusive monarch pursued his own system of policy with more eagerness than before. He published amnesties, granted honours and rewards to his followers, took many of the opposite party into his service, and treated the people generally with mildness. But he was guided principally by his Spanish ministers, who being tainted with the national weaknesses of character were, especially Orquijo, continually making exaggerated reports, intriguing against the French generals, and striving, sometimes with, sometimes without justice, to incense the king against them. This course, which was almost the inevitable consequence of his situation, excited angry feelings in the military, which, joined to the natural haughtiness of soldiers in command, produced constant disputes. In the conquered provinces, Joseph's civil agents endeavoured to obtain more of the spoil than comported with the wants of the armies, and hence bickerings between the French officers and the Spanish authorities were as unceasing as they were violent. The prefects, royal commissaries, and intendants would not act under military orders, with respect to the supplies, nor would they furnish sums for the military chests. On the other hand the generals often seized the king's revenue, raised extraordinary and forced contributions, disregarded legal forms, and even threatened to arrest the royal agents when they refused compliance with their wishes. Neither was Joseph's own conduct always free from violence, for in the latter part of 1811 he obliged the merchants of Madrid, to draw bills, for two millions of dollars, on their correspondents in London, to supply him with a forced loan.

Mr Stuart's Papers, MSS.

He was always complaining to the emperor that the niggardly allowances from France, the exactions of the generals, and the misery of the country left him no means of existence as a monarch; and during the greatest part of 1810 and the beginning of 1811, Santa Fé, Almenara, and Orquijo, succeeding each other as ambassadors at Paris, were in angry negotiations, with Napoleon's ministers, relating to this subject, and to a project for ceding the provinces of the Ebro in exchange for Portugal. Against this project Joseph protested, on the grounds that it was contrary to the constitution of Bayonne, that it would alienate the Spaniards, was degrading to himself, and unjust as a bargain; seeing that Portugal, was neither so rich, so industrious, so pleasant, nor so well affected to him as the provinces to be taken away, and the well-known hatred between the Spaniards and Portuguese would never allow the latter to be quiet subjects.

Joseph's papers captured at Vittoria, MSS.

Ibid.

To these complaints, Napoleon answered with his usual force and clearness of judgment. He insisted that the cost of the war had drained the

BOOK XIV. 1811. January.

French exchequer; that he had employed nearly four hundred thousand men for the king's interest, and that rather than increase the expenses he would withdraw some of the troops. He reproached Joseph with the feebleness of his operations, the waste and luxury of his court, his ill-judged schemes of conciliation, his extravagant rewards, his too great generosity to the opposite party, and his raising, contrary to the opinion of the marshals, a Spanish army which would desert on the first reverse. The constitution of Bayonne, he said, was rendered null by the war, nevertheless he had not taken a single village from Spain, and he had no wish to seize the provinces of the Ebro, unless the state of the contest obliged him to do so. He required indeed a guarantee for the repayment of the money France had expended for the Spanish crown, yet the real wishes of the people were to be ascertained before any cession of territory could take place, and to talk of Portugal before it was conquered was folly. As this last observation was Joseph's own argument, an explanation ensued, when it appeared that Almenara, thinking the seizure of the Ebro provinces a settled plan, had, of his own accord, asked for Portugal as an indemnification; a fact that marks the character of the Spanish cabinet.

Joseph's papers captured at Vittoria, MSS.

Ibid.

Napoleon also assured the king that there must be a great deal of money in Spain, for, besides the sums sent from France, the plate of the suppressed convents, and the silver received by the Spaniards from America, there were the subsidies from England, and the enormous expenditure of her troops. Then, the seizure and sale of national domains, and of confiscated colonial produce, were to be taken into calculation, and if the king wanted more, he must extract it from the country, or go without. France would only continue her subsidy of two millions of franks monthly. The emperor had always supported his wars by the resources of the territory in which it was carried on, and the king might do the same.

Joseph replied that his court was neither luxurious nor magnificent; that he recompensed services, by giving bills on the contingent sales of national domains, which could not be applied to the wants of the soldiers; that he could scarcely keep the public servants alive, and that his own expenses were not greater than the splendour of the crown required. That many of the best generals approved of his raising a Spanish army, desertions from it were less frequent than was imagined, and were daily diminishing; and these native troops served to garrison towns while the French were in the field. He wished, he said, to obtain large loans rather than small gifts from the French treasury, and desired that the confiscated property of the Spanish noblemen who had been declared traitors in 1808, should be paid to him; but with regard to harsh measures, the people could not pay the contributions, and the proceedings of a king with his subjects should not be like those of a foreign general. Lenity was necessary to tranquillize the provinces subdued, and as an example to those which resisted. The first thing was to conciliate the people's affections. The plate of the suppressed convents was not so valuable as it appeared at a distance, the greater part of it was already plundered by the guerillas, or by the French troops. The French marshals intercepted his revenues, disregarded his orders, in-

Joseph's papers captured at Vittoria, MSS.

BOOK XIV. 1811. January. sulted his government, and oppressed the country. He was degraded as a monarch and would endure it no longer. He had been appointed to the throne of Spain without his own consent, and although he would never oppose his brother's will, he would not live a degraded king, and was therefore ready to resign, unless the emperor would come in person and remedy the present evils.

Joseph's papers captured at Vittoria, MSS.

Napoleon, while he admitted the reasonableness of some of the king's statements, still insisted, and with propriety of argument, that it was necessary to subdue the people before they could be conciliated. Yet to prevent wanton abuses of power, he fixed the exact sum which each person, from the general governors down to the lowest subaltern was to receive, and he ordered every person violating this regulation to be dismissed upon the spot, and a report of the circumstance sent to Paris within twenty hours after. Before this, Bessieres, acknowledged by all to be a just and mild man, had been sent to remedy the mischief said to have been done by Kellerman, and others in the northern provinces. And in respect of conciliation, the emperor remarked that he had himself, at first, intended to open secret negotiations with the Cortes, but on finding what an obscure rabble they were, he had desisted. He therefore recommended Joseph to assemble at Madrid a counter-cortes, composed of men of influence and reputation, wherein (adverting to the insane insolence of the Spaniards towards their colonies) he might by the discussion of really liberal institutions, and by exposing the bad faith with which the English encouraged the Americans, improve public opinion, and conciliate the Spaniards with

Appendix, No. III. Section 3.

February.

April.

hopes of preserving the integrity of the empire, so rudely shaken by the revolt of the colonies. CHAP. I.

1811. April. An additional subsidy was peremptorily refused, but the emperor finally consented to furnish Joseph with half a million of franks monthly, for the particular support of his court; and it is worthy of notice, as illustrating the character of Napoleon, that in the course of these disputes, Joseph's friends at Paris, repeatedly advised him, that the diplomatic style of his letters incensed and hardened the emperor, whereas his familiar style as a brother always softened and disposed him to concede what was demanded. Joseph, however, could not endure the decree for establishing the military governments, by which the administration was placed entirely in the hands of the generals, and their reports upon the civil and judicial administration referred entirely to the emperor. It was a measure assailing at once his pride, his power, and his purse. His mind, therefore, became daily more embittered, and his prefects and commissaries, emboldened by his opinions, absolutely refused to act under the French marshal's orders. Many of these complaints, founded on the reports of his Spanish servants, were untrue and others distorted. We have seen how the habitual exaggerations, and even downright falsehoods of the juntas and the regency, thwarted the English general's operations, and the king, as well as the French generals, must have encountered a like disposition in the Spanish ministers. Nevertheless, the nature of the war rendered it impossible but that much ground of complaint should exist.

Appendix, No. III.

May.

Joseph's personal sentiments, abstractedly viewed, were high-minded and benevolent; but they sorted

BOOK XIV. 1811. May. ill with his situation as an usurper. He had neither patience nor profundity in his policy, and at last such was his irritation, that having drawn up a private but formal renunciation of the crown, he took an escort of five thousand men, and about the period of the battle of Fuentes Onoro, passed out of Spain and reached Paris: there Ney, Massena, Junot, St. Cyr, Kellerman, Augereau, Loison, and Sebastiani, were also assembled, and all discontented with the war, and with each other.

Appendix, No. III. Section 2.

By this rash and ill-timed proceeding, the intrusive government was left without a head, and the army of the centre was rendered nearly useless at the critical moment, when Soult, engaged in the Albuera operations, had a right to expect support from Madrid. The northern army also was in a great measure paralysed, and the army of Portugal, besides having just failed at Fuentes, was in all the disorganization attendant upon the retreat from Santarem, and upon a change of commanders. This was the principal cause why Bessieres abandoned the Asturias and concentrated his forces in Leon and Castile on the communications with France; for it behoved the French generals, everywhere to hold their troops in hand, and to be on the defensive, until the emperor's resolution in this extraordinary conjuncture should be known.

See Chap. I.

Napoleon astounded at this precipitate action of the king, complained, with reason, that having promised not to quit the country without due notice, Joseph had failed to him, both as a monarch and as a general, and that he should at least have better chosen his time; for if he had retired in January, when the armies were all inactive, the evil would have been less, as the emperor might then

Appendix, No. III. Section 3.

have abandoned Andalusia, and concentrated Soult's and Massena's troops on the Tagus; which would have been in accord with the policy fitting for the occasion. But now when the armies had suffered reverses, when they were widely separated, and in pursuit of different objects, the mischief was great, and the king's conduct not to be justified!

Joseph replied that he had taken good measures to prevent confusion during his absence, and then reiterating his complaints and declaring his resolution to retire into obscurity, he finished by observing, with equal truth and simplicity of mind, that it would be better for the emperor that he should do so, inasmuch as in France he would be a good subject, but in Spain a bad king.

Appendix, No. III. Section 2.

The emperor had however too powerful an intellect for his brother to contend with. Partly by reason, partly by authority, partly by concession, he obliged him to return again in July, furnished with a species of private treaty, by which the army of the centre was placed entirely at his disposal. He was also empowered to punish delinquents, to change the organization, and to remove officers who were offensive to him, even the chief of the staff, general Belliard, who had been represented by Orquijo as inimical to his system. And if any of the other armies should, by the chances of war, arrive within the district of the centre army, they also, while there, were to be under the king; and at all times, even in their own districts, when he placed himself at their head. The army of the north was to remain with its actual organization and under a marshal, but Joseph had liberty to change Bessieres for Jourdan.

To prevent the oppression of the people, espe-

BOOK XIV. 1811. June. Appendix, No. II. Section 3.

cially in the north, Napoleon required the French military authorities, to send daily reports, to the king, of all requisitions and contributions exacted. And he advised his brother to keep a Spanish commissary at the head-quarters of each army, to watch over Spanish interests; promising that whenever a province should have the means, and the will, to resist the incursions of the guerillas, it should revert entirely to the government of the king, and be subjected to no charges, save those made by the Spanish civil authorities for general purposes. The armies of the south and of Aragon were placed in a like situation on the same terms, and meanwhile Joseph was to receive a quarter of the contributions from each, for the support of his court and of the central army.

The entire command of the forces in Spain the emperor would not grant, observing that the marshal directing from Madrid, as major-general, would naturally claim the glory, as well as the responsibility of arranging the operations; and hence the other marshals, finding themselves, in reality, under his, instead of the king's command, would obey badly or not at all. All their reports and the intelligence necessary to the understanding of affairs were therefore to be addressed directly to Berthier, for the emperor's information. Finally the half million of francs hitherto given monthly to the king was to be increased to a million for the year 1811; and it was expected that Joseph would immediately reorganize the army of the centre, restore its discipline, and make it, what it had not yet been, of weight in the contest.

Ibid. The king afterwards obtained some further concessions, the most important of which related to the employment and assembling of Spaniards according to his own directions and plans. This final arrangement and the importance given to Joseph's return, for by the emperor's orders, he was received as if he had only been to Paris to concert a great plan, produced a good effect for a short time; but after the fall of Figueras, Napoleon fearing to trust Spanish civilians, extended the plan, hitherto confined to Catalonia, of employing French intendants in all the provinces on the left of the Ebro. Then the king's jealousy was again excited, and the old bickerings between him and the marshals were revived.

POLITICAL SITUATION OF FRANCE.

In 1811 the emperor's power over the continent, as far as the frontier of Russia, was in fact, absolute; and in France internal prosperity was enjoyed with external glory. But the emperor of Russia, stimulated by English diplomacy, and by a personal discontent; in dread also of his nobles, who were impatient under the losses which the continental system inflicted upon them, was plainly in opposition to the ascendancy of France, and Napoleon, although wishing to avoid a rupture, was too long-sighted, not to perceive, that it was time to prepare for a more gigantic contest than any he had hitherto engaged in. He therefore husbanded his money and soldiers, and would no longer lavish them upon the Spanish war. He had poured men indeed continually into that country, but these were generally conscripts, while in the north of France he was forming a reserve of two hundred thousand old

BOOK XIV. 1811.

soldiers; but with that art that it was doubtful whether they were intended for the Peninsula or for ulterior objects, being ready for either, according to circumstances.

Such an uncertain state of affairs, prevented him from taking more decided steps, in person, with relation to Spain, which he would undoubtedly have done if the war there, had been the only great matter on his hands, and therefore the aspect of French politics, both in Spain and other places, was favourable to lord Wellington's views. A Russian war, sooner or later, was one of the principal chances upon which he rested his hopes of final success; yet his anticipations were dashed with fear, for the situation of the Spanish and Portuguese governments, and of their armies, and the condition of the English government, were by no means so favourable to his plans, as shall be shewn in the next chapter.

CHAPTER II.

POLITICAL STATE OF ENGLAND WITH REFERENCE TO THE WAR.

CHAP. II. 1811.

It was very clear that merely to defend Portugal, with enormous loss of treasure and of blood, would be a ruinous policy; and that to redeem the Peninsula the Spaniards must be brought to act more reasonably than they had hitherto done. But this the national character and the extreme ignorance of public business, whether military or civil, which distinguished the generals and statesmen, rendered a very difficult task.

Lord Wellington, finding the English power weak to control, and its influence as weak to sway, the councils of Spain, could only hope by industry, patience, and the glory of his successes in Portugal, to acquire that personal ascendancy, which would enable him to direct the resources of the whole Peninsula in a vigorous manner, and towards a common object. And the difficulty of attaining that ascendancy can only be made clear by a review of the intercourse between the British government and the Spanish authorities, from the first bursting out of the insurrection, to the period now treated of; a review which will disclose the utter unfitness of Mr. Canning to conduct great affairs. Heaping treasure, stores, arms, and flattery, upon those who were unable to bear the latter, or use the former

BOOK XIV.

1811.

beneficially, he neglected all those persons who were capable of forwarding the cause; and neither in the choice of his agents, nor in his instructions to them, nor in his estimation of the value of events, did he discover wisdom or diligence, although he covered his misconduct, at the moment, by his glittering oratory.

1808. Soon after the Spanish deputies had first applied for the assistance of England, Mr. Charles Stuart, who was the only regular diplomatist sent to Spain, carried, to Coruña, such a sum, as, with previous subsidies made up one million of dollars for Gallicia alone. The deputies from Asturias had at the same time demanded five millions of dollars, and one was paid in part of their demand; but when this was known, two millions more were demanded for Gallicia, which were not refused; and yet the first point in Mr. Canning's instructions to Mr. Stuart, was, *to enter into "no political engagements."*

Appendix, No. IV. Section 1.

Mr. Duff, the consul for Cadiz, carried out a million of dollars for Andalusia, the junta asked for three or four millions more, and the demands of Portugal, although less extravagant, were very great. Thus above sixteen millions of dollars were craved, and more than four millions, including the gift to Portugal, had been sent; the remainder was not denied; and the amount of arms, and other stores given, may be estimated by the fact, that eighty-two pieces of artillery, ninety-six thousand muskets, eight hundred thousand flints, six millions and a half of ball-cartridges, seven thousand five hundred barrels of powder, and thirty thousand swords and belts had been sent to Coruña and Cadiz; and the supply to the Asturias was in proportion. But Mr. Canning's instructions to Mr. Duff and to the other agents were still the same as to Mr. Stuart, "*His Majesty had no desire to annex any conditions to the pecuniary assistance which he furnished to Spain.*" 1811. Ibid.

Mr. Canning observed that he considered the amount of money as nothing! but acknowledged that *specie* was at this time so scarce that it was only by a direct and secret understanding with the former government of Spain, under the connivance of France, that any considerable amount of dollars had been collected in England. And "each province of Spain," he said, "had made its own particular application, and the whole occasioned a call for specie such as had never before been made upon England at any period of its existence. There was a rivalry between the provinces with reference to the amount of sums demanded which rendered the greatest caution necessary." And the more so, that "the deputies were incompetent to furnish either information or advice upon the state of affairs in Spain;" yet Mr. Duff was commanded, while representing these astounding things to the junta of Seville, "*to avoid any appearance of a desire to overrate the merit and value of the exertions then making by Great Britain in favour of the Spanish nation, or to lay the grounds for restraining or limiting those exertions within any other bounds than those which were prescribed by the limits of the actual means of the country.*" In proof of Mr. Canning's sincerity upon this head, he afterwards sent two millions of dollars by Mr. Frere, while the British army was left without any funds at all! Moreover the supplies, so recklessly granted, being transmitted through subordinates and irresponsible persons were absurdly and unequally distributed.

This obsequious extravagance, produced the utmost

BOOK XIV. 1811.

arrogance on the part of the Spanish leaders, who treated the English minister's humble policy with the insolence it courted. When Mr. Stuart reached Madrid, after the establishment of the supreme junta, that body, raising its demands upon England, in proportion to its superior importance, required, and in the most peremptory language, additional succours so enormous as to startle even the prodigality of the English government.

Ten millions of dollars instantly, five hundred thousand yards of cloth, four million yards of linen for shirts and for the hospitals, three hundred thousand pair of shoes, thirty thousand pair of boots, twelve million of cartridges, two hundred thousand muskets, twelve thousand pair of pistols, fifty thousand swords, one hundred thousand arobas of flour, besides salt meat and fish! These were their demands! and when Mr. Stuart's remonstrance obliged them to alter the insulting language of their note, they insisted the more strenuously upon having the succours; observing that England had as yet only done enough to set their force afloat, and that she might *naturally expect demands like the present to follow the first.* They desired also that the money should be furnished at once, by bills on the British treasury, and at the same time required the confiscation of Godoy's property in the English funds!

Such was Mr. Canning's opening policy, and the sequel was worthy of the commencement. His proceedings with respect to the Erfurth proposals for peace, his injudicious choice of Mr. Frere, his leaving of Mr. Stuart without instructions for three months at the most critical period of the insurrection, and his management of affairs in Portugal and at Cadiz, during sir John Cradock's command, have been already noticed; and that he was not misled by any curious accordance in the reports of his agents, is certain, for he was early and constantly informed of the real state of affairs by Mr. Stuart. That gentleman was the accredited diplomatist, and in all important points, his reports were very exactly corroborated by the letters of sir John Moore, and by the running course of events; yet Mr. Canning neither acted upon them nor published them, but he received all the idle, vaunting, accounts of the subordinate civil and military agents, with complacency, and published them with ostentation; thus encouraging the misrepresentations of ignorant men, increasing the arrogance of the Spaniards, deceiving the English nation, and as far as he was able misleading the English general.

Mr. Stuart reached Coruña in July 1808, and on the 22d of that month informed Mr. Canning that the reports of successes in the south were not to be depended upon, seeing that they increased exactly in proportion to the difficulty of commucating with the alledged scenes of action, and with the dearth of events, or the recurrence of disasters in the northern parts. He also assured him, that the numbers of the Spanish armies, within his knowledge, were by no means so great as they were represented.

On the 26th of July he gave a detailed history of the Gallician insurrection, by which he plainly shewed that every species of violence, disorder, intrigue, and deceit were to be expected from the leading people; that the junta's object was to separate Gallicia from Spain; and that so inappropriate was the affected delicacy of abstaining from

Appendix, No. IV. Section 1.

BOOK XIV. 1811.

conditions, while furnishing succours; that the junta of Gallicia was only kept in power, by the countenance of England, evinced in her lavish supplies, and the residence of her envoy at Coruña. The interference of the British naval officers to quell a political tumult had even been asked for, and had been successful; and Mr. Stuart himself had been intreated to meddle in the appointments of the governing members, and in other contests for power, which were daily taking place. In fine, before the end of August the system of folly, peculation, waste, and improvidence which characterized Spanish proceedings, was completely detected by Mr. Stuart, and laid before Mr. Canning, without in the slightest degree altering the latter's egregious system, or even attracting his notice; nay, he even intimated to the ambitious junta of Seville, that England would willingly acknowledge its supremacy, if the consent of the other provinces could be obtained; thus holding out a premium for the continuation of that anarchy, which it should have been his first object to suppress.

Appendix, No. IV. Section 1.

Mr. Stuart was kept in a corner of the peninsula, whence he could not communicate freely with any other province, and where his presence materially contributed to cherish the project of separating Gallicia; and this without the shadow of a pretence, because there was also a British admiral and consul, and a military mission at Coruña, all capable of transmitting the necessary local intelligence. But so little did Mr. Canning care to receive his envoy's reports, that the packet, conveying his despatches, was ordered to touch at Gihon to receive the consul's letters, which caused the delay of a week when every moment was big with important events; a delay not to be remedied by the admiral on the station, because he had not even been officially informed that Mr. Stuart was an accredited person!

When the latter, thinking it time to look to the public affairs, on his own responsibility, proceeded See Vol. I. to Madrid, and finally to Andalusia, he found the evils springing from Mr. Canning's inconsiderate conduct every where prominent. In the capital the supreme junta had regarded England as a bonded debtor; and the influence of her diplomatist at Seville may be estimated from the following note, written by Mr. Stuart to Mr. Frere, upon the subject of permitting British troops to enter Cadiz.

"When the junta refused to admit general Mackenzie's detachment, you tell me it was merely from alarm respecting the disposition of the inhabitants of Seville and Cadiz. I am not aware of the feelings which prevail in Seville, but with respect to this town, whatever the navy or the English travellers, may assert to the contrary, I am perfectly convinced that there exists only a wish to receive them, and general regret and surprise at their continuance on board."

Nor was the mischief confined to Spain. Mr. Frere, apparently tired of the presence of a man whose energy and talent were a continued reflection upon his own imbecile diplomacy, ordered Mr. Stuart, either to join Cuesta's army or to go by Trieste to Vienna; he chose the latter, because there was not even a subordinate political agent there, although this was the critical period, which preceded the Austrian declaration of war against

BOOK XIV. 1811.

France in 1809. He was without formal powers as an envoy, but his knowledge of the affairs of Spain, and his intimate personal acquaintance with many of the leading statesmen at Vienna, enabled him at once to send home the most exact information of the proceedings, the wants, the wishes, and intentions of the Austrian government, in respect to the impending war.

That great diversion for Spain, which with infinite pains had been brought to maturity by count Stadion, was on the point of being abandoned because of Mr. Canning's conduct. He had sent no minister to Vienna, and while he was lavishing millions upon the Spaniards, without conditions, refused in the most haughty and repulsive terms, the prayers of Austria for a subsidy or even a loan, without which, she could not pass her own frontier. And when Mr. Stuart suggested the resource of borrowing some of the twenty-five millions of dollars which were then accumulated at Cadiz, it was rejected because Mr. Frere said it would alarm the Spaniards. Thus, the aid of a great empire with four hundred thousand good troops, was in a manner rejected in favour of a few miserable self-elected juntas in the peninsula, while one-half the succours which they received and misused, would have sent the whole Austrian nation headlong upon France; for all their landwehr was in arms, and where the emperor had only calculated upon one hundred and fifty battalions three hundred had come forward, voluntarily, besides the Hungarian insurrection. In this way Mr. Canning proved his narrow capacity for business, and how little he knew either the strength of France, the value of Austria, the weakness of Spain, or the true interests of England at the moment; although he had not scrupled by his petulant answers to the proposals of Erfurth to confirm a war which he was so incapable of conducting. Instead of improving the great occasion thus offered, he angrily recalled Mr. Stuart, for having proceeded to Vienna without his permission. In his eyes the breach of form was of much higher importance than the success of the object. Yet it is capable of proof, that had Mr. Stuart remained, the Austrians would have been slower to negotiate after the battle of Wagram; and the Walcheren expedition would have been turned towards Germany, where a great northern confederation was then ready to take arms against France. The Prussian cabinet in defiance of the king, or rather of the queen, whose fears influenced the king's resolutions, only waited for these troops, to declare war; and there was every reason to believe that Russia would then also have adopted that side. The misfortunes of Moore's campaign, the folly and arrogance of the Spaniards, the loss of the great British army which perished in Walcheren, the exhausting of England both of troops and specie, when she most needed both; finally the throwing of Austria entirely into the hands of France, may thus be distinctly traced to Mr. Canning's incapacity as a statesman.

But through the whole of the Napoleonic wars this man was the evil genius of the Peninsula; for passing over the misplaced military powers which he gave to Mr. Villiers' legation in Portugal, while he neglected the political affairs in that country, it was he who sent lord Strangford to Rio Janeiro whence all manner of mischief flowed. And when Mr. Stuart succeeded Mr. Villiers at Lisbon, Mr.

BOOK XIV. 1811.

Canning insisted upon having the enormous mass of intelligence, received from different parts of the Peninsula, translated before it was sent home; an act of undisguised indolence, which retarded the real business of the embassy, prevented important information from being transmitted rapidly, and exposed the secrets of the hour to the activity of the enemy's emissaries at Lisbon. In after times when by a notorious abuse of government he was himself sent ambassador to Lisbon, he complained that there were no archives of the former embassies, and he obliged Mr. Stuart, then minister at the Hague, to employ several hundred soldiers, as clerks, to copy all his papers relating to the previous war; these, at a great public expense, were sent to Lisbon; and there they were to be seen unexamined and unpacked in the year 1826! And while this folly was passing, the interests of Europe in general were neglected, and the particular welfare of Portugal seriously injured by another display of official importance still more culpable.

It had been arranged that a Portuguese auxiliary force was to have joined the duke of Wellington's army, previous to the battle of Waterloo; and to have this agreement executed, was the only business of real importance which Mr. Canning had to transact during his embassy. Marshal Beresford well acquainted with the characters, of the members of the Portuguese regency, had assembled fifteen thousand men, the flower of the old troops, perfectly equipped, with artillery, baggage, and all things needful to take the field; the ships were ready, the men willing to embark, and the marshal informed the English ambassador, that he had only to give the order, and in a few hours the whole would be on board, warning him at the same time, that in no other way could the thing be effected. But as this summary proceeding did not give Mr. Canning an opportunity to record his own talents for negotiation, he replied that it must be done by diplomacy; the Souza faction eagerly seized the opportunity of displaying their talents in the same line, and being more expert, beat Mr. Canning at his own weapons, and as Beresford had foreseen no troops were embarked at all. Lord Wellington was thus deprived of important reinforcements; the Portuguese were deprived of the advantage of supporting their army, for several years, on the resources of France, and of their share of the contributions from that country; last and worst, those veterans of the Peninsular war, the strength of the country, were sent to the Brazils, were they all perished by disease or by the sword in the obscure wars of Don Pedro! If such errors may be redeemed by an eloquence, always used in defence of public corruption, and a wit, that made human sufferings its sport, Mr. Canning was an English statesman, and wisdom has little to do with the affairs of nations.

When the issue of the Walcheren expedition caused a change of ministry, lord Wellesley obtained the foreign office. Mr. Henry Wellesley then replaced Mr. Frere at Cadiz, and he and Mr. Stuart received orders to make conditions and to demand guarantees for the due application of the British succours; those succours were more sparingly granted, and the envoys were directed to interfere with advice and remonstrances, in all the proceedings of the respective governments to which they were accredited: Mr. Stuart was even desired to

Appendix, No. IV. Section 2.

BOOK XIV. 1811.

meddle with the internal administration of the Portuguese nation,—the exertions and sacrifices of Great Britain, far from being kept out of sight, were magnified, and the system adopted was in every thing a contrast to that of Mr. Canning.

But there was in England a powerful, and as recent events have proved, a most unprincipled parliamentary opposition, and there were two parties in the cabinet. The one headed by lord Wellesley, who was anxious to push the war vigorously in the Peninsula, without much regard to the ultimate pressure upon the people of his own country; the other, headed by Mr. Perceval, who sought only to maintain himself in power. Narrow, harsh, factious, and illiberal, in every thing relating to public matters, this man's career was one of unmixed evil. His bigotry taught him to oppress Ireland, but his religion did not deter him from passing a law to prevent the introduction of medicines into France during a pestilence. He lived by faction; he had neither the wisdom to support, nor the manliness to put an end to, the war in the Peninsula, and his crooked, contemptible policy was shown, by withholding what was necessary to sustain the contest, and throwing on the general the responsibility of failure.

With all the fears of little minds, he and his coadjutors awaited the result of lord Wellington's operations in 1810. They affected to dread his rashness, yet could give no reasonable ground for their alarm; and their private letters were at variance with their public instructions, that they might be prepared for either event. They deprived him, without notice, of his command over the troops at Cadiz; they gave Graham power to furnish pecuniary succours to the Spaniards at that place, which

Appendix, No. IV.

threw another difficulty in the way of obtaining money for Portugal; and when Wellington complained of the attention paid to the unfounded apprehension of some superior officers more immediately about him, he was plainly told that those officers were better generals than himself. At the same time he was, from a pitiful economy, ordered to dismiss the transports on which the safety of the army depended in the event of failure. CHAP. II. 1811.

Between these factions there was a constant struggle, and lord Wellington's successes in the field, only furthered the views of Mr. Perceval, because they furnished ground for asserting that due support had been given to him. Indeed such a result is to be always apprehended by English commanders. The slightest movement in war requires a great effort, and is attended with many vexations, which the general feels acutely and unceasingly; but the politician, believing in no difficulties because he feels none, neglects the supplies, charges disaster on the general, and covers his misdeeds with words. The inefficient state of the cabinet under both Mr. Canning and Mr. Perceval may however be judged of by the following extracts, the writers of which as it is easy to perceive were in official situations.

"I hope by next mail will be sent, something more satisfactory and useful than we have yet done in the way of instructions. But I am afraid the late O. P. riots have occupied all the thoughts of our great men here, so as to make them, or at least some of them, forget more distant but not less interesting concerns." A. April. 1810.

"With respect to the evils you allude to as arising from the inefficiency of the Portuguese government, the people here are by no means so A. April. 1811.

BOOK XIV. 1811. April. satisfied of their existence (to a great degree) as you who are on the spot. Here we judge only of the results, the details we read over, but being unable to remedy forget them the next day; and in the mean time be the tools you have to work with good or bad, so it is that you have produced results so far beyond the most sanguine expectations entertained here by all who have not been in Portugal within the last eight months, that none inquire the causes which prevented more being done in a shorter time; of which indeed there seems to have been a great probability, if the government could have stepped forward at an earlier period with one hand in their pockets, and in the other strong energetic declarations of the indispensable necessity of a change of measures, and principles, in the government."

B. Sept. 1811. "I have done every thing in my power to get people here to attend to their real interests in Portugal, and I have clamoured for money! money! money! in every office to which I have had access. To all my clamour and all my arguments I have invariably received the same answer, '*that the thing is impossible.*' The prince himself certainly appears to be *à la hauteur des circonstances*, and has expressed his determination to make every exertion to promote the good cause in the Peninsula. Lord Wellesley has a perfect comprehension of the subject in its fullest extent, and is fully aware of the several measures which Great Britain ought and could adopt. But such is the state of parties and such the condition of the present government, that I really despair of witnessing any decided and adequate effect, on our part, to save the Peninsula. The present feeling appears to be that we have done mighty things, and all that is in our power, that the rest must be left to all-bounteous Providence, and that if we do not succeed we must console ourselves by the reflection that Providence has not been so propitious to us as we deserved. This feeling you must allow is wonderfully moral and christian-like, but still nothing will be done until we have a more vigorous military system and a ministry capable of directing the resources of the nation to something nobler than a war of descents and embarkations."

A more perfect picture of an imbecile administration could scarcely be exhibited, and it was not wonderful, that lord Wellington, oppressed with the folly of the peninsular governments, should have often resolved to relinquish a contest that was one of constant risks, difficulties, and cares, when he had no better support from England. In the next chapter shall be shewn the ultimate effects of Canning's policy in the Spanish and Portuguese affairs.

CHAPTER III.

POLITICAL STATE OF SPAIN.

BOOK XIV.

1811.

As the military operations were, by the defeat of the regular armies, broken into a multitude of petty and disconnected actions, so the political affairs were, by the species of anarchy which prevailed, rendered exceedingly diversified and incongruous. Notwithstanding the restoration of the captain-generals, the provincial juntas remained very powerful; and while nominally responsible, to the Cortes and the regency, acted independently of either, except when interested views urged them to a seeming obedience. The disputes that arose between them and the generals, who were, for the most part, the creatures of the regency, or of the Cortes, were constant. In Gallicia, in the Asturias, in Catalonia, in Valencia, and in Murcia, disputes were increasing. Mahi, Abadia, Moscoso, Campo Verde, Lacy, Sarsfield, Eroles, Milans, Bassecour, Coupigny, Castaños, and Blake, were always in controversy with each other or with the juntas. Palacios dismissed from the regency for his high monarchical opinions, was made captain-general of Valencia, where he immediately joined the church-party against the cortes. In the Condado de Niebla the junta of Seville claimed superior authority, and Ballesteros of his own motion placed the county under martial law. The junta, strangely enough, then appealed to colonel Austin the British governor of the Algarves, but he refused to interfere. CHAP. III. 1811. Appendix, No. I. Section 4.

The cortes often annulled the decrees of the regency, and the latter, of whomsoever composed, always hating and fearing the cortes, were only intent upon increasing their own power, and entirely neglected the general cause; their conduct was at once haughty and mean, violent and intriguing, and it was impossible ever to satisfy them. Thus confusion was every where perpetuated, and it is proved by the intercepted papers of Joseph, as well as by the testimony of the British officers, and diplomatists, that with the Spaniards, the only moral resource left for keeping up the war, was their personal hatred of the French, partially called into action by particular oppression. Sir John Moore, with that keen and sure judgement which marked all his views, had early described Spain as being "*without armies, generals, or government.*" And in 1811, after three years of war, lord Wellington complained that "*there was no head in Spain, neither generals, nor officers, nor disciplined troops, and no cavalry; that the government had commenced the war without a magazine or military resource of any kind, without money or financial resource, and that the people at the head of affairs were as feeble as their resources were small.*" But the miserable state of the armies and the unquenchable vanity of the officers, have been too frequently exposed to need further illustration. They hated and ill-used the peasantry, while their own want of discipline and subordination rendered them odious to their country. The poorer people, much as they detested the French, almost wished for the

Ibid.

Letter to General Dumouriez 1811. MSS.

BOOK XIV. 1811.

establishment of Joseph, and all spirit and enthusiasm had long been extinct.

The real points of interest affecting England in her prosecution of the contest were, therefore, 1°. the improvement and the better guidance of the military power; 2°. the preventing a war between Portugal and Spain; 3°. the pretensions of the princess Carlotta of Portugal; 4°. the dispute with the American colonies.

With respect to the first, lord Wellington had made strenuous efforts, and his advice, and remonstrances, had at times saved the armies in the field from destruction; some partial attempts were also made to form troops under British officers in the Spanish service, but to a system like that which England exercised in Portugal, the leading Spaniards would never listen. This was one result of Mr. Canning's impolitic fostering of the Spanish pride, for it was by no means apparent that the people would have objected to such an arrangement, if it had been prudently urged, before the republican party in the cortes, and the popular press, had filled their minds with alarm upon the subject. The Catalans openly and repeatedly desired to have an English general, and in 1812 colonel Green did organize a small corps there, while Whittingham and Roche formed in the Balearic isles large divisions; colonel Cox had before proposed a like scheme for the north, but it was rejected by lord Wellington, and I have been unable to trace any important service rendered by those officers with their divisions. Their reputation was however quite eclipsed by one Downie, who had passed from the British commissariat into the Spanish service, and the English ministers, taken with his

CHAP. III. 1811.

boasting manner, supplied him with uniforms and equipments for a body of cavalry, called the Estremadura Legion, of such an expensive and absurd nature, as to induce a general officer to exclaim on seeing them that "he blushed for the folly of his government."

When the British ministers found themselves unable to deal with the Spanish regulars, they endeavoured to prop the war by the irregulars. But the increase of this force, which however never exceeded thirty thousand men in arms, gave offence to the regular officers, and amidst these distractions, the soldiers, ill-organized, ill-fed, and quite incapable of moving in the field in large bodies, lost all confidence in their generals. The latter, as in the case of Freire with the Murcian army, generally expected to be beaten in every action, and cared very little about it, because the regency were sure to affirm that they were victorious; and another of those wandering starved naked bands, which they called armies, could be formed from new levies in a month.

Appendix. No. I, Section 4.

The chances of a war with Portugal were by no means slight, the early ravages of the Spanish insurgent forces when Junot was in Lisbon, the violence of Romana's soldiers, and the burning of the village of San Fernando, together with the disputes between the people of Algarves and the Andalusians had revived all the national hatred on both sides. The two governments indeed entered into a treaty for recruiting in their respective territories; but it was with the utmost difficulty that the united exertions of Mr. Stuart and lord Wellington could prevent the Portuguese regency first, and afterwards the court of the Brazils, from provoking

BOOK XIV. 1811.

a war by re-annexing Olivença to Portugal, when it was taken from the French by marshal Beresford. And so little were the passions of these people subordinate to their policy that this design was formed at the very moment when the princess Carlotta, was, strenuously, and with good prospect of success, pushing her claim to the regency of Spain.

The intrigues of this princess were constant sources of evil; she laboured against the influence of the British at Cadiz, and her agent Pedro Souza, proffering gold to vulgar baseness, diamonds to delicate consciences, and promises to all, was adroit and persevering. In August 1810 a paper signed by only one member, but with an intimation that it contained the sentiments of the whole cortes, was secretly given to Mr. Wellesley, as a guide for his conduct. It purported that the impossibility of releasing Ferdinand and his brother from their captivity being apparent, the princess Carlotta should be called to the throne, and it was proposed to marry her eldest son, Pedro, to the princess of Wales, or some other princess of the House of Brunswick, that a "sudden and mortal blow might be given to the French empire." Mr. Wellesley was also told that a note, of the same tendency, would in the first session of the cortes be transmitted to the English legation. This, however, did not happen, chiefly because Arguelles openly and eloquently expressed his reasons against the appointment of a royal person as regent, and some months later procured a decree, rendering such persons ineligible, to pass in the cortes. This seemed to quash Carlotta's intrigue, nevertheless her pretensions, although continually overborne by

MrStuart's Papers, MSS.

the English influence, were as continually renewed, and often on the point of being publicly admitted.

The assumption that it was hopeless to expect Ferdinand's release was founded partly on the great influence which it was known Napoleon had acquired over his mind, and partly on his extreme personal timidity, which rendered any attempt to release him hopeless. Otherwise there were at Lisbon one Francisco Sagas, and his brother, daring men, who were only deterred from undertaking the enterprize by a previous experiment made at Bayonne, where they had for an hour implored Ferdinand to escape, all things being ready, yet in vain, because Escoiquez who ruled the prince, and was as timid as himself opposed it. To prevent ill effects from this well-known weakness, the cortes passed a decree to render null every act of Ferdinand while in captivity.

These intrigues of Carlotta were, however, of minor consequence compared to the conduct of the American colonies, which was one of the highest interest and importance. The causes and the nature of their revolt have been already touched upon, and the violence and injustice of the juntas, the regency, and the cortes, with relation to them, having been also exposed in a general way, need not be repeated here. When the Spanish insurrection first commenced, the leading men of Mexico signed a paper which was sent to the peninsula in November 1808, urging the immediate appointment of the duke of Infantado to the vice-royalty. He was averse to quitting Spain, but his wife persuaded him to consent, provided the central junta, just then established, was not

See Vols. I. & III.

BOOK XIV. 1811. opposed to it. Mr. Stuart foreseeing great advantage from this appointment laboured to persuade Mr. Frere to support it; but the latter, always narrow in his views, refused, because Infantado was personally disliked in England! and this, joined to the duke's own reluctance, seemed to end the matter. Meanwhile the disturbances in the colonies went on, and Carlotta of Portugal, urged her claim to be regent, and ultimately, queen of that country, as well as of Spain; and her interests were strongly supported there, until May 1809, when Cisneros, the Spanish viceroy, arrived at Monte Video, and spoiled her schemes.

Sept. The cry for a free trade with England, was then raised by the colonists, and Cisneros assented, but under conditions, presenting a curious contrast to the affected generosity of Mr. Canning, and affording an additional proof how little the latter knew the temper of the people he was dealing with. After detailing the dangers of his situation from the disposition of the colonists to revolt, and the impoverishment of the royal treasury in consequence of the disturbances which had already taken place, Cisneros observed that the only mode of relief was a temporary permission to trade with England for the sake of the duties. Necessity, he said, drove him to this measure; he regretted it, and directed that the ordinary laws relative to the residence of foreigners, most rigorous in themselves, should be most rigorously executed; and he added others of such a nature, that at first sight, they appear to be directed against some common enemy of mankind, rather than against the subjects and vessels of a nation which was then supporting the mother-country with troops and treasure in the most prodigal manner. Englishmen were not to be suffered to possess property, to have a residence, to keep an hotel, or even to remain on shore except for a fixed period. Any property already acquired by them was to be confiscated, and when the goods by which he hoped to raise his revenue were landed, the owners were not to be permitted to have them carried to the warehouses by their own sailors!

In April 1810 the disposition to revolt spread; the Caraccas and Porto Rico declared for independence, and the British governor of Curaçoa expressed his approval of their proceedings. This naturally gave great jealousy and alarm to the Spaniards, who looked upon it as a secret continuation of Miranda's affair. Lord Liverpool, indeed, immediately disavowed the governor's manifesto, but being very desirous to retain the trade, to conciliate the Spaniards, and to oblige the colonists to acknowledge Ferdinand and oppose France, three things incompatible, his policy produced no good result. Mexico indeed still remained obedient in outward appearance, but the desire to have Infantado existed, and a strong party of the Mexicans even purposed raising him to the throne, if Napoleon's success should separate the two countries; but the Spanish regency, with characteristic folly, chose this moment to appoint Venegas, who was the avowed enemy of Infantado, viceroy of Mexico, and thus the revolt was forced on in that country also.

This state of affairs had a bad effect upon the war in Spain in many ways. The Spaniards, thinking to retain the colonies by violence, sent out a

BOOK XIV. 1811.

Appendix, No. I. Section 1.

small squadron at first, and at a later period employed the succours received from England, in fitting out large expeditions of their best troops; and that, when the enemy were most closely, pressing them in the Peninsula. The remonstrances of the British on this head were considered as indications of a faithless policy; and Carlotta also wrote to Elio, the governor of Buenos Ayres, and to the cortes, warning both, to beware of the English as "a people capable of any baseness where their own interests were concerned." Hence there was a prevalent suspicion, that England had a design of connecting itself with the colonies independently of Spain, which greatly diminished the English influence at Cadiz.

By this dispute with America the supply of specie for the Peninsula was endangered, which involved the very existence of the war; all things therefore conduced to make lord Wellesley desire his brother, Mr. Wellesley, to offer the mediation of England, and to please the Spaniards he also removed the governor of Curaçoa; but his plans, like lord Liverpool's, were based upon the desire to preserve the trade with the colonies, and this feeling pervaded and vitiated his instructions to Mr. Wellesley.

Lord Wellesley's despatch to Mr. H. Wellesley, May, 1811. MSS.

That gentleman was directed to enter into a full discussion of the subject, on principles founded on cordial amity and good faith; and to endeavour to convince the regency that the British course of proceeding had hitherto been the best for all parties. For the primary object being to keep France from forming a party in America, the revolted colonies had been by England received into an amicable intercourse of trade, a measure not inconsistent with good faith to Spain, inasmuch as the colonists would otherwise have had recourse to France, whereas now England was considered by them as a safe and honourable channel of reconciliation with the mother-country. There had been, it was said, no formal recognition of the self-constituted governments, or if any had taken place by subordinate officers they would be disavowed. Protection and mediation had indeed been offered, but the rights of Ferdinand had been supported, and as war between Spain and America would only injure the great cause, a mediatory policy was pressed upon the latter.—The blockade of Buenos Ayres and the Caraccas had already diverted money and forces from Spain, and driven the Americans to seek for French officers to assist them. The trade was essential to enable England to continue her assistance to Spain, and although this had been frequently represented to the regency, the latter had sent ships (which had been fitted out in English ports and stored at the expense of Great Britain for the war with France) to blockade the colonies and to cut off the English trade; and it was done also at a moment, when the regency was unable to transport Blake's army from Cadiz to the Condado di Niebla without the assistance of British vessels. It was difficult," Lord Wellesley said, "to state an instance in which the prejudices and jealousy of individuals had occasioned so much confusion of every maxim of discretion and good policy, and so much danger to the acknowledged mutual interests of two great states engaged in a defensive alliance against the assaults of a foreign foe:"—"Spain could not expect England to concur in a continuance of a system by which, at her own expense, her

BOOK XIV. 1811. May.

trade was injured, and by which Spain was making efforts not against the French but against the main sources of her own strength."

After these instructions, which were given before the constitution of Spain was arranged by the cortes, Mr. Wellesley pressed the mediation upon

June.

Mr. Bardaxi the Spanish minister, who agreed to accept it upon condition, that Mexico, which had not yet declared a form of government, should be excepted,—that England should immediately break off all intercourse with the colonies, and, if the mediation failed, should assist Spain to reconquer them. When the injustice and bad policy of this proposition was objected to, Mr. Bardaxi maintained that it was just and politic, and pressed it as a secret article; he however finally offered to accept the mediation, if Mr. Wellesley would only pledge England to break off the intercourse of trade. This was refused, and the negotiation continued, but as Bardaxi asserted, that lord Wellington had before agreed to the propriety of England going to war with the colonies, Mr. Wellesley referred to the latter, and that extraordinary man, while actually engaged with the enemy, under most critical circumstances, was thus called upon to discuss so grave and extensive a subject. But it was on such occasions that all his power of mind was displayed, and his manner of treating this question proved, that in political, and even in commercial affairs, his reach of thought and enlarged conceptions, immeasurably surpassed the cabinet he served. And when we consider that his opinions, stated in 1811, have been since verified in all points to the very letter, it is impossible not to be filled with admiration of his foresight and judgment.

" He denied that he had ever given grounds for Bardaxi's observation. His opinion had always been that Great Britain should follow, as he hoped she had, liberal counsels towards Spain, by laying aside, at least during the existence of the war, all consideration of merchants' profits. He felt certain that such a policy would equally suit her commercial interests and her warlike policy, as well as add greatly to her character. The immediate advantages extorted from an open trade with the colonies he had always considered ideal. Profit was undoubtedly to be made there, and eventually the commerce would be very great; but its value must arise from the increasing riches of the colonies and the growth of luxury there, and the period at which this would happen was more likely to be checked than forwarded by the extravagant speculations of English traders. Whatever might be the final particular relations established between Spain and her colonies, the general result must be, the relaxation, if not the annihilation, of their colonial commercial system, and Great Britain was then sure to be the greatest gainer.

" In expectation of this ultimate advantage, her policy ought to have been liberal throughout, that is, the colonies themselves should have been checked, and the endeavours of traders and captains of ships to separate them from Spain ought to have been repressed. England should, when the colonies first showed a disposition to revolt, have considered not only what they could do but what Great Britain could assist them to effect. His knowledge of the Spanish government and its means enabled him to say she could not reduce even one of the weakest of her colonies, and to make the attempt would be

BOOK XIV. 1811. June.

a gross folly and misapplication of means. Nay England could not, in justice to the great object in the Peninsula, give Spain any effectual assistance; for it was but too true that distant colonies could always separate from the mother country when they willed it, and certainly it would be the highest madness, in Spain, to attempt at that time to prevent such a separation by force, and in England, to assist, or even encourage her in such an attempt.

"The conduct of the latter should then have been by her influence and advice to have prevented the disputes from coming to extremity, and *now* should be to divert Spain from such an absurdity as having recourse to violence. But the reception of the deputies from America which the Spaniards so much complained of, was useful to the latter. It prevented those deputies from going to France, and if they had gone, the fact, that colonies have the power to separate if they have the will, would have been at once verified.

"Great Britain, although late, had at last *offered* that mediation which he wished had been *asked* for, and it remained to consider on what terms it ought to be accepted. It would have been better if Spain had come forward with an explicit declaration of what her intentions towards the colonies in respect to constitution and commerce were. England could then have had something intelligible to mediate upon; but now Spain only desired her to procure the submission of Buenos Ayres and the Caraccas; and if she failed in that impracticable object she was to aid Spain in forcing them to submission! and he, lord Wellington, was said to have approved of this! One would really, he exclaimed, believe that Mr. Bardaxi has never adverted to the means and resources of his own country, to the object they have acquired at home, nor to the efforts making by England in the Peninsula; and that he imagines I have considered these facts as little as he appears to have done! Great Britain cannot agree to that condition!

See Vol. III p. 419.

"In respect to constitution" (alluding to the acknowledgement of the civil rights of the Americans by the cortes) "the Spaniards had gone a great way, but not so far as some of her colonies would require, they would probably ask her to have separate local representative bodies for their interior concerns, such as the English colonial assemblies, yet this important point had not been considered in the treaty of mediation, and in respect of commerce the Spanish government had said nothing; although it was quite certain her prohibitory system could not continue, and the necessary consequence of the actual state of affairs required that in the treaty of mediation the colonies should be put, with respect to trade, exactly on the same footing as the provinces of Old Spain. If that was not done it would be useless to talk to the colonists of equal rights and interests; they would feel that their interests were sacrificed to those of the mother country.

"It was true that the latter would lose immediately, though probably not eventually, very largely in revenue and commercial profit by such a concession. This was the unavoidable result of the circumstances of the times, she had therefore a fair claim to participate in the advantages the colonies would enjoy from it. To this object the treaty of mediation should have adverted. Spain should have confidentially declared to Great Britain

BOOK XIV. 1811. June.

her intended course, what system she would follow, what duties impose, and what proportion she would demand for general imperial purposes. Upon such materials England might have worked with a prospect of permanently maintaining the integrity of the Spanish empire on just and fair principles; or at all events have allayed the present disputes and so removed the difficulties they occasioned in the Peninsula, and in either case have insured her own real interests. Spain had however taken a narrow view both of her own and the relative situation of others, and *if she did not enlarge it, matters would grow worse and worse. It would be useless for England to interfere, and after a long contest which would only tend to weaken the mother country and deprive her of the resources which she would otherwise find in the colonies for her war with France, the business would end in the separation of the colonies from Spain.*"

The mediation was, however, after many discussions, finally accepted by the cortes, Mexico only being excepted, and an English commission of mediation, of which Mr. Stuart was the head, was even appointed in September 1811, but from various causes it never proceeded beyond Cadiz. The Spaniards continued to send out expeditions, Mr. Wellesley's remonstrances were unheeded, and although the regency afterwards offered to open the trade under certain duties, in return for a subsidy, nothing was concluded.

CHAPTER IV.

POLITICAL STATE OF PORTUGAL.

THE power and crafty projects of the Souzas, their influence over their weak-minded prince, their cabal to place the duke of Brunswick at the head of the Portuguese army, the personal violence of the patriarch, the resignation of Das Minas, and the disputes with lord Wellington, have been already touched upon; but the extent of the difficulties engendered by those things, cannot be understood without a more detailed exposition. CHAP. IV. 1811. Vol. III.

Mr. Villiers's mission, like all those emanating from Mr. Canning, had been expensive in style, tainted by intrigues, useless in business, and productive of disorders. When Mr. Stuart arrived, he found every thing, except the army under Beresford, in a state of disorganization; and the influence of England was decreasing, because of the vacillating system hitherto pursued by the British government. As early as 1808 lord Wellington had advised the ministers not only to adopt Portugal as the base of operations in the Peninsula, but to assume in reality the whole administration of that country; to draw forth all its resources, both of men and money, and to make up any deficiency, by the power of England. This advice had been neglected, and an entirely different policy pursued, which, in execution, was also feeble and uncertain. Feb. 1810.

BOOK XIV. 1811.

The Portuguese constitution, like most of those springing from the feudal system, was excellent in theory, as far as regarded the defence of the kingdom: but it was overwhelmed with abuses in practice; and it was a favourite maxim with the authorities that it did not become a paternal government to punish neglect in the subordinates. When court intrigues were to be effected, or poor men to be oppressed, there was no want of vigour or of severity; but in all that regarded the admistration of affairs, it was considered sufficient to give orders without looking to their execution, and no animadversion, much less punishment, followed disobedience. The character of the government was extreme weakness; the taxes, partially levied, produced only half their just amount; the payments from the treasury were in arrears; the army was neglected in all things dependent on the civil administration, and a bad navy was kept up, at an expense of a quarter of a million, to meet a war with Algiers. This last question was, however, a knife with a double edge, for in peace, a tribute paid in coin, drained the treasury already too empty, and in war the fleet did nothing; meanwhile the feeding of Cadiz was rendered precarious by it; and of Lisbon also, for the whole produce of Portugal was only equal to four months' consumption. In commercial affairs, the usual peninsular jealousy was displayed; the imports of British goods were prohibited to the advantage of smugglers only, while the government which thus neglected its own resources to the injury of both countries, clamoured for subsidies. Finally, the power of the Souzas was so great, and the regency was so entirely subservient to them, that although Mr. Stuart had been assured by Mr. Canning, that a note forbidding Domingo Souza to meddle with affairs at Lisbon, had been procured from the Brazils, all representations, to the regency, were met by references to that nobleman, who was in London, and the business of the mission was thus paralysed.

In March 1809 the British government had taken ten thousand Portuguese troops into pay. In May they were increased to twenty thousand, and in June to thirty thousand. The cost of these forces, and the increased pay to Portuguese officers, added to the subsidy, amounted to two millions sterling; but this subsidy partly from negligence, partly from the exhaustion of England in consequence of Mr. Canning's prodigal donations to Spain, was in arrears. However, as this mode of proceeding was perfectly in unison with their own method, the regency did not much regard it, but they were eager to obtain a loan from England, in the disposal of which they would have been quite uncontrolled, and for this very reason lord Wellington strenuously opposed it. In revenge, the regency, by a wilful misunderstanding of the debates of parliament, and by the distortion of facts, endeavoured to throw a doubt upon the sincerity of England, and this, with the encouragement given to all Portuguese malcontents by the Whigs, whose clamour, just, as applied to the ministers, was unjustly extended to the generals, greatly increased the disorder of the times.

In this state of affairs Mr. Canning being happily removed from office, lord Wellesley, who succeeded him, changed the instructions of the diplomatic agents in the Peninsula. They were now directed to make conditions with respect to the

BOOK XIV. 1811.

succours, and in Portugal they were vigorously to interfere in all civil changes, augmentations of revenue, and military resources; and even to demand monthly reports of the condition of the army, and the expenditure of the subsidy. Lord Wellesley also, thinking that the example of a cortes in Spain, might create a desire for a more temperate government in Portugal, was prepared to forward such a change, provided old forms were preserved, and that all appeared to flow from the prince regent, whose consent he undertook to secure. Resistance to the enemy, he said, would be in proportion to the attachment of the people, and hence it was advisable to make timely concessions, giving however no more than was absolutely necessary.

The regency were strongly opposed to this notion of a cortes, and Mr. Suart and lord Wellington affirmed, and truly, that the docility of the people, and their hatred of the French, were motives powerful enough, without any other stimulus, to urge them to action. Thus the project fell to the ground, and the time was perhaps inconvenient to effect a revolution of this nature, which the people themselves certainly did not contemplate, and which, as Spain had shewn, was not a certain help to the war. Lord Wellington, who only considered what would conduce to the success of the war, was therefore consistent upon this occasion, but it is curious to observe the course of the English cabinet. The enforcement in France of a military conscription, authorized by the laws, was an unheard-of oppression on the part of Napoleon; but in Portugal a conscription, enforced by foreigners, was a wise and vigorous measure; and lord Wellesley admitting that the Portuguese government had been harsh and oppressive, as well as weak and capricious, was content to withhold a better system from the people, expressly because they loved their country and were obedient subjects; for he would have readily granted it to them if they had been unruly and of doubtful patriotism.

Mr. Stuart in concert with lord Wellington diligently endeavoured to remedy the evils of the hour, but whenever he complained of any particular disorder, he was, by the regency, offered arbitrary power to punish, which being only an expedient to render the British odious to the people he refused. The intrigues of the Fidalgos then became apparent, and the first regency was broken up in 1810. The marquis of Das Minas retired from it under the pretext of ill health, but really because he found himself too weak to support Mr. De Mello, a Fidalgo officer, who was thrust forward to oppose the legal authority of marshal Beresford. Mr. Cypriano Freire was then made minister of finance, and of foreign affairs, and Mr. Forjas secretary-at-war, with a vote in the regency on matters of war. But the former soon after Mr. Stuart's arrival resigned his situation in consequence of some disgust, and the Conde Redondo, having undertaken the office, commenced, with the advice of Mr. Stuart, a better arrangement of the taxes, especially the "*decima*" or income tax, which was neither impartially nor strictly enforced on the rich towns, nor on the powerful people of the Fidalgo faction. The clergy also evaded the imposts, and the British merchants, although profiting enormously from the war, sought exemption under the factory privileges, not only from the taxes, which in certain cases they could legally do, but from the

BOOK XIV. 1811.

billets, and from those recruiting laws affecting their servants, which they could not justly demand, and which all other classes in the community were liable to.

The working of the Souzas, in the Brazils, where the minister of finance wished to have the regulation of the Portuguese treasury under his control, soon changed this arrangement. Freire's resignation was not accepted, Redondo was excluded from the government, and Forjas, who was the most efficient member of the government, was deprived of his functions. The remaining members then proposed to fill up Das Minas' vacancy themselves, but this was resisted by lord Wellington, on the ground, that, without the prince's order, the proceeding would be illegal, and involve the regency in an indefensible quarrel at the Brazils. The order for removing Redondo, and cramping the utility of Forjas, he, in concert with Mr. Stuart, withstood; and this, for the moment, prevented a change, which would have impeded the ameliorations begun. Such, however, was the disorder in the finances, that Mr. Stuart proposed, as the least difficult mode of arranging them, to take the whole direction himself, England becoming answerable for the expenditure of the country; lord Wellington thought this could not be done, without assuming, at the same time, the whole government of the country, which he had previously proposed to the British cabinet, but which it was now too late to attempt, and Mr. Stuart's project fell to the ground.

Another spring of mischief soon bubbled up, lord Strangford, whose diplomatic dexterity evinced by his Bruton-street despatch, had been rewarded by the situation of minister at the Brazils, was there bestirring himself. It had been the policy of Mr. Stuart and the English general, to keep the regency permanent, and to support the secretariats as they were placed in the hands of Mr. de Forjas and the Conde de Redondo; for these men had been found by experience, to be better qualified to co-operate with the British authorities than any other persons, and hence lord Wellington had resisted the prince's orders for Cypriano Freire's resumption of office, and had continued the functions of Forjas and Redondo, until his own remonstrances could reach the Brazils. In this state of affairs lord Strangford informed Mr. Stuart that he had persuaded the prince to accede to the following propositions. 1°. That the British plenipotentiary at Lisbon, the count Redondo, doctor Nogueras, and the principal Souza, should be added to the old regency. 2°. That admiral Berkeley should be naval commander-in-chief. 3°. That all traitorous correspondence should be prevented, and that measures should be taken to limit the exuberant power assumed by subordinates. This last article was directed against Forjas, and the whole went to establish the preponderance of the Souza faction. The only useful part was the appointment of Mr. Stuart to the regency, but this was arranged before it was known that Mr. Villiers had been recalled, and consequently had the same object of favouring the Souzas in view.

Mr. Stuart and lord Wellington strongly objected to this change, although they submitted to it as not wishing to appear regardless of the prince regent's rights. Mr. Stuart, however, reflecting that a government composed of men having different views and feelings, and without any casting vote, the number being even, could not go on use-

BOOK XIV. 1811.

fully, was at first averse to join the regency, but was finally persuaded to do so by lord Wellington, who justly considered that his presence there would give the only chance of success.

Doctor Nogueras' appointment was described, by lord Strangford, as a tribute to democracy, the object being to counteract the power of those very secretariats which lord Wellington and Mr. Stuart were labouring to preserve. But lord Strangford prided himself chiefly upon the appointment of the principal Souza, who, he said, had been recommended to him by Mr. Villiers, an avowal of great import, as shewing at once the spirit of the new arrangement: for this Souza had, in a subordinate situation, hitherto opposed every proceeding of the British in Portugal; he was the avowed enemy of Beresford, the contriver of all confusion, and the most mischievous person in Portugal; and his absence from that country was so desirable, that intimations to that effect had been formally given to him, by lord Wellesley, through Mr. Stuart. This factious person was now, however, armed with additional power, to thwart the English authorities in Portugal, and thus lord Strangford's diplomacy tended, in effect, to ruin that cause which he had been sent to the Brazils to support.

In relating these proceedings I have, following his own letter, announcing the change, described lord Strangford as acting voluntarily; but in a subsequent despatch he affirmed, that it was under Mr. Canning's instructions, he had pressed for this incorporating of the British minister in the regency, and that Nogueras' appointment sprang entirely from the prince regent's own will, which he did not choose to oppose. In like manner, when lord

Wellesley was intent upon assembling a cortes, lord Strangford called it "*a great and essential measure strongly and wisely urged by the government*," and yet afterwards acknowleged that he neglected to press it, because he thought it "*useless and even hurtful*," which inconsistency renders it difficult to determine on whom these affairs rested. As affecting Mr. Canning's policy, however, it is to be observed that if he originally arranged this change, his object was to put Mr. Villiers in the regency, not with any view to the more complete controul of Portugal for the purposes of war, but, as the instructions to sir John Cradock prove, to ensure a proponderance to the diplomatic department over the military in that country. See Vol. II. Appendix.

The principal reforms, in the administration, which had been sought for by lord Wellington, were a better arrangement of the financial system—the execution of the laws without favour to the fidalgos—the suppression of the "*junta di viveres*," a negligent and fraudulent board, for which he wished to establish a Portuguese commissariat—the due supply of provisions and stores, for the national troops and fortresses—the consolidation of the arsenal department under one head—the formation of a military chest, distinct from the treasury, which was always diverting the funds to other purposes—the enforcing of the regulations about the means of transport—the repairs of the roads and bridges—the reformation of the hospitals—the succouring of the starving people, and the revival of agriculture in the parts desolated by the war.

These things he had hoped to accomplish; but from the moment the change effected by lord Strangford took place, unceasing acrimonious disputes ensued

BOOK XIV. 1811. between the British commander and the Portuguese government, and no species of falsehood or intrigue, not even personal insult, and the writing of anonymous threatening letters, were spared by the Souza faction. In the beginning of 1811 they had organized an anti-English party, and a plot was laid to force the British out of the country, which would have succeeded if less vigilance had been used by Mr. Stuart, or less vigour of control by lord Wellington. This plot however required that the patriarch should go to the northern provinces, a journey which the envoy always dexterously prevented.

The first complaint of the British authorities, accompanied with a demand for the removal of the principal Souza, reached the Brazils in February 1811, and Das Minas died about the same time; but so strongly was the faction supported at Rio
May. Janeiro, that in May, the prince regent expressed his entire approval of the Souzas' proceedings and his high displeasure with Forjas and Mr. Stuart. His minister, the Conde de Linhares, wrote, that the capture of Massena with his whole army, which he expected to hear of each day, would not make amends for the destruction of the country during the retreat of the allies; and in an official note to lord Strangford, he declared, that the prince regent could not permit Mr. Stuart to vote in matters concerning the internal government of the kingdom, because he was influenced by, and consulted persons suspected of disaffection, which expression lord Strangford said referred solely to Forjas.

The prince himself also wrote to lord Wellington, accusing Mr. Stuart of acting separately from the commander-in-chief, and of being the cause of all the factions which had sprung up, and he declared that he would not remove Souza, unless Mr. Stuart was recalled. He desired that Forjas, who he affirmed to be the real author of the opposition complained of by the British, should be sent to the Brazils, to answer for his conduct; and finally he announced his intention to write in a like strain to the king of England. To this lord Wellington answered that finding his conduct disapproved and Souza's applauded, he proposed to quit Portugal. June. Forjas immediately sent in his resignation, admiral Berkeley proposed to do the same, and Mr. Stuart withdrew from the council until the pleasure of his own cabinet should be made known: the war was then on the point of finishing, but the crisis was not perceived by the public, because the resolution of the English general was kept secret, to avoid disturbing the public mind, and in the hopes of submission on the part of the prince.

Meanwhile other embarrassments were superadded, of a nature to leave the English general little hope of being able to continue the contest, should he even defeat the intrigues at Rio Janeiro; for besides the quarrel with the Souza faction, in which he and Mr. Stuart supported Forjas, Nogueira, and Redondo, against their enemies in the Brazils, these very persons, although the best that could be found, and men of undoubted ability, influenced partly by national habits, partly by fears of ultimate consequences, continually harassed him in the execution of the details belonging to their offices. No delinquent was ever punished, no fortress ever stored in due time and quantity, the suffering people were uncared for, disorders were unrepressed, the troops were starved, and the fa-

BOOK XIV. 1811.

vouring of the fidalgos constant. The "*junta de viveres*" was supported, the formation of a military chest, and commissariat, delayed; many wild and foolish schemes daily broached; and the natural weakness of the government was, by instability, increased, because the prince regent had early in 1811 intimated an intention of immediately returning to Europe.

I have said that it was a favourite maxim with the regency that a paternal government should not punish delinquents in the public service, and they added to this another still more absurd, namely, that the Portuguese troops could thrive under privations of food, which would kill men of another nation; with these two follies they excused neglect, whenever the repetition, that there had been no neglect, became fatiguing to them. Besides this, collisions between the British commissariat and the "*junta de viveres*" were frequent and very hurtful, because the former able to outbid, and more in fear of failure, overbought the latter; this contracted the already too small sphere of their activity, and lord Wellington was prevented feeding the whole Portuguese army himself by a curious obstacle. His principal dependance for the support of his own troops was upon the Spanish muleteers attached to the army, they were the very life and sustenance of the war, and their patience, hardiness, and fidelity to the British were remarkable; but they so abhorred the Portuguese people that they would not carry provisions for their soldiers, and lord Wellington only obtained their services, for those brigades which were attached to the English divisions, by making them think the food was entirely for the latter. Upon such nice management even in apparently trifling matters did this war depend. And yet it is not uncommon for politicians, versed only in the classic puerilities of public schools, and the tricks of parliamentary faction, to hold the rugged experience of Wellington's camp as nothing in the formation of a statesman.

The effects of these complicated affairs were soon and severely felt. Abrantes had like to have been abandoned, from want, at the time Massena held Santarem, and the Portuguese troops were starved during that general's retreat; Beresford's operations in the Alemtejo were impeded, and his hospitals were left without succour; at Fuentes Onoro ammunition failed, and the Portuguese artillery were forced to supply themselves by picking up the enemy's bullets; the cavalry of that nation were quite ruined, and out of more than forty thousand regular troops, formed by Beresford, only nineteen thousand were to be found under arms after the battle of Albuera, the rest had deserted or died from extreme want.

When Massena retreated the provincial organization of the country was restored, and to encourage the people to sow the devastated districts before the season passed, Mr. Stuart had furnished seed corn on the credit of the coming subsidy; an amnesty for deserters was also published, the feudal imposts for the year were remitted, and fairs were established to supply tools of husbandry; but notwithstanding these efforts, such was the distress, that at Caldas eighty persons died daily, and at Figueras where twelve thousand people, chiefly from Portuguese Estremadura, had taken refuge, the daily deaths were above a hundred, and the whole would have perished but for the active benevolence of major Von Linstow, an officer of general Trant's staff. Meanwhile the country was so overrun with robbers that the detached officers could not travel in safety upon the service of the army, and Wellington was fearful of being obliged to employ his troops against them. British officers were daily insulted at Lisbon, and even assassinated while on duty with impunity; the whole army was disgusted, the letters to England were engendering in that country a general dislike to the war, and the British soldiers, when not with their regiments, committed a thousand outrages on the line of operations.

As a climax to these scenes of misery and mischief, the harvest which had failed in Portugal, failed also in England; and no corn was to be got from the Baltic because there was no specie to pay for it, and bills were refused. Hence the famine spread in a terrible manner until Mr. Stuart obtained leave to license fifty American vessels with corn, whose cargoes were paid for out of funds provided partly by the charity of the people of England, and partly by a parliamentary grant which passed when Massena retreated.

In this crisis the British cabinet granted an additional subsidy to Portugal, but from the scarcity of specie, the greatest part of it was paid in kind, and the distress of the regency for money was scarcely lessened; for these supplies merely stood in the place of the plunder which had hitherto prevailed in the country. Thus Mr. Canning's prodigality, Mr. Vansittart's paper system, and Mr. Perceval's economy, all combined to press upon the British general, and to use his own words, he was supplied with only one-sixth part of the money necessary to keep the great machine going which had been set in motion. Mr. Perceval however, in answer to his remonstrances, employed a secretary of the Treasury to prove in a laboured paper, founded entirely upon false data, that the army had been over-supplied, and must have money to spare. But that minister, whose speeches breathed nothing but the final destruction of France, designed to confine the efforts of England to the defence of Portugal alone, without any regard to the rest of the Peninsula.

Amongst the other follies of the Portuguese regency was a resolution to issue proclamations, filled with bombastic adulation of themselves, vulgar abuse of the French, and altogether unsuited to the object of raising the public feeling, which flagged under their system. To the English general's remonstrances on this head, Forjas replied, that praise of themselves and abuse of the French, was the national custom, and could not be dispensed with! a circumstance which certain English writers who have implicitly followed the accounts of the Portuguese authors, such as Accursio de Neves, and men of his stamp, relative to French enormities, would do well to consider. And here it is right to observe, that so many complaints were made of the cruelty committed by Massena's army while at Santarem, that lord Wellington had some thoughts of reprisals; but having first caused strict inquiry to be made, it was discovered that in most cases, the *ordenança,* after having submitted to the French, and received their protection, took advantage of it to destroy the stragglers and small detachments, and the cruelty complained of was only the infliction of legitimate punishment for such conduct: the projected retaliation was therefore

Mr. Stuart's papers, MSS.

BOOK XIV. 1811.

changed for an injunction to the *ordenanças* to cease from such a warfare.

The character of the regency was, however, most openly shewn in their proceedings connected with the convention of Cintra. All the advantages which that treaty ensured to Portugal, they complacently reaped, but overlooked or annulled those points in which the character of England was concerned. In violation of the convention, and in despite of the remonstrances of lord Wellington and Mr. Stuart, they cast the French residents at Lisbon into loathsome dungeons, without any cause of complaint; and in the affair of Mascarheñas their conduct was distinguished alike by wanton cruelty and useless treachery. This youth, when only fifteen, had with many others entered the French service in Junot's time, under the permission of his own prince; and he and the Conde de Sabugal, were taken by the peasantry in 1810 endeavouring to pass from Massena's army into Spain, Sabugal in uniform, Mascarheñas in disguise. They were both tried as traitors. The first, a general officer, and with powerful friends amongst the Fidalgos, was acquitted, as indeed was only just; but he was then appointed to a situation under the regency, which was disgraceful, as arising from faction: Mascarheñas was a boy, and had no powerful friends, and he was condemned to death. Lord Wellington and Mr. Stuart represented the injustice of this sentence, and they desired that if humanity was unheeded the government would put him to death as a spy, for being in disguise, and so prevent the danger of reprisals, already threatened by Massena. The young man's mother and sisters, grovelling in the dust, implored the regency to spare him, but to shew their hatred of lord Wellington and Mr. Stuart, for the disputes with the regency were then highest, the government told the miserable women, that it was the British general and minister who demanded his death, and they were sent, with this brutal falsehood, to weep and to ask grace from persons who had no power to grant it. Mascarheñas was publicly executed as a traitor, for entering the French service under the authority of his native prince, while Sabugal was acquitted, and even rewarded, although precisely in the same circumstances, when the excuse of the disguise had been rejected.

In 1810 one Corea, calling himself an aide-de-camp of Massena, was likewise seized in disguise within the British lines, and, having given useful information, was by lord Wellington confined in St. Julians, to protect him from the Portuguese government. After a time he became deranged, and was released, whereupon the regency, rather than keep him, desired that he might be sent as a prisoner of war to England; thus for convenience admitting the very principle which they had rejected when only honour and humanity were concerned. A process against the marquis d'Alorna had also been commenced, but his family being powerful it was soon dropped, and yet the government refused madame d'Alorna leave to join her husband, thus shewing themselves spiteful and contemptible as well as cowardly and bloody. Even the court of Brazil was shocked. The prince rebuked the regency severely for the death of Mascarheñas, reversed the sentences on some others, and banished Sabugal to Terceira.

This was the political state of Portugal.

BOOK XIV. 1811. May.

Lord Liverpool's intimation, that neither corn nor specie could be had from England, threw lord Wellington on his own resources for feeding his troops. He had before created a paper money by means of commissariat bills, which, being paid regularly at certain periods, passed current with the people when the national bonds called "Apolocies" were at an enormous discount. He now in concert with Mr. Stuart, entered into commerce to supply his necessities. For having ascertained that grain in different parts of the world, especially in South America, could be bought by bills, cheaper than it sold for hard cash in Lisbon; and that in Egypt, although only to be bought with specie, it was at a reduced price; they employed mercantile agents to purchase it for the army account, and after filling the magazines sold the overplus to the inhabitants. This transaction was, however, greatly impeded by the disputes with North America, which were now rapidly hastening to a rupture; the American ships which frequented the Tagus being prevented by the non-importation act from bringing back merchandize, were forced to demand coin, which helped to drain the country of specie.

As Mr. Stuart could obtain no assistance from the English merchants of Lisbon, to aid him in a traffic which interfered with their profits, he wrote circular letters to the consuls in the Mediterranean, and in the Portuguese islands, and to the English minister at Washington, desiring them to negotiate treasury bills; to increase the shipments of corn to Lisbon, and pay with new bills, to be invested in such articles of British manufacture as the non-importation law still permitted to go to

America. By this complicated process he contrived to keep something in the military chest; and this commerce, which lord Wellington truly observed, was not what ought to have occupied his time and attention, saved the army, and the people, when the proceedings of Mr. Perceval would have destroyed both. Yet it was afterwards cavilled at and censured by the ministers, on the representations of the merchants who found their exorbitant gains interrupted by it.

Pressed by such accumulated difficulties, and not supported in England as he deserved, the general, who had more than once intimated his resolution to withdraw from the Peninsula, now seriously thought of executing it. Yet when he considered, that the cause was one even of more interest to England than to the Peninsula; that the embarrassments of the French might be even greater than his own, and that Napoleon himself, gigantic as his exertions had been, and were likely to be, was scarcely aware of the difficulty of conquering the Peninsula while an English army held Portugal; when he considered also, that light was breaking in the north of Europe, that the chances of war are many, even in the worst of times, and above all, when his mental eye caught the beams of his own coming glory, he quelled his rising indignation, and retempered his mighty energies to bear the buffet of the tempest.

But he could not remove the obstacles that choked his path, nor could he stand still, lest the ground should open beneath his feet. If he moved in the north, Marmont's army and the army under Bessieres were ready to oppose him, and he must take Ciudad Rodrigo or blockade it

BOOK XIV. 1811. May.

before he could even advance against them. To take that place required a battering-train, to be brought up through a mountainous country from Lamego, and there was no covering position for the army during the siege. To blockade and pass it, would so weaken his forces, already inferior to the enemy, that he could do nothing effectual; meanwhile Soult would have again advanced from Llerena, and perhaps have added Elvas to his former conquests.

To act on the defensive in Beira, and follow up the blow against Soult, by invading Andalusia, in concert with the Murcians and the corps of Blake, Beguines, and Graham, while Joseph's absence paralysed the army of the centre; while the army of Portugal was being reorganized in Castile; and while Suchet was still engaged with Taragona, would have been an operation suitable to lord Wellington's fame and to the circumstances of the moment. But then Badajos must have been blockaded with a corps powerful enough to have defied the army of the centre, and the conduct of the Portuguese government had so reduced the allied forces, that this would not have left a sufficient army to encounter Soult. Hence, after the battle of Albuera, the only thing to be done, was to renew the siege of Badajos, which, besides its local interest, contained the enemy's bridge equipage and battering train; but which, on common military calculations, could scarcely be expected to fall before Soult and Marmont would succour it: yet it was only by the taking of that town that Portugal itself could be secured beyond the precincts of Lisbon, and a base for further operations obtained.

According to the regular rules of art, Soult

should have been driven over the mountains before the siege was begun, but there was no time to do this, and Marmont was equally to be dreaded on the other side; wherefore lord Wellington could only try, as it were, to snatch away the fortress from between them, and he who, knowing his real situation, censures him for the attempt, is neither a general nor a statesman. The question was, whether the attempt should be made or the contest in the Peninsula be resigned. It failed, indeed, and the Peninsula was not lost, but no argument can be thence derived, because it was the attempt, rather than the success, which was necessary to keep the war alive; moreover the French did not push their advantages as far as they might have done, and the unforeseen circumstance of a large sum of money being brought to Lisbon, by private speculation, at the moment of failure, enabled the English general to support the crisis.

CHAPTER V.

SECOND ENGLISH SIEGE OF BADAJOS.

BOOK XIV.

1811. May.

There is no operation in war so certain as a modern siege, provided the rules of art are strictly followed, but, unlike the ancient sieges in that particular, it is also different in this; that no operation is less open to irregular daring, because the course of the engineer can neither be hurried nor delayed without danger. Lord Wellington knew that a siege of Badajos, in form, required longer time, and better means, than were at his disposal, but he was forced to incur danger and loss of reputation, which is loss of strength, or to adopt some compendious mode of taking that place. The time that he could command, and time is in all sieges the greatest point, was precisely that which the French required to bring up a force sufficient to disturb the operation; and this depended on the movements of the army of Portugal, whose march from Salamanca to Badajos, by the pass of Baños, or even through that of Gata, could not be stopped by general Spencer, because the mouths of those defiles were commanded by Marmont's positions. It was possible also at that season, for an army to pass the Tagus by fords near Alcantara, and hence more than twenty days of free action against the place were not to be calculated upon.

Now the carriages of the battering guns used in

Beresford's siege were so much damaged, that the artillery officers asked eleven days to repair them; and the scanty means of transport for stores was much diminished by carrying the wounded from Albuera to the different hospitals. Thus more than fifteen days of open trenches, and nine days of fire could not be expected. With good guns, plentiful stores, and a corps of regular sappers and miners, this time would probably have sufficed; but none of these things were in the camp, and it was a keen jest of Picton to say, that "lord Wellington sued Badajos in forma pauperis."

The guns, some of them cast in Philip the Second's reign, were of soft brass, and false in their bore; the shot were of different sizes, and the largest too small; the Portuguese gunners were inexperienced, there were but few British artillery-men, few engineers, no sappers or miners, and no time to teach the troops of the line how to make fascines and gabions. Regular and sure approaches against the body of the place, by the Pardaleras and the Picurina outworks, could not be attempted; but it was judged that Beresford's lines of attack on the castle and Fort Christoval, might be successfully renewed, avoiding the errors of that general; that is to say, by pushing the double attacks simultaneously, and with more powerful means. San Christoval might thus be taken, and batteries from thence could sweep the interior of the castle, which was meanwhile to be breached. Something also was hoped from the inhabitants, and something from the effect of Soult's retreat after Albuera.

This determination once taken, every thing was put in motion with the greatest energy. Major Dickson, an artillery officer whose talents were very conspicuous during the whole war, had, with unexpected rapidity, prepared a battering train of thirty twenty-four-pounders, four sixteen-pounders, and twelve eight and ten-inch howitzers made to serve as mortars by taking off the wheels and placing them on trucks. Six iron Portuguese ship-guns were forwarded from Salvatierra, making altogether fifty-two pieces, a considerable convoy of engineer's stores had already arrived from Alcacer do Sal, and a company of British artillery marched from Lisbon to be mixed with the Portuguese, making a total of six hundred gunners. The regular engineer-officers present, were only twenty-one in number; but eleven volunteers from the line were joined as assistant-engineers, and a draft of three hundred intelligent men from the line, including twenty-five artificers of the staff corps, strengthened the force immediately under their command.

Hamilton's Portuguese division was already before the town, and on the 24th of May, at the close of evening, general Houston's division, increased to five thousand men, by the addition of the seventeenth Portuguese regiment, and the Tavira and Lagos militia, invested San Christoval. The flying bridge was then laid down on the Guadiana, and on the 27th Picton's division, arriving from Campo Mayor, crossed the river, by the ford above the town, and joined Hamilton, their united force being about ten thousand men. General Hill commanded the covering army which, including the Spaniards, was spread from Merida to Albuera. The cavalry was pushed forward in observation of Soult, and a few days after, intelligence having arrived that Drouet's division was on the point of effecting a junction with that marshal, two regiments of cavalry and two brigades of infantry, which had been quartered at Coria, as posts of communication with Spencer, were called up to reinforce the covering army.

While the allies were engaged at Albuera, Phillipon, the governor of Badajos, had levelled their trenches, repaired his own damages, and obtained a small supply of wine and vegetables from the people of Estremadura, who were still awed by the presence of Soult's army; and within the place all was quiet, for the citizens did not now exceed five thousand souls. He had also mounted more guns, and when the place was invested, parties of the townsmen mixed with soldiers, were observed working to improve the defences; wherefore, as any retrenchments made in the castle, behind the intended points of attack, would have frustrated the besiegers' object by prolonging the siege, lord Wellington had a large telescope placed in the tower of La Lyppe, near Elvas, by which the interior of the castle could be plainly looked into, and all preparations discovered.

In the night of the 29th, ground was broken for a false attack against the Pardaleras, and the following night sixteen hundred workmen, with a covering party of twelve hundred, sank a parallel against the castle, on an extent of eleven hundred yards, without being discovered by the enemy, who did not fire until after daylight. The same night twelve hundred workmen, covered by eight hundred men under arms, opened a parallel four hundred and fifty yards from San Christoval, and seven hundred yards from the bridge-head. On this line one breaching, and two counter batteries, were

BOOK XIV. 1811. June.

raised against the fort and against the bridge-head, to prevent a sally from that point; and a fourth battery was also commenced to search the defences of the castle, but the workmen were discovered, and a heavy fire struck down many of them.

On the 31st the attack against the castle, the soil being very soft, was pushed forward without much interruption, and rapidly; but the Christoval attack, being carried on in a rocky soil, and the earth brought up from the rear, proceeded slowly, and with considerable loss. This day the British artillery company came up on mules from Estremos, and the engineer hastened the works. The direction of the parallel against the castle was such, that the right gradually approached the point of attack by which the heaviest fire of the place was avoided; yet, so great was the desire to save time, that before the suitable point of distance was attained, a battery of fourteen twenty-four-pounders with six large howitzers was marked out.

On the Christoval side, the batteries were not finished before the night of the 1st of June, for the soil was so rocky, that the miner was employed to level the ground for the platforms; and the garrison having mortars of sixteen and eighteen inches' diameter mounted on the castle, sent every shell amongst the workmen. These huge missiles would have ruined the batteries on that side altogether, if the latter had not been on the edge of a ridge, from whence most of the shells rolled off before bursting, yet so difficult is it to judge rightly in war, that Phillipon stopped this fire, thinking it was thrown away! The progress

French Register of the Siege, MSS.

of the works was also delayed by the bringing of earth from a distance, and woolpacks purchased at Elvas, were found to be an excellent substitute.

CHAP. V.

1811. June.

In the night of the 2d, the batteries on both sides were completed, and armed with forty-three pieces of different sizes, of which twenty were pointed against the castle; the next day the fire of the besiegers opened, but the windage caused by the smallness of the shot, rendered it very ineffectual at first, and five pieces became unserviceable. However, before evening the practice was steadier, the fire of the fort was nearly silenced, and the covering of masonry fell from the castle-wall, discovering a perpendicular bank of clay.

In the night of the 3d the parallel against the castle was prolonged, and a fresh battery for seven guns traced out at six hundred and fifty yards from the breach. On the 4th the garrison's fire was increased by several additional guns, and six more pieces of the besiegers were disabled, principally by their own fire. Meanwhile the batteries told but slightly against the bank of clay.

At Christoval, the fort was much injured, and some damage was done to the castle, from one of the batteries on that side; but the guns were so soft and bad that the rate of firing was of necessity greatly reduced in all the batteries. In the night the new battery was armed, all the damaged works were repaired, and the next day the enemy having brought a gun in Christoval to plunge into the trenches on the castle side, the parallel there was deepened and traverses were constructed to protect the troops.

Fifteen pieces still played against the castle, but

BOOK XIV. 1811. June.

the bank of clay, although falling away in flakes, always remained perpendicular. One damaged gun was repaired on the Christoval side, but two more had become unserviceable.

In the night the parallel against the castle was again extended, a fresh battery was traced out, at only five hundred and twenty yards from the breach, to receive the Portuguese iron guns, which had arrived at Elvas; and on the Christoval side some new batteries were opened and some old ones were abandoned. During this night the garrison began to entrench themselves behind the castle breach, before morning their labourers were well covered, and two additional pieces, from Christoval, were made to plunge into the trenches with great effect. On the other hand the fire of the besiegers had broken the clay bank, which took such a slope as to appear nearly practicable, and the stray shells and shots set fire to the houses nearest the castle, but three more guns were disabled.

On the 6th there were two breaches in Christoval, and the principal one being found practicable, a company of grenadiers with twelve ladders were directed to assault it, while a second company turned the fort by the east to divert the enemy's attention. Three hundred men from the trenches were at the same time pushed forward by the west side to cut the communication between the fort and the bridge-head; and a detachment, with a six-pounder, moved into the valley of the Gebora, to prevent any passage of the Guadiana by boats.

FIRST ASSAULT OF CHRISTOVAL.

The storming party, commanded by major M'Intosh, of the 85th regiment, was preceded by a forlorn hope under Mr. Dyas, of the 51st, and this gallant gentleman, guided by the engineer Forster, a young man of uncommon bravery, reached the glacis about midnight, and descended the ditch without being discovered. The French had, however, cleared all the rubbish away, the breach had still seven feet of perpendicular wall, many obstacles, such as carts chained together and pointed beams of wood, were placed above it, and large shells were ranged along the ramparts to roll down upon the assailants. The forlorn hope finding the opening impracticable, was retiring with little loss, when the main body, which had been exposed to a flank fire, from the town as well as a direct fire from the fort, came leaping into the ditch with ladders, and another effort was made to escalade at different points; the ladders were too short, and the garrison, consisting of only seventy-five men, besides the cannoneers, made so stout a resistance, and the confusion and mischief occasioned by the bursting of the shells was so great, that the assailants again retired with the loss of more than one hundred men.

Bad success always produces disputes, and the causes of this failure were attributed by some to the breach being impracticable from the first; by others to the confusion which arose after the main body had entered. French writers affirm that the breach was certainly practicable on the night of Lamarre's Sieges.

BOOK XIV. 1811. June.

the 5th, but repaired on the 6th; that as the besiegers did not attack until midnight, the workmen had time to clear the ruins away and to raise fresh obstacles, and the bravery of the soldiers, who were provided with three muskets each, did the rest. But it is also evident, that whether from inexperience, accident, or other causes, the combinations for the assault were not very well calculated; the storming party was too weak, the ladders few and short, and the breach not sufficiently scoured by the fire of the batteries. The attack itself was also irregular and ill-combined, for the leading troops were certainly repulsed before the main body had descended the ditch. The intrepidity of the assailants was admitted by all sides, yet it is a great point in such attacks that the supports should form almost one body with the leaders, because the sense of power derived from numbers is a strong incentive to valour, and obstacles which would be insurmountable to a few, seem to vanish before a multitude. It is also to be recollected that this was a case where not loss of men, but time was to be considered.

During this night the iron guns were placed in battery against the castle, but two more of the brass pieces became unserviceable, and the following day three others were disabled. However, the bank of clay at the castle at last offered a practicable slope, and during the night captain Patton of the engineers examined it closely; he was mortally wounded in returning, yet lived to make his report that it was practicable. Nevertheless the garrison continued, as they had done every night at both breaches, to clear away the ruins, and with bales of wool and other materials to form defences behind the opening. They ranged also a number of huge shells and barrels of powder, with matches fastened to them, along the ramparts, and placed chosen men to defend the breach, each man being supplied with four muskets.

In this order they fearlessly awaited another attack, which was soon made. For intelligence now arrived that Drouet's corps was close to Llerena, and that Marmont was on the move from Salamanca, and hence lord Wellington, seeing that his prey was likely to escape, as a last effort resolved to assault Christoval again. But this time four hundred British, Portuguese, and French men of the Chasseurs Britanniques, carrying sixteen long ladders, were destined for the attack; the supports were better closed up; the appointed hour was nine instead of twelve, and a greater number of detachments than before were distributed to the right and left to distract the enemy's attention, to cut off his communication with the town, and to be ready to improve any success which might be obtained. On the other side Phillipon increased the garrison of the fort to two hundred men.

SECOND ASSAULT OF CHRISTOVAL.

The storming party was commanded by major M'Geechy; the forlorn hope, again led by the gallant Dyas, was accompanied by Mr. Hunt, an engineer officer, and a little after nine o'clock the leading troops bounding forward, were immediately followed by the support, amidst a shattering fire of musketry which killed major M'Geechy, Mr. Hunt, and many men upon the glacis. The troops with loud

BOOK XIV. 1811. June.

shouts jumped into the ditch, but the French scoffingly called to them to come on, and at the same time rolled the barrels of powder and shells down, while the musketry made fearful and rapid havoc. In a little time the two leading columns united at the main breach, the supports also came up, confusion arose about the ladders, of which only a few could be reared, and the enemy standing on the ramparts, bayonetted the foremost of the assailants, overturned the ladders, and again poured their destructive fire upon the crowd below. When a hundred and forty men had fallen the order to retire was given.

An assault on the castle breach might still have been tried, but the troops could not have formed between the top, and the retrenchments behind the breach, until Christoval was taken, and the guns from thence used to clear the interior of the castle; hence the siege was of necessity raised, because to take Christoval, required several days more, and Soult was now ready to advance. The stores were removed on the 10th, and the attack was turned into a blockade.

OBSERVATIONS.

1°. The allies lost, during this unfortunate siege, nearly four hundred men and officers, and the whole of their proceedings were against rules. The working parties were too weak, the guns and stores too few, and the points of attack, chosen, not the best; the defences were untouched by counter-batteries, and the breaching batteries were at too great a distance for the bad guns employed; howitzers mounted on trucks were but a poor substitute for mortars, and the sap was not practised; lastly, the assaults were made before the glacis had been crowned, and a musketry fire established against the breach.

2°. That a siege so conducted should fail against such a brave and intelligent garrison is not strange; but it is most strange and culpable that a government, which had been so long engaged in war as the British, should have left the engineer department, with respect to organization and equipment, in such a state as to make it, in despite of the officers' experience, bravery, and zeal, a very inefficient arm of war. The skill displayed belonged to particular persons, rather than to the corps at large; and the very tools with which they worked, especially those sent from the storekeeper's department, were so shamefully bad that the work required could scarcely be performed; the captured French cutting-tools were eagerly sought for by the engineers as being infinitely better than the British; when the soldiers' lives and the honour of England's arms, were at stake, the English cutlery was found worse than the French.

3°. The neglect of rules, above noticed, was for the most part a matter of absolute necessity; yet censure might attach to the general, inasmuch as he could have previously sent to England for a battering train. But then the conduct of the Portuguese and British governments when lord Wellington was in the lines, left him so little hope of besieging any place on the frontier, that he was hourly in fear of being obliged to embark: moreover, the badness of the Portuguese guns was not

BOOK XIV.

1811.

known, and the space of time that elapsed between the fall of Badajos and this siege, was insufficient to procure artillery from England; neither would the Portuguese have furnished the means of carriage. It may however at all times be taken as a maxim, that the difficulties of war are so innumerable that no head was ever yet strong enough to fore-calculate them all.

CHAPTER VI.

CHAP. VI. 1811. June.

It will be remembered, that Soult instead of retiring into Andalusia, took a flank position at Llerena, and awaited the arrival of Drouet's division, which had been detached from Massena's army. At Llerena, although closely watched by general Hill, the French marshal, with an army, oppressed by its losses and rendered unruly by want, maintained an attitude of offence until assured of Drouet's approach, when he again advanced to Los Santos, near which place a slight cavalry skirmish took place to the disadvantage of the French.

Intercepted despatch from Soult to Marmont.

On the 14th, Drouet, whose march had been very rapid, arrived, and then Soult, who knew that lord Wellington expected large reinforcements, and was desirous to forestal them, advanced to Fuente del Maestro, whereupon Hill took measures to concentrate the covering army on the position of Albuera. Meanwhile Marmont, who had reorganized the army of Portugal, in six divisions of infantry and five brigades of cavalry, received Napoleon's orders to co-operate with Soult; and in this view had sent Reynier with two divisions by the pass of Baños, while himself with a considerable force of infantry and cavalry and ten guns escorted a convoy to Ciudad Rodrigo. General Spencer, with the first, fifth, sixth, and light divisions, and one brigade of cavalry, was then behind the Agueda; and

BOOK XIV. 1811. June.

Pack's Portuguese brigade was above Almeida, which had been again placed in a condition to resist an irregular assault. Spencer's orders were to make his marches correspond with those of the enemy, if the latter should point towards the Tagus ; but if the French attacked, he was to take the line of the Coa, and to blow up Almeida if the movements went to isolate that fortress. On the morning of the 6th, Marmont, having introduced his convoy, marched out of Rodrigo in two columns, one moving upon Gallegos, the other upon Espeja. The light division fell back before the latter, and Slade's cavalry before the former; but in this retrograde movement, the latter gave its flank obliquely to the line of the enemy's advance, which soon closed upon, and cannonaded it, with eight pieces of artillery. Unfortunately the British rear-guard got jammed in between the French and a piece of marshy ground, and in this situation the whole must have been destroyed, if captain Purvis, with a squadron of the fourth dragoons, had not charged the enemy while the other troopers, with strong horses and a knowledge of the firmest parts, got through the marsh. Purvis then passed also, and the French horses could not follow. Thus the retreat was effected with a loss of only twenty men. After the action an officer calling himself Montbrun's aid-du-camp deserted to the allies.

General Spencer, more distinguished for great personal intrepidity than for quickness of military conception, was now undecided as to his measures ; and the army was by no means in a safe situation, for the country was covered with baggage, the movements of the divisions were wide, and without concert, and general Pack who had the charge of

Almeida too hastily blew it up. In this uncertainty the adjutant-general Pakenham pointed out that the French did not advance as if to give battle, that their numbers were evidently small, their movements more ostentatious than vigorous, and probably intended to cover a flank movement by the passes leading to the Tagus: he therefore urged Spencer either to take up a position of battle which would make the enemy discover his real numbers and intentions, or retire at once behind the Coa, with a view to march to lord Wellington's assistance. These arguments were supported by colonel Waters, who, having closely watched the infantry coming out of Ciudad Rodrigo, observed that they were too clean and well dressed to have come off a long march, and must therefore be a part of the garrison. He had also ascertained that a large body was actually in movement towards the passes.

Spencer yielding to these representations marched in the evening by Alfayates to Soito, and the next day behind the Coa. Here certain intelligence, that Marmont was in the passes, reached him, and he continued his march to the Alemtejo by Penamacor, but detached one division and his cavalry to Coria, as flankers, while he passed with the main body by Castello Branco, Vilha Velha, Niza, and Portalegre. The season was burning and the marches long, yet so hardened by constant service were the light division, and so well organized by general Craufurd, that, although covering from eighteen to eight-and-twenty miles daily, they did not leave a single straggler behind. The flanking troops, who had been rather unnecessarily exposed at Coria, then followed, and Marmont having imposed upon

BOOK XIV. 1811. June.

Spencer and Pack by his demonstration in front of Ciudad Rodrigo, filed off by the pass of Perales, while Reynier moved by the passes of Bejar and Baños, and the whole were by forced marches soon united at the bridge of Almaraz. Here a pontoon bridge expected from Madrid had not arrived, and the passage of the Tagus was made with only one ferry-boat which caused a delay of four days, which would have proved fatal to Badajos, if the battering guns employed in that siege had been really effective.

When the river was crossed, the French army marched in two columns with the greatest rapidity upon Merida and Medellin, where they arrived the 18th, and opened their communications with Soult.

On the other side, lord Wellington had been attentively watching these movements; he had never intended to press Badajos beyond the 10th, because he knew that when reinforced with Drouet's division, Soult alone would be strong enough to raise the siege, and hence the hurried assaults; but he was resolved to fight Soult, and although he raised the siege on the 10th, yet, by a deciphered intercepted letter, that Phillipon's provisions would be exhausted on the 20th, he continued the blockade of the place, in hopes that some such accident of war as the delay at Almaraz might impede Marmont. It may be here asked, why, as he knew a few days would suffice to reduce Badajos, he did not retrench his whole army and persist in the siege? The answer is that Elvas being out of repair, and exhausted both of provisions and ammunition, by the siege of Badajos, the enemy would immediately have taken that fortress.

When Soult's advanced guard had reached Los Santos, the covering army, consisting of the second and fourth divisions and Blake's Spaniards was concentrated at Albuera, Hamilton's Portuguese were also directed there from Badajos; meanwhile the third and seventh divisions maintained the blockade, and Wellington expecting a battle repaired in person to Albuera, but, unlike Beresford, he had that position entrenched, and did not forget to occupy the hill on the right.

CHAP. VI.

1811. June.

On the 14th, it was known that Marmont was at Truxillo, and that in four days he could unite with Soult, wherefore the blockade was also raised with a view to repass the Guadiana, yet Wellington still lingered at Albuera hoping to fall on Soult separately, but the cautious manner in which the latter moved, continually refusing his left and edging with his right, towards Almendralejos, soon extinguished this chance; on the 17th, the blockade having been raised the day before, the allies repassed the Guadiana in two columns. The British and Portuguese moved by the pontoon bridge near Badajos, the Spaniards crossed at Jerumenha;—this movement, not an easy one, was executed without any loss of men or stores, and without accident, save that general William Stewart by some error, took the same line as Blake, and at night fell in with the Spaniards, who thought his division French and were like to have fired.

The 19th the united French armies entered Badajos, which was thus succoured after two most honourable defences, and at a moment when Phillipon, despairing of aid and without provisions, was preparing his means of breaking out and escaping.

The 21st Godinot's division which had marched

BOOK XIV. 1811. June.

by Valverde took possession of Olivenza; the 22d he pushed a detachment under the guns of Jerumenha, and the same day the whole of the French cavalry crossed the Guadiana in two columns, advancing towards Villa Viciosa and Elvas on one side, and Campo Mayor on the other.

Lord Wellington being now joined by the head of Spencer's corps, had placed his army on both sides of the Caya, with cavalry posts towards the mouth of that river and on the Guadiana in front of Elvas. His right wing was extended behind the Caya to the lower bridge on that river, and his left wing had a field of battle on some high ground resting on the Gebora, a little beyond Campo Mayor, which fortress was occupied, and the open space between it and the high ground strongly entrenched. On this side also cavalry were posted in observation beyond the Gebora and about Albuquerque, the whole position forming an irregular arch embracing the bridge of Badajos. The wood and town of Aronches were behind the centre of the position and the little fortified place of Ouguella was behind the left; but the right wing was much more numerous than the left, and the Monte Reguingo, a wooded ridge between Campo Mayor and the Caya, was occupied by the light division, whose position could not be recognized by the enemy.

If the French attacked the left of the allies, a short movement would have sufficed to bring the bulk of the troops into action on the menaced point, because the whole extent of country occupied did not exceed ten or twelve miles: the communications also were good, and from Campo Mayor open plains, reaching to Badajos, exposed the French movements which could be distinguished both from

Elvas, from Campo Mayor, and from the many atalayas or watch-towers on that frontier.

The chief merit of this position was the difficulty of recognizing it from the enemy's side, and to protect the rear, the first division was retained at Portalegre: from thence it could intercept the enemy at Marvão or Castello de Vide if he should attempt to turn the allies by Albuquerque; and was ready to oppose Soult if he should move between Elvas and Estremos; but the march from Portalegre was too long to hope for the assistance of this division in a battle near Elvas or Campo Mayor.

The French cavalry, as I have said, passed the Guadiana on the 21st, both by the bridge of Badajos and by two fords, where the road of Olivenza crosses that river, below the confluence of the Caya. The right column after driving back the outposts of the allies, was opposed by the heavy dragoons, and by Madden's Portuguese, and retired without seeing the position on the Campo Mayor side; but the horsemen of the left column, while patrolling towards Villa Viciosa and Elvas, cut off a squadron of the eleventh dragoons, and the second German hussars which were on the Guadiana escaped to Elvas with difficulty and loss. The cause of this misfortune in which nearly a hundred and fifty men were killed or taken is not very clear, for the French aver that colonel Lallemand, by a feigned retreat drew the cavalry into an ambuscade, and the rumours in the English camp were various and discordant.

After this action the French troops were quartered along the Guadiana above and below Badajos from Xeres de los Cavalheiros to Montijo, and proceeded to collect provisions for themselves and for

BOOK XIV. 1811. June.

the fortress, hence, with the exception of a vain attempt on the 26th to cut off the cavalry detachments on the side of Albuquerque, no farther operations took place.

Appendix, No. III. Section 3.

All things had seemed to tend to a great and decisive battle, and, although the crisis glided away without any event of importance, this was one of the most critical periods of the war. For Marmont brought down, including a detachment of the army of the centre, thirty-one thousand infantry, four thousand five hundred cavalry, and fifty-four guns; Soult about twenty-five thousand infantry, three thousand cavalry, and thirty-six guns;—to effect this, Andalusia and Castile had been nearly stripped of troops. Bessieres had abandoned the Asturias, Bonnet united with general Mayer, who had succeeded Serras in Leon, was scarcely able, as we have seen, to keep the Gallicians in check on the Orbijo, the chief armies of the Peninsular were in presence, a great battle seemed to be the interest of the French, and it was in their option to fight or not. Their success at Badajos, and the surprise of the cavalry on the Caya had made ample amends for their losses at Los Santos and Usagre, and now, when Badajos was succoured, and the allied army in a manner driven into Portugal, Albuera seemed to be a victory. The general result of the Estremadura campaign had been favourable to them, and the political state of their affairs seemed to require some dazzling action to impose upon the peninsulars. Their army was powerful, and as they were especially strong in cavalry, and on favourable ground for that arm, there could scarcely be a better opportunity for a blow, which would, if successful, have revenged

Massena's disasters, and sent lord Wellington back to Lisbon, perhaps from the Peninsula altogether; if unsuccessful not involving any very serious consequences, because from their strength of horse and artillery, and nearness to Badajos, a fatal defeat was not to be expected. But the allied army was thought to be stronger by the whole amount of the Spanish troops, than it really was; the position very difficult to be examined was confidently held by lord Wellington, and no battle took place.

Napoleon's estimation of the weight of moral over physical force in war was here finely exemplified. Both the French armies were conscious of recent defeats, Busaco, Sabugal, Fuentes, and the horrid field of Albuera, were fresh in their memory; the fierce blood there spilled, still reeked in their nostrils, and if Cæsar after a partial check at Dyrrachiaum held it unsafe to fight a pitched battle with recently defeated soldiers, however experienced or brave, Soult may well be excused, seeing that he knew there were divisions on the Caya, as good in all points, and more experienced, than those he had fought with on the banks of the Albuera. The stern nature of the British soldier had been often before proved by him, and he could now draw no hope from the unskilfulness of the general. Lord Wellington's resolution to accept battle on the banks of the Caya, was nevertheless, one of as unmixed greatness, as the crisis was one of unmixed danger to the cause he supported. For the Portuguese government, following up the system which I have already described, had reduced their troops to the lowest degree of misery, and the fortresses were, at times, only not abandoned to the enemy. The British government had taken the

BOOK XIV. 1811. June.

native troops into pay, but it had not undertaken to feed them; yet such was the suffering of those brave men that Wellington, after repeatedly refusing to assist them from the English stores, unable longer to endure the sight of their misfortunes, and to prevent them from disbanding, at last fed the six brigades, or three-fourths of the whole army, the English commissariat charging the expense to the subsidy. He hoped that the government would then supply the remnant, but they starved it likewise, and during the siege of Badajos these troops were of necessity thrown for subsistence upon the magazines of Elvas, which were thus exhausted; and what with desertion, famine, and sickness, that flourishing army which had mustered more than forty thousand good soldiers in line, at the time of Massena's invasion, could now scarcely produce fourteen thousand for a battle on which the fate of their country depended. The British troops, although large reinforcements had come out, and more were arriving, had so many sick and wounded, that scarcely twenty-eight thousand sabres and bayonets were in the field. The enemy had therefore a superiority, of one fourth in artillery and infantry, and the strength of his cavalry was double that of the British.

To accept battle in such circumstances, military considerations only being had in view, would have been rash in the extreme, but the Portuguese government besides throwing the subsistence of the troops upon Elvas, had utterly neglected that place, and Jerumenha, Campo Mayor, and Ouguella, Aronches and Santa Olaya, which were the fortresses covering this frontier; neither had they drawn forth any means of transport from the

CHAP. VI.

1811. June.

country. The siege of Badajos had been entirely furnished from Elvas; but all the carts and animals of burthen that could be found in the vicinity, or as far as the British detachments could go; and all the commissariat means to boot, were scarcely sufficient to convey the ammunition, the stores, and the subsistence of the native troops, day by day, from Elvas to the camp; there was consequently no possibility of replacing these things from the British magazines at Abrantes and Lisbon.

When the allies crossed the Guadiana in retreat, Elvas had only ten thousand rounds of shot left, and not a fortnight's provisions in store, even for her own garrison; her works were mouldering in many places, from want of care, houses and enclosures encumbered her glacis, most of her guns were rendered unserviceable by the fire at Badajos, the remainder were very bad, and her garrison was composed of untried soldiers and militia. Jerumenha was not better looked to; Olaya, Campo Mayor, and Ouguella had nothing but their walls. It would appear then, that if Soult had been aware of this state of affairs, he might under cover of the Guadiana, have collected his army below the confluence of the Caya, and then by means of the pontoon train from Badajos, and by the fords at which his cavalry did pass, have crossed the Guadiana, overpowered the right of the allies, and suddenly investing Elvas, have coveied his army with lines, which would have ensured the fall of that place; unless the English general, anticipating such an attempt, had, with very inferior numbers, defeated him between the Caya and Elvas. But this, in a perfectly open country, offering no advantages to the weaker army, would not have

BOOK XIV. 1811. June.

been easy. Soult also, by marching on the side of Estremos, could have turned the right, and menaced the communications of the allies with Abrantes, which would have obliged him to retreat and abandon Elvas or fight to disadvantage. The position on the Caya was therefore taken up solely with reference to the state of political affairs. It was intended to impose upon the enemy, and it did so; Elvas and Jerumenha must otherwise have fallen.

While a front of battle was thus presented, the rear was cleared of all the hospitals and heavy baggage; workmen were day and night employed to restore the fortifications of the strong places, and guns, ammunition, and provisions were brought up from Abrantes, by means of the animals and carts before employed in the siege of Badajos. Until all this was effected Portugal was on the brink of perdition, but the true peninsular character was now displayed, and in a manner that proclaims most forcibly the difficulties overcome by the English general, difficulties which have been little appreciated in his own country. The danger of Elvas had aroused all the bustle of the Portuguese government, and the regency were at first frightened at the consequences of their own conduct; but when they found their own tardy efforts were forestalled by the diligence of lord Wellington, they with prodigious effrontery asserted, that he had exhausted Elvas for the supply of the British troops, and that they had replenished it!

His imperturbable firmness at this crisis was wonderful, and the more admirable, because Mr. Perceval's policy, prevailing in the cabinet, had left him without a halfpenny in the military chest, and almost without a hope of support in his own country: yet his daring was not a wild cast of the net for fortune; it was supported by great circumspection, and a penetration and activity that let no advantages escape. He had thrown a wide glance over the Peninsula, knew his true situation, had pointed out to the Spaniards how to push their war to advantage, while the French were thus concentrated in Estremadura, and at this period had a right to expect assistance from them; for Soult and Marmont were united at Badajos, the army of the north and the army of the centre were paralysed by the flight of the king, and this was the moment, when Figueras having been surprised by Rovira, and Taragona besieged by Suchet, the French armies of Catalonia and Aragon were entirely occupied with those places. Thus, nearly the whole of the Peninsula was open to the enterprizes of the Spaniards. They could have collected, of Murcians and Valencians only, above forty thousand regulars, besides partizans, with which they might have marched against Madrid, while the Gallicians operated in Castile, and the Asturian army supported the enterprizes of the northern partidas.

This favourable occasion was not seized. Julian Sanchez, indeed, cut off a convoy, menaced Salamanca, and blockaded Ciudad Rodrigo; Santocildes came down to Astorga, and as I have before observed, Mina and the northern chiefs harassed the French communications; some stir also was made by the guerillas near Madrid, and Suchet was harassed, but the commotion soon subsided; and a detachment from Madrid having surprised a congregation of partidas at Peneranda, killed many and

See Book XIII. Chap. I.

BOOK XIV.

1811. June.

recovered a large convoy which they had taken; and in this complicated war, which being spread like a spider's web over the whole Peninsula, any drag upon one part would have made the whole quiver to the most distant extremities, the regular armies effected nothing. Nor did any general insurrection of the people take place in the rear of the French, who retained all their fortified posts, while their civil administrations continued to rule in the great towns as tranquilly as if there was no war!

Lord Wellington's principal measure for dissipating the storm in his front had rested upon Blake. That general had wished him to fight beyond the Guadiana, and was not well pleased at being refused; wherefore the English general, instead of taking ten or twelve thousand Spaniards, and an uneasy colleague, into the line of battle at Campo Mayor, where he knew by experience that they would quarrel with the Portuguese, and by their slowness, insubordination, and folly, would rather weaken than strengthen himself, delivered to Blake the pontoons used at Badajos, and concerted with him a movement down the right bank of the Guadiana. He was to recross that river at Mertola, and to fall upon Seville, which was but slightly guarded by a mixed force of French and Spaniards in Joseph's service; and this blow, apparently easy of execution, would have destroyed all the arsenals and magazines, which supported the blockade of Cadiz. Lord Wellington had therefore good reason to expect the raising of that siege, as well as the dispersion of the French army in its front. He likewise urged the regency at Cadiz to push forward general Beguines from San Roque, against Seville, while the insurgents in the Ronda pressed the few troops, left in Grenada, on one side, and Freire, with the Murcian army, pressed them on the other.

Blake marched the 18th, recrossed the river at Mertola the 22d, remained inactive at Castillegos until the 30th, and sent his heavy artillery to Ayamonte by water; then, instead of moving direct with his whole force upon Seville, he detached only a small body, and with a kind of infatuation wasted two successive days in assaulting the castle of Niebla; a contemptible work garrisoned by three hundred Swiss, who had in the early part of the war abandoned the Spanish service. Being without artillery he could not succeed, and meanwhile Soult, hearing of his march, ordered Olivenza to be blown up, and taking some cavalry, and Godinot's division which formed the left of his army, passed the Morena by Santa Ollalla and moved rapidly upon Seville. From Monasterio he sent a detachment to relieve the castle of Niebla; and at the same time, general Conroux, whose division was at Xeres de los Cavalheiro, crossed the mountain by the Aracena road, and endeavoured to cut off Blake from Ayamonte.

Thus far, notwithstanding the failure at Niebla, the English general's project was crowned with success. The great army in his front was broken up, Soult was gone, Marmont was preparing to retire, and Portugal was safe. Blake's cavalry under Penne Villemur, and some infantry under Ballesteros, had also, during the attack on Niebla, appeared in front of Seville on the right of the Guadalquivir, and a slight insurrection took place at Carmona on the left bank. The Serranos, always in arms, were assisted by Beguines with three thou-

BOOK XIV. 1811. July.

sand men, and blockaded the town of Ronda; and Freire advancing with his Murcians beyond Lorca, menaced general Laval, who had succeeded Sebastiani in command of the fourth corps. In this crisis, general Daricau, unable to keep the field, shut himself up in a great convent, which Soult had, in anticipation of such a crisis, fortified in the Triana suburb, before his first invasion of Estremadura. But the Spanish troops of Joseph, shewed no disposition to quit him, the people of Seville remained tranquil, and Blake's incapacity ruined the whole combination.

Soult approached on the 6th of July, Ballesteros and Villemur immediately retired, and the insurrection at Carmona ceased. Blake, hearing of Conroux's march, precipitately fled from Niebla, and only escaped into Portugal by the assistance of a bridge laid for him at San Lucar de Guadiana by colonel Austin. He then resolved to embark some of his forces and sail to attack San Lucar de Barameda; but scarcely had a few men got on board, when the French advanced guard appeared, and he again fled in disorder to Ayamonte, and got into the island of Canelas, where fortunately a Spanish frigate and three hundred transports had unexpectedly arrived. While Ballesteros, with the cavalry and three thousand infantry, protected the embarkation, by taking a position on the Rio Piedra, Blake got on board with great confusion, and sailed to Cadiz, for the French had reinforced San Lucar de Barameda, and entered Ayamonte. The Portuguese militia, of the Algarves, were then called out; and Ballesteros after losing some men on the Piedra, took post in the mountains of Aroches on his left, until the French retired, when he came back with his infantry and entrenched himself in Canelas. On this island he remained until August, and then embarked under the protection of the Portuguese militia at Villa Real, while his cavalry marched up the Guadiana to rejoin Castaños, who with a few troops still remained in Estremadura. A small battalion left in the castle of Paymago was soon after unsuccessfully attacked by the French, and this finished the long partizan warfare of the Condado de Niebla.

There was now nothing to prevent the French from again pressing the allies on the Caya, except the timid operations of Freire on the side of Grenada, and these Soult was in march to repress. With indefatigable activity he had recalled the troops of the fourth corps, from Estremadura, to supply the place of the detachments which he had already sent, from Seville, Cadiz, Grenada, and Malaga, to quell the insurrection in the Ronda; and while he thus prepared the means of attacking Freire, Beguines was driven back to San Roque, and the Serranos as I have before observed, disgusted with the Spanish general's ill conduct, were upon the point of capitulating with the French. During these events in the Ronda, Godinot returned, from the pursuit of Blake, to Jaen, whence on the 7th of August, he was directed to march against Pozalçon and Baza, where the Murcian army was posted. Meanwhile Blake, re-landing his troops at Almeria, joined Freire; his intention was to have commenced active operations against Grenada, but thinking it necessary to go first to Valencia where Palacio was making mischief, he left the army,

BOOK XIV. 1811. August.

which was above twenty-seven thousand strong, under Freire, and before he could return it was utterly dispersed.

ROUT OF BAZA.

General Quadra, who commanded the right wing of the Murcians, was at Pozalçon, and it is said, had orders to rejoin Freire, but disobeyed. The centre and left under Freire himself, were at Venta de Bahul in front of Baza. The 8th, Soult, at the head of a mixed force of French and Spanish troops in Joseph's service, drove back the advanced guards from Guadix. The 9th he appeared in front of Bahul, where he discerned the Spanish army on strong ground, their front being covered by a deep ravine. As his object was to cut off the retreat upon Lorca, and the city of Murcia, he only shewed a few troops at first, and skirmished slightly, to draw Freire's attention, while Godinot attacked his right at Pozalçon and got in his rear. Godinot wasted time. His advanced guard, alone, had defeated Quadra with great loss, but instead of entering Baza, he halted for the night near it; and during the darkness, the Spaniards, who had no other line of retreat, and were now falling back in confusion before Soult, passed through that place, and made for Lorca and Caravalha. Soult's cavalry, however, soon cut this line, and the fugitives took to the by-roads, followed and severely harassed by the French horse.

At this time the whole province was in a defenceless state, but the people generally took arms to protect the city of Murcia. That place was entrenched, and the French marshal, whose troops were few, and fatigued by constant marching, not thinking fit to persevere, especially as the yellow fever was raging at Carthagena, returned to Grenada, whence he sent detachments to disperse some insurgents who had gathered under the Conde de Montijo in the Alpuxaras. Thus Grenada was entirely quieted.

Here it is impossible to refrain from admiring Soult's vigour and ability. We see him in the latter end of 1810, with a small force and in the depth of winter, taking Olivenza, Badajos, Albuquerque, Valencia d'Alcantara, and Campo Mayor; defeating a great army, and capturing above twenty thousand men. Again when unexpectedly assailed by Beresford in the north, by the Murcians in the east, by Ballesteros in the west, and by Lapeña and Graham in the south, he found means to repel three of them, to persevere in the blockade of Cadiz, and to keep Seville tranquil, while he marched against the fourth. At Albuera he lost one of the fiercest battles upon human record, and that at a moment when the king by abandoning his throne had doubled every embarrassment; nevertheless, holding fast to Estremadura, he still maintained the struggle, and again taking the offensive obliged the allies to repass the Guadiana. If he did not then push his fortune to the utmost, it must be considered that his command was divided, that his troops were still impressed with the recollection of Albuera, and that the genius of his adversary had worked out new troubles for him in Andalusia. With how much resolution and activity he repressed those troubles

BOOK XIV.

1811.

I have just shewn; but above all things he is to be commended for the prudent vigour of his administration, which, in despite of the opposition of Joseph's Spanish counsellors, had impressed the Andalusians with such a notion of his power and resources, that no revolt of any real consequence took place, and none of his civic guards or "Escopeteros" failed him in the hour of need.

Let any man observe the wide extent of country he had to maintain; the frontiers fringed as it were with hostile armies, the interior suffering under war requisitions, the people secretly hating the French, a constant insurrection in the Ronda, and a national government and a powerful army in the Isla de Leon. Innumerable English and Spanish agents prodigal of money, and of arms, continually instigating the people of Andalusia to revolt; the coast covered with hostile vessels, Gibraltar sheltering beaten armies on one side, Cadiz on another, Portugal on a third, Murcia on a fourth; the communication with France difficult, two battles lost, few reinforcements, and all the material means to be created in the country. Let any man, I say, consider this, and he will be convinced that it was no common genius that could remain unshaken amidst such difficulties; yet Soult not only sustained himself, but contemplated the most gigantic offensive enterprises, and was at all times an adversary to be dreaded. What though his skill in actual combat was not so remarkable as in some of his contemporaries; who can deny him firmness, activity, vigour, foresight, grand perception, and admirable arrangement? It is this combination of high qualities that forms a great captain.

CHAPTER VII.

CHAP. VII. 1811. July.

While Soult was clearing the eastern frontier of Andalusia, Marmont retired gradually from Badajos and quartered his troops in the valley of the Tagus, with exception of one division which he left, at Truxillo. At the same time the fifth corps retired to Zafra, and thus lord Wellington found himself relieved from the presence of the French, at the very moment when he had most reason to fear their efforts. He had by this time secured the fortresses on the frontier, his troops were beginning to suffer from the terrible pestilence of the Guadiana, this was sufficient to prevent him from renewing the siege of Badajos, if Marmont's position had not forbid that measure, he therefore resolved to adopt a new system of operations. But to judge of the motives which influenced his conduct we must again cast a hasty glance over the general state of the Peninsula, which was hourly changing.

In Catalonia Suchet had stormed Taragona, seized Montserrat, and dispersed the Catalan army. A division of the army of the centre had chased the Partidas from Guadalaxara and Cuença, and re-established the communications with Aragon. Valencia and Murcia were in fear and confusion, both from internal intrigue and from the double disasters on each side of their frontier, at Baza and Taragona.

The French emperor was pouring reinforcements

BOOK XIV.

1811. July.

into Spain by the northern line; these troops as usual scoured the country to put down the Guerillas on each side of their march, and nearly forty thousand fresh men, mostly old soldiers from the army of the reserve, were come, or coming into the north of Spain. The young guard which was at Burgos, under general Dorsenne, was increased to seventeen thousand men; and as no efforts, except those already noticed, were made by the Spaniards, to shake the French hold of the country while Soult and Marmont were on the Guadiana, the French generals were enabled to plan extensive measures of further conquest: and the more readily, because the king was now on his return from Paris, in apparent harmony with his brother, and the powers and duties of all parties were defined.

Suchet urged by Napoleon to hasten his preparations for the invasion of Valencia, was resolved to be under the walls of that city in the middle of September, and Soult was secretly planning a gigantic enterprise, calculated to change the whole aspect of the war. In the north when the king, who re-entered Madrid the 14th, had passed Valladolid, the imperial guards entered Leon; thirteen thousand men of the army of the north were concentrated at Benevente on the 17th, and Santocildes retired into the mountains. Bessieres then sent a large convoy to Ciudad Rodrigo, but following the treaty between Joseph and Napoleon, returned himself to France, and general Dorsenne taking the command of the army of the north, prepared to invade Gallicia.

Appendix, No. III. Section 3.

Meanwhile Marmont was directed to resign the whole of Castile and Leon, to the protection of the army of the north, and to withdraw all his posts and depots, with the exception of the garrison of Ciudad Rodrigo, which was to be changed at a more convenient time. His line of communication was to be with Madrid, and that city was to be his chief depot and base; he was to take positions in the valley of the Tagus, and at Truxillo; to fortify either Alcantara or Almaraz, and to secure the communication across the river.

Thus posted, the emperor judged that Marmont could more effectually arrest the progress of the allies than in any other. The invasion of Andalusia, for the purpose of raising the siege of Cadiz, was, he said, the only object the allies had at the moment, but it could always be frustrated by Marmont's moving against their flank; and with respect to the north, the allies having no object on that side, would be unlikely to make any serious attempt, because they must in time be overmatched, as the French fell back upon their resources. Marmont could also act against their right flank, as he could do against their left flank, if they marched upon Andalusia; and while stationary he protected Madrid, and gave power and activity to the king's administration.

In pursuance of these instructions, Marmont, who had remained in Estremadura, to cover Soult's operations against Blake and the Murcians, now proceeded to occupy Talavera, and other posts in the valley of the Tagus; and he placed a division at Truxillo, the castle of which place, as well as that of Medellin, was repaired. Another division occupied Placentia, with posts in the passes of Bejar and Baños; Girard's division of the fifth corps, remained at Zafra, to serve as a point of connexion

BOOK XIV. 1811. July.

between Marmont and Soult, and to support Badajos, which, by a wise provision of Napoleon's, was now garrisoned with detachments from the three armies, of the centre, of Portugal and of the south. This gave each general a direct interest in moving to its succour, and in the same policy Ciudad Rodrigo was to be wholly garrisoned by the army of the north, that Marmont might have no temptation to neglect the army of the south, under pretence of succouring Ciudad.

To restore and maintain Alcantara was beyond the means of the duke of Ragusa; he therefore repaired the bridge of Almaraz, and constructed two strong forts, one at each side, to protect it, and to serve as an intermediate field depot; a third and more considerable fort was also built on the high ridge of Mirabete, to insure a passage over the hills from Almaraz to Truxillo. A free intercourse with the army of the south was thus secured on one side, and on the other, the passes of Baños and Bejar, and the Roman road of Puerto Pico, which had been restored in 1810, served for communication with the army of the north.

The French affairs had now assumed a very favourable aspect. There was indeed a want of money, but the generals were obeyed with scrupulous attention by the people of Spain, not only within the districts occupied by them, but even in those villages where the guerillas were posted. This obedience lord Wellington attributed entirely to fear, and hoped as the exactions were heavy, that the people would at last fight or fly from their habitations on the approach of a French soldier; but this did not happen generally, and to me it appears, that the obedience was rather a symptom of the subjection of the nation, and that with a judicious mixture of mildness and severity perfect submission would have followed if England had not kept the war alive. CHAP VII. 1811. July.

On the other hand the weakness and anarchy of the Spaniards were daily increasing, and the disputes, between the British general and the Portuguese government, had arrived to such a height, that lord Wellington, having drawn up powerful and clear statements of his grievous situation, sent one to the Brazils and the other to his own government, with a positive intimation that if an entirely new system was not immediately adopted he would no longer attempt to carry on the contest. Lord Wellesley, taking his stand upon this ground, made strenuous exertions in both countries to prevent the ruin of the cause; but lord Wellington, while expecting the benefit of his brother's interference, had to contend with the most surprising difficulties, and to seek in his own personal resources for the means of even defending Portugal. He had sent marshal Beresford to Lisbon, immediately after Albuera, to superintend the reorganization and restoration of the Portuguese forces, and Beresford had sent Mr. De Lemos, an officer of his own staff, to the Brazils, to represent the inconveniences arising from the interference of the regency in the military affairs. On the other hand the Souzas sent one Vasconcellos, who had been about the British head-quarters as their spy, to Rio Janeiro, and thus the political intrigues became more complicated than ever.

But with respect to the war Wellington had penetrated Napoleon's object, when he saw Marmont's position in the valley of the Tagus; he felt the full force of the emperor's military reasoning,

BOOK XIV. 1811. July.

yet he did not despair, if he could overcome the political obstacles, to gain some advantage. He had now a powerful and experienced British force under his command, the different departments and the staff of the army were every day becoming more skilful and ready, and he had also seen enough of his adversaries to estimate their powers. The king he knew to be no general, and discontented with the marshals; Soult he had found able and vast in his plans, but too cautious in their execution; Marmont, with considerable vigour, had already shown some rashness in the manner he had pushed Reynier's division forward, after passing the Tagus, and it was, therefore, easy to conceive that no very strict concert would be maintained in their combined operations.

Lord Wellington had also established some good channels of information. He had a number of spies amongst the Spaniards who were living within the French lines; a British officer in disguise, constantly visited the French armies in the field; a Spanish state-counsellor, living at the head-quarters of the first corps, gave intelligence from that side, and a guitar-player of celebrity, named Fuentes, repeatedly making his way to Madrid, brought advice from thence. Mr. Stuart, under cover of vessels licensed to fetch corn for France, kept *chasse marées* constantly plying along the Biscay coast, by which he not only acquired direct information, but facilitated the transmission of intelligence from the land spies, amongst whom the most remarkable was a cobbler, living in a little hutch at the end of the bridge of Irun. This man while plying his trade, continued for years, without being suspected, to count every French soldier, that passed in or out of Spain by that passage, and transmitted their numbers by the *chasse marées* to Lisbon.

With the exception of the state spy at Victor's head-quarters, who being a double traitor was infamous, all the persons thus employed were very meritorious. The greater number, and the cleverest also, were Spanish gentlemen, alcaldes, or poor men, who disdaining rewards and disregarding danger, acted from a pure spirit of patriotism, and are to be lauded alike for their boldness, their talent, and their virtue. Many are dead. Fuentes was drowned in passing a river, on one of his expeditions; and the alcalde of Caceres, a man, of the clearest courage and patriotism, who expended his own property in the cause, and spurned at remuneration, was on Ferdinand's restoration cast into a dungeon, where he perished; a victim to the unbounded ingratitude and baseness of the monarch he had served so well!

With such means lord Wellington did not despair of baffling the deep policy of the emperor in the field. He thought that the saying of Henry the Fourth of France, that "*large armies would starve and small ones be beaten in Spain*," was still applicable. He felt that a solid possession of Portugal and her resources, which, through his brother's aid, he hoped to have, would enable him either to strike partial blows against the French, or oblige them to concentrate in large masses, which, confident in his own martial genius he felt he could hold in check, while the Spaniards ruined the small posts, and disorganized the civil administrations in their rear. Hitherto, indeed, the Spaniards had not made any such efforts except by the partidas, which were insufficient; but time, his own remonstrances, and the palpable advan-

BOOK XIV. 1811. July.

tages of the system, he trusted would yet teach them what to do.

Having deeply meditated upon these matters and received his reinforcements from England, he resolved to leave Hill with ten thousand infantry, a division of cavalry, and four brigades of artillery, about Portalegre, Villa Viciosa, and Estremos. From these rich towns which were beyond the influence of the Guadiana fever, the troops could rapidly concentrate either for an advance or retreat; and the latter was secured upon Abrantes, or upon the communications with Beira, by Niza, and Vilha Velha, where a permanent boat-bridge had now been established. The front was protected by Elvas, Jerumenha, Campo Mayor, and Ouguella; and Castaños also remained in Estremadura with the fifth army, which by the return of the cavalry from Ayamonte and the formation of Downie's legion now amounted to about a thousand infantry and nine hundred horse. This force placed on the side of Montijo, had Albuquerque and Valencia de Alcantara as posts of support, and a retreat either by the fords of the Tagus near the bridge of Alcantara, or upon Portugal by Marvão and Castello de Vide. Hill's position was thus so well covered, that he could not be surprised, nor even pressed except by a very strong army; and he was always on the watch as we shall hereafter find, to make incursions against the division of the fifth corps, which remained in Estremadura. The rest of the army was then placed in quarters of refreshment at Castello de Vide, Marvão and other places near the Tagus, partly to avoid the Guadiana fever, partly to meet Marmont's movement to that river.

When this disposition was made, the English general arranged his other measures of offence. The conduct of the Portuguese government and the new positions of the French armies had, as Napoleon had foreseen, left him no means of undertaking any sustained operation; but, as he was ignorant of the great strength of the army of the north, he hoped to find an opportunity of taking Ciudad Rodrigo before Marmont could come to its assistance. For this purpose he had caused a fine train of iron battering guns, and mortars, together with a reinforcement of British artillerymen, which had arrived at Lisbon from England, to be shipped in large vessels, and then with some ostentation made them sail as it were for Cadiz; at sea they were however shifted on board small craft, and while the original vessels actually arrived at Cadiz and Gibraltar, the guns were secretly brought first to Oporto and then in boats to Lamego. During this process, several engineer, artillery, and commissariat officers, were sent to meet and transport these guns, and the necessary stores for a siege, to Villaponte near Celerico; and as one of the principal magazines of the army was at Lamego, and a constant intercourse was kept up between it and Celerico, another great depot, the arrival, and passage of the guns and stores to their destination was not likely to attract the attention of the French spies.

Other combinations were also employed, both to deceive the enemy and to prepare the means for a sudden attack, before the troops commenced their march for Beira; but the hiding of such extensive preparations from the French would have been scarcely possible, if the personal hatred borne to the invaders by the peninsulars, combined with the latter's peculiar subtlety of character, had not prevented any information spreading abroad, beyond the

BOOK XIV. 1811. July.

fact that artillery had arrived at Oporto. The operation of bringing sixty-eight huge guns, with proportionate stores, across nearly fifty miles of mountain, was however one of no mean magnitude; five thousand draft bullocks were required for the train alone, and above a thousand militia were for several weeks employed merely to repair the road.

Appendix, No. V. Section 1.

The allies broke up from the Caya the 21st of July, and they had received considerable reinforcements, especially in cavalry, but they were sickly and required a change of cantonments; hence when an intercepted despatch gave reason to believe that Ciudad Rodrigo was in want of provisions, Wellington suddenly crossed the Tagus at Vilha Velha, and marched in the beginning of August by Castello Branco and Penamacor towards Rodrigo, hoping to surprise it in a starving state, but giving out that his movement was for the sake of healthy quarters. His movement was unmolested save by some French dragoons, from the side of Placentia, who captured a convoy of seventy mules loaded with wine near Pedrogoa, and getting drunk with their booty attacked some Portuguese infantry, who repulsed them and recovered the mules; but there were other ostensible objects besides the obvious one of removing from the well-known pestilence of the Guadiana, which contributed to blind the French as to the secret motives of the English general. We have seen that Dorsenne was menacing Gallicia, and that Soult was in full operation against the Murcians; it was supposed that he intended to invade Murcia itself, and therefore the march of the allies had the double object, of saving Gallicia, by menacing the rear of the invading army; and of relieving Murcia by forcing Marmont to look after

General Harvey's Journal.

Ciudad Rodrigo, and thus draw him away from the support of Soult, who would not, it was supposed, then quit Andalusia. CHAP. VII. 1811. July.

Gallicia was meanwhile in great danger, for the Partidas of the north had been vigorously repressed by Caffarelli and Reille, which enabled Dorsenne to collect about twenty thousand men on the Esla. Abadia, who had succeeded Santocildes, was posted with about seven thousand disciplined men behind this river, and he had a reserve of fifteen hundred at Foncebadon; but he could make no head, for to this number the Gallician army had again dwindled, and these were starving. The 25th the French, having passed the river in four columns, made a concentric march upon Astorga. Abadia, whose rear-guard sustained a sharp conflict near La Baneza, retreated, precisely by the same line as sir John Moore had done in 1809, and with about the same relative proportion of force; but as he only took the Foncebadon road and did not use the same diligence and skill as that general, the enemy forestalling him by Manzanal and Bembibre, cut him off from Villa Franca del Bierzo and from the road to Lugo, and on the 27th drove him into the Val des Orres. During this operation the division of the army of the north, which Bessieres had sent with the convoy to Ciudad Rodrigo, entered that place and returned to Salamanca.

General Walker's Correspondence, MSS. Abadia's ditto, MSS.

Appendix, No. V. Section 1.

The Spanish general having thus lost his line of communication with Lugo, and the few stores he possessed at Villa Franca, took post at Domingo Flores in the Val des Orres, where he entered a strong country, and, under the worst circumstances, could retire upon Portugal and save his troops if not his province. But his army which was in the

Sir H. Douglas's Correspondence, MSS.

BOOK XIV. 1811. August.

utmost distress before, for shoes and clothing, was now ready to disband from misery, and the consternation in Gallicia was excessive. That province torn by faction, stood helpless before the invader, who could, and would, have taken both Coruña and Ferrol, but for the sudden arrival of the allies on the Coa, which obliged him, for his own safety, to return to the plains. Souham, also, who was coming from Burgos, by forced marches, to support Dorsenne, halted at Rio Seco, and Abadia did not fail to ascribe all this to the loss he had inflicted, but his vanity was laughed at.

To have thus saved Gallicia was a great thing. That kingdom was the base of all the operations against the line of communication with France; from thence went forth, those British squadrons which nourished the guerilla warfare in Biscay, in the Montaña, in Navarre, in the Rioja, and the Asturias; it was the chief resource for the supply of cattle to the allied army, it was the outwork of Portugal, and honestly and vigorously governed, would have been more important than Catalonia. But like the rest of Spain it was always weak from disorders, and, if the allies had remained in Alemtejo, there was nothing to prevent Dorsenne from conquering it; for though he should not have taken Ferrol and Coruña, the points of St. Jago, Lugo, Villa Franca, and Orense would have given him an entire command of the interior, and the Spaniards holding the ports only would not have been able to dislodge him.

Lord Wellington arrived upon the Coa about the 8th of August, intending, as I have said, first a close blockade of Ciudad Rodrigo, and finally a siege; it was however soon known that the French had on the 6th supplied the place for two months, and the first part of the design was therefore relinquished. The troops were then quartered near the sources of the Coa and Agueda, close to the line of communication between Marmont and Dorsenne, and in a country where there was still some corn. If the enemy advanced in superior numbers, the army could retire through a strong country to a position of battle near Sabugal, whence the communication with Hill was direct. Nor was the rest of Beira left unprotected, because the French would have exposed their left flank, by any advance in the direction of Almeida, and the allies could, by Guarda, send detachments to the valley of the Mondego in time to secure the magazines at Celerico. The line of supply from Lamego along which the battering-train was now moving, was however rather exposed.

While the army was in this position, the preparations for the siege went on briskly, until Wellington learned, contrary to his former belief, that the disposable force of the army of the north, was above twenty thousand good troops; and consequently, that Ciudad Rodrigo could not be attacked in face of that corps, and of Marmont's army. Then changing his plan, he resolved to blockade the place, and wait for some opportunity to strike a sudden blow, either against the fortress, or against the enemy's troops; for it was the foundation of his hopes, that as the French could not long remain in masses, for want of provisions, and that he could check those masses on the frontier of Portugal, so he could always force them to concentrate, or suffer the loss of some important post. But it is worthy of observation, that his plans were based on calculations which did not comprise the Gallician army. He had no expec-

BOOK XIV. 1811. August. tation that it would act at all, or if it did, that it would act effectually. It had no cavalry, and the infantry being undisciplined dared not enter the plains in face of the enemy's horsemen; yet this was in August 1811, and Gallicia had not seen the face of an enemy since June 1809!

Early in September, Marmont, pushing a detachment from Placencia through the passes, surprised a British cavalry piquet, at St. Martin de Trebejo, and opened his communications with Dorsenne. Nevertheless lord Wellington formed the blockade. His head-quarters were fixed at Guinaldo, the fifth division was placed at Perales, in observation of Marmont, and the first division, now commanded by general Graham, occupied Penamacor. A battery of artillery, was withdrawn from Hill, and three brigades of that general's corps, reinforced by a Portuguese regiment, passed the Tagus, and were placed on the Ponçul, in advance of Castello Branco, to protect the magazines on that line of communication. Meanwhile the battering-train was collected at Villa de Ponte, the troops were employed to prepare gabions and fascines, and the engineers instructed two hundred men of the line, in the duties of sappers. The bridge over the Coa at Almeida which had been broken by Massena, was permanently repaired, and the works of Almeida itself, were ordered to be once more restored to form a place of arms for the battering-train and stores; Carlos d'España came also to Leon to form a new army under the protection of the allies, but he was without officers, arms, money, or stores, and his force was a mere name.

CHAPTER VIII.

CHAP. VIII.

1811. Sept.

During the first arrangements, for the blockade of Ciudad Rodrigo, the garrison made some excursions, to beat up the quarters of the British cavalry, and to forage the villages; and some lancers from Salamanca drove Julian Sanchez from Ledesma. Meanwhile in Estremadura, Morillo chased the enemy from Caceres, and advancing to Montanches, menaced Truxillo, but being beaten there by general Foy, he returned to Montijo, where some French cavalry, arriving from Zafra, again defeated him and drove him to Albuquerque. Other military operations, worth relating, there were none, but the civil transactions in Portugal were very important.

Mr. Stuart's exertions had produced some improvement in the Portuguese revenue; the ranks of the infantry were again filling by the return of deserters, and by fresh recruits, which, with the reinforcements from England had raised the actual number of the allied army to upwards of eighty thousand men, fifty-six thousand of which were British; the number under arms did not however exceed twenty-four thousand Portuguese and thirty-three thousand British, of whom five thousand were cavalry, with about ninety pieces of artillery. The previous operations in Alemtejo had produced sickness, which was increasing, and twenty-two thousand men were in hospital; and hence, Hill's

Appendix, No. IX. Section 1.

BOOK XIV. 1811. Sept.

corps being deducted, lord Wellington could not bring to the blockade of Ciudad above forty-four thousand of all arms, including Sanchez's Partida. But Marmont, alone, could in a few days bring as many to its succour, and Dorsenne always had from twenty to twenty-five thousand men in hand; because the French reinforcements had relieved the old garrisons in the north and the latter had joined the army in the field.

At this time the British military chest was quite bankrupt, even the muleteers, upon whose fidelity and efficiency the war absolutely depended, were six months in arrears for wages; and the disputes with the Portuguese government were more acrimonious than ever. The regency had proposed a new system of military regulations, calculated to throw the burthen of feeding the native troops entirely upon the British commissariat, without any reform of abuses, and lord Wellington had rejected it, hence renewed violence; and as Beresford had fallen sick at Cintra, Mr. Stuart deprived of his support on military questions, and himself no longer a member of the regency, was unable to restrain the triumphant faction of the Souzas. The prince regent's return to Portugal was prevented by troubles in the Brazils, and the regency expecting a long hold of power, and foolishly imagining that the war was no longer doubtful, were, after the custom of all people who employ powerful auxiliaries, devising how to get rid of the British army. With this view they objected to or neglected every necessary measure, and made many absurd demands, such as that the British general should pay the expenses of the Portuguese post office; and at the same time they preferred various vexatious, and unfounded charges against British officers, while gross corruption, and oppression of the poorer people, marked the conduct of their own magistrates.

CHAP. VIII.

1811. Sept.

But the fate of Portugal, which to these people appeared fixed, was in the eyes of the English general more doubtful than ever. Intercepted letters gave reasons to believe that the emperor was coming to Spain. And this notion was confirmed by the assembling of an army of reserve in France, and by the formation of great magazines at Burgos, and other places, to supply which, and to obtain money, the French generals were exacting the fourth of the harvest, and selling the overplus of corn again even by retail. Miunte reports of the state of these magazines were demanded by Napoleon; reinforcements, especially of the imperial guards, were pouring into Spain, and Wellington judging that the emperor must either drive the British from the Peninsula, or lower his tone with the world, thought that he would invade Portugal from the side of Rodrigo, the valley of the Tagus, and Alemtejo at the same time; and that he would risk his fleet in a combined attack upon Lisbon by sea and land.

Whether Napoleon really meant this; or whether he only spread the report, with a view to restrain the allies from any offensive operations during the summer, and to mislead the English cabinet as to the real state of his negotiations with Russia, intending if the latter proved favourable to turn his whole force against the Peninsula, does not very clearly appear; yet it is certain that every thing in Spain at this time indicated his approach. Lord Wellington's opinion that the emperor was bound to drive the British army away or lose his influence in the world does not however seem quite

BOOK XIV.

1811. Sept.

just; because the mighty expedition to Moscow, proved, that Napoleon did not want force to conquer Spain; and success in Russia would have enabled him to prolong the war in the Peninsula as a drain on the English resources for many years; which was so obvious a policy, that the rest of Europe could not from thence draw conclusions unfavourable to his influence.

Under the notion that Napoleon's coming was probable, the English general, with characteristic prudence, turned his own attention to the security of his ancient refuge within the lines, and therefore urgently desired the government to put the fortresses in order, repair the roads, and restore the bridges broken during Massena's invasion. An increased number of workmen were also put to the lines, for the engineers had never ceased to improve those on the northern bank of the Tagus, and on the southern bank the double lines of Almada had been continued on a gigantic scale. The defensive canal there was planned to float ships of three hundred tons, and to serve as a passage from the Tagus to Setuval by joining the navigation of the Sadao and Marateca rivers; thus conducing to objects of general utility as well as the military defence; as it will be found that lord Wellington did at all times sustain, not only the political, and financial, and military affairs, but also the agricultural, the commercial, and charitable interests of Portugal. The batteries at the mouth of the Tagus were likewise put into complete order, they were provided with furnaces for heating shot, and captain Holloway of the engineers, at a trifling expense, constructed four jetties at St. Julian's, in such an ingenious manner, that they withstood the most tempestuous gales and secured the embarkation

Colonel Jones's History of the Peninsular War.

of the army in any season. Finally the militia were again called out, a measure of greater import, in the actual state of affairs, than would at first appear; for the expense was a very heavy drain upon the finances, and the number of hands thus taken away from agriculture was a serious evil.

CHAP. VIII.

1811. Sept.

Had all these preparations been duly executed, lord Wellington would not have feared even Napoleon; but all that depended upon the Portuguese government, if that can be called government which was but a faction, was, as usual, entirely neglected. The regency refused to publish any proclamation to display the danger, or to call upon the people to prepare for future efforts; and although the ancient laws of Portugal provided the most ample means for meeting such emergencies, the bridges over the Ceira, the Alva and other rivers, on the line of retreat, were left unrepaired. The roads were therefore impassable, and as the rainy season was coming on, the safety of the army would have been seriously endangered if it had been obliged to retire before the emperor. The regency pleaded want of money, but this also could be traced to their own negligence in the collection of the taxes, for which there was no solid reason; because, with the exception of the devastated districts, the people were actually richer than they had ever been, not indeed in goods, but in hard cash, derived from the enormous sums expended by the British army. To add to these embarrassments the secret correspondents of the army on the side of Salamanca suddenly ceased their communications, and it was at first feared they had paid with their lives for the culpable indiscretion of the Portuguese government; for the latter had published, in the Lisbon Gazette, all the secret information sent to

BOOK XIV.

1811. Sept.

Silveira, which being copied into the English newspapers, drew the enemy's attention. Fortunately this alarm proved false, but a sense of the other difficulties was greatly aggravated to the English general, by comparison of his situation with that of the enemy; neither necessity nor remuneration, could procure for him due assistance from the Portuguese people, while the French generals had merely to issue their orders to the Spaniards through the prefects of the provinces, and all means of transport or other succour, possible to be obtained, were sure to be provided on the day and at the place indicated.

Wellington's correspondence with Lord Liverpool, MSS.

In the midst of these cares lord Wellington was suddenly called into military action by the approach of the enemy. Ciudad Rodrigo having been blockaded for six weeks wanted food, and Marmont, who had received a reinforcement of eleven thousand men from France, and had now fifty thousand, present under arms, in the valley of the Tagus, being in pain for the garrison, had concerted with Dorsenne a great combined operation for its succour. In this view Truxillo had been occupied by a part of the fifth corps, and Girard with the remainder had advanced to Merida, while Foy, reinforced by a strong division of the army of the centre, occupied Placentia. Marmont himself quitting Talavera, had passed the mountains and collected a large convoy at Bejar; at the same time Dorsenne reinforced by eight thousand men under Souham, had collected another convoy at Salamanca, and leaving Bonnet's division, which now included Mayer's troops, at Astorga, to watch the Gallicians, came down to Tamames. They met on the 21st, their united armies presenting a mass of sixty thousand men, of which six thousand were cavalry; and they had above a hundred pieces of artillery.

1811. Sept.

The English general, who had expected this movement, immediately concentrated his scattered troops. He could not fight beyond the Agueda, but he did not think fit to retreat until he had seen their whole army, lest a detachment should relieve the place to his dishonour. Hence to make the enemy display his force, he established himself in the following positions near the fortress.

The third division, reinforced by three squadrons of German and British cavalry, formed his centre. It was posted on the heights of Elbodon and Pastores, on the left of the Agueda, and within three miles of Ciudad, commanding a complete prospect of the plains round that place.

The right wing, composed of the light division, some squadrons of cavalry, and six guns, was posted beyond the Agueda, and behind the Vadillo, a river rising in the Peña de Francia, and flowing in a rugged channel to the Agueda, which it joins about three miles above Rodrigo; from this line an enemy coming from the eastern passes of the hills could be discerned.

The left wing, composed of the sixth division and Anson's brigade of cavalry, the whole under general Graham, was placed at Espeja, on the lower Azava, with advanced posts at Carpio and Marialva. From thence to Ciudad Rodrigo was about eight miles over a plain, and on Graham's left, Julian Sanchez's Partida, nominally commanded by Carlos d'España, was spread along the lower Agueda in observation. The heads of the columns were therefore presented on three

BOOK XIV. 1811. Sept.

points to the fortress; namely, at the ford of the Vadillo; and the heights of Pastores and Espeja. The communication between the left and centre was kept up by two brigades of heavy cavalry, posted on the Upper Azava, and supported at Campillo by Pack's Portuguese brigade. But the left of the army was very distant from Guinaldo, which was the pivot of operations, and to obviate the danger of making a flank march in retreat, should the enemy advance, the seventh division was placed in reserve at Alamedillo, and the first division at Nava d'Aver. Thus the allied army was spread out on the different roads which led, like the sticks of a fan, to one point on the Coa.

The fifth division remained at St. Payo, watching the passes from Estremadura, lest Foy should from that direction fall on the rear of the right wing; and as Marmont's movement affected the line of communication along the eastern frontier, general Hill first sent Hamilton's Portuguese towards Alburquerque, to support the Spanish cavalry, which was menaced by the fifth corps, and then brought the remainder of his troops nearer to the Tagus, in readiness to take the place of his third brigade, which now marched from the Ponçul to Penamacor.

Wellington's position before Rodrigo was very extensive, and therefore very weak. The Agueda, although fordable in many places during fine weather, was liable to sudden freshes, and was on both sides lined with high ridges. The heights, occupied by the troops, on the left bank, were about three miles wide, ending rather abruptly above Pastores and Elbodon, and they were flanked by the great plains and woods, which extend from Ciudad to the bed of the Coa. The position of Elbodon itself, which was held by the centre of the army, was, therefore, not tenable against an enemy commanding these plains; and as the wings were distant their lines of retreat were liable to be cut, if the centre should be briskly pushed back beyond Guinaldo. But, at the latter place, three field redoubts had been constructed, on the high land, with a view to impose upon the enemy, and so gain time to assemble and feel Marmont's disposition for a battle, because a retreat behind the Coa was to be avoided if possible.

On the 23d the French advanced from Tamames, and encamped behind the hills to the north-east of Ciudad Rodrigo. Then a strong detachment entered the plain, and having communicated with the garrison, and examined the position of the light division on the Vadillo returned.

The 24th, six thousand cavalry, with four divisions of infantry, crossed the hills in two columns, and placing some troops in observation on the Vadillo, introduced the convoy. On this day the fourth division of the allies, was brought up to the position of Guinaldo, and the redoubts were completed, yet no other change was made, for it was thought the French would not advance further. But the 25th, soon after daybreak, fourteen squadrons of the imperial guards drove the outposts of the left wing from Carpio across the Azava, and the lancers of Berg crossed that river in pursuit, they were however flanked by some infantry in a wood, and then charged and beaten by two squadrons of the fourteenth, and sixteenth, dragoons, who reoccupied the post at Carpio.

During this skirmish, fourteen battalions of infantry, thirty squadrons of cavalry, and twelve

BOOK XIV. 1811. Sept.

guns, the whole under Montbrun, passed the Agueda by the bridge of Rodrigo and the fords above it, and marched towards Guinaldo. The road soon divided, one branch turning the Elbodon heights on the right hand, the other leading nearer to the Agueda, and passing through the villages of Pastores, La Encina, and Elbodon; and as the point of divarication was covered by a gentle ridge, it was for some time doubtful which branch the French would follow. In a short time this doubt was decided. Their cavalry poured along the right-hand road leading directly to Guinaldo, the small advanced posts which the allied squadrons had on the plain were rapidly driven in, and the enemy's horsemen without waiting for their infantry commenced the

COMBAT OF ELBODON.

The position of the third division was completely turned by this movement, and the action began very disadvantageously, for the seventy-fourth and sixtieth regiments, being at Pastores, on the right, were too distant to be called in, and Picton being with three other regiments, at Elbodon, could not take any immediate part in the fight. Hence, as the French force was considerable, Wellington sent to Guinaldo for a brigade of the fourth division, and meanwhile directed general Colville to draw up the seventy-seventh and fifth British regiments, the twenty-first Portuguese, and two brigades of artillery of the same nation, on the hill over which the road to Guinaldo passed, supporting their flanks with Alten's three squadrons. The height, thus occupied by the allies, was convex towards the enemy, and covered in front and on both flanks, by deep ravines, but it was too extensive for their numbers; and before Picton could bring in the troops from the village of Elbodon, the crisis of the combat passed. The Portuguese guns had sent their shot amongst the thickest of Montbrun's horsemen in the plain, but the latter passed the front ravine in half squadrons, and with amazing vigour riding up the rough height, on three sides, fell vehemently upon the allies. Neither the loose fire of the infantry, nor of the artillery, could stop them, but they were checked by the fine fighting of the cavalry, who charged the heads of the ascending masses, not once but twenty times, and always with a good will, thus maintaining the upper ground for above an hour.

It was astonishing to see so few troopers bearing up against that surging multitude, even favoured as the former were by the steep rocky nature of the ground; but Montbrun obstinate to win soon brought up his artillery, and his horsemen gaining ground in the centre, cut down some of the gunners and captured the guns; and one of the British squadrons by charging too far got entangled in the intricacy of the ravines. The danger was then imminent, when suddenly the fifth regiment, led by major Ridge, a daring spirit, darted into the midst of the French cavalry, and retook the artillery, which again opened its fire; and nearly at the same time the seventy-seventh, supported by the twenty-first Portuguese, repulsed the enemy on the left. However, this charging of a weak line of infantry against a powerful cavalry, could only check the foe at that particular point. Montbrun still pressed onwards

BOOK XIV.

1811. Sept.

with fresh masses, against the left flank of the allies, while other squadrons penetrated between the right flank and the village of Elbodon. From the enclosures and vineyards of that village, Picton was at this time with difficulty and some confusion extricating his regiments; the expected brigade of the fourth division was not yet in sight, and the French infantry was rapidly approaching: the position was no longer tenable, and lord Wellington directed both Picton and Colville to fall back and unite in the plain behind.

Colville forming his battalions in two squares immediately descended from the hill, but Picton had a considerable distance to move, and at this moment, the allied squadrons, fearing to be surrounded by the French, who had completely turned their right, galloped away, and took refuge with the Portuguese regiment, which was farthest in retreat. Then the fifth and seventy-seventh, two weak battalions formed in one square, were quite exposed, and in an instant the whole of the French cavalry came thundering down upon them. But how vain, how fruitless to match the sword with the musket! To send the charging horseman against the steadfast veteran! The multitudinous squadrons, rending the skies with their shouts, and closing upon the glowing squares, like the falling edges of a burning crater, were as instantly rejected, scorched, and scattered abroad; and the rolling peal of musketry had scarcely ceased to echo in the hills, when bayonets glittered at the edge of the smoke, and with firm and even step, the British regiments came forth like the holy men from the Assyrian's furnace.

Picton now effected his junction and the whole

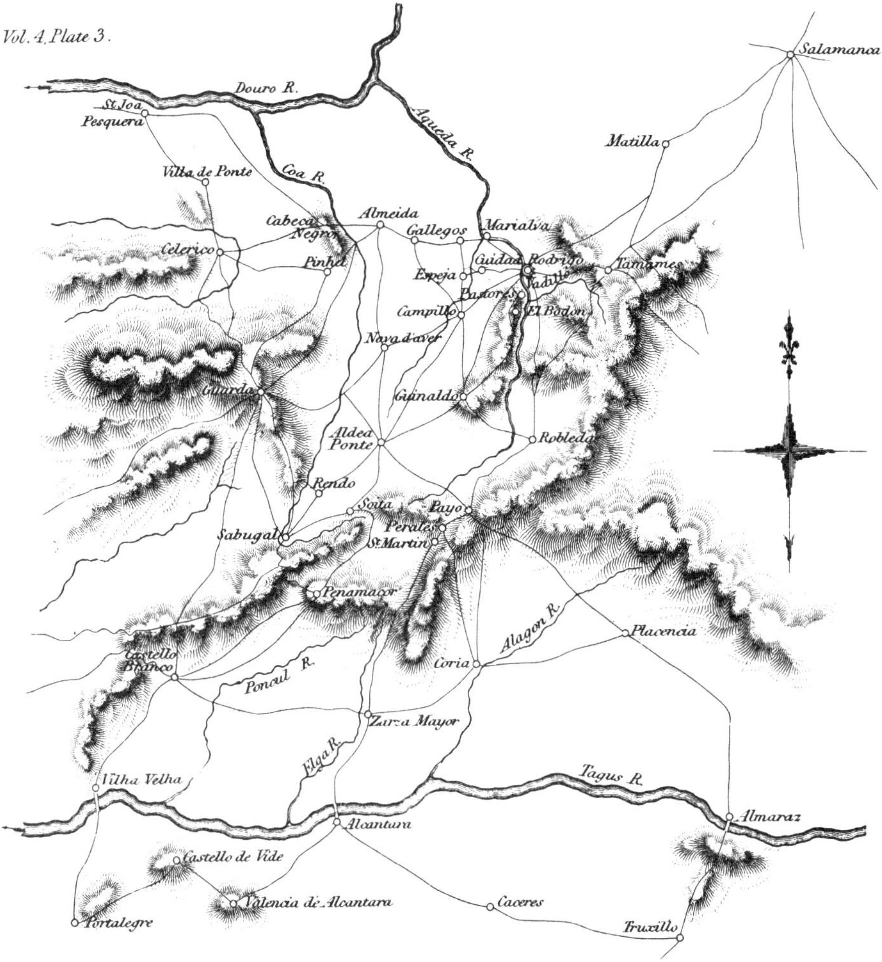

EXPLANATORY SKETCH
of the
OPERATIONS AND *COMBAT*
of
EL BODON.

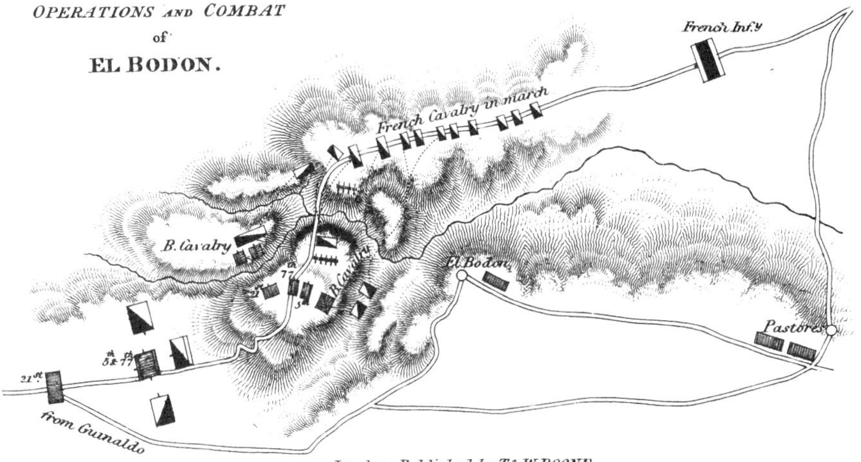

London: Published by T. & W. BOONE.

retired over the plain to the position at Guinaldo, which was about six miles distant. The French, although fearing to renew the close attack, followed, and plied the troops with shot and shell, until about four o'clock in the evening, when the entrenched camp was gained. Here the fourth division presented a fresh front, Pack's brigade came up from Campillo, and the heavy cavalry from the Upper Azava, being also brought into line, the action ceased. By this retrograde movement of the left and centre of the third division, the seventy-fourth and the sixtieth regiments, posted at Pastores, were cut off; they however crossed the Agueda by a ford, and moving up the right bank happily reached Guinaldo in the night, after a march of fifteen hours, in the course of which they captured a French cavalry patrol.

During the retreat from Elbodon, the left wing of the army was ordered to fall back on the first division, at Nava d'Aver, but to keep posts in observation on the Azava. Carlos d'España retired with Sanchez's infantry behind the Coa, and the guerilla chief himself passed with his cavalry into the French rear. The seventh division was withdrawn from Allemadilla to Albergaria, and the head-quarters baggage moved to Casilla de Flores. The light division should have marched to Guinaldo; general Craufurd received the order at two o'clock, he plainly heard the cannonade, and might easily have reached Guinaldo before midnight, but he only marched to Cespedosa, one league from the Vadillo, which river was immediately passed by fifteen hundred French. The position at Guinaldo was therefore occupied by only fourteen thousand men, of which about two thousand six

BOOK XIV. 1811. Sept.

hundred were cavalry. The left of the army, concentrated at Nava d'Aver, under Graham, was ten miles distant; the light division being at Cespedosa and debarred the direct route by the ford of Carros, was sixteen miles distant, and the fifth division, posted at Payo in the mountains, was twelve miles distant. Meanwhile Marmont brought up a second division of infantry, and in the course of the night, and the following day, united sixty thousand men in front of Guinaldo. The situation of the English general was become most critical, yet he would not abandon the light division, which did not arrive until after three o'clock in the evening. Marmont's fortune was fixed in that hour! He knew nothing of the allies' true situation, and having detached a strong column by the valley of the Azava to menace their left, contented himself with making an ostentatious display of the imperial guards in the plain, instead of attacking an adversary who was too weak to fight, and laughing to see him so employed, soon changed the state of affairs.

In the night, Wellington by a skilful concentric movement from Guinaldo, Nava d'Aver, Perales, and Payo, united the whole army on new ground, between the Coa and the sources of the Agueda, twelve miles behind Guinaldo; and it is a curious fact that Marmont had so little knowledge of his own advantages, that instead of harassing the allies in this difficult movement, he also retired during the night, and was actually in march to the rear, when the scouts of the column, which had marched by the valley of Azava, brought word that the allies were in retreat, and their divisions still widely separated. Dorsenne then insisted that Marmont should wheel round and pursue, but lord Wellington was already in a strong position behind the stream of the Villa Maior.

The fifth division, coming up from Payo, was now on the right at Aldea Velha, the fourth and light divisions, with Victor Alten's cavalry, and the heavy dragoons, under sir Stapleton Cotton, were in the centre in front of Alfayates; the convent of Sacaparte was on their left, and the line was prolonged to Rebulon by Pack's and M'Mahon's Portuguese brigades; the sixth division with Anson's cavalry closed the line at Bismula. The cavalry picquets were pushed beyond the Villa Maior in front of Aldea Ponte, in the centre, and towards Furcalhos on the right; and the third and seventh divisions were in reserve behind Alfayates. This position was extensive, but the days were short, serious dispositions were required for a general attack, and the allies could not be turned, because they covered all the practicable roads leading to the bridges and fords of the Coa.

COMBAT OF ALDEA DE PONTE.

The French, moving by the roads of Furcalhos and of Aldea de Ponte, were checked by the picquets of the light division on the former; but on the latter their horsemen drove the cavalry posts from the hills, and across the stream of the Villa Maior, and about ten o'clock took possession of Aldea de Ponte.

At twelve o'clock the head of the infantry came up and immediately attacked general Pakenham, then commanding a brigade of the fourth division, which was posted on the opposite heights. Lord Wellington arrived at the same moment, and directed the seventh fuzileers to charge in line, and he supported them on each flank with a Portuguese regiment in column. The French, who had advanced well up the hill, were driven back, and though they afterwards attempted to turn the brigade by a wood, which was distant about musket-shot from the right, while their cavalry advanced to the foot of the hills, the artillery sufficed to baffle the effort. Then the English general taking the offensive, directed the twenty-third fuzileers and Portuguese caçadores to turn the French left, and seize the opposite hills, which finished the action, and Aldea de Ponte was again occupied by the allies. Wellington, who had been much exposed to the fire, rode to another part of the position, but scarcely had he departed when the French from the Forcalhos road joined those near Aldea de Ponte, and at five o'clock renewing the attack retook the village. Pakenham, with his fuzileers, immediately recovered it, but the French were very numerous, the country rugged, and so wooded, that he could not tell what was passing on the flanks, wherefore, knowing that the chosen ground of battle was behind the Coa, he abandoned Aldea de Ponte and regained his original post.

In the night the allies retreated, and on the morning of the 28th occupied a new and very strong position in front of the Coa, the right resting on the Sierra de Mesas, the centre covered by the village of Soita, the left at Rendo upon the Coa. The whole army thus enclosed, as it were in a deep loop of the Coa river could only be attacked on a narrow front, and Marmont, who had brought up but a few days' provisions and could gather none in that country, retired the same day. This terminated the operations. The French placed a fresh garrison in Ciudad Rodrigo; Dorsenne marched to Salamanca; a strong division was posted at Alba de Tormes to communicate with Marmont, and the latter resumed his old position in the valley of the Tagus. At the same time Foy, who had advanced with his two divisions as far as Zarza Mayor, in the direction of Castello Branco, returned to Placentia; Girard also, being threatened by Hamilton's Portuguese division, which Hill had sent to check his advance, left two thousand men of the fifth corps at Merida, and retired to Zafra; and when these movements were known, the light division reinforced by some cavalry resumed the nominal blockade of Ciudad Rodrigo, in concert with Julian Sanchez. The rest of the army was cantoned on both sides of the Coa, and head-quarters were fixed at Frenada.

Nearly a month had been employed by the French in the preparation and execution of this great operation, which terminated so feebly and so abruptly, because the generals were as usual at variance. They had victualled Ciudad Rodrigo, but they had lost the favourable opportunity of invading Gallicia. Nothing had been gained in the field, time was lost, and the English general's plans were forwarded.

Victoires et Conquêtes des François.

OBSERVATIONS.

1°. Lord Wellington's position behind the Soita has been noticed by two recent authors. The one condemns the imprudence of offering battle on

Londonderry's Narrative.

BOOK XIV.

1811. Sept.

Annals of the Peninsular Campaigns

ground whence there was no retreat; the other intimates that it was assumed in contempt of the adversary's prowess. This last appears a mere shift to evade what was not understood, for if lord Wellington had despised Marmont, he would have fought him beyond the Agueda. But sixty thousand French soldiers were never to be despised, neither was Wellington a man to put an army in jeopardy from any overweening confidence; and it is not difficult to show that his position was chosen well, without imprudence, and without presumption.

The space between the Sierra de Mesas and the Coa was less than six miles, and the part open to attack was very much reduced by the rugged bed of a torrent which covered the left. Forty thousand men were quite able to defend this line, which was scarcely more than one-third of their full front; and as the roads were bad, the country hilly and much broken with woods and ravines, the superiority of the enemy's horse and guns would have availed him little. Lord Wellington had a right to be bold against an adversary who had not molested him at Guinaldo, and it is always of importance to show a menacing front. It was also certain that great combinations must have been made by Marmont, before he could fight a general battle on such ground; it was equally certain that he could only have a few days' provisions with his army, and that the neighbourhood could not supply him. It was, therefore, reasonable to expect that he would retire rather than fight, and he did so.

Let us however, take the other side, and suppose that Marmont was prepared and resolute to bring on a great battle. The position behind Soita would still have been good. The French were indeed too strong to be fought with on a plain, yet not strong enough to warrant a retreat indicating fear; hence the allies had retired slowly for three days, each day engaged, and the enemy's powerful horse and artillery was always close upon their rear. Now the bed of the Coa, which was extremely rugged, furnished only a few points for crossing, of which the principal were, the ford of Serraleira behind the right of the allies; the ford of Rapoulha de Coa behind their left; and the bridge of Sabugal behind their centre. The ways to those points were narrow, and the passage of the river, with all the baggage, could not have been easily effected in face of an enemy without some loss and perhaps dishonour: and had lord Wellington been unable to hold his position in a battle, the difficulty of passing the river would not have been very much increased, because his incumbrances would all have been at the other side, and there was a second range of heights half-a-mile in front of Sabugal favourable for a rear-guard. The position of Soita appears therefore to have been chosen with good judgment in regard to the immediate object of opposing the enemy; but it is certain that the battering train, then between Pinhel and Villa Ponte, was completely exposed to the enemy. Marmont, however, had not sufficiently considered his enterprize, and knew not where or how to strike.

2°. The position of Aldea Ponte, was equally well chosen. Had the allies retreated at once from Guinaldo, to Soita, baggage and stores would have been lost, and the retrograde movement have had the appearance of a flight; the road from Payo would have been uncovered, and the junction of the fifth division endangered. But in the position taken up, the points of junction of all the roads were occupied, and as each point was strong in itself, it was not difficult for a quick-sighted general, perfectly acquainted with the country, and having excellent troops, to check the heads of the enemy's columns, until the baggage had gained a sufficient offing, and the fifth division had taken its place in line.

3°. The position at Guinaldo was very different from the others. The previous entrenching of it proved lord Wellington's foresight, and he remained there thirty-six hours, that is, from mid-day of the 25th until mid-night of the 26th, which proved his firmness. It is said that sir George Murray advised him to abandon it in the night of the 25th, and that arrangements were actually made in that view, yet anxious for the safety of the light division he would not stir. The object was certainly one of an importance sufficient to justify the resolution, but the resolution itself was one of those daring strokes of genius which the ordinary rules of art were never made to controul. The position was contracted, of no great natural strength in front, and easily to be turned; the entrenchments constructed were only a few breastworks and two weak field redoubts, open in rear, and without palisades; not more than fourteen thousand British and Portuguese troops were in line, and sixty thousand French veterans with a hundred pieces of artillery were before them! When Marmont heard of the escape of the light division, and discovered the deceit, he prophetically exclaimed, alluding to Napoleon's fortune, "*And Wellington's star, it also is bright!*"

4°. The positions of Aldea Ponte and Soita are

to be commended, that at Guinaldo to be admired rather than imitated, but the preceding operations are censurable. The country immediately beyond Ciudad Rodrigo offered no covering position for a siege or blockade; and the sudden floods, to which the Agueda is subject, rendered the communications with the left bank precarious. Nor though bridges had been secured, could Wellington have ventured to encamp round the place with lines of contravallation and circumvallation, on both sides of the river; because Marmont's army would then have advanced from Placencia to Castello Branco, have seized the passage over the Tagus at Vilha Velha, and in concert with the fifth corps endangered the safety of Hill. This would have obliged the allies to quit their entrenched camp, and Dorsenne could then have revictualled the place. It was therefore necessary to hold a strong central position with respect to Marmont and Dorsenne, to keep both in check while separate, and to oppose them when united. This position was on the Coa, and as Salamanca or Bejar, the nearest points where convoys could be collected for Ciudad Rodrigo, were from fifty to sixty miles distant, lord Wellington's object, namely the forcing the French to assemble in large bodies without any adequate result, could be, and was obtained by a distant as well as by a close investment.

So far all was well calculated, but when Marmont and Dorsenne arrived with sixty thousand men at Ciudad Rodrigo, the aspect of affairs entirely changed, and as the English general could not dispute the entrance of the convoy, he should have concentrated his army at once behind Guinaldo. Instead of doing this he kept it extended on a line of

BOOK XIV. 1811. Sept.

many miles and the right wing separated from the centre by a difficult river. In his despatch, he says, that, from some uncertainty in his estimate of the enemy's numbers, it was necessary to ascertain their exact strength by actual observation; but this is rather an excuse than a valid reason, because, for this object, which could be obtained by other means, he risked the loss of his whole army, and violated two vital rules of war which forbid—

1°. The parcelling of an army before a concentrated enemy.

2°. The fixing of your own point of concentration within the enemy's reach.

Now lord Wellington's position on the 24th and 25th extended from the ford of the Vadillo on the right of the Agueda, to Marialva on the Azava; the distance either from the Vadillo, or Marialva, to Guinaldo, was as great as that from Ciudad to Guinaldo, and by worse roads; and the distance from Ciudad to Elbodon was as nothing, compared to the distance of the wings from the same place. Wherefore when Montbrun attacked, at Elbodon, the allies' wings were cut off, and the escape of the third and light divisions, and of the troops at Pastores, was a matter of fortune and gallantry, rather than of generalship; that is, in the enlarged sense of the last word, for it cannot be denied that the actual movements of the troops were conducted with consummate skill.

But what if Marmont, instead of being drawn by circumstances into a series of ill-combined, and partial attacks, had previously made dispositions for a great battle? He certainly knew, through the garrison, the real situation of the allies, and he also

Appendix, No. V. Section 1.

knew of the camp at Guinaldo, which being on their line of retreat was the important point. If he had issued from the fortress before daybreak on the 25th with the whole or even half of his forces, he could have reached Campillo in two hours with one column, while another fell on the position at Pastores and Elbodon; the third division, thus attacked, would have been enveloped and captured, or broken and driven over the Agueda, by the ford of Zamara, and would have been irretrievably separated from Guinaldo. And if this division had even reached Guinaldo, the French army would have arrived with it in such overwhelming numbers, that the fourth division could not have restored the battle; meanwhile a few thousand men thrown across the ford of Caros near Robleda would have sufficed to keep the light division at bay, because the channel of the Robleda torrent, over which their retreat lay, was a very deep and rugged ravine. The centre being broken the French could, at choice, have either surrounded the light division, or directed the mass of their forces against the reserves, and then the left wing under Graham would have had to retreat from the Azava over the plains towards Almeida.

It may be said that all the French were not up on the 25th, but they might have been so, and as lord Wellington was resolved to see their number he would have been in the same position the 26th. It is however sufficient to remark that the allies exclusive of the fifth division, which was at Payo, did not exceed thirty-five thousand men of all arms; that they were on an irregular line of at least twenty miles, and mostly in an open country; that at no point were the troops more than eight,

BOOK XIV. 1811. Sept.

and at the principal point, namely Pastores, only three, miles, from a fortress from whence sixty thousand infantry and six thousand cavalry, with one hundred and twenty guns were ready to issue. Finally the point of concentration at Guinaldo was only twelve miles from that fortress. The allies escaped because their adversary was blind! Lord Wellington's conduct at Guinaldo was above rules, but at Elbodon it was against rules, which is just the difference between genius and error.

4°. In these operations Marmont gave proof that as a general he was rather shining than great. He was in error throughout. Before he commenced his march he had desired Girard to advance on the side of the Alemtejo, assuring him that the whole of the allied army, and even the Spanish troops under Castaños, had crossed the Tagus to operate against Rodrigo; but in fact only one brigade of Hill's corps had moved, and Girard would have been destroyed, if, fortunately for him, the allies had not intercepted the original and duplicate of the letter containing this false information.

Appendix, No. V. Section 1.

5°. When Marmont brought his convoy into Ciudad, it would appear he had no intention of fighting, but tempted by the false position of the allies, and angry at the repulse of his cavalry on the Lower Azava, he turned his scouting troops into columns of attack. And yet he permitted his adversary to throw dust in his eyes for thirty-six hours at Guinaldo; and at Aldea Ponte his attack was a useless waste of men, because there was no local advantage offered, and he did not intend a great battle.

6°. The loss incurred in the different combats was not great. About three hundred men and officers fell on the part of the allies, and on that of the French rather more, because of the fire of the squares and artillery at Elbodon. But the movements during the three days were full of interest, and instruction, and diversified also by brilliant examples of heroism. Ridge's daring charge has been already noticed, and it was in one of the cavalry encounters, that a French officer in the act of striking at the gallant Felton Harvey of the fourteenth dragoons, perceived that he had only one arm, and with a rapid movement brought down his sword into a salute and passed on! Such was the state of the war on the frontier of Portugal; in the next book will be found the contemporary events in Spain.

CHAP. VIII.

1811. Sept.

BOOK XV.

CHAPTER I.

STATE OF THE WAR IN SPAIN.

BOOK XV. 1811.

Northern Provinces. The invasion of Gallicia, which had been arrested by the arrival of the allies on the Coa, would have been a most serious calamity. Abadia, a weak man, with troops, distressed for provisions and clothing, was on bad terms with the chief of his staff Moscosa, whom he feared, and on worse terms with the junta. The great road to Coruña was open, and although general Walker, seeing the danger, advised that Ferrol, which was indefensible, should be dismantled, and the guns, amounting to fifteen hundred, with the timber and vessels of war in the harbour, transferred to Coruña, neither that nor any other useful measure was executed.

Appendix, No. V. Section 1.

Before this, overtures had been made to the Spanish government, to take Spanish troops into British pay after the manner of the Portuguese; but the regency remembering the prodigality of Canning demanded three millions yearly, besides arms and clothing, without which they said the Spaniards could make no efficient exertions! To introduce British officers into the service on any other terms was not possible, because the Spanish military were indignant at what they termed the degradation of such a proposal. The Perceval faction finding it thus, and wanting greatness of mind to support Wellington, on a scale commensurate with his talents, then turned their attention to the encouragement of the Partidas, as being less expensive, and affording an example to the continental nations of popular and protracted resistance to France.

Sir Howard Douglas, who succeeded general Walker as military agent, (these officers must not be confounded with the military agents originally sent out, and whose mischievous proceedings I have had occasion to notice,) was directed to encourage those bodies by increased supplies, and to combine their movements better with each other and with the British squadron in the Bay of Biscay. Lord Wellington at the desire of government, sent to the guerilla chiefs, military presents, with a letter acknowledging the importance of their services, and this was not mere compliment, for he had indeed derived great advantages from their exertions, and thought he had derived more, because he only knew of their exploits by hearsay. When he afterwards advanced into Spain and saw them closely, he was forced to acknowledge that the guerillas, although active and willing, and although their operations in general occasioned the utmost annoyance to the enemy, were so little disciplined that they could do nothing against the French troops unless the latter were very inferior in numbers. If the French took post in a house or church of which they only barricadoed the entrance, both regular troops and guerillas were so ill equipped as military bodies, that their enemy could remain in security until

Sir H. Douglas's Correspondence, MSS.

BOOK XV. 1811. Sept.

relieved. In like manner Napoleon reprimanding his generals for suffering the Partidas to gain any head, observed, that when cut off from communication with the English ships they were a nullity!

Sir H. Douglas's Correspondence, MSS.

Douglas arrived just as Dorsenne's retreat enabled Abadia to resume his position on the frontier, but the army was in a miserable state; the wet season was setting in upon men, destitute of even the necessaries of life, although the province abounded in cattle and goods, which could be easily procured, because money, although plentiful, was generally hoarded, and commodities were therefore cheap, and could be obtained in lieu of taxes at the market-price. An extraordinary increase of the customs, arising from the trade of Santander and Bilbao being transferred to Coruña by the war, also offered a valuable resource; the harbour was filled with colonial goods, and as the appetites of men generally stifle patriotism, and baffle power, a licensed commerce was carried on with the enemy's ports in Biscay; yet without judgment as related to the war, for the return was iron, to re-export to the colonies, whereas by an internal traffic of the same kind, clothes and grain for the troops might have been had from Castile and Leon. But confusion and corruption every where prevailed, the exigences of the war were always the last things cared for, and the starving soldiers committed a thousand excesses with impunity, for where there is no food or pay, there can be no discipline.

The people were oppressed with imposts, legal and illegal, and yet the defalcation in the revenue was great, and the monopoly of tobacco the principal financial resource, was injured by the smuggling arising from the unsettled nature of the times.

The annual charge on the province was about £1,300,000, the actual receipts were less than £500,000, and the junta endeavoured to supply the deficiency by an extraordinary contribution from all property, save that of day-labourers, which they expected would produce sixty millions of reals (£750,000). But a corrupt and vexatious collection of this tax tormented the people without filling the treasury; the clergy, and the richer classes, were, as in Portugal, favoured, and it yielded, in six months, less than a seventh part.

From this state of affairs two inferences may be safely drawn:—1°. That England and not Gallicia had hitherto supported the war here, as in other parts of the Peninsula. 2°. That as England had in 1808–9 paid to Gallicia three millions of hard dollars, and given other succours sufficient for double the number of troops employed, the deficiency of the revenue had been amply compensated, and the causes of distress must be sought for in the proceedings of the authorities, and in the anomalous nature of the war itself. The successive juntas, apprehensive of offending the people, were always inert in the civil administration, and either too corrupt, or too incapable, to apply the succours from England, justly or wisely. The junta of this period was, like its predecessors, factious and intriguing; it was hostile to the junta of Leon, unfriendly to that of Asturias, jealous and contemptuous of the military leaders; in return these last abhorred the junta, and were tormented with factions of their own. The regular officers hated the guerillas, and endeavoured to get the controul of the succours granted, by England, to the latter; and as they necessarily lived by plundering their own

BOOK XV. 1811.

countrymen, they strenuously opposed the arming of the peasants, partly from fear lest the latter should resist this license, partly because the republican, and anti-English spirit, which was growing up in the cortes had also reached this quarter.

The clergy clung to the peasantry, with whom they had great influence, but the army, which had imbibed liberal words, rather than principles, was inimical to them. A press had been established at head-quarters, from whence issued political papers either original, or repeated from the libels at Cadiz, in which, the Portuguese were called slaves, for submitting to British influence; and it was openly avowed that the French yoke was preferable to that of England; the guerilla system, and the arming of the people were also attacked, and these writings were met by other political papers from the civil press at Coruña and St. Jago. The frequent changes of commanders rendered all the evils more prominent; for the local government had legal power to meddle with the military arrangements, and every change of commander produced a new difficulty. Thus the junta refused to acknowledge Abadia as their president during the absence of Castaños, he in return complained alike of their neglect and of their interference; and when they proposed to establish a general depôt at Lugo he marched a part of his army there to prevent it.

But the occult source of most of these difficulties is to be found in the inconsistent attempts of the British cabinet, to uphold, national independence with internal slavery, against foreign aggression, with an ameliorated government. The clergy who led the mass of the people, clung to the English, because they supported aristocracy and church domination;

and they were also strongly for the Partidas, because these were commanded by men who sprung directly from the church itself, or from people who were attached to the church, while the regular armies being officered by the friends of the cortes, disliked the Partidas, both as interlopers and as political enemies. The English ministers, hating Napoleon, not because he was the enemy of England, but because he was the champion of equality, cared not for Spain, unless her people were enslaved. They were willing enough to use a liberal cortes to defeat Napoleon, but they also desired to put down that cortes, by the aid of the clergy, and of the bigoted part of the people: nevertheless as liberty will always have more charms than slavery, they would have missed of both objects, if the exigences of the continental system had not induced the emperor to go to Moscow, where the snow destroyed him; and if the very advocates of liberty in Spain had not in their madness, resolved to oppress the Americans. The cortes, by discovering a rabid love of power in practice, rendered their democratic doctrines suspected, and lost partizans; but lord Wellington, in support of aristocracy, used the greatest prudence in policy, and in his actions was considerate and just.

In the first conference held at Coruña, after sir Howard Douglas's arrival, the junta, as the usual preliminary, demanded more money from England; but he advised, instead, a better management of their own resources, and pointed out the military measures requisite to render the army efficient. He recommended the adoption of the line of retreat upon Orense, rather than upon Lugo and Coruña; and he endeavoured to establish a permanent depôt

BOOK XV.

1811. Sept.

in the island of Arosa, on the Vigo coast, as a secure resource in the event of defeat; he also furnished the soldiers with shoes and great coats, the hospitals with blankets, and completed the fire-locks of the army to twenty-five thousand. There were however abuses, which he could not remedy, and which would seem rather to belong to the army of an Asiatic despot, than to an European force fighting for independence. Innumerable baggage animals devoured all the forage, and the personal servants and cooks, who from custom never did duty, were above five thousand! a sixth part of the whole force! When the sick men were deducted, scarcely sixteen thousand infantry and three squadrons of cavalry remained for service. Then there was so little organization or arrangement that, although young, robust, patient, and docile to the greatest degree, the troops could scarcely be moved, even from one quarter to another, as a military body; and the generals, unable to feed them on the frontier, more than once, menaced, and in December did actually retire to Lugo, leaving the province open to invasion.

Appendix, No. I. Section 1.

Abadia at first exerted himself with activity, and appeared to enter loyally into the ameliorations proposed. He gave the command of the troops to Portasgo, repaired to Coruña himself, and organized the province in seven military governments, under as many chiefs, one for each division of the army. Every government was to raise a reserve, and to supply and clothe the corresponding division on the frontier. But in a little time this activity relaxed; he entered into various intrigues, displayed jealousy, both of the peasantry and the English, and no real improvement took place, save in that select part of the army, which the Cadiz regency had destined for South America, and had ordered him to equip from the English stores. This was done at the very moment when a French army on the frontier was again preparing to invade Gallicia, and sir Howard Douglas vehemently opposed the disloyal proceeding; the junta also were really averse to it, and Abadia pretended to be so; but he had a personal interest in the colonies and secretly forwarded the preparations. The regency, to evade Mr. Wellesley's reproaches, promised to suspend the embarkation of these troops, but the expedition sailed from Vigo, and the organization of another, three times its strength, including all the best artillery in the province, was immediately commenced, and also sailed a few months later. This then was the state of Gallicia in the latter end of 1811. She was without magazines, hospitals, or system, whether civil or military, and torn by faction, her people were oppressed, her governors foolish, her generals bad: she had no cavalry, and the infantry were starving, although the province easily supplied cattle for the allies in Portugal. As a natural consequence, those famished soldiers were too undisciplined to descend into the plains of Leon, and were consequently of little weight in the general contest.

Under these circumstances, sir Howard Douglas had nothing to work upon, save the Guerilla leaders, whose activity he very considerably increased. His policy was to augment the number of chiefs, but to keep the force of each low, lest, growing proud of their command, they should consider themselves generals, and become useless, as indeed had already happened to Campillo, Longa, and Porlier, when

BOOK XV. 1811. Nov.

they were made a part of the seventh army. Nevertheless the advantage of this policy may be doubted, for of all the numerous bands in the north, seven only were not supported entirely by robbery. Mina, Pastor, Salazar, Pinto, Amor, and the curate, whose united forces did not exceed ten thousand men, were sustained by regular taxes, customs, convent revenues, and donations; Longa supported his from the produce of the salt-mines of Paza, but all the rest were bandits, whose extinction was one of the advantages expected from the formation of the seventh army.

Mr. Stuart's Papers. MSS.

It is now convenient to resume the narrative of military events.

In the Asturias, previous to Mendizabal's arrival, and when Bonet had marched to the Orbijo, Porlier surprised Santander, and plundered some houses; but being followed by general Caucault, a very active officer, he retired again to his stronghold of Liebana. The British cruizers, in concert with whom he acted, then destroyed several coast-batteries, and the Iris frigate having arms on board, came to the Bay of Biscay for the purpose of arranging an intercourse with the Partidas of that province. But this was the period when Reille and Caffarelli, were, as I have before noticed, chasing Mina and Longa, whom they drove from the coast, into the mountains of Leon, and thus marred the object of the Iris. Nevertheless, when Mina was reinforced by the Valencians and other fugitives from Catalonia, he returned to Navarre, and there performed very considerable exploits, which, as belonging to other combinations of the war, will be hereafter noticed.

While Caffarelli and Reille thus scoured the line

of communication, Dorsenne having the invasion of Gallicia in view, relieved Bonet on the Esla, and sent him early in November, with eight thousand men to re-occupy the Asturias as a preliminary measure. The Gallicians foreseeing this, had detached Moscoso with three thousand five hundred men to reinforce San Pol, who was at Pagares, below the passes leading from Leon; and on the other hand Mendizabal uniting the bands of Porlier and other chiefs, concentrated five thousand men to the eastward on the Xalon. Eleven thousand men were therefore ready to oppose the entrance of Bonet, but with the usual improvidence of the Spaniards, the passes of Cubillas and Ventana, to the westward of Pagares, were left unguarded. By these roads, Bonet, an excellent officer, turned Moscoso, and drove him down the Lena with loss and disgrace; then turning upon Mendizabal, he chased him also in disorder from Lanes into the Liebana.

All the civil authorities immediately fled to Castropol, the Spanish magazines fell into the hands of the French, and Bonet having resumed his old positions at Oviedo, Gihon, and Grado, fortified several posts in the passes leading to Leon, raised contributions, and effectually ruined all the military resources of the Asturias. The organization of the seventh army was thus for the time crushed, and in Gallicia great mischief ensued. For the return of Moscoso's division and the want of provisions in the Bierzo, which had obliged Abadia to retire to Lugo, while Dorsenne was menacing the frontier, had thrown that kingdom into a ferment, which was increased by the imposition of the new contributions. The people

BOOK XV. 1811. Nov.

became exceedingly exasperated and so unfavourably disposed, that it was common to hear them say, "the exactions of a French army were a relief in comparison to the depredations of the Spanish troops."

Sir H. Douglas's Correspondence, MSS.

During these transactions in the north, Drouet had joined Girard at Merida, and menaced the allies in the Alemtejo, hoping thus to draw Wellington from the Coa; but the demonstration was too feeble, and the English general thought it sufficient to reinforce Hill with his own brigade from Castello Branco. These movements were undoubtedly part of a grand plan for invading Portugal, if the emperor could have arranged his affairs peaceably with Russia. For to move once more against Lisbon, by Massena's route, was not promising, unless the northern provinces of Portugal were likewise invaded, which required the preliminary occupation of Gallicia, at least of the interior. In the south also, it was advisable to invade Alemtejo, simultaneously with Beira; and the occupation of Valencia and Murcia was necessary to protect Andalusia during the operation. The plan was vast, dangerous, and ready for execution; for though the wet season had set in, an attack on the northern parts of Portugal, and the invasion of Gallicia, were openly talked of in Dorsenne's army, Caffarelli was to join in the expedition, and Monthion's reserve, which was to replace Caffarelli's on the line of communication, was already six thousand strong. Ney or Oudinot were spoken of to command the whole, and a strong division was already in march to reinforce the army of the south, arrangements which could have reference only to Napoleon's arrival; but the Russian war soon baulked the project, and Wellington's operations, to be hereafter noticed, obliged Dorsenne to relinquish the invasion of Gallicia, and caused Bonet once more to abandon the Asturias.

CHAP. I.

1811. Nov.

Thus, with various turns of fortune, the war was managed in the northern provinces, and no great success attended the French arms, because the English general was always at hand to remedy the faults of the Spaniards. It was not so on the eastern line of invasion. There Suchet, meeting with no opponent capable of resisting him, had continued his career of victory, and the insufficiency of the Spaniards to save their own country was made manifest; but these things shall be clearly shewn in the next chapter, which will treat of the conquest of Valencia.

CHAPTER II.

CONQUEST OF VALENCIA.

BOOK XV.

1811. August.

In August, and the beginning of September, Suchet, while preparing for this great enterprise, had dispersed the bands of Villa Campa and the other chiefs, who during the siege of Taragona vexed Aragon. He had sent his feeble soldiers to France, receiving conscripts in their places, and although the harvest was very bad, formed large magazines in Morella and Tortoza. Eight thousand men had been left in Catalonia under general Frere, another eight thousand were placed under general Musnier, to protect Aragon, and twenty-four thousand of all arms remained for the invasion of Valencia, but this force Suchet thought inadequate, and demanded a reinforcement from the army of reserve, then in Navarre. Napoleon, whose system of war, whatever has been said to the contrary, was eminently methodical, refused. He loved better to try a bold push, at a distant point, with a few men, than to make an overwhelming attack, if he thereby weakened his communications; he judged courage and enterprise fittest for the attack, prudence and force for the support. And yet he designed to aid Suchet's operations vigorously when the decisive blow could be struck. Then not only the divisions of the reserve were to march, but combined movements, of detachments from nearly all the armies in the

Peninsula, were arranged; and we shall find, that if Wellington, by menacing Ciudad Rodrigo, saved Gallicia, the French army of the north, in return, by menacing Gallicia, fixed the allies on the Agueda, and so protected Suchet's invasion of Valencia.

Three roads led to the Guadalaviar, one from Tortoza by the sea-coast, one by Teruel and Segorbe, and one by Morella and San Mateo. That from Tortoza, and that by Teruel, were carriage-roads, but the first only was fit for heavy artillery, and it was blocked, partially by the fortress of Peniscola, and completed by the fort of Oropesa. Wherefore, though the infantry and cavalry could move on a bye-road to the right, the convoys and the guns, which were at Tortoza, could not pass until Oropesa was reduced. Nevertheless the French general, well knowing the value of boldness in war, resolved to mask Penisçola, to avoid Oropesa, to send his field artillery by Teruel, and uniting his troops near Saguntum, to offer battle to Blake; and if the latter declined it, to reduce Oropesa and Saguntum, trusting for subsistence to the "*huerta*" or garden of Valencia, until the arrival of his convoys.

He had, however, organized his system of supply with care. From Morella and Tortoza, brigades of mules, after the manner adopted in the British army, were to carry provisions to the troops, and sheep and cattle were delivered to each regiment for its subsistence in advance. This last plan, which sir John Moore had also projected in his campaign, Suchet found advantageous; and I am persuaded that the principle should be extended, so that all things requisite for the subsistence, and fighting of troops should

BOOK XV.

1811. Sept.

be organized regimentally, and the persons employed wear the uniform of their different corps. Jealousies between the functionaries, of different branches of the service, would then be unknown; and the character of all subordinate persons, being under the guardianship of the battalions to which they belonged, would be equally praiseworthy, which caanot now be said.

While Suchet was thus gathering his strength, Valencia was a prey to disorder. About the period of the siege of Taragona, Palacios, notwithstanding his high monarchical principles, which caused him to be dismissed from the regency, had been appointed captain-general of Valencia, Murcia, and Aragon; and he immediately raised a strong party amongst the friars and other opponents of the cortes. When after the dispersion of the Murcian army at Baza, Blake had rallied the fugitives, and in virtue of his power as regent, assumed the chief command at Valencia, Palacios' faction opposed him, and endeavoured to draw the soldiers and the populace to their side, by proposing to inundate the plain of Murviedro, and to defend the strong country in advance. Blake, however, resolved to act on the flanks of the French army by detachments, and, in this view, sent C. O'Donnel, with the divisions of Obispo and Villa Campa, to Albaracin, supporting them with four thousand men at Segorbe and Liria. He charged Mahy, who commanded five thousand infantry, and seven hundred cavalry of the Murcian army, to surprise the French detachment of the army of the centre, posted at Cuenca. He detached Bassecour with two thousand men to Requeña, and the same time, directed Duran and the Empe-

Capt. Codrington's papers, MSS.

cinado, to unite, and invade Aragon; and it was to aid in this expedition that Mina quitted the mountains of Leon.

CHAP. II.

1811. Sept.

Blake had, exclusive of Mahy's and Bassecour's divisions, about twenty thousand infantry, and two thousand cavalry. Three thousand five hundred men were placed in Saguntum, which was provisioned for three months; two hundred were in Oropesa, and fifteen hundred in Peniscola; and there were so many Partidas, that the whole country seemed to be in arms, but the assembling of these people being very uncertain, Blake could not depend upon having a permanent partizan force, of more than eight thousand. The Valencian army contained the Albuera divisions, St. Juan's, Miranda's, and Villa Campa's veterans; it was therefore, not only numerous, but the best Spain had yet produced; and Valencia itself was exceedingly rich in all things necessary for its supply: but there was no real power, the building, though fair enough outside, had the dry rot within. The French had many secret friends, faction was as usual at work, the populace were not favourable to Blake, and that general had rather collected than organized his forces, and was quite incapable of leading them. He was unpopular, both at Cadiz and Valencia, and the regency of which he formed a part was tottering. The Cortes had quashed Mahy's command of the Murcian army, and even recalled Blake himself; but the order, which did not reach him until he was engaged with Suchet, was not obeyed. Meanwhile that part of the Murcian army, which should have formed a reserve, after Mahy's division had marched for Cuenca, fell into the greatest disorder: above eight thousand men deserted in a few weeks,

Roche, MSS.

Tupper, MSS.

Mr. Wellesley, MSS.

Doyle, MSS.

Appendix, No. I. Section 3.

BOOK XV. 1811. Sept.

and those who remained were exceedingly dispirited. Thus all interest became concentrated in the city of Valencia; which was in fact the key of all the eastern coast because Carthagena required an army to defend it, and could only be fed from Valencia, and Alicant was then quite defenceless.

It was in this state of affairs, that Suchet commenced the invasion. His army was divided into three columns, and, on the 15th of September one moved by the coast-road, one by Morella and San Mateo, and one by Teruel, where an intermediate magazine was established; but this latter column instead of proceeding directly to Segorbe, turned off to its left, and passed over the Sierra de Gudar to Castellon de la Plana, where the whole three were united on the 20th. The main column, commanded by Suchet in person, had masked Peniscola on the 15th, and invested Oropesa by a detachment on the 19th; but as the road run directly under the fire of the last place, the main body moved by the rugged route of Cabanes to Villa Franca, leaving the battering-train still at Tortoza.

Suchet. Vacani.

During these operations Blake appeared inclined to fight, for he brought Zayas up in front of Murviedro, and called in Obispo; Mahy, who had done nothing on the side of Cuenca, was also in march to join him; but all these divisions marched slowly, and with confusion; and a slight skirmish at Almansora, on the Mingares, where a few French dragoons put a great body of Spanish infantry to flight, made Blake doubt the firmness of his troops. He therefore left O'Donnel with four thousand men on the side of Segorbe, and then retired himself with fifteen thousand behind the Guadalaviar. Valencia was thus thrown into great confusion, but

Roche, MSS.

Tupper, MSS.

Bassecour's division was at hand, and Suchet fearing to attack so large an army in an entrenched camp (which had cost two years to construct), while his own communication with Tortoza was intercepted, merely dispersed the armed peasants which had assembled on his flank, and then turned against Murviedro.

SIEGE OF SAGUNTUM.

This celebrated place, situated about four leagues from Valencia, was a rocky mountain, covered with the ruins of the ancient city, and the remains of Moorish towers and walls, which being connected by modern works, formed four distinct posts covering the whole summit of the rock: but in consequence of the usual Spanish procrastination the heavy guns prepared to arm it were not yet mounted, and only seventeen pieces of inferior size were available for defence. The modern town of Murviedro, situated at the foot of the rock, was covered by the river Palancia, and by a canal, and occupied by some Spanish picquets; but the 23d Habert, having passed the water, invested the rock on the east, while Harispe invested it on the west and south, and a third division drove the Spanish posts from Murviedro and entrenched itself in the houses. The rest of the army was disposed in villages, on the hills to the north west, and patroles were pushed towards Valencia. Thus the rock of Saguntum was invested, but it was inaccessible to the engineer, save on the west, where the ascent, although practicable, was very rough and difficult. It would have been impregnable, if the Spaniards had mounted their large guns; for the French were

BOOK XV. 1811. Sept.

obliged to bring earth from a distance, to form the batteries and parallels, and to set the miner to level the approaches, and their parapets were too thin to withstand heavy shot.

The first point of resistance was an ancient tower called San Pedro, and immediately above it was the fort of San Fernando, which could not be attacked until San Pedro fell, and, from its height, then only by the miner. But near the eastern extremity of the rock, there were two ancient breaches which the Spaniards were still engaged repairing, and had only stopped with timber; a large tank offered cover for the assembling of troops close to these breaches, and Suchet resolved to try an escalade. To effect this, three columns were assembled before daybreak on the 28th in the tank, a strong reserve was held in support, and a false attack was directed against the San Pedro to distract the attention of the besieged: but in the previous part of the night, the Spaniards having sallied were repulsed, and the action having excited both sides. a French soldier fired from the tank before the appointed time, whereupon the columns rushing forward, in disorder, planted their ladders, and the garrison would have carried the place by noise, but the garrison thrust the ladders from the walls, and drove the stormers back, with the loss of three hundred men. After this check, as the artillery was still at Tortoza, Suchet ordered a part of his army to attack Oropesa, employed another part in making a road, for the guns, to reach the battery raised against the tower of San Pedro, and then turned his own attention to the movements of Blake.

That general following his first plan of action against the French flanks, had during the investment of Saguntum, sent C. O'Donnel with Villa Campa's division and St. Juan's cavalry, to Betera, and Beneguazil, and Obispo's division to Segorbe; thus forming a half circle round the French army, and cutting its communication with Teruel, near which place Mahy had by this time arrived. Suchet however caused Palombini to attack Obispo, whose whole division dispersed after a skirmish with the advanced guard, and the Italians then returned to the siege. The next night Harispe marched against O'Donnel, who was well posted at Beneguazil behind a canal, having his centre protected by a chapel and some houses; nevertheless the Spaniards were beaten with loss at the first shock, and fled in disorder over the Guadalaviar. During these events Blake remained an idle spectator of the defeat of his division, although he had a large body of troops in hand, and was within a few miles of the field of battle.

The French train now advanced from Tortoza, and four pieces were placed in battery against Oropesa. On the 10th Suchet took the direction of the attack in person, and the fort situated upon an isolated rock, was breached in a few hours; but the garrison of the King's Tower (a separate work placed on a small promontory, and commanding the harbour) refused to surrender, and was carried off, on the 11th, under the French fire, by the Magnificent. The French general having thus with a loss of only thirty men opened the road for his artillery, returned to Saguntum and pushed the siege of that place; but the difficulties were very great, the formation of the road to the batteries was itself a work of pain, and although his indefatigable troops had formed a breaching battery on

BOOK XV. 1811. October.

the 12th, while seven small mortars and howitzers, placed on the right and left, had nearly silenced the Spanish fire, the muskets of the besiegers alone brought down from fifteen to twenty men.

On the 17th the breaching battery being armed, opened its fire against the tower, and the new masonry crumbled away at once; yet the ancient work resisted the guns like a rock. On the 18th the fire recommenced, when the wall gave way to the stroke of the guns, and the assault was ordered; but from the height of the tower, which overlooked the works at a short distance, the preparations were early discovered, the Spaniards collecting on the breach repaired it with sand-bags, and regardless of the French fire, with loud cries provoked the attack. At five o'clock, four hundred men rushed forward as swiftly as the steepness of the ascent would permit. Soon, however, the head of the column was checked, the rear began to fire, the whole got into confusion, and when one-half had fallen without making the slightest impression on the defenders, the attempt was abandoned. After this signal failure the French erected a second battery of six pieces, one hundred and forty yards from the tower, and endeavoured to push the approach close to the foot of the breach, yet the plunging fire of the besieged baffled them; meanwhile Andriani the governor, having communication by signal with the ships in the Grao, was encouraged to continue his gallant defence, and was informed that he was already promoted for what he had done. But to understand Suchet's embarrassments, from the protracted resistance of Saguntum, we must take a view of Lacy's contemporary operations in Catalonia, and the proceedings of the Partidas against the French communications and posts in Aragon. CHAP. II. 1811. October.

CATALONIA.

It will be recollected that the blockade of Figueiras produced sickness in M'Donald's army, and that the return of Suchet to Aragon, and the parcelling of his troops on the lines, from Lerida to Montserrat, Tortoza, and Taragona, had completely extinguished the French power in the field; because the divisions of the army of Aragon which still remained in Lower Catalonia, being destined for the enterprize against Valencia, could not be employed in harassing expeditions. Lacy was therefore enabled, notwithstanding the troubles which followed the fall of Taragona, to reorganize about eight thousand men in two divisions, the one under Eroles, the other under Sarsfield; the junta also called out the tercios of reserve, and arms and ammunition being supplied by the English navy, Lacy was soon in a condition to act offensively. Thus the taking of Montserrat was very injurious to the French, for it is generally supposed that Friere's division, if held together in the field, would have prevented this reaction in the principality. Lacy at first suggested to the British navy the recapture of the Medas Islands, and it was effected in the latter end of August, by the Undaunted, Lavinia, and Blossom, aided by a small party of Spaniards, the whole under the command of captain Thomas. The enterprise itself was one of more labour than danger, and the Spanish allies were of little use, but the naval officers to whose exer- August.

BOOK XV. 1811. August. Appendix, No. II. Section 2.

tions the success was entirely due, were indignant at finding that colonel Green, who served as a volunteer, endeavoured to raise his own reputation with the Catalans by injuring the character of those under whom he served.

Memoir upon Busa, by Capt. Zeupfinning, MSS.

Immediately after the fall of Montserrat, Lacy and the junta had proposed the fortifying of Palamos or Blanes, to be held as a marine depôt and strong-hold, in common with the British navy, but with a strange folly expected that sir E. Pellew, who had no troops, would defend them from the enemy while establishing this post. Finding this scheme received coldly by the admiral, they turned their attention inland, and blowing up the works of Berga, fixed upon the position of Busa, as a place of strength and refuge. This remarkable rock which is situated between the Cardener and Bindasaes rivers and about twenty miles from Cardona could be reached by one road only, and that a very rugged one. The rock itself fourteen miles in circumference, healthy and full of springs, is fertile, and produces abundance of forage, and fuel. It is cut off from the rest of the world by frightful precipices, and could neither be forced, nor starved into a surrender. Busa, Cardona, Solsona, and Seu d'Urgel were therefore guarded by the tercios of reserve and Lacy soon commenced offensive excursions with the regular army, against the long lines of the French communication.

In September while the Somatenes interrupted the passage of the convoys to Montserrat, Eroles made an unsuccessful attack on the fort of Moncada near Barcelona; Lacy who had returned from an incursion in the French Cerdaña where he had gathered some booty, then united Eroles and Sarsfield's troops, and surprised the town of Igualada, where he killed two hundred French, but not daring to attack the castle retired to Calaf, and from thence again detached Eroles to Jorbas, to attack a French convoy coming to Igualada. Eroles beat the escort, and captured the convoy, and then the French quitted the fortified convent of Igualada, and joined the garrison of Montserrat, when the whole, fearful of being invested and so starved, abandoned that important point, and marched through Barcelona to Taragona; the Spaniards immediately occupied Montserrat, and recovered a large store of clothing and cavalry equipments, which had been hidden in a vault and were undiscovered by the enemy. Eroles, pursuing his success, forced the garrisons of Belpuig, and Cervera, about five hundred in all, to surrender, and thus the whole line of communication, between Lerida and Barcelona, fell into the power of the Catalonians. The confidence of the people then revived; Sarsfield occupied Granollers, and the passes leading into the valley of Vich; Manso and Rovira menaced the Ampurdan; and Eroles suddenly passing by Seu d'Urgel into the Cerdaña, defeated, at Puigcerda, some national guards commanded by general Gareau, who had been sent there after Lacy's invasion. He afterwards raised large contributions on the frontier, burnt a French town, and returning with his spoil by the way of Ribas, and Ripol, took post in the pass of Garriga, while Milans occupied Mataro, and both watched to intercept a convoy which M'Donald was preparing for Barcelona.

Sarsfield at the same time embarked his division and sailed to the coast of the Ampurdan, but the weather would not permit him to land. Nevertheless the attention of the French general was distracted, and the convoy did not move. Lacy then recalled Sarsfield, and projected the surprise of Barcelona itself, but after putting his troops in march, feared the execution and relinquished the attempt. Meanwhile one swarm of the smaller Partidas menaced the French communication between Mequinenza and Tortoza, and another swarm settled on the plains about Lerida.

The state of Aragon was equally alarming. Duran and the Empecinado had received Blake's orders to unite near Cuença, for the purpose of invading Aragon; but the secret junta of the district were averse to the plan, and the troops of the latter chief refused to move, and even came to blows with the junta's people. In this confusion general d'Armanac, who had retired from Cuença, returned, and dispersed the whole. The Empecinado however collected them again, and having joined Duran, their united powers being about six thousand infantry and two thousand five hundred horse, moved against Calatayud; Mina also acting in concert with them, quitted the mountains of Leon and entered Navarre with about five thousand men, and some minor partisans were already acting against different parts of Aragon. The whole were in want of clothing and ammunition, but Mr. Tupper, the consul at Valencia, having safe means of communication with the interior supplied them.

General Musnier's force was so scattered that he could not fight either of the large Partidas, without exposing some important point to the other, and the 29th of September the Empecinado took possession of the pass of Frasno, while Duran invested the fortified convent of Calatayud. This place was garrisoned by some French and Italian troops, who differed upon the defence, and when the explosion of two mines had killed a number of them they surrendered. Musnier collected some men to succour the place, but unable to force the pass of Frasno, retired; yet being reinforced on the 5th, he again advanced, and a column sent from Navarre by general Reille also came up; whereupon the Spaniards disappeared until the French retired, and then reoccupied Calatayud. They were now in full communication with Mina and a general plan of invasion was discussed, but as Duran and Mina could not accord each acted separately.

Severoli's division eight thousand strong and just arrived from Italy, then reinforced Musnier, and on the 9th driving the Spaniards from Calatayud pursued them on the roads to Molino, Daroca, and Medinaceli. On the other side of the Ebro however Mina fell on the post of Exca in the Cinco Villas; the garrison broke through his investment in the night, but he pursued them almost to the gates of Zaragosa, and then turning off towards Ayerbe, attacked that post and menaced the communication by Jaca. The commandant of Zaragosa had sent an Italian battalion to look after the flying garrison of Exca, which was found at Zuera, and the united forces amounting to eleven hundred infantry and sixty cavalry followed Mina and came up with him at Ayerbe; the guerilla chief instantly turned with a part of his troops, and the Italians retreated towards Huesca, but having to cross a plain were all killed or taken.

Reille and Musnier hearing of this misfortune spread their columns in all directions to intercept Mina, but he evaded their toils, and although

BOOK XV.

1811. October.

sharply chased and several times engaged, reached Motrico on the Biscay coast with his prisoners. The Iris frigate which was then harassing the enemy's coast line took some of them off his hands, and the remainder, three hundred in number, were sent to Corunna by the Asturian mountains, but only thirty-six arrived, the rest were shot by the escort, under pretence that they made a noise near a French post!

While these events were passing on the left of the Ebro, Mazzuchelli's brigade followed the Empecinado, and having defeated him in a sharp action, at Cubiliejos de la Sierra, brought off the garrison of Molino and dismantled that fort; but the smaller Partidas infested the road between Tortoza and Oropesa, and in this disturbed state of affairs reports were rife that an English force was to disembark at Peniscola. Blake also sent Obispo's division against Teruel, which was thus menaced on all sides, for Mahy was still in those parts. Thus the partizan warfare seemed interminable, and Suchet's situation would really have been very dangerous, if he had been opposed by a man of ability. He had an inferior force and was cooped up between the enemy's fortresses; his communications were all interrupted; he had just met with two signal failures at Saguntum, and he was menaced by a formidable army which was entirely master of its operations. Blake however soon relieved him of his difficulties.

Palacios with the junta had retired to Alcira, and in concert with the friars of his faction had issued a manifesto, intended to raise a popular commotion to favour his own restoration to the command, but Blake was now become popular;

the Valencians elated by the successful resistance of Saguntum, called for a battle, and the Spanish general urged partly by his courage, the only military qualification he possessed, partly that he found his operations on the French rear had not disturbed the siege, acceded to their desire. Mahy and Bassecour's divisions had arrived at Valencia, Obispo was called in to Betera, eight thousand irregulars were thrown upon the French communications, and the whole Spanish army amounting to about twenty-two thousand infantry, two thousand good cavalry, and thirty-six guns made ready for battle.

Previous to this, Suchet, although expecting such an event, had detached several parties to scour the road of Tortoza, and had directed Palombini's division to attack Obispo and relieve Teruel. Obispo skirmished at Xerica on the 21st, and then rapidly marched upon Liria with a view to assist in the approaching battle; but Blake, who might have attacked while Palombini was absent, took little heed of the opportunity, and Suchet, now aware of his adversary's object, instantly recalled the Italians who arrived the very morning of the action.

The ground between Murviedro and Valencia was a low flat, interspersed here and there with rugged isolated hills; it was also intersected by ravines, torrents, and water-cuts, and thickly studded with olive-trees; but near Saguntum it became straitened by the mountain and the sea, so as to leave an opening of not more than three miles, behind which it again spread out. In this narrow part Suchet resolved to receive the attack, without relinquishing the siege of Saguntum; and he left a strong detachment in the trenches with orders to open the

BOOK XV.

1811. October.

fire of a new battery, the moment the Spanish army appeared.

His left, consisting of Habert's division, and some squadrons of dragoons, was refused, to avoid the fire of some vessels of war and gun-boats which flanked Blake's march. The centre under Harispe, was extended to the foot of the mountains, so that he offered an oblique front, crossing the main road from Valencia to Murviedro. Palombini's division and the dragoons, were placed in second line behind the centre, and behind them the cuirassiers were held in reserve.

This narrow front was favourable for an action in the plain, but the right flank of the French, and the troops left to carry on the siege, were liable to be turned by the pass of Espiritus, through which, the roads from Betera led to Gilet, directly upon the line of retreat. To prevent such an attempt Suchet posted Chlopiski with a strong detachment of infantry and the Italian dragoons in the pass, and placed the Neapolitan brigade of reserve at Gilet: in this situation, although his fighting troops did not exceed seventeen thousand men, and those cooped up between two fortresses, hemmed in by the mountain on one side, the sea on the other, and with only one narrow line of retreat, the French general did not hesitate to engage a very numerous army. He trusted to his superiority in moral resources, and what would have been madness in other circumstances, was here a proof of skilful daring.

Blake having issued a fine address to his soldiers on the 25th of October advanced to fight. His right wing under Zayas, composed of the Albuera divisions, marched by a road leading upon the village of Puzzol; and Blake followed in person, with a weak reserve, commanded by general Velasco.

The centre under Lardizabal supported by the cavalry of Loy and Caro, moved by the main road.

The left consisting of Miranda's, and Villa Campa's infantry, and of St. Juan's cavalry, and supported by Mahy's division which came from the side of Betera moved against the defile of Espiritus. Obispo, also coming from Betera, acted as a flanking corps, and entering the mountains by Naquera, menaced the right of Chlopiski, but he was met by a brigade under general Robert.

The Spaniards moved on rapidly and in good order, driving the French outposts over a ravine called the Piccador, which covered Suchet's front. Zayas and Lardizabal immediately passed this obstacle as did also Caro and Loy, and the first took possession of Puzzol while the flotilla ranged along the coast and protected his right flank. Blake with Velasco's reserve halted at El Puig, an isolated hill on the sea-coast behind the Piccador, but Lardizabal and the cavalry forming an oblique line, in order to face the French front, occupied the ground between Puzzol and the Piccador. Thus the Spanish order of battle was cut in two by the ravine, for on the hither side of it St. Juan, Miranda, and Villa Campa were drawn up, and Mahy took possession of a height called the Germanels, which was opposite the mouth of St. Espiritus.

By this disposition the Spanish line, extending from Puzzol to the Germanels, was not less than six miles, and the division of Obispo was separated from the left by about the same distance. Blake's order of battle was therefore feeble, and he

BOOK XV. 1811. October. was without any efficient reserve, for Velasco was distant and weak and Mahy's was actually in the line. The French order of battle covering less than three miles was compressed and strong, the reserves were well placed and close at hand; and Chlopiski's division, although a league distant from the main body, was firmly posted, and able to take a direct part in the battle, while the interval between him and Suchet was closed by impassable heights.

BATTLE OF SAGUNTUM.

The fight was commenced by Villa Campa, who was advancing against the pass of Espiritus, when the Italian dragoons galloping out overthrew his advanced guard, and put his division into confusion. Chlopiski seeing this, moved down with the infantry, drove Mahy from the Germanels, and then detached a regiment to the succour of the centre, where a brisk battle was going on, to the disadvantage of Suchet.

That general had not judged his ground well at first, and when the Spaniards had crossed the Piccador, he too late perceived that an isolated height in advance of Harispe's division, could command all that part of the field. Prompt however to remedy his error, he ordered the infantry to advance, and galloped forward himself with an escort of hussars to seize the hill; the enemy was already in possession, and their guns opened from the summit, but the head of Harispe's infantry then attacked, and after a sharp fight, in which general Paris and several superior officers were wounded, gained the height.

Vol. 4 Plate 4.

Explanatory Sketch
OF THE SIEGE & BATTLE OF
SAGUNTUM,
1811.

London: Published by T. & W. BOONE.

1811. October.

At this time Obispo's guns were heard on the hills far to the right, and Zayas passing through Puzzol endeavoured to turn the French left, and as the day was fine, and the field of battle distinctly seen by the soldiers in Saguntum, they crowded on the ramparts, regardless of the besiegers' fire, and uttering loud cries of Victory! Victory! by their gestures seemed to encourage their countrymen to press forward. The critical moment of the battle was evidently approaching. Suchet ordered Palombini's Italians, and the dragoons, to support Harispe, and although wounded himself galloped to the cuirassiers and brought them into action. Meanwhile the French hussars had pursued the Spaniards from the height to the Piccador, where however the latter rallied upon their second line and again advanced; and it was in vain that the French artillery poured grape-shot into their ranks, their march was not checked. Loy and Caro's horsemen overthrew the French hussars in a moment, and in the same charge sabred the French gunners and captured their battery. The crisis would have been fatal, if Harispe's infantry had not stood firm while Palombini's division marching on the left under cover of a small rise of ground, suddenly opened a fire upon the flank of the Spanish cavalry, which was still in pursuit of the hussars. These last immediately turned, and the Spaniards thus placed between two fires, and thinking the flight of the hussars had been feigned, to draw them into an ambuscade, hesitated; the next moment a tremendous charge of the cuirassiers put every thing into confusion. Caro was wounded and taken, Loy fled with the remainder of the cavalry over the Piccador, the French guns were recovered, the Spanish artillery was taken, and Lardizabal's infantry being quite broken, laid down their arms, or throwing them away, saved themselves as they could. Harispe's division immediately joined Chlopiski's, and both together pursued the beaten troops.

This great, and nearly simultaneous success in the centre, and on the right, having cut the Spanish line in two, Zaya's position became exceedingly dangerous. Suchet was on his flank, Habert advancing against his front, and Blake had no reserve in hand to restore the battle, for the few troops and guns under Velasco, remained inactive at El Puig. However such had been the vigour of the action in the centre, and so inferior were Suchet's numbers, that it required two hours to secure his prisoners and to rally Palombini's division for another effort. Meanwhile Zayas, whose left flank was covered in some measure by the water-cuts, fought stoutly, maintained the village of Puzzol for a long time, and when finally driven out, although he was charged several times, by some squadrons attached to Habert's division, effected his retreat across the Piccador, and gained El Puig. Suchet had however re-formed his troops, and Zayas now attacked in front and flank, fled along the sea-coast to the Grao of Valencia, leaving his artillery and eight hundred prisoners.

During this time, Chlopiski and Harispe, had pursued Mahy, Miranda, Villa Campa, and Lardizabal, as far as the torrent of Caraixet, where many prisoners were made; but the rest being joined by Obispo, rallied behind the torrent, and the French cavalry having outstripped their infantry, were unable to prevent the Spaniards from reaching the line of the Guadalaviar. The victors had about a thousand killed and wounded, and the Spaniards had not more, but two generals, five thousand prisoners, and twelve guns were taken; and Blake's inability to oppose Suchet in the field, being made manifest by this battle, the troops engaged were totally dispirited, and the effect reached even to Saguntum, for the garrison surrendered that night.

OBSERVATIONS.

1°. In this campaign the main object on both sides was Valencia. That city could not be invested until Saguntum was taken, and the Spanish army defeated; hence to protect Saguntum without endangering his army, was the problem for Blake to solve, and it was not very difficult. He had at least twenty-five thousand troops, besides the garrisons of Peniscola, Oropesa, and Segorbe, and he could either command or influence the movements of nearly twenty thousand irregulars; his line of operations was direct, and secure, and he had a fleet to assist him, and several secure harbours. On the other hand the French general could not bring twenty thousand men into action, and his line of operation, which was long, and difficult, was intercepted by the Spanish fortresses. It was for Blake therefore to choose the nature of his defence: he could fight, or he could protract the war.

2°. If he had resolved to fight, he should have taken post at Castellon de la Plana, keeping a corps of observation at Segorbe, and strong detachments towards Villa Franca, and Cabanes, holding his

BOOK XV. 1811.

army in readiness to fall on the heads of Suchet's columns, as they came out of the mountains. But experience had, or should have, taught Blake, that a battle in the open field between the French and Spanish troops, whatever might be the apparent advantage, was uncertain; and this last and best army of the country ought not to have been risked. He should therefore have resolved upon protracting the war, and have merely held that position to check the heads of the French columns, without engaging in a pitched battle.

3°. From Castellon de la Plana and Segorbe, the army might have been withdrawn, and concentrated at Murviedro, in one march, and Blake should have prepared an intrenched camp in the hills close to Saguntum, placing a corps of observation in the plain behind that fortress. These hills were rugged, very difficult of access, and the numerous water-cuts and the power of forming inundations in the place, were so favourable for defence, that it would have been nearly impossible for the French to have dislodged him; nor could they have invested Saguntum while he remained in this camp.

4°. In such a strong position, with his retreat secure upon the Guadalaviar, the Spanish general would have covered the fertile plains from the French foragers, and would have held their army at bay while the irregulars operated upon their communication. He might then have safely detached a division to his left, to assist the Partidas, or to his right, by sea, to land at Peniscola. His forces would soon have been increased and the invasion would have been frustrated.

5°. Instead of following this simple principle of defensive warfare consecrated since the days of

Fabius, Blake abandoned Saguntum, and from behind the Guadalaviar, sent unconnected detachments on a half circle round the French army, which being concentrated, and nearer to each detachment than the latter was to its own base at Valencia, could and did, as we have seen, defeat them all in detail.

6°. Blake, like all the Spanish generals, indulged vast military conceptions far beyond his means, and, from want of knowledge, generally in violation of strategic principles. Thus his project of cutting the communication with Madrid, invading Aragon, and connecting Mina's operations between Zaragoza and the Pyrenees, with Lacy's in Catalonia, was gigantic in design, but without any chance of success. The division of Severoli being added to Musnier's, had secured Aragon; and if it had not been so, the reinforcements then marching through Navarre, to different parts of Spain, rendered the time chosen for these attempts peculiarly unfavourable. But the chief objection was, that Blake had lost the favourable occasion of protracting the war about Saguntum; and the operations against Valencia, were sure to be brought to a crisis, before the affair of Aragon could have been sufficiently embarrassing, to recal the French general. The true way of using the large guerilla forces, was to bring them down close upon the rear of Suchet's army, especially on the side of Teruel, where he had magazines; which could have been done safely, because these Partidas had an open retreat, and if followed would have effected their object, of weakening and distressing the army before Valencia. This would have been quite a different operation from that which Blake adopted, when he posted

BOOK XV. 1811.

Obispo and O'Donnel at Benaguazil and Segorbe; because those generals' lines of operations, springing from the Guadalaviar, were within the power of the French; and this error alone proves that Blake was entirely ignorant of the principles of strategy.

7°. Urged by the cries of the Valencian population, the Spanish general delivered the battle of the 25th, which was another great error, and an error exaggerated by the mode of execution. He who had so much experience, who had now commanded in four or five pitched battles, was still so ignorant of his art, that with twice as many men as his adversary, and with the choice of time and place, he made three simultaneous attacks, on an extended front, without any connection or support; and he had no reserves to restore the fight or to cover his retreat. A wide sweep of the net without regard to the strength or fierceness of his prey, was Blake's only notion, and the result was his own destruction.

8°. Suchet's operations, especially his advance against Saguntum, leaving Oropesa behind him, were able and rapid. He saw the errors of his adversary, and made them fatal. To fight in front of Saguntum was no fault; the French general acted with a just confidence in his own genius, and the valour of his troops. He gained that fortress by the battle, but he acknowledged that such were the difficulties of the siege, the place could only have been taken by a blockade, which would have required two months.

CHAPTER III.

CHAP. III. 1811. Nov.

SAGUNTUM having fallen, Suchet conceived the plan of enclosing and capturing the whole of Blake's force, together with the city of Valencia, round which it was encamped; and he was not deterred from this project by the desultory operations of the Partidas in Aragon, nor by the state of Catalonia. Blake however, reverting to his former system, called up to Valencia, all the garrisons and depôts of Murcia, and directed the conde de Montijo, who had been expelled by Soult from Grenada, to join Duran. He likewise ordered Freire to move upon Cuença, with the Murcian army, to support Montijo, Duran, and the Partida chiefs, who remained near Aragon after the defeat of the Empecinado. But the innumerable small bands, or rather armed peasants, immediately about Valencia, he made no use of, neither harassing the French nor in any manner accustoming these people to action.

In Aragon his affairs turned out ill. Mazuchelli entirely defeated Duran in a hard fight, near Almunia, on the 7th of November; on the 23d Campillo was defeated at Añadon, and a Partida having appeared at Peñarova, near Morella, the people rose against it. Finally Napoleon, seeing that the contest in Valencia was coming to a crisis, ordered general Reille to reinforce Suchet not only with Severoli's Italians, but with his own French division, in all fifteen thousand good troops.

BOOK XV. 1811. Nov.

Meanwhile in Catalonia Lacy's activity had greatly diminished. He had, including the Tercios, above sixteen thousand troops, of which about twelve thousand were armed, and in conjunction with the junta he had classed the whole population in reserves; but he was jealous of the people, who were generally of the church party, and, as he had before done in the Ronda, deprived them of their arms, although they had purchased them, in obedience to his own proclamation. He also discountenanced as much as possible the popular insurrection, and he was not without plausible reasons for this, although he could not justify the faithless and oppressive mode of execution.

He complained that the Somatenes always lost their arms and ammunition, that they were turbulent, expensive, and bad soldiers, and that his object was to incorporate them by just degrees with the regular army, where they could be of service; but then he made no good use of the latter himself, and hence he impeded the irregulars without helping the regular warfare. His conduct disgusted the Catalonians. That people had always possessed a certain freedom and loved it; but they had been treated despotically and unjustly, by all the different commanders who had been placed at their head, since the commencement of the war; and now finding, that Lacy was even worse than his predecessors, their ardour sensibly diminished; many went over to the French, and this feeling of discouragement was increased by some unfortunate events.

Henriod governor of Lerida had on the 25th of October surprised and destroyed, in Balaguer, a swarm of Partidas which had settled on the plain of Urgel, and the Partizans on the left bank of the Ebro had been defeated by the escort of one of the convoys. The French also entrenched a post before the Medas Islands, in November, which prevented all communication by land, and in the same month Maurice Mathieu surprised Mattaro. The war had also now fatigued so many persons, that several towns were ready to receive the enemy as friends. Villa Nueva de Sitjes and other places were in constant communication with Barcelona; and the people of Cadaques openly refused to pay their contributions to Lacy, declaring that they had already paid the French and meant to side with the strongest. One Guinart, a member of the junta, was detected corresponding with the enemy; counter guerillas, or rather freebooting bands, made their appearance near Berga; privateers of all nations infested the coast, and these pirates of the ocean, the disgrace of civilized warfare, generally agreed not to molest each other, but robbed all defenceless flags without distinction. Then the continued bickerings between Sarsfield, Eroles, and Milans, and of all three with Lacy, who was, besides, on bad terms with captain Codrington, greatly affected the patriotic ardour of the people, and relieved the French armies from the alarm which the first operations had created.

Appendix, No. I. Section 3.

In Catalonia the generals in chief were never natives, nor identified in feeling with the natives. Lacy was unfitted for open warfare, and had recourse to the infamous methods of assassination. Campo Verde had given some countenance to this horrible system, but Lacy and his coadjutors have been accused of instigating the murder of French officers in their quarters, the poisoning of wells,

BOOK XV. 1811. Nov.

the drugging of wines and flour, and the firing of powder-magazines, regardless of the safety even of the Spaniards who might be within reach of the explosion; and if any man shall doubt the truth of this allegation, let him read "*The History of the Conspiracies against the French Armies in Catalonia.*" That work, printed in 1813 at Barcelona, contains the official reports of the military police, upon the different attempts, many successful, to destroy the French troops; and when due allowance for an enemy's tale and for the habitual falsifications of police agents is made, ample proof will remain that Lacy's warfare was one of assassination.

The facility which the great size of Barcelona afforded for these attempts, together with its continual cravings and large garrison, induced Napoleon to think of dismantling the walls of the city, preserving only the forts. This simple military precaution has been noted by some writers as an indication that he even then secretly despaired of final success in the Peninsula; but the weakness of this remark will appear evident, if we consider, that he had just augmented his immense army, that his generals were invading Valencia, and menacing Gallicia, after having relieved Badajos and Ciudad Rodrigo; and that he was himself preparing to lead four hundred thousand men to the most distant extremity of Europe. However the place was not dismantled, and Maurice Mathieu contrived both to maintain the city in obedience and to take an important part in the field operations.

It was under these circumstances that Suchet advanced to the Guadalaviar, although his losses and the escorts for his numerous prisoners had diminished his force to eighteen thousand men while Blake's army including Freire's division was above twenty-five thousand, of which near three thousand were cavalry. He first summoned the city, to ascertain the public spirit; he was answered in lofty terms, yet he knew by his secret communications, that the enthusiasm of the people was not very strong; and on the 3d of November he seized the Grao, and the suburb of Serranos on the left of the Guadalaviar. Blake had broken two, out of five, stone bridges on the river, had occupied some houses and convents which covered them on the left bank, and protected those bridges, which remained whole, with regular works. Suchet immediately carried the convents which covered the broken bridges in the Serranos, and fortified his position there and at the Grao, and thus blocked the Spaniards on that side with a small force, while he prepared to pass the river higher up with the remainder of his army.

The Spanish defences on the right bank consisted of three posts.

1°. The city itself which was surrounded by a circular wall thirty feet in height, and ten in thickness with a road along the summit, the platforms of the bastions being supported from within by timber scaffolding. There was also a wet ditch and a covered way with earthen works in front of the gates.

2°. An intrenched camp of an irregular form five miles in extent. It enclosed the city and the three suburbs of Quarte, San Vincente, and Ruzafa. The slope of this work was so steep as to require scaling ladders, and there was a ditch in front twelve feet deep.

BOOK XV. 1811. Nov.

3°. The lines, which extended along the banks of the river to the sea at one side, and to the villages of Quarte and Manisses on the other.

The whole line, including the city and camp, was about eight miles; the ground was broken with deep and wide canals of irrigation, which branched off from the river just above the village of Quarte, and the Spanish cavalry was posted at Aldaya behind the left wing to observe the open country. Suchet could not venture to force the passage of the river until Reille had joined him, and therefore contented himself with sending parties over to skirmish, while he increased his secret communications in the city, and employed detachments to scour the country in his rear. In this manner, nearly two months passed; the French waited for reinforcements, and Blake hoped that while he thus occupied his enemy a general insurrection would save Valencia. But in December, Reille, having given over the charge of Navarre and Aragon to general Caffarelli, marched to Teruel where Severoli with his Italians had already arrived.

The vicinity of Freire, and Montijo, who now appeared near Cuenca, obliged Reille to halt at Teruel until general D'Armañac with a detachment of the army of the centre, had driven those Spanish generals away, but then he advanced to Segorbe, and as Freire did not rejoin Blake, and as the latter was ignorant of Reille's arrival, Suchet resolved to force the passage of the Guadalaviar instantly.

On the 25th, the Neapolitan division being placed in the camp at the Serranos, to hold the Spaniards in check, Habert took post at the Grao, and Palombini's division was placed opposite the

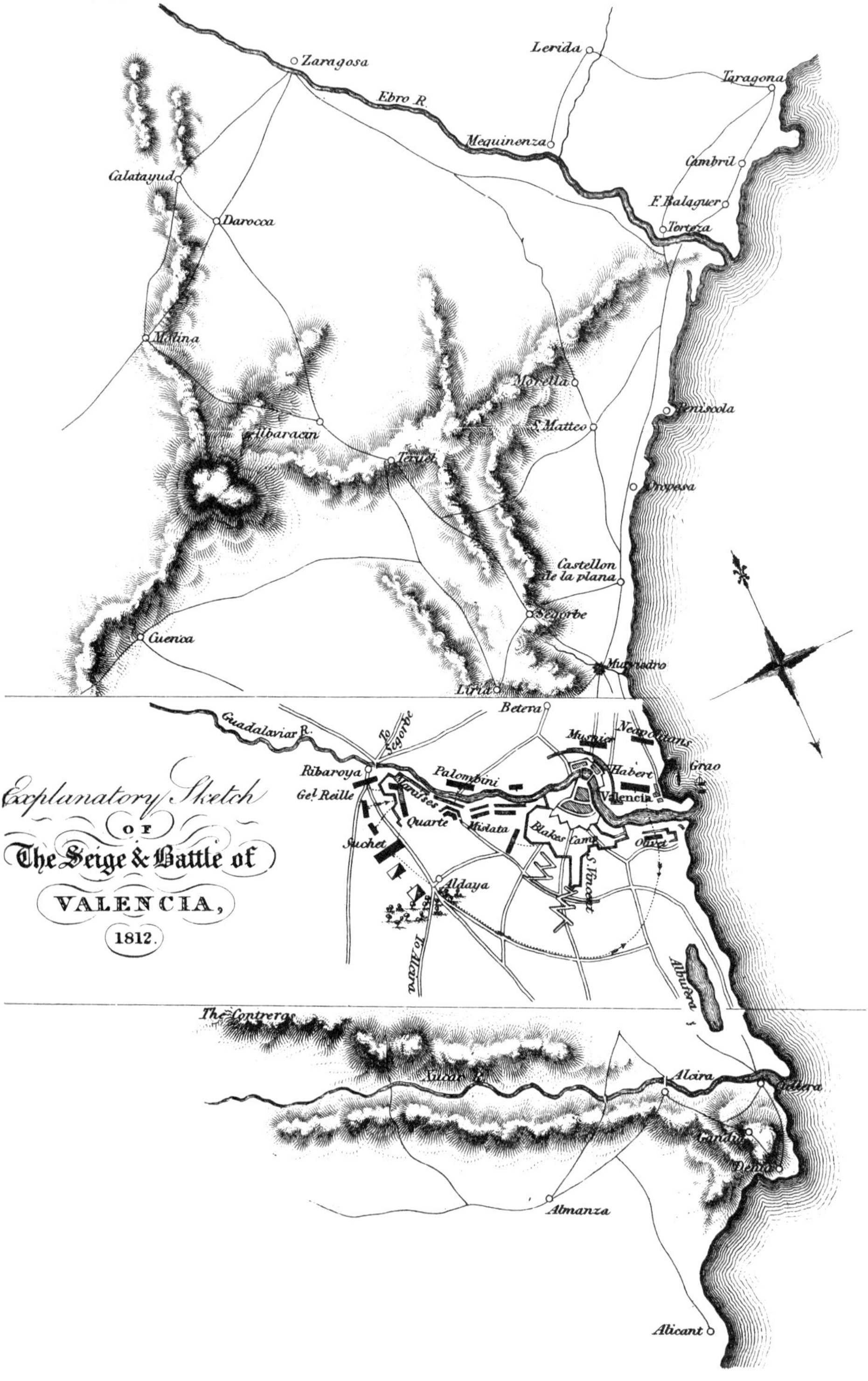

London. Published by T. & W. BOONE.

village of Mislata, which was about half way between Valencia and the village of Quarte. Reille at the same time made a forced march by Liria and Benaguazil, and three bridges being thrown in the night, above the sources of the canals, opposite Ribaroya, the rest of the army crossed the Guadalaviar with all diligence on the 26th and formed in order of battle on the other side. It was then eight o'clock and Reille had not arrived, but Suchet, whose plan was to drive all Blake's army within the entrenched camp, fearing that the Spanish general, would evade the danger, if he saw the French divisions in march, resolved to push at once with Harispe's infantry and the cavalry to the Albufera or salt-lake, beyond Valencia, and so cut off Blake's retreat to the Xucar river. Robert's brigade therefore halted to secure the bridges, until Reille should come up, and while the troops, left on the other bank of the Guadalaviar, attacked all the Spanish river line of entrenchments, Suchet marched towards the lake as rapidly as the thick woods would permit.

The French hussars soon fell in with the Spanish cavalry at Aldaya and were defeated, but this charge was stopped by the fire of the infantry, and the remainder of the French horsemen coming up overthrew the Spaniards. During this time Blake instead of falling on Suchet with his reserve, was occupied with the defence of the river, especially at the village of Mislata, where a false attack, to cover the passage at Ribaroya, had first given him the alarm. Palombini, who was at this point, had passed over some skirmishers and then throwing two bridges, attacked the entrenchments; but his troops were repulsed by Zayas, and driven back on the

BOOK XV.

1811. Dec.

river in disorder; they rallied and had effected the passage of the canals, when a Spanish reserve coming up restored the fight, and the French were finally driven quite over the river. At that moment Reille's division, save one brigade which could not arrive in time, crossed at Ribaroya, and in concert with Robert, attacked Mahy in the villages of Manisses and Quarte, which had been fortified carefully in front, but were quite neglected on the rear, and on the side of Aldaya. Suchet who had been somewhat delayed at Aldaya by the aspect of affairs at Mislata, then continued his march to the lake, while Reille meeting with a feeble resistance at Manisses and Quarte, carried both at one sweep, and turned Mislata where he united with Palombini. Blake and Zayas retired towards the city but Mahy driven from Quarte took the road to Alcira, on the Xucar, and thus passing behind Suchet's division, was entirely cut off from Valencia.

All the Spanish army, on the upper Guadalaviar, was now entirely beaten with the loss of its artillery and baggage, and below the city, Habert was likewise victorious. He had first opened a cannonade against the Spanish gun-boats near the Grao, and this flotilla although in sight of an English seventy-four and a frigate, and closely supported by the Papillon sloop, fled without returning a shot; the French then passed the water, and carried the entrenchment, which consisted of a feeble breastwork, defended by the irregulars who had only two guns. When the passage was effected Habert fixed his right, as a pivot, on the river, and sweeping round with his left, drove the Spaniards towards the camp; but before he could connect his flank with Harispe's troops, who were on the lake, Obispo's division, flying from Suchet's cavalry, passed over the rice grounds between the lake and the sea, and so escaped to Cullera. The remainder of Blake's army about eighteen thousand of all kinds retired to the camp and were closely invested during the night.

Three detachments of French dragoons, each man having an infantry soldier behind him, were then sent by different roads of Alcira, Cullera, and Cuenca, the two first in pursuit of Mahy and Obispo, the latter to observe Freire. Mahy was found in a position at Alcira, and Blake had already sent him orders to maintain the line of the Xucar; but he had lost his artillery, his troops were disheartened, and at the first shot he fled although the ground was strong and he had three thousand men while the French were not above a thousand. Obispo likewise abandoned Cullera and endeavoured to rejoin Mahy, when a very heavy and unusual fall of snow not only prevented their junction, but offered a fine advantage to the French. For the British consul thinking the Xucar would be defended, had landed large stores of provisions and ammunition at Denia and was endeavouring to re-embark them, when the storm drove the ships of war off the coast, and for three days fifty cavalry could have captured Denia and all the stores.

In this battle which cost the French less than five hundred men, Zayas alone displayed his usual vigour and spirit, and while retiring upon the city, he repeatedly proposed to Blake to retreat by the road Mahy had followed, which would have saved the army; yet the other was silent, for he was in every way incapable as an officer. With

BOOK XV. 1811. Dec.

twenty-three thousand infantry, a powerful cavalry, and a wide river in his front—with the command of several bridges by which he could have operated on either side; with strong entrenchments, a secure camp—with a fortified city in the centre, whence his reserves could have reached the most distant point of the scene of operation, in less than two hours—with all these advantages he had permitted Suchet whose force, seeing that one of Reille's brigades had not arrived, scarcely exceeded his own, to force the passage of the river, to beat him at all points, and to enclose him, by a march, which spread the French troops on a circuit of more than fifteen miles or five hours march; and he now rejected the only means of saving his army. But Suchet's operations which indeed were of the nature of a surprise, proves that he must have had a supreme contempt for his adversary's talents, and the country people partook of the sentiment; the French parties which spread over the country for provisions, as far as Xativa, were every where well received, and Blake complained that Valencia contained a bad people.

The 2d of December, the Spanish general, finding his error, attempted at the head of ten thousand men to break out by the left bank of the Guadalaviar; but his arrangements were unskilful, and when his advanced guard of five thousand men had made way, it was abandoned, and the main column returned to the city. The next day many deserters went over to the French, and Reille's absent brigade, now arrived and reinforced the posts on the left bank of the river. Suchet fortified his camp on the right bank, and having in the night of the 30th repulsed two thousand Spaniards who made a sally, commenced regular approaches against the camp and city.

CHAP. III.

1812. January.

SIEGE OF VALENCIA.

It was impossible for Blake to remain long in the camp; the city contained one hundred and fifty thousand souls besides the troops, and there was no means of provisioning them, because Suchet's investment was complete. Sixty heavy guns with their parcs of ammunition which had reached Saguntum, were transported across the river Guadalaviar to batter the works; and as the suburb of San Vincente, and the Olivet offered two projecting points of the entrenched camp, which possessed but feeble means of defence, the trenches were opened against them in the night of the 1st of January.

The fire killed colonel Henri, the chief engineer, but in the night of the 5th the Spaniards abandoned the camp and took refuge in the city; the French, perceiving the movement, escaladed the works, and seized two of the suburbs so suddenly, that they captured eighty pieces of artillery and established themselves within twenty yards of the town wall, when their mortar batteries opened upon the place. In the evening, Suchet sent a summons to Blake, who replied, that he would have accepted certain terms the day before, but that the bombardment had convinced him, that he might now depend upon both the citizens and the troops.

This answer satisfied Suchet. He was convinced the place would not make any defence, and he continued to throw shells until the 8th; after which he

BOOK XV. 1812. January.

made an attack upon the suburb of Quarte, but the Spaniards still held out and he was defeated. However, the bombardment killed many persons, and set fire to the houses in several quarters; and as there were no cellars or caves, as at Zaragoza, the chief citizens begged Blake to capitulate. While he was debating with them, a friar bearing a flag, which he called the Standard of the Faith, came up with a mob, and insisted upon fighting to the last, and when a picquet of soldiers was sent against him, he routed it and shot the officer; nevertheless his party was soon dispersed. Finally, when a convent of Dominicans close to the walls was taken, and five batteries ready to open, Blake demanded leave to retire to Alicant with arms, baggage, and four guns.

These terms were refused, but a capitulation guaranteeing property and oblivion of the past, and providing that the unfortunate prisoners in the island of Cabrera should be exchanged against an equal number of Blake's army, was negotiated and ratified on the 9th. Then Blake complaining bitterly of the people, gave up the city. Above eighteen thousand regular troops, with eighty stand of colours, two thousand horses, three hundred and ninety guns, forty thousand muskets, and enormous stores of powder were taken; and it is not one of the least remarkable features of this extraordinary war, that intelligence of the fall of so great a city took a week to reach Madrid, and it was not known in Cadiz until one month after!

On the 14th of January Suchet made his triumphal entry into Valencia, having completed a series of campaigns in which the feebleness of his adversaries somewhat diminished his glory, but in which his own activity and skill were not the less conspicuous. Napoleon created him duke of Albufera, and his civil administration was strictly in unison with his conduct in the field, that is to say vigorous and prudent. He arrested all dangerous persons, especially the friars, and sent them to France, and he rigorously deprived the people of their military resources; but he proportioned his demands to their real ability, kept his troops in perfect discipline, was careful not to offend the citizens by violating their customs, or shocking their religious prejudices, and endeavoured, as much as possible, to govern through the native authorities. The archbishop and many of the clergy aided him, and the submission of the people was secured.

The errors of the Spaniards contributed as much to this object, as the prudent vigilance of Suchet; for although the city was lost, the kingdom of Valencia might have recovered from the blow, under the guidance of able men. The convents and churches were full of riches, the towns and villages abounded in resources, the line of the Xucar was very strong, and several fortified places and good harbours remained unsubdued; the Partidas in the hills were still numerous, the people were willing to fight, and the British agents and the British fleets were ready to aid, and to supply arms and stores. The junta however dissolved itself, the magistrates fled from their posts, the populace were left without chiefs; and when the consul, Tupper, proposed to establish a commission of government, having at its head the padre Rico, the author of Valencia's first defence against Moncey, and the most able and energetic man in those parts, Mahy evaded the

BOOK XV. 1812. January.

proposition; he would not give Rico power, and shewed every disposition to impede useful exertion. Then the leading people either openly submitted or secretly entered into connection with the French, who were thus enabled tranquilly to secure the resources of the country; and as the regency at Cadiz refused the stipulated exchange of prisoners, the Spanish army was sent to France, and the horrors of the Cabrera were prolonged.

During the siege of Valencia, Freire, with his Murcians, including a body of cavalry, had abandoned the passes of the Contreras district and retired across the Xucar to Almanza; Mahy occupied Alcoy, and Villa Campa had marched to Carthagena. Suchet wished to leave them undisturbed until he was ready to attack Alicant itself. But to ensure the fall of Valencia, Napoleon had directed Soult to hold ten thousand men in the Despeñas Peros, ready to march if necessary to Suchet's assistance; and at the same time Marmont was ordered to detach Montbrun with two divisions of infantry and one of cavalry, from the valley of the Tagus, to co-operate with the army of Aragon. These last-named troops should have interposed between Valencia and Alicant before the battle of the 26th, but they were delayed, and only reached Almanza on the 9th, the very day Valencia surrendered. Freire retreated before them, and Mahy, who was preparing to advance again to Alcira, took shelter in Alicant. Montbrun knew that Valencia had fallen, and was advised by Suchet to return immediately, but ambitious to share in the glory of the hour he marched against Alicant, and throwing a few shells summoned it to surrender.

The municipal authorities, the governor and many of the leading people, were disposed to yield, yet Montbrun did not press them, and when he retired the place was, as Suchet had foreseen, put into a state of defence. The consul, Tupper, and Roche, the military agent, by distributing clothes and food to the naked famishing soldiers, restored their courage, drew many more to Alicant, and stopped the desertion, which was so great that in one month Freire's division alone had lost two thousand men. Montbrun's attempt therefore, hurt the French interests, and his troops on their return to Toledo wasted and pillaged the country through which they passed in a shameful manner.

Villa Campa now abandoned Carthagena and returned to the mountains of Albarazin; and Suchet, embarrassed by the failure at Alicant, and dreading the fever at Carthagena, posted Harispe's division on the Xucar, to guard against the pestilence rather than to watch the enemy. Yet he seized Gandia and Denia, which last was strangely neglected both by the Spaniards and by the British squadron after the stores were removed; for the castle had sixty guns mounted, and many vessels were in the port; and as a post it was important, and might easily have been secured until a Spanish garrison could be thrown in. When these points were secured Suchet detached a brigade on the side of Cabrillas to preserve the communication with Cuenca, and then directed Musnier's division to form the siege of Peniscola; but at the moment of investing that place, intelligence arrived that Taragona, the garrison of which, contrary to orders, had consumed the reserve-provisions, was menaced by Lacy; wherefore Severoli's division moved from Valencia

BOOK XV. 1812. January.

to replace Musnier, and the latter marched to Tortoza in aid of Taragona. Previous to Musnier's arrival, Lafosse, governor of Tortoza, had advanced with some cavalry and a battalion of infantry to the fort of Balaguer, to observe Lacy, and being falsely told that the Spaniards were in retreat, entered Cambril the 19th, and from thence pushed on with his cavalry to Taragona. Lacy was nearer than he imagined.

It will be remembered that the Catalan army was posted in the valley of the Congosta and at Mattaro, to intercept the French convoy to Barcelona. In December Maurice Mathieu seized Mattaro, while Dacaen, who had received some reinforcements, brought down the long expected convoy, and the Spaniards being thus placed between two fires, after a slight action, opened the road. When Dacaen returned to Gerona they resumed their position, but Lacy after proposing several new projects, which he generally relinquished at the moment of execution, at last decided to fall on Taragona, and afterwards to invade Aragon. With this view, he drew off Eroles' division and some cavalry, in all about six thousand men, from the Congosta, and took post about the 18th of January, at Reus. Stores from Cadiz were landed from the English vessels at Cape Salou; captain Codrington repaired to the Spanish quarters on the 19th to concert a combined operation with the fleet, and it was at this moment the scouts brought word that Lafosse had entered Taragona with the cavalry, and that the French infantry, about eight hundred in number, were at Villa Seca, ignorant of the vicinity of the Spanish army.

Lacy immediately put his troops in motion, and

captain Codrington would have returned to his ship, but a patrol of French dragoons chased him back, and another patrol pushing to Salou made two captains and a lieutenant of the squadron prisoners, and brought them to Villa Seca. By this time, however, Lacy had fallen upon the French infantry in front, and Eroles turning both their flanks, and closing upon their rear, killed or wounded two hundred when the remainder surrendered.

The naval officers, thus freed, immediately regained their ships, and the squadron was that night before Taragona; but a gale of wind off shore impeded its fire, the Spaniards did not appear on the land-side, and the next day the increasing gale obliged the ships to anchor to the eastward. Lacy had meanwhile abandoned the project against Taragona, and after sending his prisoners to Busa, went off himself towards Montserrat, leaving Eroles' division, reinforced by a considerable body of armed peasantry, in a position at Altafulla, behind the Gaya. Here the bridge in front being broken, and the position strong, Eroles, who had been also promised the aid of Sarsfield's division, awaited the attack of three thousand men who were coming from Barcelona. He was however ignorant that Dacaen, finding the ways from Gerona open, because Sarsfield had moved to the side of Vich, had sent general Lamarque with five thousand men to Barcelona, and that Maurice Mathieu was thus in march not with three but eight thousand good troops.

BATTLE OF ALTAFULLA.

The French generals, anxious to surprise Eroles, took pains to conceal their numbers, and while

BOOK XV.

1812. January.

Maurice Mathieu appeared in front, Lamarque was turning the left flank. They marched all night, and at day-break on the 24th, having forded the river, made a well combined and vigorous attack, by which the Spaniards were defeated with a loss of more than one thousand killed and wounded. The total dispersion of the beaten troops baffled pursuit, and the French in returning to Barcelona suffered from the fire of the British squadron, but Eroles complained that Sarsfield had kept away with a settled design to sacrifice him.

While this was passing in Lower Catalonia, Dacaen scoured the higher country about Olot, and then descending into the valley of Vich defeated Sarsfield at Centellas, and that general himself was taken, but rescued by one of his soldiers. From Centellas, Dacaen marched by Caldas and Sabadel upon Barcelona, where he arrived the 27th January, meanwhile Musnier re-victualled Taragona. Thus the Catalans were again reduced to great straits, for the French knowing that they were soon to be reinforced, occupied all the sea-coast, made new roads out of reach of fire from the ships, established fresh posts at Moncado, Mattaro, Palamos, and Cadaques, placed detachments in the higher valleys, and obliged their enemies to resort once more to an irregular warfare; which was however but a feeble resource, because from Lacy's policy the people were now generally disarmed and discontented.

Milans, Manso, Eroles, Sarsfield, and Rovira, indeed, although continually quarrelling, kept the field; and being still supplied with arms and stores which the British navy contrived to land, and send into the interior, sustained the war as partizans until new combinations were produced by the efforts of England; but Lacy's intrigues and unpopularity increased, a general gloom prevailed, and the foundations of strength in the principality were shaken. The patriots indeed still possessed the mountains, but the French held all the towns, all the ports, and most of the lines of communication; and their moveable columns without difficulty gathered the harvests of the valleys, and chased the most daring of the partizans. Meanwhile Suchet, seeing that Taragona was secure, renewed his operations.

1812. January.

SIEGE OF PENISCOLA.

This fortress, crowning the summit of a lofty rock in the sea, was nearly impregnable; and the only communication with the shore, was by a neck of land sixty yards wide and two hundred and fifty long. In the middle of the town there was a strong castle, well furnished with guns and provisions, and some British ships of war were at hand to aid the defence; the rock yielded copious springs of water, and deep marshes covered the approach to the neck of land, which being covered by the waves in heavy gales, had also an artifical cut defended by batteries and flanked by gun-boats. Garcia Navarro, who had been taken during the siege of Tortoza, but had escaped from France, was now governor of Peniscola, and his garrison was sufficiently numerous.

On the 20th ground was broken, and mortar-batteries being established twelve hundred yards from the fort, opened their fire on the 28th.

In the night of the 31st a parallel five hundred

BOOK XV.

yards long was built of fascines and gabions, and batteries were commenced on either flank.

1812. February.

In the night of the 2d of February the approaches were pushed beyond the first parallel, and the breaching batteries being finished and armed were going to open when a privateer captured a despatch from the governor, who complained in it that the English wished to take the command of the place, and declared his resolution rather to surrender than suffer them to do so. On this hint Suchet opened negotiations which terminated in the capitulation of the fortress, the troops being allowed to go where they pleased. The French found sixty guns mounted, and the easy reduction of such a strong place, which secured their line of communication, produced a general disposition in the Valencians to submit to fortune. Such is Suchet's account of this affair, but the colour which he thought it necessary to give to a transaction, full of shame and dishonour, to Navarro, can only be considered as part of the price paid for Peniscola. The true causes of its fall were treachery and cowardice. The garrison were from the first desponding and divided in opinion, and the British naval officers did but stimulate the troops and general to do their duty to their country.

After this capture, six thousand Poles quitted Suchet, for Napoleon required all the troops of that nation for his Russian expedition. These veterans marched by Jaca, taking with them the prisoners of Blake's army, at the same time Reille's two French divisions were ordered to form a separate corps of observation on the Lower Ebro, and Palombini's Italian division was sent towards Soria and Catalayud to oppose Montijo,

Villa Campa, and Bassecour, who were still in joint operation on that side. But Reille soon marched towards Aragon, and Severoli's division took his place on the Lower Ebro; for the Partidas of Duran, Empecinado, and those numerous bands from the Asturias and La Montaña composing the seventh army, harassed Navarre and Aragon and were too powerful for Caffarelli. Mina's also re-entered Aragon in January, surprised Huesca, and being attacked during his retreat at Lumbiar repulsed the enemy and carried off his prisoners.

Suchet's field force in Valencia was thus reduced by twenty thousand men, he had only fifteen thousand left, and consequently could not push the invasion on the side of Murcia. The approaching departure of Napoleon from Paris also altered the situation of the French armies in the Peninsula. The king was again appointed the emperor's lieutenant, and he extended the right wing of Suchet's army to Cuenca, and concentrated the army of the centre at Madrid; thus Valencia was made, as it were, a mere head of cantonments, in front of which fresh Spanish armies soon assembled, and Alicant then became an object of interest to the English government. Suchet, who had neglected the wound he received at the battle of Saguntum, now fell into a dangerous disorder, and that fierce flame of war which seemed destined to lick up all the remains of the Spanish power, was suddenly extinguished.

OBSERVATIONS.

1°. The events which led to the capitulation of

BOOK XV. 1811.

Valencia, were but a continuation of those faults which had before ruined the Spanish cause in every part of the Peninsula, namely, the neglect of all good military usages, and the mania for fighting great battles with bad troops.

2°. Blake needed not to have fought a serious action during any part of the campaign. He might have succoured Saguntum without a dangerous battle, and might have retreated in safety behind the Guadalaviar; he might have defended that river without risking his whole army, and then have retreated behind the Xucar. He should never have shut up his army in Valencia, but having done so he should never have capitulated. Eighteen thousand men, well conducted, could always have broken through the thin circle of investment, drawn by Suchet, especially as the Spaniards had the power of operating on both banks of the river. But the campaign was one huge error throughout, and was pithily summed up in one sentence by the duke of Wellington. Being accused by the regency at Cadiz of having caused the catastrophe, by permitting the army of the north and that of Portugal to send reinforcements to Suchet, he replied thus—"The misfortunes of Valencia are to be attributed to Blake's ignorance of his profession, and to Mahi's cowardice and treachery!"

CHAPTER IV.

OPERATIONS IN ANDALUSIA AND ESTREMADURA.

CHAP. IV. 1811.

THE affairs of these provinces were so intimately connected, that they cannot be treated separately, wherefore, taking Soult's position at Seville as the centre of a vast system, I will show how, from thence, he dealt his powerful blows around, and struggled, even as a consuming fire, which none could smother though many tried.

Seville the base of his movements, and the storehouse of his army, was fortified with temporary citadels, which, the people being generally submissive, were tenable against desultory attacks. From this point he maintained his line of communication, with the army of Portugal, through Estremadura, and with Madrid through La Mancha; and from this point he sustained the most diversified operations on all parts of a circle, which embraced the Condado de Niebla, Cadiz, Grenada, Cordoba, and Estremadura.

The Niebla, which furnished large supplies, was the most vulnerable point, because from thence the allies might intercept the navigation of the river Guadalquivir, and so raise the blockade of Cadiz; and the frontier of Portugal would cover the assembly of the troops until the moment of attack. Moreover, expeditions from Cadiz to the mouth of the Guadiana were as we have seen frequent. Ne-

BOOK XV. 1811.

vertheless, when Blake and Ballesteros had been driven from Ayamonte, in July and August, the French were masters of the Condado with the exception of the castle of Paymago, wherefore Soult, dreading the autumnal pestilence, did not keep more than twelve hundred men on that side.

The blockade of the Isla was always maintained by Victor, whose position formed an irregular crescent, extending from San Lucar de Barameda on the right, to Conil on the left, and running through Xeres, Arcos, Medina, Sidonia, and Chiclana. But that marshal while thus posted was in a manner blockaded himself. In the Isla, including the Anglo-Portuguese division, there were never less than sixteen thousand troops, who, having the command of the sea, could at any moment land on the flanks of the French. The Partidas, although neither numerous nor powerful, often impeded the intercourse with Seville; the Serranos of the Ronda and the regular forces at Algeziras issuing, as it were, from the fortress of Gibraltar, cut the communication with Grenada; and as Tarifa was still held by the allies, for general Campbell would never relinquish that important point, the fresh supplies of cattle, drawn from the great plain called the Campiña de Tarifa, were straightened. Meanwhile the expeditions to Estremadura and Murcia, the battles of Barosa and Albuera, and the rout of Baza, had employed all the disposable part of the army of the south; hence Victor's corps, scarcely strong enough to preserve its own fortified position, could make no progress in the attack of the Isla. This weakness of the French army being well known in Cadiz, the safety of that city was no longer doubtful, a part of the British garrison therefore joined lord

Wellington's army, and Blake as we have seen carried his Albuera soldiers to Valencia.

In Grenada the fourth corps, which, after the departure of Sebastiani, was commanded by general Laval, had two distinct tasks to fulfil. The one to defend the eastern frontier from the Murcian army; the other to maintain the coast line, beyond the Alpuxaras, against the efforts of the Partidas of those mountains, against the Serranos of the Ronda, and against the expeditionary armies from Cadiz and from Algeziras. However, the defeat at Baza, and the calling off of Mahi, Freire, and Montijo to aid the Valencian operations, secured the Grenadan frontier; and Martin Carera, who was left there with a small force, having pushed his partizan excursions rashly, was killed in a skirmish at Lorca about the period when Valencia surrendered.

Cordoba was generally occupied by a division of five or six thousand men, who were ready to operate on the side of Estremadura, or on that of Murcia, and meanwhile chased the Partidas, who were more numerous there than in other parts, and were also connected with those of La Mancha.

Estremadura was the most difficult field of operation. There Badajos, an advanced point, was to be supplied and defended from the most formidable army in the Peninsula; there the communications with Madrid, and with the army of Portugal, were to be maintained by the way of Truxillo; and there the fifth French corps, commanded by Drouet, had to collect its subsistence from a ravaged country; to preserve its communications over the Sierra Morena with Seville; to protect the march of monthly convoys to Badajos; to observe the corps of general Hill, and to oppose the enterprises

BOOK XV. 1811. of Morillo's Spanish army, which was becoming numerous and bold.

Neither the Spanish nor British divisions could prevent Drouet from sending convoys to Badajos, because of the want of bridges on the Guadiana, below the fortress, but Morillo incommoded his foraging parties; for being posted at Valencia de Alcantara, and having his retreat upon Portugal always secure, he vexed the country about Caceres, and even pushed his incursions to Truxillo. The French general, therefore, kept a strong detachment beyond the Guadiana, but this exposed his troops to Hill's enterprises; and that bold and vigilant commander having ten thousand excellent troops, and being well instructed by Wellington, was a very dangerous neighbour.

Marmont's position in the valley of the Tagus; the construction of the forts and bridge at Almaraz, which enabled him to keep a division at Truxillo, and connected him with the army of the south, tended indeed to hold Hill in check, and strengthened the French position in Estremadura; nevertheless, Drouet generally remained near Zafra with his main body, because from thence he could more easily make his retreat good to the Morena, or advance to Merida and Badajos as occasion required.

Such was the state of military affairs on the different parts of the circle round Seville, at the period when Suchet invaded Valencia, and Wellington blockaded Ciudad Rodrigo; and to support his extensive operations, the duke of Dalmatia, if his share of the reinforcements which entered Spain in July and August had joined him, would have had about a hundred thousand troops, of which ninety

Appendix, No. IX. Section 3.

thousand men and fourteen thousand horses were French. But the reinforcements were detained in the different governments, and the actual number of French present with the eagles was not more than sixty-seven thousand.

The first corps contained twenty thousand; the fourth and fifth about eleven thousand each; the garrison of Badajos was five thousand; twenty thousand formed a disposable reserve, and the rest of the force consisted of "*Escopeteros*" and civic guards, who were chiefly employed in the garrisons and police. Upon pressing occasions, Soult could therefore take the field, at any point, with twenty-four or twenty-five thousand men, and in Estremadura, on very pressing occasions, with even a greater number of excellent troops well and powerfully organized. The manner in which this great army was paralysed in the latter part of 1811, shall now be shown.

In October, Drouet was in the Morena, and Girard at Merida, watching Morillo, who was in Caceres, when Soult, who had just returned to Seville after his Murcian expedition, sent three thousand men to Fregenal, seemingly to menace the Alemtejo. General Hill therefore recalled his brigades from the right bank of the Tagus, and concentrated his whole corps behind the Campo Maior on the 9th.

The 11th Girard and Drouet advanced, the Spanish cavalry retired from Caceres, the French drove Morillo to Caza de Cantellaña, and every thing indicated a serious attack; but at this moment Soult's attention was attracted by the appearance of Ballesteros in the Ronda, and he recalled the force from Fregenal. Drouet, who had reached

BOOK XV. 1811. October.

Merida, then retired to Zafra, leaving Girard with a division and some cavalry near Caceres.

Ballesteros had disembarked at Algeziras on the 11th of September, and immediately marched with his own and Beguine's troops, in all four thousand men, to Ximena, raising fresh levies and collecting the Serranos of the Ronda as he advanced. On the 18th he had endeavoured to succour the castle of Alcala de Gazúles, where Beguines had a garrison, but a French detachment from Chiclana had already reduced that post, and after some skirmishing both sides fell back, the one to Chiclana, the other to Ximena.

At this time six thousand French were collected at Ubrique, intending to occupy the sea-coast, from Algeziras to Conil, in furtherance of a great project which Soult was then meditating, and by which he hoped to effect, not only the entire subjection of Andalusia, but the destruction of the British power in the Peninsula. But this design, which shall be hereafter explained more fully, required several preliminary operations, amongst the most important of which was the capture of Tarifa; for that place, situated in the narrowest part of the straits, furnished either a protection, or a dangerous point of offence, to the Mediterranean trade, following the relations of its possessor with England. It affected, as we have seen, the supplies of the French before the Isla; it was from its nearness, and from the run of the current, the most convenient and customary point for trading with Morocco; it menaced the security of Ceuta, and it possessed, from ancient recollections, a species of feudal superiority over the smaller towns, and ports along the coast, which would have given the French, if they had taken it, a moral influence of some consequence.

1811. October.

Soult had in August despatched a confidental officer from Conil to the African coast to negotiate with the Barbaric emperor, and the latter had agreed to a convention, by which he engaged to exclude British agents from his court; and to permit vessels of all nations to use the Moorish flag to cover their cargoes, while carrying to the French those supplies hitherto sent to the allies, provided Soult would occupy Tarifa as a depôt. This important convention was on the point of being ratified, when the opportune arrival of some unusually magnificent presents from England, turned the scale against the French: their agent was then dismissed, the English supplies were increased, and Mr. Stuart entered into a treaty for the purchase of horses to remount the allied cavalry.

Although foiled in this attempt, Soult, calculating on the capricious nature of barbarians, resolved to fulfil his part by the capture of Tarifa; hence it was, that when Ballesteros appeared at Ximena, he arrested the movement of Drouet against the Alemtejo, and sent troops from Seville by Ubrique against the Spanish general, whose position besides being extremely inconvenient to the first and fourth corps, was likely to affect the taking of Tarifa. Ballesteros, if reinforced, might also have become very dangerous to the blockade of Cadiz, by intercepting the supplies from the Campiña de Tarifa, and still more by menacing Victor's communications with Seville, along the Guadalquiver. A demonstration by the allies in the Isla de Leon arrested the march of these French troops for a moment, but on the 14th eight thousand men under generals Godinot and Se-

BOOK XV. 1811. October. mélé advanced upon St. Roque and Algeziras. The inhabitants of those places immediately fled to the green island, and Ballesteros took refuge under Gibraltar, where his flanks were covered by the gun-boats of the place. The garrison was too weak to assist him with men, and thus cooped up, he lived upon the resources of the place, while efforts were therefore made to draw off the French by harassing their flanks. The naval means were not sufficient to remove his whole army to another quarter, but seven hundred were transported to Manilba, where the Serranos and some Partidas had assembled on the left of the French, and at the same time twelve hundred British troops with four guns, under colonel Skerrett, and two thousand Spaniards, under Copons, sailed from Cadiz to Tarifa to act upon the French right.

Copons was driven back by a gale of wind, but Skerrett arrived the 17th. The next day Godinot sent a detachment against him, but the sea-road by which it marched was so swept with the guns of the Tuscan frigate, aided by the boats of the Stately, that the French after losing some men returned. Then Godinot and Semélé being in dispute, and without provisions, retreated; they were followed by Ballesteros' cavalry as far as Ximena, where the two generals separated in great anger, and Godinot having reached Seville shot himself. This failure in the south unsettled Soult's plans, and was followed by a heavier disaster in Estremadura.

CHAP. IV.

SURPRISE OF AROYO MOLINO.

1811. October.

When Drouet had retired to Zafra, Hill received orders from Wellington to drive Girard away from Caceres, that Morillo might forage that country. For this purpose he assembled his corps at Albuquerque on the 23d, and Morillo brought the fifth Spanish army to Aliseda on the Salor. Girard was then at Caceres with an advanced guard at Aroyo de Puerco, but on the 24th Hill occupied Aliseda and Casa de Cantillana, and the Spanish cavalry drove the French from Aroyo de Puerco. The 26th at day-break Hill entered Malpartida de Caceres, and his cavalry pushed back that of the enemy. Girard then abandoned Caceres, but the weather was wet and stormy, and Hill, having no certain knowledge of the enemy's movements, halted for the night at Malpartida.

On the morning of the 27th the Spaniards entered Caceres; the enemy was tracked to Torre Mocha on the road to Merida; and the British general, hoping to intercept their line of march, pursued by a cross road, through Aldea de Cano and Casa de Don Antonio. During this movement intelligence was received that the French general had halted at Aroyo Molino, leaving a rear-guard at Albala, on the main road to Caceres, which proved that he was ignorant of the new direction taken by the allies, and only looked to a pursuit from Caceres. Hill immediately seized the advantage, and by a forced march reached Alcuesca in the night, being then within a league of Aroyo de Molinos.

This village was situated in a plain, and be-

BOOK XV. 1811. October.

hind it a sierra or ridge of rocks, rose in the form of a crescent, about two miles wide on the chord. One road led directly from Alcuesca upon Aroyo, another entered it from the left, and three led from it to the right. The most distant of the last was the Truxillo road, which rounded the extremity of the sierra; the nearest was the Merida road, and between them was that of Medellin.

During the night, though the weather was dreadful, no fires were permitted in the allied camp; and at two o'clock in the morning of the 28th, the troops moved to a low ridge, half a mile from Aroyo, under cover of which they formed three bodies; the infantry on the wings and the cavalry in the centre. The left column then marched straight upon the village, the right marched towards the extreme point of the sierra, where the road to Truxillo turned the horn of the crescent; the cavalry kept its due place between both.

One brigade of Girard's division, having marched at four o'clock by the road of Medellin, was already safe, but Dombrouski's brigade and the cavalry of Briche were still in the place; the horses of the rear-guard, unbridled, were tied to the olive-trees, and the infantry were only gathering to form on the Medellin road outside the village. Girard himself was in his quarters, waiting for his horse, when two British officers galloped down the street, and in an instant all was confusion; the cavalry bridled their horses, and the infantry run to their alarming posts. But a thick mist rolled down the craggy mountain, a terrifying shout, drowning even the clatter of the elements arose on the blast, and with the driving storm came the seventy-first and ninety-second regiments, charging down the street. Then the French rear-guard of cavalry, fighting and struggling hard, were driven to the end of the village, and the infantry, hastily forming their squares, covered the main body of the horsemen which gathered on their left.

The seventy-first immediately lined the garden-walls, and opened a galling fire on the nearest square, while the ninety-second filing out of the streets formed upon the French right; the fiftieth regiment closely following, secured the prisoners in the village, and the rest of the column, headed by the Spanish cavalry, skirted the outside of the houses, and endeavoured to intercept the line of retreat. The guns soon opened on the French squares, the thirteenth dragoons captured their artillery, the ninth dragoons and German hussars, charged their cavalry and entirely dispersed it with great loss; but Girard, an intrepid officer, although wounded, still kept his infantry together, and continued his retreat by the Truxillo road. The right column of the allies was however already in possession of that line, the cavalry and artillery were close upon the French flank, and the left column, having re-formed, was again coming up fast; Girard's men were falling by fifties, and his situation was desperate, yet he would not surrender, but giving the word to disperse, endeavoured to escape by scaling the almost inaccessible rocks of the sierra. His pursuers, not less obstinate, immediately divided. The Spaniards ascended the hills at an easier part beyond his left, the thirty-ninth regiment and Ashworth's Portuguese turned the mountain by the Truxillo road; the twenty-eighth and thirty-fourth, led by general Howard, followed him step by step up the

BOOK XV. 1811. October.

rocks, and prisoners were taken every moment, until the pursuers, heavily loaded, were unable to continue the trial of speed with men who had thrown away their arms and packs. Girard, Dombrouski, and Briche, escaped at first to San Hernando, and Zorita, in the Guadalupe mountains, after which, crossing the Guadiana at Orellano on the 9th of November, they rejoined Drouet with about six hundred men, the remains of three thousand. They were said to be the finest troops then in Spain, and indeed their resolution not to surrender in such an appalling situation was no mean proof of their excellence.

The trophies of this action were the capture of twelve or thirteen hundred prisoners, including general Bron, and the prince of Aremberg; all the French artillery, baggage, and commissariat, together with a contribution just raised; and during the fight, a Portuguese brigade, being united to Penne Villamur's cavalry was sent to Merida, where some stores were found. The loss of the allies was not more than seventy killed and wounded, but one officer, lieutenant Strenowitz, was taken. He was distinguished by his courage and successful enterprises, but he was an Austrian, who having abandoned the French army in Spain to join Julian Sanchez' Partida, was liable to death by the laws of war; having been however originally forced into the French service he was, in reality, no deserter. General Hill, anxious to save him, applied frankly to general Drouet, and such was the latter's good temper, that while smarting under this disaster he released his prisoner.

Girard was only deprived of his division, which was given to general Barois, yet in a military

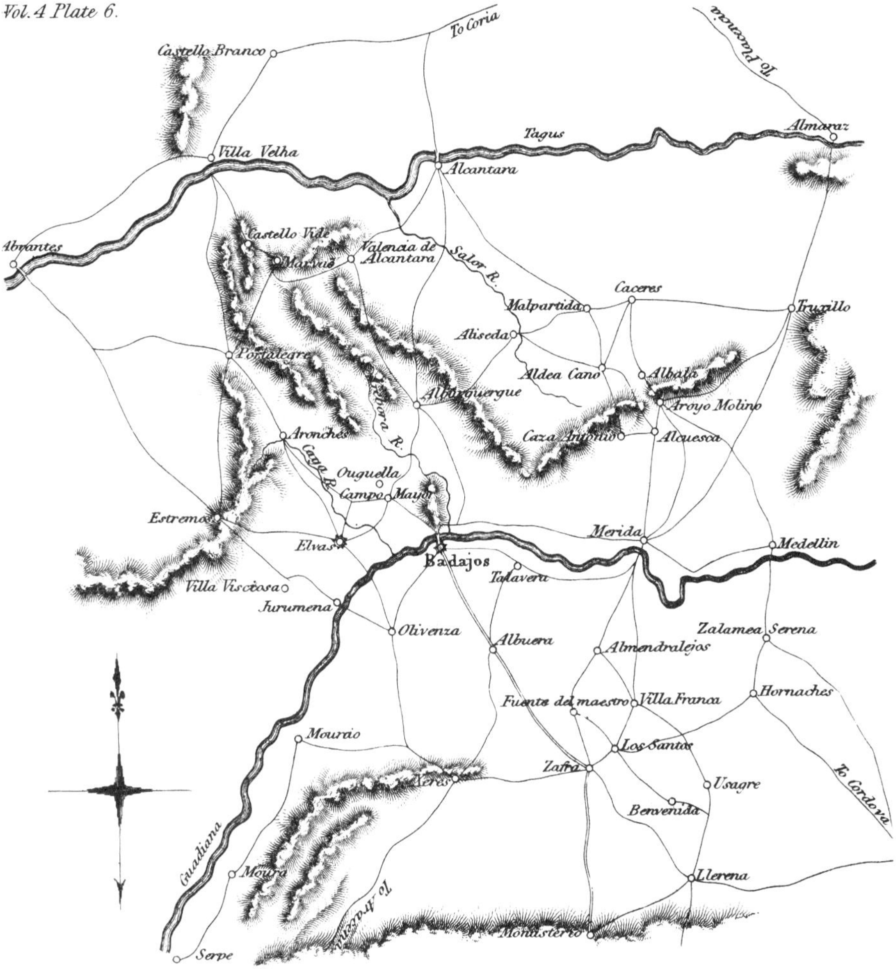

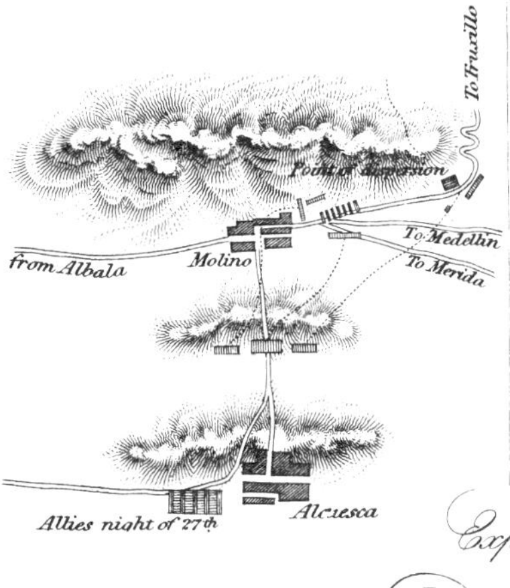

Explanatory Sketch of

GENL HILL'S OPERATIONS,

1811.

London: Published by T. & W. BOONE.

point of view his offence was unpardonable. He knew two or three days before, that general Hill was near him; he knew that there was a good road from Malpartida to Alcuesca, because he had himself passed it coming from Caceres; and yet he halted at Aroyo de Molino without necessity, and without sending out even a patrole upon his flank, thus sacrificing two thousand brave men. Napoleon's clemency was therefore great, and yet not misplaced, for Girard, afterwards, repaid it by his devotion at the battle of Lutzen when the emperor's star was on the wane. On the other hand general Hill neglected no precaution, let no advantage escape; and to good arrangements added celerity of movement, with the utmost firmness and vigour of execution. His troops seconded him as he merited; and here was made manifest the advantage of possessing the friendship of a people so strongly influenced by the instincts of revenge as the Peninsulars; for, during the night of the 27th, every Spaniard in Aroya, as well as in Alcuesca, knew that the allies were at hand, and not one was found so base or so indiscreet as to betray the fact.

This blow being struck, Hill returned to his old quarters, and the Spanish troops fell back behind the Salor, but the report of Girard's disaster set all the French corps in motion. Drouet re-occupied Caceres with a thousand men; Foy passed the Tagus at Almaraz on the 15th of November, and moved to Truxillo; a convoy entered Badajos from Zafra on the 12th, a second on the 20th, and Soult, while collecting troops in Seville, directed Phillipon to plant all the ground under the guns at Badajos with potatoes and corn. Every thing seemed to

BOOK XV. 1811. Nov.

indicate a powerful attack upon Hill, when a serious disturbance amongst the Polish troops, at Ronquillo, obliged Soult to detach men from Seville to quell it. When that was effected, a division of four thousand entered Estremadura, and Drouet, whose corps was thus raised to fourteen thousand infantry and three thousand cavalry, on the 5th of December advanced to Almendralejos, and the 18th his advanced guard occupied Merida. At the same time Marmont concentrated part of his army at Toledo, from whence Montbrun, as we have seen, was directed to aid Suchet at Valencia, and Soult with the same view sent ten thousand men to the Despeños Peros.

Mr Stuart's papers, MSS.

Drouet's movements were, however, again stopped by some insubordination in the fifth corps. And as it was now known that Soult's principal object was to destroy Ballesteros, and take Tarifa, Hill again advanced, partly to protect Morillo from Drouet, partly to save the resources of Estremadura, partly to make a diversion in favour of Ballesteros and Tarifa, and in some sort also for Valencia. With this view he entered Estremadura by Albuquerque on the 27th of December, and having received information that the French, untaught by their former misfortunes were not vigilant, he made a forced march in hopes to surprise them. On the 28th he passed Villar del Rey and San Vincente and reached Nava de Membrillos, where he fell in with three hundred French infantry, and a few hussars, part of a foraging party, the remainder of which was at a village two leagues distant. A patrole gave an alarm, the French retreated towards Merida, and were closely followed by four hundred of the allied cavalry, who had orders to make every effort to stop their march; but to use the words of general Hill, "the intrepid and admirable manner in which the enemy retreated, the infantry formed in square, and favoured as he was by the nature of the country of which he knew how to take the fullest advantage, prevented the cavalry alone from effecting any thing against him." Captain Neveux, the able officer who commanded on this occasion, reached Merida with a loss of only forty men, all killed or wounded by the fire of the artillery; but the French at Merida immediately abandoned their unfinished works, and evacuated that town in the night, leaving behind some bread and a quantity of wheat. 1811. Dec.

From Merida, Hill, intending to fight Drouet, 1812. marched on the 1st of January to Almendralejos, where he captured another field store; but the French general, whose troops were scattered, fell back towards Zafra; the weather was so bad, and the roads so deep, that general Hill with the main body halted while colonel Abercrombie with a detachment of Portuguese and German cavalry followed the enemy's rear-guard. Meanwhile Phillipon, who never lost an advantage, sent, either the detachment which had escorted the convoy to Badajos, or some Polish troops with whom he was discontented, down the Portuguese frontier on the right of the Guadiana, by Moura, Mourão, and Serpe, with orders to drive the herds of cattle from those places into the sierra Morena.

Abercrombie reached Fuente del Maestro, on the evening of the 3d, where, meeting with a stout squadron of the enemy, a stiff charge took place, and the French out-numbered and flanked on both sides

BOOK XV.

1812. January.

were overthrown with a loss of thirty men. But Drouet was now in full retreat for Monasterio, and Morillo moving upon Medellin, took post at San Benito. Thus the allies remained masters of Estremadura until the 13th of January, when Marmont's divisions moved by the valley of the Tagus towards the eastern frontier of Portugal; Hill then returned to Portalegre and sent a division over the Tagus to Castello Branco. Drouet immediately returned to Llerena and his cavalry supported by a detachment of infantry marched against Morillo, but that general, instead of falling back when Hill did, had made a sudden incursion to La Mancha, and was then attacking the castle of Almagro. There, however, he was so completely defeated by general Treillard that, flying to Horcajo in the Guadaloupe mountains, although he reached it on the 18th, his fugitives were still coming in on the 21st, and his army remained for a long time in the greatest disorder.

CHAPTER V.

CHAP. V. 1811. Nov.

While the events, recorded in the foregoing chapter, were passing in Estremadura, the south of Andalusia was the scene of more important operations. Soult, persisting in his design against Tarifa, had given orders to assemble a battering train, and directed general Laval with a strong division of the 4th corps to move from Antequera upon San Roque. Skerrett was then menacing the communications of general Semélé on the side of Vejer de Frontera, and Ballesteros had obtained some success against that general at Bornos on the 5th of November ; but Skerrett finding that Copons instead of four thousand had only brought seven hundred men, returned to Tarifa on the approach of some French from Conil.

Semélé, being thus reinforced, obliged Ballesteros, on the 27th, again to take refuge under the walls of Gibraltar, which he reached just in time, to avoid a collision with Laval's column from Antequera. Semélé's troops did not follow very close, and a combined attack upon Laval by the divisions of Ballesteros, Skerrett, and Copons, was projected. The two latter with a part of the troops under Ballesteros, were actually embarked on the 29th of November for the purpose of landing at Manilba, in pursuance of this scheme, when Semélé's column came in sight, and Skerrett and Copons instantly returned to Tarifa.

Ballesteros remained at Gibraltar, a heavy

BOOK XV. 1811. Dec.

burthen upon that fortress, and his own troops without shelter from the winter rain, wherefore general Campbell proposed to send them, in British vessels, to renew the attempt against Malaga, which had formerly failed under Lord Blayney. On the 12th of January, at the very moment of embarking, the French retired from before Gibraltar, by the Puerto de Ojen, a grand pass connecting the plains of Gibraltar and the vallies of the Guadaranque, with the great and rich plain called the Campiña de Tarifa; and with the gorge of Los Pedragosos, which is the eastern entrance to the pastures called the Vega de Tarifa. This movement was preparatory to the siege of Tarifa; and as the battering train was already within five leagues of that place, Skerrett proposed to seize it by a combined operation from Cadiz, Tarifa, Gibraltar, and Los Barios, where Ballesteros had now taken post. This combination was however on too wide a scale to be adopted in all its parts; Ballesteros indeed fell on the enemy by surprise at the pass of Ojen, and Skerrett and Copons received orders from general Campbell to take advantage of this diversion; but the former, seeing that his own plan was not adopted to its full extent, would not stir, and the Spaniards after a skirmish of six hours retired. Laval then left fifteen hundred men to observe Ballesteros, and placing a detachment at Vejes to cover his right flank, threaded Los Pedragosos and advanced against Tarifa.

This town was scarcely expected by the French to make any resistance. It was encircled with towers, which were connected by an ancient archery wall, irregular in form without a ditch, and so thin as to offer no resistance even to field artillery. To the north and east, some high ridges flanked, and seemed

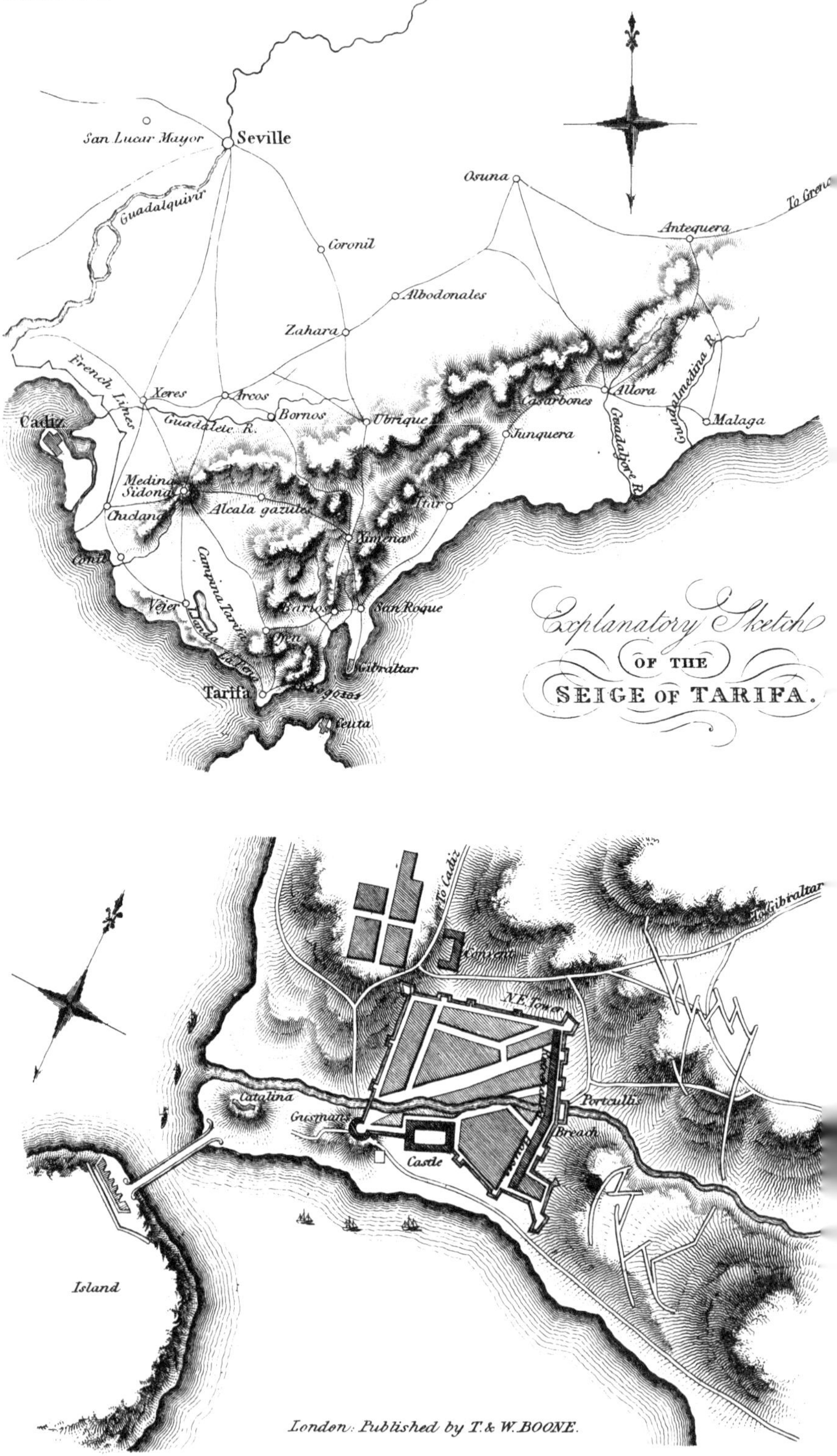

London: Published by T. & W. BOONE.

entirely to command the weak rampart; but the English engineer had observed that the nearest ridges formed, at half pistol-shot, a natural glacis, the plane of which, one point excepted, intersected the crest of the parapet with great nicety; and to this advantage was added a greater number of towers, better flanks, and more powerful resources for an interior defence. He judged therefore that the seemingly favourable nature of the ridges combined with other circumstances, would scarcely fail to tempt the enemy to commence their trenches on that side. With a view to render the delusion unavoidable, he strengthened the western front of the place, rendered the access to it uneasy, by demolishing the main walls and removing the flooring of an isolated suburb on the north west; and an out-work, of a convent which was situated about a hundred yards from the place, and to the east of the suburb. This done, he prepared an internal defence, which rendered the storming of the breach the smallest difficulty to be encountered; but to appreciate his design the local peculiarities must be described.

Tarifa was cloven in two by the bed of a periodical torrent which entering at the east, passed out at the opposite point. This stream was barred, at its entrance, by a tower with a portcullis, in front of which pallisades were planted across the bed of the water. The houses within the walls were strongly built and occupied inclined planes rising from each side of the torrent, and at the exit of the latter there were two massive structures, forming part of the walls called the tower and castle of the Gusmans, both of which looked up the hollow formed by the meeting of the inclined planes at the stream. From these structures, first a sandy neck

BOOK XV. 1811. Dec.

of land, and then a causeway, the whole being about six hundred yards long, joined the town to an island, or rather promontory, about two thousand yards in circumference, with perpendicular sides, which forbade any entrance save by the causeway; and at the island end of the latter there was an unfinished entrenchment and battery.

On the connecting neck of land were some sand hills, the highest of which, called the Catalina, was scarped and crowned with a slight field work, containing a twelve-pounder. This hill covered the causeway, and in conjunction with the tower of the Gusmans, which was armed with a ship eighteen-pounder, flanked the western front, and commanded all the ground between the walls and the island. The gun in the tower of the Gusmans also shot clear over the town on to the slope where the French batteries were expected to be raised; and in addition to these posts, the stately ship of the line, the Druid frigate, and several gun and mortar-boats were anchored in the most favourable situation for flanking the enemy's approaches.

Reverting then to the head of the defence, it will be seen, that while the ridges on the eastern fronts, and the hollow bed of the torrent, which offered cover for troops moving to the assault, deceitfully tempted the enemy to that side; the flanking fire of the convent, the ruins of the suburb, the hill of the Catalina, and the appearance of the shipping deterred them even from examining the western side, and as it were, forcibly urged them towards the eastern ridge where the English engineer wished to find them. There he had even marked their ground, and indicated the situation of the breach; that is to say, close to the entrance of the torrent, where the hollow meeting of the inclined planes rendered the inner depth of the walls far greater than the outer depth; where he had loop-holed the houses, opened communications to the rear, barricaded the streets, and accumulated obstacles. The enemy after forcing the breach would thus have been confined between the houses on the inclined planes, exposed on each side to the musketry from the loop-holes and windows, and in front to the fire of the tower of the Gusmans, which looked up the bed of the torrent. Thus disputing every inch of ground, the garrison could at worst have reached the castle and tower of the Gusmans, which being high and massive were fitted for rear-guards to cover the evacuation of the place, and were provided with ladders for the troops to descend and retreat to the island under cover of the Catalina.

The artillery available for the defence appeared very powerful, for besides that of the shipping, and the guns in the Catalina, there were in the island twelve pieces, comprising four twenty-four-pounders, and two ten-inch mortars; and in the town there were six field-pieces and four coehorns on the east front. An eighteen-pounder was on the Gusmans, a howitzer on the portcullis tower, and two field-pieces were kept behind the town in reserve for sallies; but most of the artillery in the island was mounted after the investment, so that two twenty-four-pounders and two mortars only, could take part in the defence of the town; and as the walls and towers of the latter were too weak and narrow to sustain heavy guns, only three field-pieces and the coehorns did in fact reply to the enemy's fire.

BOOK XV.

1811. Dec.

SIEGE OF TARIFA.

The garrison, including six hundred Spanish infantry and one hundred horse of that nation, amounted to two thousand five hundred men, and was posted in the following manner. Seven hundred were in the island, one hundred in the Catalina, two hundred in the convent, and fifteen hundred in the town.

On the 19th of December the enemy having driven in the advanced posts, were encountered with a sharp skirmish, and designedly led towards the eastern front.

The 20th the place was invested, but on the 21st a picquet of French troops having incautiously advanced towards the western front, captain Wren of the eleventh suddenly descended from the Catalina and carried them off. In the night the enemy approached close to the walls, but the next morning captain Wren again came down from the Catalina, and, at the same time, the troops sallied from the convent, with a view to discover the position of the French advanced posts. So daring was this sally that Mr. Welstead of the eighty-second actually pushed into one of their camps and captured a field-piece there; and although he was unable to bring it off, in face of the French reserves, the latter were drawn by the skirmish under the fire of the ships, of the island, and of the town, whereby they suffered severely and could with difficulty recover the captured piece of artillery from under the guns of the north-east tower.

In the night of the 22d the anticipations of the British engineer were realized. The enemy broke ground in two places, five hundred yards from the eastern front, and assiduously pushed forward their approaches until the 26th; but always under a destructive fire, to which they replied with musketry, and with their wall-pieces, which killed several men, and would have been very dangerous, but for the sand-bags which captain Nicholas, the chief engineer at Cadiz, had copiously supplied. This advantage was however counterbalanced by the absence of the ships which were all driven away in a gale on the 23rd.

On the 27th the French battering-train arrived, and on the 29th the sixteen-pounders opened against the town, and the howitzers against the island. These last did little damage beyond dismounting the gun in the tower of the Gusmans, which was however quickly re-established; but the sixteen-pounders brought the old wall down in such flakes, that in a few hours a wide breach was effected, a little to the left of the portcullis tower, looking from the camp.

The place was now exposed both to assault and escalade, but behind the breach the depth to the street was above fourteen feet, the space below was covered with iron window-gratings, having every second bar turned up, the houses there, and behind all points liable to escalade, were completely prepared and garrisoned, and the troops were dispersed all round the ramparts, each regiment having its own quarter assigned. The Spanish and forty-seventh British regiment guarded the breach, and on their right some riflemen prolonged the line. The eighty-seventh regiment occupied the portcullis tower and extended along the rampart to the left.

BOOK XV. 1811. Dec.

In the night of the 29th the enemy fired salvos of grape on the breach, but the besieged cleared the foot of it between the discharges.

The 30th the breaching fire was renewed, the wall was broken for sixty feet, and the whole breach offered an easy ascent, yet the besieged again cleared away the rubbish, and in the night were fast augmenting the defences behind, when a heavy rain filled the bed of the river, and the torrent bringing down, from the French camp, planks, fascines, gabions, and dead bodies, broke the palisades with a shock, bent the portcullis backward, and with the surge of the waters even injured the defences behind the breach: a new passage was thus opened in the wall, yet such was the vigour of the besieged, that the damage was repaired before the morning, and the troops calmly and confidently awaited

THE ASSAULT.

The waters subsided in the night as quickly as they had risen, but at daylight a living stream of French grenadiers glided swiftly down the bed of the river, and as if assured of victory, arrived, without shout or tumult, within a few yards of the walls, when, instead of quitting the hollow, to reach the breach, they, like the torrent of the night, continued their rapid course and dashed against the portcullis. The British soldiers, who had hitherto been silent and observant, as if at a spectacle which they were expected to applaud, now arose, and with a crashing volley smote the head of the French column! The leading officer, covered with wounds, fell against the portcullis and gave up his sword through the bars to colonel Gough; the French drummer, a gallant boy, who was beating the charge, dropped lifeless by his officer's side, and the dead and wounded filled the hollow. The remainder of the assailants then breaking out to the right and left, spread along the slopes of ground under the ramparts and opened a quick irregular musketry. At the same time, a number of men coming out of the trenches, leaped into pits digged in front, and shot fast at the garrison, but no escalade or diversion at the other points was made, and the storming column was dreadfully shattered. For the ramparts streamed forth fire, and from the north-eastern tower a field-piece, held in reserve expressly for the occasion, sent, at pistol-shot distance, a tempest of grape whistling through the French masses, which were swept away in such a dreadful manner, that they could no longer endure the destruction, but plunging once more into the hollow returned to their camp, while a shout of victory, mingled with the sound of musical instruments, passed round the wall of the town.

In this combat the allies lost five officers and thirty-one men, but the French dead covered all the slopes in front of the rampart, and choked the bed of the river, and ten wounded officers, of whom only one survived, were brought in by the breach. Skerrett, compassionating their sufferings and admiring their bravery, permitted Laval to fetch off the remainder; and the operations of the siege were then suspended, for both sides suffered severely from the weather. The rain partially ruined the French batteries, interrupted their communications,

BOOK XV.

1812. January.

and stopped their supplies; on the other hand the torrent, again swelling, broke the stockades of the allies and injured their retrenchments, and some vessels, coming from Gibraltar with ammunition, were wrecked on the coast. Nevertheless a fresh assault was hourly expected until the night of the 4th, when, several cannon-shots being heard in the French camp, without any bullets reaching the town, it was judged that the enemy were destroying the guns previous to retreating. Soon afterwards large fires were observed, and at daylight the troops issuing out of the convent, drove the enemy from the batteries, and commenced a skirmish with the rear-guard; but a heavy storm impeded the action; the French conducted their retreat skilfully, and the British, after making a few prisoners, relinquished the pursuit. Nevertheless Laval's misfortunes did not end here. The privations his troops had endured in the trenches produced sickness; many men deserted, and it was computed, at the time, that the expedition cost the French not less than a thousand men, while the whole loss of the allies did not exceed one hundred and fifty.

General Campbell's Correspondence, MSS.

Such is the simple tale of Tarifa, but the true history of its defence cannot there be found. To hide the errors of the dead is not always a virtue, and when it involves injustice to the living it becomes a crime; colonel Skerrett has obtained the credit, but he was not the author of the success at Tarifa. He, and lord Proby, the second in command, were from the first impressed with a notion, that the place could not be defended and ought to be abandoned; all their proceedings tended to that end, and they would even have abandoned the island. At colonel Skerrett's express desire general

Appendix, No. VI. Section 3.

Cooke had recalled him on the 18th, that is to say, the day before the siege commenced; and during its progress he neither evinced hopes of final success, nor made exertions to obtain it; in some instances he even took measures tending directly towards failure. To whom then was England indebted for this splendid achievement? The merit of the conception is undoubtedly due to general Campbell, the lieutenant-governor of Gibraltar. He first occupied Tarifa, and he also engaged the Spaniards to admit an English garrison into Ceuta, that the navigation of the straits and the coasting trade might be secured; for he was the only authority in the south of the Peninsula who appeared to understand the true value of those points. Finally, it was his imperious and even menacing orders, which prevented colonel Skerrett from abandoning Tarifa before the siege commenced.

General Campbell's resolution is the more to be admired, because Tarifa was, strictly speaking, not within his command, which did not extend beyond the walls of his own fortress; and he had also to contend against general Cooke, who claimed the controul of a garrison which was chiefly composed of troops from Cadiz. He acted also contrary to the opinion of lord Wellington, who, always averse to any serious co-operation with the Spaniards, as well knowing the latter would inevitably fail, and throw the burthen on the British in the hour of need, was in this instance more strongly influenced, because the reports of general Cooke, founded on colonel Skerrett's and lord Proby's representations, reprobated the defence of Tarifa. Thus misinformed of the real resources, and having no local knowledge of the

BOOK XV. 1812. January.

place, lord Wellington judged, that the island only could be held—that Skerrett's detachment was not wanting for that purpose—and that without the island the enemy could not keep possession of Tarifa. Were they even to take both, he thought they could not retain them, while Ballesteros was in strength and succoured from Gibraltar, unless they also kept a strong force in those parts; finally, that the defence of the island was the least costly and the most certain. However, with that prudence, which always marked his proceedings, although he gave his opinion, he would not interfere from a distance, in a matter which could only be accurately judged of on the spot.

Appendix, No. VI. Section 5.

But the island had not a single house, and was defenceless; the rain alone, without reckoning the effects of the enemy's shells, would have gone near to force the troops away; and as the shipping could not always remain in the road-stead, the building of casemates and barracks, and storehouses for provisions and ammunition, would have been more expensive than the defence of the town. Tarifa was therefore an out-work to the island, and one so capable of a good defence that a much more powerful attack had been expected, and a more powerful resistance prepared by the English engineer; a defence not resting on the valour of the troops alone, but upon a skilful calculation of all the real resources, and all the chances.

That the value of the object was worth the risk may be gathered from this, that Soult, three months after the siege, thus expressed himself, "The taking of Tarifa will be more hurtful to the English and to the defenders of Cadiz, than the taking of Alicant or even Badajos, where I cannot

Intercepted despatches, 17th April, 1812.

CHAP. V. 1812. January.

go without first securing my left and taking Tarifa." And, besides the advantages already noticed as belonging to the possession of this place, it was close to Ceuta where there were a few British soldiers, but many French prisoners, and above two thousand discontented Spanish troops and galley-slaves; Ceuta, which was so neglected by the Spanish regency that a French general, a prisoner, did not hesitate to propose to the governor to give it up to Soult as his only means of avoiding starvation. Neither would Soult have failed to strengthen himself at Tarifa in despite of Ballesteros, were it only to command the supplies of the Campiña, and those from Barbary which could but be brought to that port or to Conil: the latter was however seldom frequented by the Moors, because the run was long and precarious, whereas a favourable current always brought their craft well to Tarifa. Swarms of French gun-boats would therefore soon have given Soult the command of the coasting trade, if not of the entire straits.

General Campbell's papers, MSS.

Appendix, No. VI.

Tarifa then was worth the efforts made for its defence; and setting aside the courage and devotion of the troops, without which nothing could have been effected, the merit chiefly appertains to sir Charles Smith, the captain of engineers. That officer's vigour and capacity overmatched the enemy's strength without, and the weakness and cajolement of those who did not wish to defend it within. Skerrett could not measure a talent above his own mark, and though he yielded to Smith's energy, he did so with avowed reluctance, and dashed it with some wild actions, for which it is difficult to assign a motive; because he was not a

BOOK XV. 1812. January.

dull man, and he was a brave man, as his death at Bergem-op-Zoon proved. But his military capacity was naught, and his mind did not easily catch another's enthusiasm. Tarifa was the commentary upon Taragona.

During the siege, the engineer's works in front were constantly impeded by colonel Skerrett; he would call off the labourers to prepare posts of retreat, and Smith's desire to open the north-gate, (which had been built up,) that the troops might have egress in case of escalade, was opposed by him, although there was no other point for the garrison to sally, save by the sea-gate which was near the castle. On the 29th of December a shell, fired from the eighteen-pounder in the tower of the Gusmans, having bursted too soon, killed or wounded one of the inhabitants, and a deputation of the citizens came to complain of the accident; Colonel Skerrett, although the breach was then open, immediately ordered that gun, and a thirty-two-pound caronade, which at four hundred yards looked into the French batteries, to be dismounted and spiked! and it was done! To crown this absurd conduct, he assigned the charge of the breach entirely to the Spanish troops, and if Smith had not insisted upon posting the forty-seventh British regiment along-side of them, this alone would have ruined the defence; because hunger, nakedness, and neglect, had broken the spirit of those poor men, and during the combat general Copons alone displayed the qualities of a gallant soldier.

Appendix, No. VI. Section 3.

To the British engineer, therefore, the praise of this splendid action is chiefly due; because he saw from the first all the resources of the place, and with equal firmness and talent developed them, notwithstanding the opposition of his superiors; because at the same time he, by skilful impositions, induced the enemy (whose attack should have embraced the suburbs and the north-west salient angle of the place) to open his trenches on the east, where the besieged, under the appearance of weakness, had concentrated all their strength; finally, because he repressed despondency where he failed to infuse confidence. The second in merit was captain Mitchell, of the artillery; because in the management of that arm for the defence of the town, his talent and enterprise were conspicuous, especially during the assault; nor can the result of this last event be taken as the just measure of either officer's merits, seeing that a prolonged siege and a more skilful and powerful attack was expected. In the enemy's camp was found the French engineer's sketch for a renewed operation by a cautious and extensive system of mines and breaches; but nothing was there laid down that had not been already anticipated, and provided against by his British opponents. If then the defence of Tarifa was a great and splendid exploit, and none can doubt that it was, those who conceived, planned, and executed it should have all the glory. Amongst those persons colonel Skerrett has no right to be placed; yet, such are the errors of power, that he was highly applauded for what he did not do, and general Campbell was severely rebuked by lord Liverpool for having risked his Majesty's troops!

The French displayed courage but no skill. For two days, their heavy howitzers had been directed vaguely against the interior of the town, and the

BOOK XV. 1812. January.

distant island, whither the unfortunate people fled from their shattered and burning houses. A portion of the shells thus thrown away in cruelty would have levelled the north-east tower with the ground, and the French were aware of its importance; but throughout the siege their operations were mastered by the superior ability of the engineer and artillery officers opposed to them.

In the expectation that a more powerful attack would be made in the spring, general Campbell directed casemates and splinter proofs to be made in the island, but Skerrett's troops were recalled to Cadiz, which now contained nearly eight thousand British, exclusive of fifteen hundred of these destined for Carthagena and Alicant. This arrangement was however soon changed, because the events of the war put Carthagena out of the French line of operations, and the pestilence there caused the removal of the British troops. Neither was Tarifa again attacked; lord Wellington had predicted that it would not, and on sure grounds, for he was then contemplating a series of operations, which were calculated to change the state of the war, and which shall be set forth in the next book.

BOOK XVI.

CHAPTER I.

CHAP. I. 1811.

Up to this period, the invasion, although diversified by occasional disasters on the part of the invaders, had been progressive. The tide, sometimes flowing, sometimes ebbing, had still gained upon the land, and wherever the Spaniards had arrested its progress, it was England that urged their labour and renovated their tired strength; no firm barrier, no solid dike, had been opposed to its ravages, save by the British general in Portugal, and even there the foundation of his work, sapped by the trickling waters of folly and intrigue, was sliding away. By what a surprising effort of courage and judgment he secured it shall now be shown; and as the field operations, in this war, were always influenced more by political considerations, than by military principles, it will be necessary first to place the general's situation with respect to the former in its true light.

Political situation of king Joseph. France, abounding in riches and power, was absolute mistress of Europe from the Pyrennees to the Vistula; but Napoleon, resolute to perfect his continental system for the exclusion of British goods, now found himself, in the pursuit of that object, hasten-

BOOK XVI.

1811.

ing rapidly to a new war, and one so vast, that even his force was strained to meet it. The Peninsula already felt relief from this cause. The dread of his arrival ceased to influence the operations of the allied army in Portugal, many able French officers were recalled, and as it was known that the imperial guards, and the Polish troops, were to withdraw from Spain, the scale of offensive projects was necessarily contracted. Conscripts and young soldiers instead of veterans, and in diminished numbers, were now to be expected; and in the French army there was a general, and oppressive sense, of the enormous exertion which would be required to bring two such mighty wars to a happy conclusion. On the other hand, the Peninsulars were cheered by seeing so powerful a monarch, as the czar, rise in opposition to Napoleon, and the English general found the principal basis of his calculations realized by this diversion. He had never yet been strong enough to meet eighty thousand French troops in battle, even under a common general; but his hopes rose when he saw the great warrior of the age, not only turning himself from the contest, but withdrawing from it a reserve of four hundred thousand veterans, whose might the whole world seemed hardly able to withstand.

The most immediate effect, however, which the approaching contest with Russia produced in the Peninsula, was the necessity of restoring Joseph to his former power over the French armies. While the emperor was absent from Paris, the supreme controul of the operations could only be placed in the hands of the monarch of Spain; yet this was only to reproduce there, and with greater virulence, the former jealousies and disputes. Joseph's

Spanish policy remained unchanged; the pride of the French generals was at least equal to his, pretexts for disputes were never wanting on either side, and the mischievous nature of those disputes may be gathered from one example. In November the king being pressed for money, sold the magazines of corn collected near Toledo, for the army of Portugal, and without which the latter could not exist; Marmont, regardless of the political scandal, immediately sent troops to recover the magazines by force, and desired the purchasers to reclaim their money from the monarch.

Political state of Spain. All the intrigues and corruptions and conflicting interests before described had increased in violence. The negotiations for the mediation of England with the colonies, were not ended; Carlotta still pressed her claims; and the division between the liberals and serviles, as they were called, became daily wider. Cadiz was in 1811 the very focus of all disorder. The government was alike weak and dishonest, and used many pitiful arts to extract money from England. No subterfuge was too mean. When Blake was going with the fourth army to Estremadura, previous to the battle of Albuera, the minister Bardaxi entreated the British envoy to grant a loan, or a gift, without which, he asserted, Blake could not move; Mr. Wellesley refused, because a large debt was already due to the legation, and the next morning a Spanish ship of war from America landed a million and a half of dollars!

In July, notwithstanding the victory of Albuera, the regency was held in universal contempt, both it and the cortes were without influence, and their conduct merited it. For although vast sums were

BOOK XVI. 1811.

continually received, and every service was famished, the treasury was declared empty, and there was no probability of any further remittances from America. The temper of the public was soured towards England, the press openly assailed the British character, and all things so evidently tended towards anarchy, that Mr. Wellesley declared "Spanish affairs to be then worse than they had been at any previous period of the war."

The cortes, at first swayed by priests and lawyers, who cherished the inquisition and were opposed to all free institutions, was now chiefly led by a liberal or rather democratic party, averse to the British influence; hence, in August a new constitution, quite opposed to the aristocratic principle, was promulgated. With the excellencies and defects of that instrument the present History has indeed little concern, but the results were not in accord with the spirit of the contrivance, and the evils affecting the war were rather increased by it; the democratic basis of the new constitution excited many and bitter enemies, and the time and attention, which should have been bestowed upon the amelioration of the soldiers' condition, was occupied in factions, disputes, and corrupt intrigues.

That many sound abstract principles of government were clearly and vigorously laid down in the scheme of this constitution, cannot be denied, the complicated oppressions of the feudal system were swept away with a bold and just hand; but of what avail, as regarded the war, was the enunciation of principles which were never attempted to be reduced to practice? What encouragement was it to the soldier, to be told he was a free man, fighting for a constitution as well as for national independence, when he saw the authors of that constitution, corruptly revelling in the wealth which should have clothed, and armed, and fed him? What was nominal equality to him, when he saw incapacity rewarded, crimes and treachery unpunished in the rich, the poor and patriotic oppressed? He laughed to scorn those who could find time to form the constitution of a great empire, but could not find time or honesty to feed, or clothe, or arm the men who were to defend it!

Appendix. No. I.

The enemies of democracy soon spread many grievous reports of misfortunes and treachery, some true, some false; and at the most critical period of the war in Valencia, they endeavoured to raise a popular commotion to sweep away the cortes. The monks and friars, furious at the suppression of the inquisition, were the chief plotters every where; and the proceedings of Palacios, in concert with them, were only part of a church project, commenced all over Spain to resist the cortes. In October, Lardizabal, the other deposed regent, published at Alicant, a manifesto, in which he accused the cortes and the Cadiz writers of jacobinism, maintained the doctrine of passive obedience, and asserted, that the regents only took the oath to the cortes, because they could not count on the army or the people at Cadiz; otherwise they would cause the king's authority to be respected in their persons as his only legitimate representatives. This manifesto was declared treasonable, and a vessel was despatched to bring the offender to Cadiz; but the following day it was discovered, that the old council of Castile had also drawn up a manifesto similar in principle, and the persons sent by the cortes to seize the paper were told that it was

BOOK XVI. 1811. destroyed. The protest of three members against it was however found, and five lawyers were selected from the cortes to try the guilty councillors and Lardizabal.

In November the public cry for a new regency became general, and it was backed by the English plenipotentiary. Nevertheless the matter was deferred upon divers pretexts, and meanwhile the democratic party gained strength in the cortes, and the anti-British feeling appeared more widely diffused than it really was; because some time elapsed before the church and aristocratic party discovered that the secret policy of England was the same as their own. It was so, however, even to the upholding of the inquisition, which it was ridiculously asserted had become objectionable only in name; as if, while the frame-work of tyranny existed, there could ever be wanting the will to fill it up. Necessity alone induced the British cabinet to put on a smooth countenance towards the cortes. In this state of affairs, the negotiation for the colonial mediation, was used by the Spaniards merely as a ground for demanding loans, subsidies, and succours in kind, which they used in fitting out new expeditions against the revolted colonists; the complaints of the British legation on this point were quite disregarded. At this time also Lapeña was acquitted of misconduct at Barosa, and would have been immediately re-employed, if the English minister had not threatened to quit Cadiz, and advised general Cooke to do the same.

Mr. Wellesley seeing that the most fatal consequences to the war must ensue, if a stop was not put to the misconduct of the regency, had sent Mr. Vaughan, the secretary of legation, to acquaint the

British cabinet with the facts, and to solicit a more firm and decided course of policy. Above all things he desired to have the subsidies settled by treaty, that the people of Spain might really know what England had done and was still doing for them; for on every occasion, arms, clothing, ammunition, loans, provisions, guns, stores, and even workmen and funds, to form founderies, were demanded and obtained by the Spanish government, and then wasted or embezzled, without the people benefiting, or even knowing of the generosity, or rather extravagance, with which they were supplied; while the receivers and wasters were heaping calumnies on the donors.

The regency question was at last seriously discussed in the cortes, and the deputy, Capmany, who if we may believe the partizans of Joseph, was anti-English in his heart, argued the necessity of this change on the ground of pleasing the British. This excited great discontent, as he probably intended, and many deputies declared at first that they would not be dictated to by any foreign power; but the departure of Mr. Vaughan alarmed them, and a commission, formed to improve the mode of governing, was hastening the decision of the question, when Blake's disaster at Valencia completed the work. Carlotta's agent was active in her behalf, but the eloquent and honest Arguelles was opposed to him; and the cortes although they recognized her claim to the succession, denied her the regency, because of a previous decree which excluded all royal personages from that office.

Joseph's papers captured at Vittoria.

On the 21st of January 1812, after a secret discussion of twenty-four hours, a new regency, to consist of five members, of which two were Ame-

BOOK XVI. 1812.

ricans, was proclaimed. The men chosen, were the duke of Infantado, then in England, Henry O'Donnel, admiral Villarvicencio, Joachim de Mosquera, and Ignacios de Ribas; and each was to have the presidency by rotation for six months.

They commenced beneficially. O'Donnel was friendly to the British alliance, and proposed a military feast, to restore harmony between the English and Spanish officers; he made many changes in the department of war, and finances; consulted the British generals, and disbanding several bad regiments, incorporated the men with other battalions; he also reduced many inefficient and malignant colonels, and striking off from the pay lists all unemployed and absent officers, it was found, that they were five thousand in number! Ballesteros was appointed captain-general of Andalusia and received the command of the fourth army, whose head-quarters were prudently removed to Algeziras; the troops there were encreased, by drafts from Cadiz to ten or twelve thousand men, and a new army was set on foot in Murcia. Finally, to check trading with the French a general blockade of all the coast in their possession, from Rosas to St. Sebastian, was declared.

But it was soon discovered that the secret object was to obtain a loan from England, and as this did not succeed, and nothing good was ever permanent in Spanish affairs, the old disputes again broke out. The democratic spirit gained strength in the cortes; the anti-English party augmented; the press abounded in libels, impugning the good faith of the British nation, especially with respect to Ceuta; for which however there was some plausible ground of suspicion, because the acquisition of that fortress had actually been proposed to lord Liverpool. The new regency, also as violent as their predecessors with respect to America, disregarded the mediation, and having secretly organized in Gallicia an expedition against the colonies, supplied it with artillery furnished from England for the French war, and then, under another pretence, demanded money of the British minister to forward this iniquitous folly.

Political state of Portugal.—In October all the evils before described still existed, and were aggravated. The old disputes remained unsettled, the return of the royal family was put off, and the reforms in the military system, which Beresford had repaired to Lisbon to effect, were either thwarted or retarded by the regency. Mr. Stuart indeed forced the government to repair the bridges and roads in Beira, to throw some provisions into the fortresses; and, in despite of Redondo, the minister of finance, who, for the first time, now opposed the British influence, he made the regency substitute a military chest and commissariat, instead of the "Junta de Viveres." But Forjas and Redondo then disputed for the custody of the new chest; and when Mr. Stuart explained to the one, that, as the intent was to separate the money of the army from that of the civil departments, his claims were incompatible with such an object; and to the other that the conduct of his own department was already more than he could manage, both were offended; and this new source of disorder was only partially closed by withholding the subsidy until they yielded.

Great malversations in the revenue were also

BOOK XVI. 1811.

discovered; and a plan, to enforce an impartial exaction of the "decima," which was drawn up by Nogueira, at the desire of Wellington, was so ill received by those whose illegal exemptions it attacked, that the Souzas immediately placed themselves at the head of the objectors out of doors. Nogueira then modified it, but the Souzas still opposed, and as Wellington, judging the modification to be an evasion of the principle, would not recede from the first plan, a permanent dispute and a permanent evil, were thus established by that pernicious faction. In fine, not the Souzas only, but the whole regency in their folly now imagined that the war was virtually decided in their favour, and were intent upon driving the British away by disgusting the general.

A new quarrel also arose in the Brazils. Lord Wellington had been created conde de Vimiero, Beresford conde de Trancoso, Silveira conde d'Amurante; and other minor rewards, of a like nature, had been conferred on subordinate officers. These honours had however been delayed in a marked manner, and lord Strangford, who appears to have been ruled entirely by the Souza faction, and was therefore opposed to Forjas, charged, or as he termed it, reported a charge, made against the latter, at the Brazils, for having culpably delayed the official return of the officers who were thus to be rewarded. Against this accusation, which had no foundation in fact, seeing that the report had been made, and that Forjas was not the person to whose department it belonged, lord Wellington and Mr. Stuart protested, because of the injustice; and because it was made in pursuance of a design to remove Forjas from the government. The English general was however thus placed in a strange position, for while his letters to Forjas were menacing rebukes to him, and his coadjutors, for their neglect of public affairs; and while his formal complaints of the conduct of the regency were transmitted to the Brazils, he was also obliged to send other letters in support of the very persons whom he was justly rebuking for misconduct.

In the midst of these embarrassments, an accidental event was like to have brought the question of the British remaining in Portugal to a very sudden decision. While Massena was before the lines, one d'Amblemont had appeared in North America, and given to Onis, the Spanish minister, a plan for burning the British fleet in the Tagus, which he pretended to have received orders from the French government to execute. This plan being transmitted to the Brazils, many persons named by d'Amblemont as implicated were, in consequence arrested at Lisbon and sent to Rio Janeiro, although Mr. Stuart had ascertained the whole affair to be a forgery. The attention paid to this man by Onis and by the court of Rio Janeiro, induced him to make farther trial of their credulity, and he then brought forward a correspondence between the principal authorities of Mexico and the French government; he even produced letters from the French ministers, directing intrigues to be commenced at Lisbon, and the French interest there to be placed in the hands of the Portuguese intendant of police.

Mr. Stuart, lamenting the ruin of many innocent persons, whom this forging villain was thus dooming, prayed lord Wellesley to interfere; but mean-

BOOK XVI. 1811.

while the court of Rio Janeiro, falling headlong into the snare, sent orders to arrest more victims; and amongst others, without assigning any cause, and without any communication with the English general, the regency seized one Borel, a clerk in the department of the British paymaster-general. This act being at once contrary to treaty, hostile to the alliance, and insulting in manner, raised lord Wellington's indignation to such a pitch, that he formally notified to the Portuguese government his resolution, unless good reasons were assigned and satisfaction made for the outrage, to order all persons attached to the British to place themselves in security under the protection of the army, as if in a hostile country, until the further pleasure of the British prince regent should be made known.

The political storm which had been so long gathering then seemed ready to break, but suddenly the horizon cleared. Lord Wellington's letter to the prince, backed up by lord Wellesley's vigorous diplomacy, had at last alarmed the court of Rio Janeiro, and in the very crisis of Borel's case came letters, in which the prince regent admitted, and approved of all the ameliorations and changes proposed by the English general; and the contradiction given by Mr. Stuart to the calumnies of the Souza faction, was taken as the ground for a complete and formal retraction, by Linhares, of his former insinuations, and insulting note relative to that gentleman's conduct. Principal Souza was however not dismissed, nor was Forjas' resignation noticed, but the prince declared that he would overlook that minister's disobedience, and retain him in office; thus proving that fear, not conviction, or justice, for Forjas had not been disobedient, was the true cause of this seeming return to friendly relations with the British.

Mr. Stuart considering the submission of the prince to be a mere nominal concession of power which was yet to be ripened into real authority, looked for further difficulties, and he was not mistaken: meanwhile he made it a point of honour to defend Forjas, and Nogueira, from the secret vengeance of the opposite faction. The present submission of the court however gave the British an imposing influence, which rendered the Souzas' opposition nugatory for the moment. Borel was released and excuses were made for his arrest; the formation of a military chest was pushed with vigour; the paper money was raised in value; the revenue was somewhat increased, and Beresford was enabled to make progress in the restoration of the army. The prince had however directed the regency to revive his claim to Olivenza immediately; and it was with difficulty that lord Wellington could stifle this absurd proceeding; neither did the forced harmony last, for the old abuses affecting the civil administration of the army rather increased, as will be shewn in the narration of military operations which are now to be treated of.

It will be remembered that after the action of El Bodon, the allied army was extensively cantoned on both sides of the Coa. Ciudad Rodrigo was distantly observed by the British, and so closely by Julian Sanchez, that on the 15th he carried off more than two hundred oxen from under the guns of the place, and at the same time captured general Renaud the governor, who had imprudently ven-

BOOK XVI. 1811. October.

tured out with a weak escort. At this time Marmont had one division in Placentia, and the rest of his infantry between that place and Madrid; but his cavalry was at Peneranda on the Salamanca side of the mountains, and his line of communication was organized on the old Roman road of the Puerto de Pico, which had been repaired after the battle of Talavera. The army of the north stretched from the Tormes to Astorga, the walls of which place, as well as those of Zamora, and other towns in Leon, were being restored, that the flat country might be held with a few troops against the Gallician army. It was this scattering of the enemy which had enabled lord Wellington to send Hill against Girard at Aroyo de Molino; but when the reinforcements from France reached the army of Portugal, the army of the north was again concentrated, and would have invaded Gallicia while Bonet attacked the Asturias, if Julian Sanchez's exploit had not rendered it necessary first to re-victual Ciudad Rodrigo.

With this view a large convoy was collected at Salamanca, in October, by general Thiebault, who spread a report that a force was to assemble towards Tamames, and that the convoy was for its support. This report did not deceive lord Wellington; but he believed that the whole army of the north and one division of the army of Portugal would be employed in the operation, and therefore made arrangements to pass the Agueda and attack them on the march. The heavy rains however rendered the fords of that river impracticable; Thiebault seized the occasion, introduced the convoy, and leaving a new governor returned on the 2nd of November before the waters had subsided. One brigade of the light division was at this time on the Vadillo, but it was too weak to meddle with the French, and it was impossible to reinforce it while the Agueda was overflowed; for such is the nature of that river that all military operations on its banks are uncertain. It is very difficult for an army to pass it, at any time in winter, because of the narrow roads, the depth of the fords and the ruggedness of the banks; it will suddenly rise from rains falling on the hills, without any previous indication in the plains, and then the violence and depth of its stream will sweep away any temporary bridge, and render it impossible to pass except by the stone bridge of Ciudad Rodrigo, which was at this time in the enemy's possession.

Early in November, Bonet, having reoccupied the Asturias, Dorsenne marched a body of troops towards the hills above Ciudad, as if to conduct another convoy; but the allied troops being immediately concentrated, passed the Agueda at the ford of Zamara, whereupon the French retired, and their rear was harassed by Carlos d'España and Julian Sanchez, who captured some provisions and money contributions they had raised. But now the provisions in the country between the Coa and the Agueda were all consumed, and the continued negligence of the Portuguese government, with respect to the means of transport, rendered it impossible to bring up the field magazines from the points of water carriage to the army. Lord Wellington was therefore, contrary to all military rules, obliged to separate his divisions in face of the enemy, and to spread the troops, especially the cavalry, even to the Mondego and the valley of the Douro, or see them starved.

BOOK XVI. 1811. Nov.

To cover this dangerous proceeding he kept a considerable body of men beyond the Coa, and the state of all the rivers and roads, at that season, together with the distance of the enemy in some measure protected him; general Hill's second expedition into Estremadura was then also drawing the attention of the French towards that quarter; finally Marmont, being about to detach Montbrun towards Valencia, had withdrawn Foy's division from Placentia, and concentrated the greatest part of his army at Toledo; all which rendered the scattering of the allies less dangerous, and in fact no evil consequences ensued. This war of positions had therefore turned entirely to the advantage of the allies, lord Wellington by taking post near Ciudad Rodrigo while Hill moved round Badajos, had in a manner paralysed three powerful armies. For Soult harassed by Hill in Estremadura, and by Ballesteros and Skerrett in Andalusia, failed in both quarters; and although Marmont in conjunction with Dorsenne, had succoured Ciudad Rodrigo, the latter general's invasion of Gallicia had been stopped short, and his enterprises confined to the reoccupation of the Asturias.

Meanwhile the works of Almeida were so far restored as to secure it from a sudden attack, and in November when the army by crossing the Agueda had occupied the attention of the French, the battering train and siege stores were brought to that fortress, without exciting the enemy's attention, because they appeared to be only the armament for the new works; a trestle bridge to throw over the Agueda was also secretly prepared in the arsenal of Almeida by major Sturgeon of the staff corps, an officer whose brilliant talents, scientific resources, and unmitigated activity continually attracted the attention of the whole army. Thus the preparation for the attack of Ciudad advanced while the English general seemed to be only intent upon defending his own positions.

CHAPTER II.

BOOK XVI. 1811.

Having now brought the story of the war to that period, when, after many changes of fortune, the chances had become more equal, and the fate of the Peninsula, thrown as it were between the contending powers, became a prize for the readiest and boldest warrior, I would, ere it is shown how Wellington seized it, recal to the reader's recollection the previous vicissitudes of the contest. I would have him remember how, when the first, or insurrectional epoch of the war, had terminated successfully for the Spaniards, Napoleon vehemently broke and dispersed their armies, and drove the British auxiliaries to embark at Coruña. How the war with Austria, and the inactivity of Joseph, rendered the emperor's victories unavailing, and revived the confidence of the Spaniards. How sir Arthur Wellesley, victorious on the Douro, then marched into Spain, and, although the concentrated force of the enemy, and the ill conduct of the Spanish government, forced him to retreat again to Portugal as sir John Moore, from the same causes, had been obliged to retreat to the ocean, he by his advance relieved Gallicia, as Moore had by a like operation before saved Andalusia, which concluded the third epoch.

How the peninsulars, owing to the exertions of their allies, still possessed a country, extending from the Asturias, through Gallicia, Portugal, Andalusia, Murcia, Valencia, and Catalonia, and including every important harbour and fortress except Santander, Santona, Barcelona, and St. Sebastian. How Wellington appreciating the advantages which an invaded people possess in their numerous lines of operation, then, counselled the Spaniards, and forced the Portuguese, to adopt a defensive war; and with the more reason that England, abounding beyond all nations in military resources, and invincible as a naval power, could form with her ships a secure exterior floating base or line of depôts round the Peninsula, and was ready to employ her armies as well as her squadrons in the struggle. How the Spaniards, unheeding these admonitions, sought great battles, and in a few months lost the Asturias, Andalusia, Estremadura, Aragon, and the best fortresses of Catalonia, and were again laid prostrate and helpless before the enemy.

How the victorious French armies then moved onwards, in swelling pride, until dashed against the rocks of Lisbon they receded, broken and refluent, and the English general once more stood a conqueror on the frontier of Spain; and had he then retaken Badajos and Rodrigo he would have gloriously finished the fourth or defensive epoch of the war. But being baffled, partly by skill, partly by fortune; factiously opposed by the Portuguese regency, thwarted by the Spanish government, only half supported by his own cabinet, and pestered by the follies of all three, he was reduced to a seeming inactivity; and meanwhile the French added Taragona and the rich kingdom of Valencia to their conquests.

These things I would have the reader reflect upon, because they are the proofs of what it is the

BOOK XVI. 1811.

main object of this history to inculcate, namely that English steel, English gold, English genius, English influence, fought and won the battle of Spanish independence; and this not as a matter of boast, although it was very glorious! but as a useful lesson of experience. On the other hand also we must wonder at the prodigious strength of France under Napoleon, that strength which could at once fight England and Austria, aim at the conquest of the Peninsula, and the reduction of Russia at the same moment of time, and all with good hope of success.

Let it not be said that the emperor's efforts in the war of Spain were feeble, for if the insurrectional epoch, which was unexpected and accidental, be set aside, the grandeur of his efforts will be found answerable to his gigantic reputation. In 1809 the French army was indeed gradually decreased by losses and drafts for the Austrian war, from three hundred and thirty-five thousand, which Napoleon had led into the country, to two hundred and twenty-six thousand. But in 1810 it was again raised to three hundred and sixty-nine thousand, and fluctuated between that number and three hundred and thirty thousand until August 1811, when it was again raised to three hundred and seventy-two thousand men with fifty-two thousand horses! And yet there are writers who assert that Napoleon neglected the war in Spain! But so great is the natural strength of that country, that had the firmness of the nation in battle and its wisdom in council, been commensurate with its constancy in resistance, even this power, backed by the four hundred thousand men who marched to Russia, would scarcely have been sufficient to

Appendix, No. IX. Section 2.

subdue it; whereas, weak in fight and steeped in folly, the Spaniards must have been trampled in the dust, but for the man whose great combinations I am now about to relate.

The nicety, the quickness, the prudence, and the audacity of Wellington's operations, cannot however be justly estimated without an exact knowledge of his political, local, and moral position. His political difficulties have been already described, and his moral situation was simply, that of a man, who felt, that all depended upon himself; that he must by some rapid and unexpected stroke effect in the field what his brother could not effect in the cabinet, while the power of the Perceval faction was prevalent in England. But to understand his local or military position, the conformation of the country and the lines of communication must be carefully considered.

The principal French magazines were at Valladolid, and their advanced troops were on the Tormes, from whence to the Agueda, where they held the important point of Ciudad Rodrigo, was four long marches through a wild forest country.

The allies' line of communication from the Agueda to Lisbon, was supplied by water to Raiva on the Mondego, after which the land carriage was at least a hundred miles, through wild mountains, or devastated valleys; it required fifteen days to bring up a convoy from Lisbon to the army.

The line of communication with Oporto on the left flank, run through eighty miles of very rugged country, before it reached the first point of water carriage on the Douro.

The line of communication with Hill's army on

the right flank, running also through a country full of strong passes and natural obstacles, offered no resources for an army, save what were furnished by the allies' field magazines, which were supplied from Abrantes, the first navigable point on the Tagus. On this line the boat-bridge of Villa Velha was a remarkable feature, as furnishing the only military passage over the Tagus between Abrantes and Almaraz.

The country between the Coa and the Agueda could not supply the troops who occupied it; and the nature of the last river, and the want of a covering position beyond, rendered it a matter of the utmost danger and difficulty to besiege or even invest Ciudad Rodrigo. The disadvantage which the French suffered in being so distant from that fortress was thus balanced.

These considerations had prevented the English general from attacking Ciudad Rodrigo in May; he had then no battering train, and Almeida and her guns, were rendered a heap of ruins by the exploit of Brenier. Badajos was at that period his object, because Beresford was actually besieging it, and the recent battle of Fuentes Onoro, the disputes of the French generals, the disorganization of Massena's army, and as proved by that battle, the inefficiency of the army of the north, rendered it improbable that a serious invasion of Portugal would be resumed on that side. And as the lines of communication with the Mondego and the Douro, were not then completely re-established, and the intermediate magazines small, no incursion of the enemy could have done much mischief; and Spencer's corps was sufficiently strong to cover the line to Vilha Velha.

Affairs however soon changed. The skill of Phillipon, the diligence of Marmont, and the generalship of Soult, in remaining at Llerena after his repulse at Albuera, had rescued Badajos. Lord Wellington's boldness in remaining on the Caya prevented further mischief, but the conduct of the Portuguese government, combined with the position which Napoleon had caused Marmont to take in the valley of the Tagus, effectually precluded a renewal of that siege; and then the fallacious hope of finding Ciudad unprovided, brought lord Wellington back to the Coa. This baffled the enemy's projects, yet the position of the army of the north, and that of Portugal, the one in front, the other on the flank, prevented the English general from undertaking any important operations in the field. For if he had advanced on Salamanca, besides the natural difficulties of the country, his communications with Hill, and even with Abrantes and Lisbon, would have been cut by Marmont; and if he turned against Marmont on the Tagus, Soult and Dorsenne would have closed upon his flanks.

This state of affairs not being well considered, had induced some able officers, at the time of the Elbodon operation, to censure the line of retreat to Sabugal, because it uncovered the line of Celerico, and exposed to capture the battering train then at Villa Ponte; but war is always a choice of difficulties, and it was better to risk guns, of whose vicinity the enemy was not aware, than to give up the communication with Hill which was threatened by the advance of Foy's two divisions on Zarza Maior.

As the French armies were reinforced after the allies came to Beira, Dorsenne and Marmont be-

BOOK XVI. 1811.

came each equal to Wellington in the field, and together infinitely too strong. Soult was then master of Andalusia, and had a moveable reserve of twenty thousand men; the army of Suchet daily gained ground in Valencia, the Asturias were re-occupied by Bonet, and the army of the centre was reorganized. Hence, to commence the siege of either Ciudad or Badajos, in form, was hopeless, and when the rumour of Napoleon's arrival became rife, the English general, whose embarrassments were hourly increasing, looked once more to the lines of Torres Vedras as a refuge. But when the certainty of the Russian war removed this fear, the aspect of affairs again changed, and the capture of Ciudad Rodrigo became possible. For, first, there was a good battering train in Almeida, and the works of that place were restored; secondly, the line of communication with Oporto was completely organized, and shortened by improving the navigation of the Douro; thirdly, Ciudad itself was very weakly garrisoned and the ignorance of the French as to the state of the allies' preparations gave hope of a surprise. It was, however, only by a surprise that success could be expected, and it was not the least of lord Wellington's merits that he so well concealed his preparations, and for so long a period. No other operation, promising any success, was open; and yet the general could no longer remain inactive, because around him the whole fabric of the war was falling to pieces from the folly of the governments he was serving. If he could not effect a blow against the French while Napoleon was engaged in the Russian war, it was clear that the Peninsula would be lost.

Now the surprise of a fortress, with a garrison of only seventeen hundred men, seems a small matter in such grave circumstances, but in reality it was of the very greatest importance, because it was the first step in a plan which saved the Peninsula when nothing else could have saved it. Lord Wellington knew that the valley of the Tagus, could not long support both the army of Portugal, and the army of the centre; he knew by intercepted letters that Marmont and the king were already at open war upon the subject, and he judged, that if he could surprise Ciudad Rodrigo, the army of Portugal would be obliged, for the sake of provisions, and to protect Leon, then weakened by the departure of the imperial guards, to concentrate in that province. This was the first step.

The French kept magazines in reserve for sudden expeditions, feeding meanwhile as they could upon the country, and therefore their distress for provisions never obstructed their moving upon important occasions. Nevertheless lord Wellington thought the tempestuous season would render it very difficult for Marmont, when thus forced into Leon, to move with great masses; wherefore he proposed when Rodrigo fell, to march by Vilha Velha to Estremadura, and suddenly besiege Badajos also, the preparations to be previously made in Elvas, under the protection of Hill's corps, and unknown to the enemy. This was the second step, and in this surprise also he hoped to be successful, because of the jealousies of the marshals, the wet season, and his own combinations, which would impede the concentration of the French armies, and prevent them from keeping together if they did unite. He had hopes likewise that as Ballesteros' corps was now augmented,

BOOK XVI. 1811. Nov.

it would vex Soult's posts on the coast, while Hill and Morillo harassed him on the Guadiana; and if Badajos fell, the English general was resolved to leave a force to cover the captured place against the army of the centre, and then fight Soult in Andalusia. For he judged that Marmont could not for want of provisions, pass beyond the Guadiana, nor follow him before the harvest was ripe; neither did he fear him in Beira, because the torrents would be full, the country a desert, and the militia, aided by a small regular corps, and covered by Almeida and Ciudad Rodrigo, would, he thought, be sufficient to prevent any serious impression being made on Portugal during the invasion of Andalusia.

This was lord Wellington's plan, and his firmness and resolution in conceiving it were the more signal because his own troops were not in good plight. The army had indeed received reinforcements, but the infantry had served at Walcheren, and exposure to night air, or even slight hardship, threw them by hundreds into the hospital, while the new regiments of cavalry, inexperienced, and not acclimated, were found, men and horses, quite unfit for duty, and were sent to the rear. The pay of the army was three months in arrear, and the supplies, brought up with difficulty, were very scanty; half and quarter rations were often served, and sometimes the troops were without any bread for three days consecutively, and their clothing was so patched, that scarcely a regiment could be known by its uniform. Chopped straw, the only forage, was so scarce that the regimental animals were dying of hunger; corn was rarely distributed save to the generals and staff, and even the horses of the artillery and of the old cavalry suffered; nay, the very mules of the commissariat were pinched by the scarcity, and the muleteers were eight months in arrears of pay. The cantonments on the Coa and Agueda were unhealthy from the continued rains, above twenty thousand men were in hospital; and deduction made for other drains, only fifty-four thousand of both nations, including garrisons and posts of communication, were under arms. To finish the picture, the sulky apathy produced in the Portuguese regency by the prince regent's letter, was now becoming more hurtful than the former active opposition.

But even these distresses so threatening to the general cause, Wellington turned to the advantage of his present designs; for the enemy were aware of the misery in the army, and in their imagination magnified it; and as the allied troops were scattered, for relief, from the Gata mountains to the Douro, and from the Agueda to the Mondego, at the very moment when the battering train entered Almeida, both armies concluded, that these guns were only to arm that fortress, as a cover to the extended country quarters which necessity had forced the British general to adopt. No person, not even the engineers employed in the preparations, knew more than that a siege or the simulation of a siege was in contemplation; but when it was to be attempted, or that it would be attempted at all, none knew; even the quarter-master general Murray, was permitted to go home on leave, with the full persuasion that no operation would take place before spring.

In the new cantonments, however, abundance of

BOOK XVI. 1811. Dec.

provisions, and dry weather (for in Beira the first rains generally subside during December,) stopped the sickness, and restored about three thousand men to the ranks; and it would be a great error to suppose, that the privations had in any manner weakened the moral courage of the troops. The old regiments had become incredibly hardy and experienced in all things necessary to sustain their strength and efficacy; the staff of the army was well practised, and lord Fitzroy Somerset, the military secretary, had established such an intercourse between the head-quarters and the commanders of battalions, that the latter had, so to speak, direct communication with the general-in-chief upon all the business of their regiments; a privilege which increased the enthusiasm and zeal of all in a very surprising manner. For the battalions being generally under very young men, the distinctions of rank were not very rigidly enforced, and the merits of each officer were consequently better known, and more earnestly supported when promotion and honours were to be obtained. By this method lord Fitzroy acquired an exact knowledge of the true moral state of each regiment, rendered his own office at once powerful and gracious to the army, and yet, such was his discretion and judgment, did in no manner weaken the military hierarchy; thus also all the daring young men were excited, and being unacquainted with the political difficulties of their general, anticipated noble triumphs which were happily realized.

The favourable moment for action so long watched for by Wellington came at last. An imperial decree had remodelled the French armies. That of Aragon was directed to give up four divisions to form a new corps, under Reille, called the "*army of the Ebro,*" whose head-quarters were at Lerida. The army of the south was recomposed in six divisions of infantry and three of cavalry, besides the garrison of Badajos, and marshal Victor returned to France, discontented, for he was one of those whose reputation had been abated by this war. His divisions were given to generals Conroux, Barrois, Villatte, Laval, Drouet, Daricau, Peyremont, Digeon, and the younger Soult, Phillipon continuing governor of Badajos. The reserve of Monthion was broken up, and the army of the north, destined to maintain the great communications with France and to reduce the Partidas, on that line, was ordered to occupy the districts round St. Ander, Sebastian, Burgos, and Pampeluna, and to communicate by the left with the new army of the Ebro: it was also exceedingly reduced in numbers; for the imperial guards, seventeen thousand strong, were required for the Russian war, and marched in December to France. And besides these troops, the Polish battalions, the skeletons of the cavalry regiments, and several thousand choice men destined to fill the ranks of the old guard were drafted; so that not less than forty thousand, of the very best soldiers, were withdrawn, and the maimed and worn-out men being sent back to France at the same time, the force in the Peninsula was diminished by sixty thousand.

The head-quarters of the army of the north arrived at Burgos in January, and a division was immediately sent to drive Mendizabel from the Montaña de St. Ander; but as this arrangement weak-

BOOK XVI.

1812. January.

ened the grand line of communication with France, Marmont was ordered to abandon the valley of the Tagus and fix his head-quarters at Valladolid or Salamanca. Ciudad Rodrigo, the sixth and seventh governments, and the Asturias, were also placed under his authority, by which Souham and Bonet's division, forming together about eighteen thousand men, were added to his army; but the former general returned to France. These divisions however, being pressed by want, were extended from the Asturias to Toledo, while Montbrun was near Valencia, and meanwhile Soult's attention was distracted by Tarifa, and by Hill's pursuit of Drouet. Thus the French armies, every where occupied, were spread over an immense tract of country; Marmont deceived by the seemingly careless winter attitude of the allies, left Ciudad Rodrigo unprotected within their reach, and Wellington jumped with both feet upon the devoted fortress.

CHAPTER III.

SIEGE OF CIUDAD RODRIGO.

CHAP. III. — 1812. January.

THE troops disposable for the attack of Ciudad Rodrigo were about thirty-five thousand, including cavalry; the materials for the siege were established at Gallegos, Villa del Ciervo, and Espeja, on the left of the Agueda, and the ammunition was at Almeida. From those places, the hired carts and mules, were to bring up the stores to the parc, and seventy pieces of ordnance had been collected at Villa de Ponte. But from the scarcity of transports only thirty-eight guns could be brought to the trenches, and these would have wanted their due supply of ammunition, if eight thousand shot had not been found amidst the ruins of Almeida.

On the 1st of January the bridge was commenced at Marialva, near the confluence of the Azava with the Agueda, about six miles below Ciudad, and piles were driven into the bed of the river, above and below, to which the trestles were tied to render the whole firm. The fortress was to have been invested on the 6th, but the native carters were two days moving over ten miles of flat and excellent road, with empty carts; the operation was thus delayed, and it was dangerous to find fault with these people, because they deserted on the slightest offence. Meanwhile the place being closely examined, it was found that the French, in addition

BOOK XVI. 1812. January.

to the old works, had fortified two convents, which flanked and strengthened the bad Spanish entrenchments round the suburbs. They had also constructed an enclosed and palisadoed redoubt upon the greater Teson; and this redoubt, called Francisco, was supported by two guns and a howitzer placed on the flat roof of the convent of that name.

The soil around was exceedingly rocky, except on the Teson itself, and though the body of the place was there better covered by the outworks, and could bring most fire to bear on the trenches, it was more assailable according to the English general's views; because elsewhere the slope of the ground was such, that batteries must have been erected on the very edge of the counterscarp before they could see low enough to breach. This would have been a tedious process, whereas the smaller Teson furnished the means of striking over the crest of the glacis at once, and a deep gully near the latter offered cover for the miners. It was therefore resolved to storm fort Francisco, form a lodgement there, and opening the first parallel along the greater Teson, to place thirty-three pieces in counter-batteries with which to ruin the defences, and drive the besieged from the convent of Francisco; then working forward by the sap to construct breaching-batteries on the lesser Teson, and blow in the counterscarp, while seven guns, by battering a weak turret on the left, opened a second breach, with a view to turn any retrenchment behind the principal breach.

The first, third, fourth, and light divisions, and Pack's Portuguese, were destined for the siege, but as the country on the right bank of the Agueda was destitute of fuel and cover, these troops were still to keep their quarters on the left bank; and although there was a very severe frost and fall of snow, yet one division carrying a day's provisions ready cooked, was to ford the river, every twenty-four hours, either above or below the town, and thus alternately carry on the works. Meanwhile to cover the siege, Julian Sanchez and Carlos d'España were posted on the Tormes in observation of the enemy.

To obviate the difficulty of obtaining country transport, the English general had previously constructed eight hundred carts drawn by horses, and these were now his surest dependence for bringing up ammunition; yet so many delays were anticipated from the irregularity of the native carters and muleteers, and the chances of weather, that he calculated upon an operation of twenty-four days, and yet hoped to steal it from his adversaries; sure, even if he failed, that the clash of his arms would again draw their scattered troops to that quarter, as tinkling bells draw swarming bees to an empty hive.

The 8th of January the light division and Pack's Portuguese forded the Agueda near Caridad, three miles above the fortress, and making a circuit, took post beyond the great Teson, where they remained quiet during the day, and as there was no regular investment, the enemy believed not that the siege was commenced. But in the evening the troops stood to their arms, and colonel Colborne commanding the fifty-second, having assembled two companies from each of the British regiments of the light division, stormed the redoubt of Francisco. This he did with so much fury, that the assailants appeared to be at one and the same time, in the ditch, mounting the parapets, fighting on the top of the rampart, and

BOOK XVI. 1812. January.

forcing the gorge of the redoubt, where the explosion of one of the French shells had burst the gate open. Of the defenders a few were killed, not many, and the remainder, about forty in number, were made prisoners. The post being thus taken with the loss of only twenty-four men and officers, working parties were set to labour on the right of it, because the fort itself was instantly covered with shot and shells from the town. This tempest continued through the night, but at day-break the parallel, six hundred yards in length, was sunk three feet deep, and four wide, the communication over the Teson to the rear was completed, and the progress of the siege was thus hastened several days by this well-managed assault.

The 9th the first division took the trenches in hand. The place was encircled by posts to prevent any external communication, and at night twelve hundred workmen commenced three counter-batteries, for eleven guns each, under a heavy fire of shells and grape. Before day-light the labourers were under cover, and a ditch was also sunk in the front to provide earth; for the batteries were made eighteen feet thick at top, to resist the very powerful artillery of the place.

On the 10th the fourth division relieved the trenches, and a thousand men laboured, but in great peril, for the besieged had a superabundance of ammunition, and did not spare it. In the night the communication from the parallel to the batteries was opened, and on the 11th the third division undertook the siege.

This day the magazines in the batteries were excavated, and the approaches widened, but the enemy's fire was destructive, and the shells came so fast into the ditch in front of the batteries, that the troops were withdrawn, and the earth was raised from the inside. Great damage was also sustained from salvos of shells, with long fuzes, whose simultaneous explosion cut away the parapets in a strange manner, and in the night the French brought a howitzer to the garden of the convent of Francisco, with which they killed many men and wounded others.

On the 12th the light division resumed the work, and the riflemen taking advantage of a thick fog, covered themselves in pits, which they digged in front of the trenches, and from thence picked off the enemy's gunners; but in the night the weather was so cold, and the besieged shot so briskly, that little progress was made.

The 13th, the first division being on duty, the same causes impeded the labourers, and now also the scarcity of transport baulked the general's operations. One third only, of the native carts, expected, had arrived, and the drivers of those present were very indolent; much of the twenty-four pound ammunition was still at Villa de Ponte, and intelligence arrived that Marmont was collecting his forces to succour the place. Wellington therefore changing his first plan, resolved to open a breach with his counter-batteries, which were not quite six hundred yards from the curtain, and then to storm the place without blowing in the counterscarp; in other words, to overstep the rules of science, and sacrifice life rather than time, for such was the capricious nature of the Agueda that in one night a flood might enable a small French force to relieve the place.

The whole army was immediately brought up

BOOK XVI.

1812. January.

from the distant quarters, and posted in the villages on the Coa, ready to cross the Agueda and give battle; and it was at this time, that Hill, who was then at Merida, returned to Portalegre, and sent a division across the Tagus, lest Marmont in despair of uniting his force in the north, in time to save Ciudad, should act against the line of communication by Castello Branco and Vilha Velha.

Vide page 328.

In the night of the 13th the batteries were armed with twenty-eight guns, the second parallel and the approaches were continued by the flying sap, and the Santa Cruz convent was surprised by the Germans of the first division, which secured the right flank of the trenches.

The 14th the enemy, who had observed that the men in the trenches always went off in a disorderly manner on the approach of the relief, made a sally and overturned the gabions of the sap; they even penetrated to the parallel, and were upon the point of entering the batteries, when a few of the workmen getting together, checked them until a support arrived, and thus the guns were saved. This affair, together with the death of the engineer on duty, and the heavy fire from the town, delayed the opening of the breaching-batteries, but at half-past four in the evening, twenty-five heavy guns battered the "*fausse braye*" and rampart, and two pieces were directed against the convent of Francisco. Then was beheld a spectacle at once fearful and sublime. The enemy replied to the assailants' fire with more than fifty pieces, the bellowing of eighty large guns shook the ground far and wide, the smoke rested in heavy volumes upon the battlements of the place, or curled in light wreaths about the numerous spires, the shells, hissing through the air, seemed fiery serpents leaping from the darkness, the walls crashed to the stroke of the bullet, and the distant mountains, faintly returning the sound, appeared to moan over the falling city. And when night put an end to this turmoil, the quick clatter of musketry was heard like the pattering of hail after a peal of thunder, for the fortieth regiment assaulted and carried the convent of Francisco, and established itself in the suburb on the left of the attack.

1812. January.

The next day the ramparts were again battered, and fell so fast that it was judged expedient to commence the small breach at the turret, and in the night of the 15th five more guns were mounted. The 16th at day-light the besiegers' batteries recommenced, but at eight o'clock a thick fog obliged them to desist, nevertheless the small breach had been opened, and the place was now summoned, but without effect. At night the parallel on the lower Teson was extended, and a sharp musketry was directed from thence against the great breach. The breaching-battery as originally projected was also commenced, and the riflemen of the light division, hidden in the pits, continued to pick off the enemy's gunners.

The 17th the fire on both sides was very heavy and the wall of the place was beaten down in large cantles; but several of the besiegers' guns were dismounted, their batteries injured, and many of their men killed; general Borthwick the commandant of artillery was wounded and the sap was entirely ruined. Even the riflemen in the pits were at first overpowered with grape, yet towards evening they recovered the upper hand, and the French could only fire from the more distant embrasures. In the night the battery, intended for the lesser

BOOK XVI.

1812. January.

breach, was armed, and that on the lower Teson raised so as to afford cover in the day-time.

On the 18th the besiegers' fire was resumed with great violence. The turret was shaken at the small breach, the large breach became practicable in the middle, and the enemy commenced retrenching it. The sap however could make no progress, the superintending engineer was badly wounded, and a twenty-four pounder having bursted in the batteries, killed several men. In the night the battery on the lower Teson was improved, and a field-piece and howitzer being placed there, kept up a constant fire on the great breach to destroy the French retrenchments.

On the 19th both breaches became practicable, major Sturgeon closely examined the place, and a plan of attack was formed on his report; the assault was then ordered, and the battering-guns were turned against the artillery of the ramparts.

ASSAULT OF CIUDAD RODRIGO.

This operation which was confided to the third and light divisions, and Pack's Portuguese, was organized in four parts.

1°. *The right attack.* The light company of the eighty-third and the second caçadores which were posted in the houses beyond the bridge on the Agueda, were directed to cross that river and escalade an outwork in front of the castle, where there was no ditch, but where two guns commanded the junction of the counterscarp with the body of the place. The fifth and ninety-fourth regiments posted behind the convent of Santa Cruz and having the seventy-seventh in reserve, were to enter the ditch at the extremity of the counterscarp; then to escalade the "*fausse braye*," and scour it on their left as far as the great breach. CHAP. III.

2°. *The centre attack or assault of the great breach.* One hundred and eighty men protected by the fire of the eighty-third regiment, and carrying hay-bags to throw into the ditch, were to move out of the second parallel and to be followed by a storming party, which was again to be supported by general Mackinnon's brigade of the third division. 1812. January.

Left attack. The light division, posted behind the convent of Francisco, was to send three companies of the ninety-fifth to scour the "*fausse braye*" to the right, and so connect the left and centre attacks. At the same time a storming party preceded by the third caçadores carrying hay-sacks, and followed by Vandeleur's and Andrew Barnard's brigades, was to make for the small breach, and when the "*fausse braye*" was carried to detach to their right, to assist the main assault, and to the left to force a passage at the Salamanca gate.

4°. *The false attack.* This was an escalade to be made by Pack's Portuguese on the St. Jago gate at the opposite side of the town.

The right attack was commanded by colonel O'Toole of the caçadores.

Five hundred volunteers commanded by major Manners of the seventy-fourth with a forlorn hope under Mr. Mackie of the eighty-eighth, composed the storming party of the third division.

Three hundred volunteers led by major George Napier of the fifty-second with a forlorn hope of twenty-five men under Mr. Gurwood, of the same regiment, composed the storming party of the light division.

All the troops reached their different posts with-

BOOK XVI. 1812. January. Appendix, No. VII. Sect. 1.

out seeming to attract the attention of the enemy, but before the signal was given, and while lord Wellington, who in person had been pointing out the lesser breach to major Napier, was still at the convent of Francisco, the attack on the right commenced, and was instantly taken up along the whole line. Then the space between the army and the ditch was covered with soldiers and ravaged by a tempest of grape from the ramparts. The storming parties of the third division jumped out of the parallel when the first shout arose, but so rapid had been the movements on their right, that before they could reach the ditch, Ridge, Dunkin, and Campbell with the fifth, seventy-seventh, and ninety-fourth regiments, had already scoured the "*fausse braye*," and were pushing up the great breach, amidst the bursting of shells, the whistling of grape and muskets, and the shrill cries of the French who were driven fighting behind the retrenchments. There however they rallied, and aided by the musketry from the houses, made hard battle for their post; none would go back on either side, and yet the British could not get forward, and men and officers, falling in heaps, choked up the passage, which from minute to minute was raked with grape, from two guns, flanking the top of the breach at the distance of a few yards; thus striving and trampling alike upon the dead and the wounded these brave men maintained the combat.

Meanwhile the stormers of the light division, who had three hundred yards of ground to clear, would not wait for the hay-bags, but with extraordinary swiftness running to the crest of the glacis, jumped down the scarp, a depth of eleven feet, and rushed up the "*fausse braye*" under a smashing discharge of grape and musketry. The bottom of the ditch was dark and intricate, and the forlorn hope took too much to their left; but the storming party went straight to the breach, which was so contracted that a gun placed lengthwise across the top nearly blocked up the opening. Here the forlorn hope rejoined the stormers, but when two-thirds of the ascent were gained, the leading men, crushed together by the narrowness of the place, staggered under the weight of the enemy's fire; and such is the instinct of self-defence, that although no man had been allowed to load, every musket in the crowd was snapped. The commander, major Napier, was at this moment stricken to the earth by a grape shot which shattered his arm, but he called on his men to trust to their bayonets, and all the officers simultaneously sprang to the front, when the charge was renewed with a furious shout, and the entrance was gained. The supporting regiments coming up in sections, abreast, then reached the rampart, the fifty-second wheeled to the left, the forty-third to the right, and the place was won. During this contest which lasted only a few minutes, after the "*fausse braye*" was passed, the fighting had continued at the great breach with unabated violence, but when the forty-third, and the stormers of the light division, came pouring down upon the right flank of the French, the latter bent before the storm; at the same moment, the explosion of three wall magazines destroyed many persons, and the third division with a mighty effort broke through the retrenchments. The garrison indeed still fought for a moment in the streets, but finally fled to the castle, where Mr. Gurwood who though wounded, had been amongst the foremost at the lesser breach, received the governor's sword.

BOOK XVI.

1812. January.

The allies now plunged into the streets from all quarters, for O'Toole's attack was also successful, and at the other side of the town Pack's Portuguese, meeting no resistance, had entered the place, and the reserves also came in. Then throwing off the restraints of discipline the troops committed frightful excesses. The town was fired in three or four places, the soldiers menaced their officers, and shot each other; many were killed in the market-place, intoxication soon increased the tumult, disorder every where prevailed, and at last, the fury rising to an absolute madness, a fire was wilfully lighted in the middle of the great magazine, when the town and all in it would have been blown to atoms, but for the energetic courage of some officers and a few soldiers who still preserved their senses.

Three hundred French had fallen, fifteen hundred were made prisoners, and besides the immense stores of ammunition, above one hundred and fifty pieces of artillery including the battering-train of Marmont's army, were captured in the place. The whole loss of the allies was about twelve hundred soldiers and ninety officers, and of these above six hundred and fifty men and sixty officers had been slain or hurt at the breaches. General Crawfurd and general Mackinnon, the former a man of great ability, were killed, and with them died many gallant men, amongst others, a captain of the forty-fifth, of whom it has been felicitously said, that "three generals and seventy other officers had fallen, but the soldiers fresh from the strife only talked of Hardyman." General Vandaleur, colonel Colborne, and a crowd of inferior rank were wounded, and unhappily the slaughter did

Captain Cooke's Memoirs, vol. i.

Explanatory Sketch OF THE SIEGE OF CIUDAD RODRIGO, 1812.

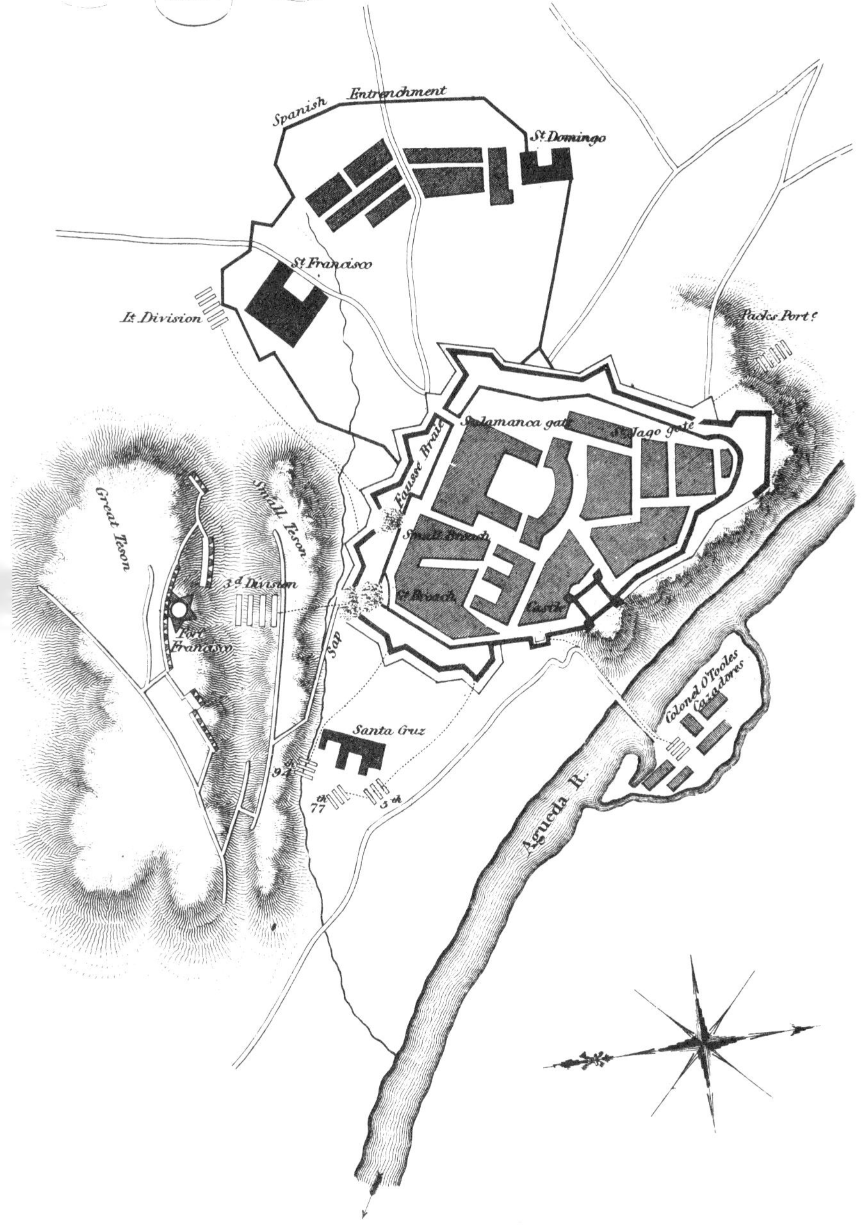

London: Published by T. & W. BOONE.

not end with the battle, for the next day as the prisoners and their escort were marching out by the breach, an accidental explosion took place and numbers of both were blown into the air. CHAP. III. 1812. January.

To recompense an exploit so boldly undertaken and so gloriously finished, lord Wellington was created duke of Ciudad Rodrigo by the Spaniards, earl of Wellington by the English, and marquis of Torres Vedras by the Portuguese; but it is to be remarked, that the prince regent of Portugal had previous to that period displayed great ingratitude in the conferring of honours upon the British officers.

OBSERVATIONS.

1°. The duration of this siege was twelve days, or half the time originally calculated upon by the English general, and yet the inexperience both of the engineer and soldier, and the very heavy fire of the place, had caused the works to be more slowly executed than might have been expected; the cold also had impeded the labourers, and yet with a less severe frost the trenches would have been overflowed, because in open weather the water rises every where to within six inches of the surface. But the worst obstacle was caused by the disgraceful badness of the cutting-tools furnished from the storekeeper-general's office in England, the profits of the contractor seemed to be the only thing respected; the engineers eagerly sought for French implements, because those provided by England were useless.

2°. The audacious manner in which Wellington stormed the redoubt of Francisco, and broke ground

BOOK XVI. 1812. January.

on the first night of the investment; the more audacious manner in which he assaulted the place before the fire of the defence had been in any manner lessened, and before the counterscarp had been blown in; were the true causes of the sudden fall of the place. Both the military and political state of affairs warranted this neglect of rules. The final success depended more upon the courage of the troops than the skill of the engineer; and when the general terminated his order for the assault, with this sentence, "Ciudad Rodrigo *must* be stormed this evening," he knew well that it would be nobly understood. Yet the French fought bravely on the breach, and by their side many British deserters, desperate men, were bayonetted.

3°. The great breach was cut off from the town by a perpendicular descent of sixteen feet, and the bottom was planted with sharp spikes, and strewn with live shells; the houses behind were all loop-hooled, and garnished with musketeers, and on the flanks there were cuts, not indeed very deep or wide and the French had left the temporary bridges over them, but behind were parapets so powerfully defended that it was said the third division could never have carried them, had not the light division taken the enemy in flank: an assertion perhaps easier made than proved.

4°. The rapid progress of the allies on this occasion, has been contrasted with the slow proceedings of Massena in 1810, and the defence of Herrasti has been compared with that of Barrié. But Massena was not pressed for time, and he would have been blameable to have spared labour at the expense of blood; Herrasti also had a garrison of six thousand men, whereas Barrié had less than two thousand, of which only seventeen hundred were able to bear arms, and he had additional works to guard. Nevertheless his neglect of the lesser breach was a great error; it was so narrow and high, that a very slight addition to its defences would have rendered it quite impracticable; and as the deserters told him in the morning of the 19th that the light division was come up, out of its turn, he must have expected the assault and had time to prepare for it. Moreover the small breach was flanked at a very short distance, by a demi-bastion with a parapet, which, though little injured, was abandoned when the head of the storming party had forced their way on to the rampart. But the true way of defending Ciudad was by external operations, and it was not until it fell, that the error of Marmont at Elbodon could be judged in its full extent. Neither can that marshal be in any manner justified for having left so few men in Ciudad Rodrigo; it is certain that with a garrison of five thousand the place would not have been taken, for when there are enough of men the engineer's art cannot be overcome by mere courage.

5°. The excesses committed by the allied troops were very disgraceful. The Spanish people were allies and friends, unarmed and helpless, and all these claims were disregarded. "The soldiers were not to be controuled." That excuse will however scarcely suffice here, because colonel Macleod of the forty-third, a young man of a most energetic spirit, placed guards at the breach and did constrain his regiment to keep its ranks for a long time after the disorders commenced; but as no previous general measures had been taken, and no organized efforts made by higher authorities, the men were finally carried away in the increasing tumult.

Captain Cooke's Memoirs, vol. i. p. 122.

CHAPTER IV.

BOOK XVI.

1812. January.

In Ciudad Rodrigo, papers were found by which it appeared, that many of the inhabitants were emissaries of the enemy: all these people Carlos d'España slew without mercy, but of the English deserters, who were taken, some were executed, some pardoned, and the rigour of the Spanish generals was thought to be overstrained.

When order had been restored workmen were set to repair the breaches and to level the trenches, and arrangements were made to provision the place quickly, for Marmont's army was gathering at Valladolid; that general was however still ignorant that Ciudad had fallen. In the latter end of December, rumour, anticipating the fact had indeed spoken of an English bridge on the Agueda, and the expedition to Alicant was countermanded; yet the report died away, and Montbrun re-commenced his march. But though the bridge was cast on the 1st and the siege commenced on the 8th, on the 12th nothing was known at Salamanca.

On the 11th Marmont arrived at Valladolid; on the 15th he for the first time heard of the siege. His army was immediately ordered to concentrate at Salamanca, Bonnet quitted the Asturias, Montbrun hastened back from Valencia, Dorsenne sent a detachment to aid, and on the 25th six divisions of infantry and one of cavalry, being about forty-five thousand in all, were assembled at Salamanca, from whence to Ciudad, was four marches.

On the 23d Souham had advanced to Matilla to ascertain the fate of the fortress, but meanwhile five thousand of Hill's troops had reached Castello Branco, and the allies were therefore strong enough to fight beyond the Agueda. Hence if the siege had even lasted twenty-four days, the place might still have been taken.

The 26th Marmont knew that the fortress was lost, and unable to comprehend his adversary's success, retired to Valladolid. His divisions were thus harassed by ruinous marches in winter; for Montbrun had already reached Arevalo on his return from Valencia, and Bonnet in repassing the Asturian mountains, had suffered much from cold and fatigue, and more from the attacks of Porlier who harassed him without cessation. Sir Howard Douglas immediately sent money and arms to the Asturians, on one flank, and on the other flank, Morillo who had remained at Horcajo in great peril after his flight from Almagro, took the opportunity to escape by Truxillo; meanwhile Saornil's band cut off a French detachment at Medina del Campo, other losses were sustained from the Partidas on the Tietar, and the operations of those in the Rioja, Navarre, and New Castile were renewed. The regular Spanish troops were likewise put in movement. Abadia and Cabrera, advancing from Gallicia, menaced Astorga and La Baneza, but the arrival of Bonnet at Benevente, soon obliged them to retire again to Puebla de Senabria and Villa Franca; and Silveira who had marched across the frontier of Tras os Montes to aid them, also fell back to Portugal.

Marmont's operations were here again ill judged. He should have taken post at Tamames, or St. Martin de Rio, and placed strong advanced guards

BOOK XVI. 1812. February.

at Tenebron and St. Espiritus, in the hills immediately above Ciudad. His troops could have been concentrated at those places the 28th and on that day such a heavy rain set in, that the trestle bridge at Marialva could not stand, and the river rose two feet over the stone bridge at the town. The allies were then on the left bank, the communication with the town was entirely cut off, the repair of the breaches was scarcely complete, and Ciudad being entirely exposed for several days might have been retaken. But the greatest warriors are the very slaves of fortune!

The English general's eyes were now turned towards Badajos, which he was desirous to invest in the second week of March; because then the flooding of the rivers in Beira, would enable him to carry nearly all his forces to the Alemtejo, without risk, and the same rains would impede the junction of the enemy's force in Estremadura. Green forage was to be had in the last province considerably earlier than on the Agueda, and the success of the contemplated campaign in Andalusia depended upon the operations taking place before the harvest upon the ground should ripen, which was the enemy's resource, and would happen much earlier there than in Leon.

Preliminary measures were already in progress. In December a pontoon bridge escorted by military artificers and some Portuguese seamen, had been ordered from Lisbon to Abrantes, where draft bullocks were collected to draw it to Elvas. After the fall of Ciudad stores and tools were sent from Lisbon to Setuval, and thence in boats to Alcacer do Sal; and a company of the military artificers. then at Cadiz, were disembarked at Ayamonte to proceed to Elvas, where an engineer officer secretly superintended the preparations for the siege. Meanwhile the repairs of Ciudad went on, two new redoubts were traced out upon the Tesons, the old one was enlarged, and the suburbs were strengthened, but the heavy storms before mentioned, impeded these works, and having entirely stopped all communication by sea and land, delayed for many days the preparations for the ulterior operations. When the weather cleared they were renewed, yet other obstacles were not wanting.

The draft bullocks, sinking from want, were unable to drag the whole battering train by the way of Vilha Velha, and only sixteen twenty-four pounders, and twenty spare carriages could be moved on that line. To supply the deficiency sixteen twenty-four pounders, then in vessels in the Tagus, were ordered up to Abrantes, and admiral Berkeley was applied to for twenty ship-guns. He had none of that calibre and offered eighteen pounders, which were accepted; but when major Dickson, who superintended the arrangements for the artillery service, arrived at Lisbon, he found that these were Russian pieces whose bore was too large for English shot, and the admiral refused to give guns from his own ship the Barfleur, in their place. This apparently capricious proceeding produced both difficulty and delay, because the artillery-men were in consequence obliged to cull the Portuguese shot in the arsenal to obtain a sufficient supply. However the energy of major Dickson overcame every obstacle, and in the beginning of March the battering guns fifty-two in number, the pontoons from Abrantes, and most of the stores

BOOK XVI. 1812. February.

from Alcaçer do Sal, were parked at Elvas, where also gabions and fascines were piled in great numbers.

Marmont having lost his emissaries at Ciudad Rodrigo, and being unable to measure his adversary's talent and energy, had during these transactions again spread his troops that he might the more easily feed them. Three divisions of infantry and part of the cavalry returned to Talavera and Toledo. Souham occupied the country from Zamora and Toro, to the banks of the Tormes; and Bonnet after driving the Gallicians back to Senabria and Villa Franca remained about Benevente and Astorga. The army of Portugal appeared to dread no further operations on the part of the allies, yet from some secret misgiving, Marmont caused general Foy to march through the Guadalupe, by the pass of St. Vincente to ascertain whether an army could march by that line from the Tagus to the Guadiana.

This scattering of the French relieved lord Wellington from a serious embarrassment. The constant difficulty of land transport, had prevented him from bringing up the clothing of the army, and he was now obliged to send the regiments to those points on the Mondego, the Douro, and the Tagus, where the clothing had arrived by boats; hence the march to the Alemtejo was necessarily long and unmilitary, and would have been too dangerous to attempt, if Marmont had kept his troops together on the Tormes, with advanced posts pushed towards Ciudad Rodrigo. The weather was now however extremely favourable to the allies, and the new Portuguese commissariat supplied the troops on this march well, and without any of those exactions and oppressions which had always before marked the movements of the native troops; nevertheless the scarcity was so great, that rations of cassava root were served to the Portuguese instead of bread. CHAP. IV. 1812. March.

The talents of lord Wellington always rose with his difficulties, but the want of specie crippled every operation. A movement into Spain, such as that now intended against Andalusia, could not be effected without magazines when there was no harvest on the ground, except by paying ready money; because it was certain that the Spaniards, however favourably disposed, would never diminish their own secret resources for mere promises of payment. The English general and Mr. Stuart, therefore, endeavoured to get British bank notes accepted as cash, by the great merchants of Lisbon and Oporto; and lord Wellington reflecting that, from the enormous sums spent in Portugal, many persons must needs have secret hoards which they would be glad to invest if they could do it safely, asked for English exchequer-bills to negotiate in the same manner; intending to pay the interest punctually and faithfully however inconvenient it might prove at the moment. This plan could not be adopted with Portuguese paper, because the finances were faithlessly managed by the regency; but some futile arguments against the proposition were advanced by lord Liverpool, and money became so scarce, that we shall find, even in the midst of victory, the war was more than once like to stop altogether from absolute inability to proceed.

On the 5th of March, the army being well on the way to the Alemtejo, lord Wellington who had

BOOK XVI. 1812. March.

maintained his head-quarters on the Coa to the last moment, that the enemy might not be awakened to his real designs, gave up Ciudad Rodrigo to Castaños. He also in person, and on the spot, explained to Vives, the governor, the plan and intention of the new works; he supplied him with money to complete them; furnished him with six weeks provision remaining from the field stores of the British troops, and gave him the reserved stores at St. Joa de Pesqueira on the Douro, from whence Carlos d'España undertook to transport them to the fortress.

As Marmont was at this time in Salamanca, and still ignorant of the allies' march, general Victor Alten's brigade of cavalry was posted on the Yeltes, to screen the allies' movement as long as possible, and he was instructed if Marmont advanced to retire on Beira, and cover the magazines at Castello Branco, by disputing all the rivers and defiles with the enemy's advanced parties. At the same time Silveira was directed to fall back upon the Douro to cover Oporto; the militia, under Trant and J. Wilson, were ordered to concentrate about Guarda; and those of Beira to unite about Castello Branco under colonel Lecor; the orders of all being the same, namely, to dispute the passage of the rivers and defiles. Trant was to defend those of the Estrella, and Lecor those of Castello Branco, on which town Victor Alten's cavalry was finally to retire if pressed. With these forces, and the Spaniards under Sanchez and España, and with the two fortresses, for Almeida was now capable of defence, Marmont's efforts were not much to be dreaded in that season, after he had lost his battering train in Ciudad.

CHAP. IV. 1812. March.

These things arranged, Wellington set off for Elvas which he reached the 11th, and prepared to invest Badajos, although neither the troops nor the stores were all arrived; but even this was ten days later than he had designed, and threw his operations into the violent equinoctial rains, by which the difficulties were augmented two-fold. This was one of the evils produced by the incredibly vexatious conduct of the Portuguese regency. There was no want of transport in the country, but as the government would not oblige the magistrates to do their duty, the latter either refused to procure carts for the army, or obliged the poorer classes to supply them, from which oppression the peasants naturally endeavoured to escape by flight. Thus, all the arrangements for the investment of Badajos on the 6th of March had been made, but the rich town of Evora, which had not seen the face of an enemy for more than three years, refused to supply any carriages at all, and the operation was necessarily put off till the 17th.

But it was in vain that Wellington threatened and remonstrated, in vain that he employed his time and wasted his mental powers in devising new laws, or remedies for bad ones; it was in vain that Mr. Stuart exerted himself, with equal vigour, to give energy to this extraordinary government; for whether in matters of small or vital importance, insolent anger and falsehood, disgraceful subterfuges and stolid indifference, upon the part of all civil functionaries, from the highest to the lowest, met them at every turn. The responsibility even in small matters became too great for subordinate officers; and the English general was forced to arrange the most trifling details of the service him-

BOOK XVI. 1812. March.

self; thus the iron-strength of his body and mind was strained, until all men wondered how they held, and in truth he did fall sick, but recovered after a few days. The critical nature of the war may be here judged of, for no man could have taken his place at such a moment, no man, however daring or skilful, would have voluntarily plunged into difficulties which were like to drive Wellington from the contest.

CHAPTER V.

CHAP. V. 1812. March.

The 15th the pontoons were laid over the Guadiana, about four miles from Elvas, at a place where the current was dull, two large Spanish boats were arranged as flying bridges; and the 16th, Beresford, who had again joined the army, crossed the river, drove in the enemy's posts, and invested Badajos with the third, fourth, and light divisions, and a brigade of Hamilton's Portuguese; in all fifteen thousand men.

Soult was then before the Isla, Drouet's division, of five thousand men, was at Villafranca, and Darricau with a like force was at Zalamea de Serena near Medellin; wherefore general Graham passing the Guadiana with the first, sixth, and seventh divisions of infantry, and two brigades of cavalry, directed his march by Valverde, and Santa Martha, upon Llerena, while Hill moved from Albuquerque by Merida upon Almendralejos. These covering corps were together thirty thousand strong, nearly five thousand including the heavy Germans who were at Estremos being cavalry; and as the fifth division was now on the march from Beira, the whole army presented about fifty-one thousand sabres and bayonets, of which twenty thousand were Portuguese. Castaños had repaired to Gallicia, but the fifth Spanish army under Morillo and Penne Villemur, being about four thousand strong, passed down the Portuguese frontier to the Lower

Appendix, No. IX. Section 1.

BOOK XVI. 1812. March.

Guadiana, intending to fall on Seville when Soult should advance to the succour of Badajos.

As the allies advanced, Drouet marched by his right to Hornaches, in the direction of La Serena and Medellin, with a view to keep open the communication with Marmont by Truxillo. Hill then halted at Almendralejos, and Graham took post at Zafra, placing Slade's cavalry at Villafranca; but Marmont had moved his sixth division from Talavera towards Castile, through the Puerto de Pico, on the 9th, and the four divisions and cavalry quartered at Toledo had recrossed the Tagus and marched over the Guadarama, the whole pointing for Valladolid. Thus it was already manifest that the army of Portugal would not act in conjunction with that of the south.

THIRD ENGLISH SIEGE OF BADAJOS.

Vol. III. Appendix, No. IX.

This fortress has before been described. The garrison composed of French, Hessian, and Spanish troops, was now near five thousand strong including sick. Phillipon had since the last siege made himself felt in all directions, for he had continually scoured the vicinity of the place, destroyed many small bands, carried off cattle, almost from under the guns of Elvas and Campo Mayor, and his spies extended their researches from Ciudad Rodrigo to Lisbon, and from Lisbon to Ayamonte.

He had also greatly improved the defences of the place. An interior retrenchment was made in the castle, and many more guns were there mounted; the rear of fort Cristoval was also better secured, and a covered communication from the fort itself, to the work at the bridge-head, was nearly completed. Two ravelins had been constructed on the south side of the town, and a third was commenced, together with counterguards for the bastions; but the eastern front next the castle, which was in other respects the weakest point, was without any outward protection save the stream of the Rivillas. A "*cunette*" or second ditch had been dug at the bottom of the great ditch, which was also in some parts filled with water; the gorge of the Pardaleras was enclosed, and that outwork was connected with the body of the place, from whence powerful batteries looked into it. The three western fronts were mined, and on the east, the arch of the bridge behind the San Roque, was built up to form an inundation, two hundred yards wide, which greatly contracted the space by which the place could be approached with troops. All the inhabitants had been obliged, on pain of being expelled, to lay up food for three months, and two convoys with provisions and ammunition had entered the place on the 10th and 16th of February, but Phillipon's stores of powder were still inadequate to his wants, and he was very scantily supplied with shells.

As the former system of attack against Cristoval and the castle, was now impracticable, lord Wellington desired to assail one of the western fronts which would have been a scientific operation; but the engineer represented that he had neither mortars nor miners, nor enough of guns, nor the means of bringing up sufficient stores for such an attack. Indeed the want of transport had again obliged the allies to draw the stores from Elvas, to the manifest hazard of that fortress, and hence, here, as at

BOOK XVI. 1812. March.

Ciudad Rodrigo, time was necessarily paid for, by the loss of life; or rather the crimes of politicians were atoned for by the blood of the soldiers.

The plan finally fixed upon, was to attack the bastion of Trinidad, because, the counterguard there being unfinished, that bastion could be battered from the hill on which the Picurina stood. The first parallel was therefore to embrace the Picurina, the San Roque, and the eastern front, in such a manner that the counter batteries there erected, might rake and destroy all the defences of the southern fronts which bore against the Picurina hill. The Picurina itself was to be battered and stormed, and from thence the Trinidad and Santa Maria bastions, were to be breached; after this all the guns were to be turned against the connecting curtain, which was known to be of weak masonry, that a third breach might be made, and a storming party employed to turn any retrenchments behind the breaches in the bastions. In this way the inundation could be avoided, and although a French deserter declared, and truly, that the ditch was there eighteen feet deep, such was the general's confidence in his troops, and in his own resources for aiding their efforts, that he resolved to storm the place without blowing in the counterscarp.

The battering train, directed by major Dickson, consisted of fifty-two pieces. This included sixteen twenty-four-pound howitzers, for throwing Shrapnel shells, but this species of missile, much talked of in the army at the time, was little prized by lord Wellington, who had early detected its insufficiency, save as a common shell; and partly to avoid expense, partly from a dislike to injure the inhabitants, neither in this, nor in any former siege, did he use mortars. Here indeed he could not have brought them up, for besides the neglect of the Portuguese government, the peasantry and even the ordenança employed to move the battering train from Alcacer do Sal, although well paid, deserted.

Of nine hundred gunners present, three hundred were British, the rest Portuguese, and there were one hundred and fifty sappers volunteers from the third divison, who were indeed rather unskilful, but of signal bravery. The engineer's parc was established behind the heights of St. Michael, and the direction of the siege was given to general Picton. General Kempt, general Colville, and general Bowes alternately commanded in the trenches.

In the night of the 17th, eighteen hundred men, protected by a guard of two thousand, broke ground one hundred and sixty yards from the Picurina. A tempest stifled the sound of their pickaxes, and though the work was commenced late, a communication, four thousand feet in length, was formed, and a parallel of six hundred yards three feet deep, and three feet six inches wide, was opened. However, when the day broke the Picurina was reinforced, and a sharp musketry interspersed with discharges from some field-pieces, aided by heavy guns from the body of the place, was directed on the trenches.

In the night of the 18th two batteries were traced out, the parallel was prolonged both on the right and left, and the previous works were improved. On the other hand the garrison raised the parapets of the Picurina, and having lined the top of the covered way with sand-bags, planted musketeers there, to gall the men in the trenches, who replied in a like manner.

BOOK XVI. 1812. March.

The 19th lord Wellington having secret intelligence that a sally was intended, ordered the guards to be reinforced. Nevertheless, at one o'clock some cavalry came out by the Talavera gate, and thirteen hundred infantry under general Vielland, the second in command, filed unobserved into the communication between the Picurina and the San Roque; a hundred men were prepared to sally from the Picurina itself, and all these troops jumping out at once, drove the workmen before them, and began to demolish the parallel. Previous to this outbreak, the French cavalry forming two parties had commenced a sham fight on the right of the parallel, and the smaller party pretending to fly, and answering Portuguese, to the challenge of the picquets, were allowed to pass. Elated by the success of their stratagem, they then galloped to the engineer's parc, which was a thousand yards in rear of the trenches, and there cut down some men, not many, for succour soon came, and meanwhile the troops at the parallel having rallied upon the relief which had just arrived, beat the enemy's infantry back even to the castle.

In this hot fight the besieged lost above three hundred men and officers, the besiegers only one hundred and fifty; but colonel Fletcher, the chief engineer, was badly wounded, and several hundred entrenching tools were carried off, for Phillipon had promised a high price for each; yet this turned out ill, because the soldiers, instead of pursuing briskly, dispersed to gather the tools. After the action a squadron of dragoons and six field-pieces were placed as a reserve-guard behind St. Michael, and a signal post was established on the Sierra de Venta to give notice of the enemy's motions.

The weather continued wet and boisterous, and the labour of the works was very harassing, but in the night of the 19th the parallel was opened in its whole length, and the 20th it was enlarged; yet a local obstacle and the flooding of the trenches, rendered the progress slow.

In the night of the 20th the parallel was extended to the left, across the Seville road, and three counter-batteries were commenced; but they were traced, in rear of the parallel, partly because the ground was too soft in front to admit of the guns moving; partly for safety, because the batteries were within three hundred yards of the San Roque, and as the parallel, eighteen hundred yards long, was only guarded by fourteen hundred men, a few bold soldiers might by a sudden rush have succeeded in spiking the guns if they had been placed in front of the trench. A slight sally was this day repulsed, and a shoulder was given to the right of the parallel to cover that flank.

The 21st the enemy placed two field-pieces on the right bank of the Guadiana, designing to rake the trenches, but the shoulder, made the night before, baffled the design, and the riflemen's fire soon sent the guns away. Indications of a similar design against the left flank, from the Pardaleras hill, were also observed, and a guard of three hundred men with two guns, was posted on that side in some broken ground.

In the night another battery against the San Roque was commenced, and the battery against the Picurina was finished; but heavy rain again retarded the works, and the besiegers having failed in an attempt to drain the lower parts of the parallel, by cuts, made an artificial bottom of sand-

BOOK XVI. 1812. March.

bags. On the other hand the besieged thinking the curtain adjoining the castle was the true object of attack, threw up an earthen entrenchment in front, and commenced clearing away the houses behind it. A covered communication from the Trinidad gate to the San Roque, intended to take this supposed attack in reverse, was also commenced; but the labour of digging being too great, it was completed by hanging up brown cloth, which appeared to be earth, and by this ingenious expedient, the garrison passed unseen between those points.

La Marre's Siege of Badajos.

Vauban's maxim, that a perfect investment is the first requisite in a siege, had been neglected at Badajos to spare labour, but the great master's art was soon vindicated by his countrymen. Phillipon finding the right bank of the Guadiana free, made a battery in the night for three field-pieces, which at daylight raked the trenches, and the shots pitching into the parallel, swept it in the most destructive manner for the whole day; there was no remedy, and the loss would have been still greater but for the soft nature of the ground, which prevented the touch and bound of the bullets. Orders were immediately sent to the fifth division, then at Campo Mayor, to invest the place on that side, but these troops were distant and misfortunes accumulated. In the evening heavy rain filled the trenches, the flood of the Guadiana ran the fixed bridge under water, sank twelve of the pontoons, and broke the tackle of the flying bridges; the provisions of the army could not then be brought over, and the guns and ammunition being still on the right bank, the siege was upon the point of being raised. In a few days, however, the river subsided, some Portuguese craft were brought up to form another flying-bridge, the pontoons saved were employed as row-boats, and in this manner the communication was secured, for the rest of the siege, without any accident.

The 23d the besieged continued to work at the entrenchments covering the front next the castle, and the besiegers were fixing their platforms, when at three o'clock the rain again filled the trenches, the earth, being completely saturated with water, fell away, the works everywhere crumbled, and the attack was entirely suspended.

The 24th the fifth division invested the place on the right bank of the Guadiana, the weather was fine, and the batteries were armed with ten twenty-fours, eleven eighteens, and seven five-and-a-half-inch howitzers. The next day, at eleven o'clock, these pieces opened, but they were so vigorously answered, that one howitzer was dismounted and several artillery and engineer officers were killed. Nevertheless the San Roque was silenced, and the garrison of the Picurina was so galled by the marksmen in the trenches, that no man dared look over the parapet; hence, as the external appearance of that fort did not indicate much strength, general Kempt was charged to assault it in the night.

The outward seeming of the Picurina was however fallacious, the fort was very strong; the fronts were well covered by the glacis, the flanks were deep, and the rampart, fourteen feet perpendicular from the bottom of the ditch, was guarded with thick slanting pales above; and from thence to the top there were sixteen feet of an earthen slope. A few palings had, indeed, been knocked off at the covered-way, and the parapet was slightly damaged

BOOK XVI.

1812. March.

on that side, but this injury was repaired with sand-bags, and the ditch was profound, narrow at the bottom, and flanked by four splinter-proof casemates. Seven guns were mounted on the works, the entrance to which by the rear was protected with three rows of thick paling, the garrison was above two hundred strong, and every man had two muskets. The top of the rampart was garnished with loaded shells to push over, a retrenched guard-house formed a second internal defence, and finally, some small mines and a loop-holed gallery, under the counterscarp, intended to take the assailants in rear, were begun but not finished.

Five hundred men of the third division being assembled for the attack, general Kempt ordered two hundred, under major Rudd of the seventy-seventh, to turn the fort on the left; an equal force, under major Shaw of the seventy-fourth, to turn the fort by the right; and one hundred from each of these bodies were directed to enter the communication with San Roque and intercept any succours coming from the town. The flanking columns were to make a joint attack on the fort, and the hundred men remaining, were placed under captain Powis of the eighty-third, to form a reserve. The engineers, Holloway, Stanway, and Gips, with twenty-four sappers bearing hatchets and ladders, guided these columns, and fifty men of the light division, likewise provided with axes, were to move out of the trenches at the moment of attack.

ASSAULT OF PICURINA.

The night was fine, the arrangements clearly and

skilfully made, and about nine o'clock the two flanking bodies moved forward. The distance was short, and the troops quickly closed on the fort, which black and silent before, now seemed one mass of fire; then the assailants running up to the palisades in the rear, with undaunted courage endeavoured to break through, and when the destructive musketry of the French, and the thickness of the pales, rendered their efforts nugatory, they turned against the faces of the work and strove to break in there; but the depth of the ditch and the slanting stakes at the top of the brick-work again baffled them.

At this time, the enemy shooting fast, and dangerously, the crisis appeared imminent, and Kempt sent the reserve headlong against the front; thus the fight was continued strongly, the carnage became terrible, and a battalion coming out from the town to the succour of the fort, was encountered and beaten by the party on the communication. The guns of Badajos, and of the castle now opened, the guard of the trenches replied with musketry, rockets were thrown up by the besieged, and the shrill sound of alarm bells, mixing with the shouts of the combatants, increased the tumult. Still the Picurina sent out streams of fire, by the light of which, dark figures were seen furiously struggling on the ramparts; for Powis first escaladed the place in front where the artillery had beaten down the pales, and the other assailants had thrown their ladders on the flanks in the manner of bridges, from the brink of the ditch to the slanting stakes, and all were fighting hand to hand with the enemy. Meanwhile the axe-men of the light division, compassing the fort like prowling wolves, discovered the gate,

Appendix, No. VII. Section 2, Letter C.

BOOK XVI. 1812. March.

and hewing it down, broke in by the rear. Nevertheless the struggle continued. Powis, Holloway, Gips, and Oates, of the eighty-eighth, fell wounded on or beyond the rampart; Nixon of the fifty-second was shot two yards within the gate; Shaw, Rudd, and nearly all the other officers had fallen outside; and it was not until half the garrison were killed, that Gaspar Thiery, the commandant, and eighty-six men, surrendered, while some, not many, rushing out of the gate, endeavoured to cross the inundation and were drowned.

The French governor hoped to have delayed the siege five or six days by the resistance of Picurina, and had the assault been a day later, this would have happened; for the loop-holed gallery in the counter-scarp, and the mines, would then have been completed, and the body of the work was too well covered by the glacis to be quickly ruined by fire. His calculations were baffled by this heroic assault, which lasted an hour, and cost four officers and fifty men killed, fifteen officers and two hundred and fifty men wounded; and so vehement was the fight throughout, that the garrison either forgot, or had not time to roll over the shells and combustibles arranged on the ramparts. Philipon did not conceal the danger accruing to Badajos from the loss of the Picurina, but he stimulated his soldiers' courage, by calling to their recollection, how infinitely worse than death it was, to be the inmate of an English hulk! an appeal which must have been deeply felt, for the annals of civilized nations, furnish nothing more inhuman towards captives of war, than the prison-ships of England.

When the Picurina was taken, three battalions of reserve advanced to secure it, and though a great turmoil and firing from the town, continued until midnight, a lodgment in the works, and a communication with the first parallel, were established, and the second parallel was commenced. However at day-light the redoubt was so overwhelmed with fire, from the town, that no troops could remain in it, and the lodgment was entirely destroyed. In the evening the sappers effected another lodgment on the flanks, the second parallel was then opened in its whole length, and the next day the counter-batteries on the right of Picurina exchanged a vigorous fire with the town; but one of the besiegers' guns was dismounted, and the Portuguese gunners, from inexperience, produced less effect on the defences than was expected.

In the night of the 27th a new communication from the first parallel to the Picurina was made, and three breaching-batteries were traced out. The first to contain twelve twenty-four pounders, occupied the space between the Picurina and the inundation, and was to breach the right face of the Trinidad bastion. The second, to contain eight eighteen pounders, was on the site of the Picurina, and was to breach the left flank of the Santa Maria bastion. The third, constructed on the prolonged line of the front to be attacked, contained three Shrapnel howitzers, to scour the ditch and prevent the garrison working in it; for Phillipon had now discovered the true line of attack, and had set strong parties in the night, to raise the counter-guard of the Trinidad and the imperfect ravelin covering the menaced front.

At day-break these works being well furnished with gabions and sand-bags, were lined with musqueteers, who severely galled the workmen em-

BOOK XVI.

1812. March.

ployed on the breaching batteries and the artillery practice also was brisk on both sides. Two of the besiegers' guns were dismounted; the gabions placed in front of the batteries to protect the workmen were knocked over, and the musquetry then became so destructive that the men were withdrawn and threw up earth from the inside.

In the night of the 27th the second parallel was extended to the right, with the view of raising batteries, to ruin the San Roque, to destroy the dam which held up the inundation, and to breach the curtain behind; but the Talavera road proved so hard, and the moon shone so brightly, that the labourers were quite exposed and the work was relinquished.

On the 28th the screen of gabions before the batteries, was restored and the workmen resumed their labours outside; the parallel was then improved, and the besieged withdrew their guns from San Roque; but their marksmen still shot from thence with great exactness, and the plunging fire from the castle dismounted two howitzers in one of the counter-batteries which was therefore dismantled. The enemy had also during the night observed the tracing string, which marked the direction of the sap in front of San Roque, and a daring fellow creeping out just before the workmen arrived, brought it in the line of the castle fire, whereby some loss was sustained ere the false direction was discovered.

In the night the dismantled howitzer battery was re-armed, with twenty-four pounders, to play on the San Roque, and a new breaching battery was traced out on the site of the Picurina, against the flank of the Santa Maria bastion. The second parallel was also carried by the sap across the Talavera road, and a trench was digged, for riflemen, in front of the batteries.

The 29th a slight sally, made on the right bank of the river, was repulsed by the Portuguese, but the sap at the San Roque was ruined by the enemy's fire, and the besieged continued to raise the counter-guard and ravelin of the Trinidad and to strengthen the front attacked. On the other hand the besiegers during the night carried the sap over the Talavera road, and armed two breaching batteries, with eighteen pounders, which the next day opened against the flank of Santa Maria; but they made little impression, and the explosion of an expense magazine killed many men and hurt others.

While the siege was thus proceeding Soult having little fear for the town, but expecting a great battle, was carefully organizing a powerful force to unite with Drouet and Daricau. Those generals had endeavoured to hold the district of La Serena with the view of keeping open the communication with Marmont by Medellin and Truxillo; but Graham and Hill marched against their flanks and forced them into the Morena by the Cordova roads; and on the other side of the country Morillo and Penne-Villemur, were lying close on the lower Guadiana waiting their opportunity to fall on Seville when Soult should advance. Nor were there wanting other combinations to embarrass and delay the French marshal; for in February, general Montes being detached, by Ballesteros, from San Roque, had defeated Maransin on the Guadajore river, driving him from Cartama into Malaga. After this the whole of the Spanish army was assembled

BOOK XVI. 1812. March.

in the Ronda hills, with a view to fall on Seville by the left of the Guadiana while Morillo assailed it on the right of that river. This had obliged Soult to send troops towards Malaga, and fatally delayed his march to Estremadura.

Meanwhile Marmont was concentrating his army in the Salamanca country, and it was rumoured that he meant to attack Ciudad Rodrigo. Lord Wellington was somewhat disturbed by this information; he knew indeed that the flooding of the rivers in the north, would prevent a blockade, and he was also assured that Marmont had not yet obtained a battering train. But the Spanish generals and engineers had neglected the new works and repairs of Ciudad Rodrigo; even the provisions at St. Joa de Pesquiera had not been brought up; the fortress had only thirty days' supply, Almeida was in as bad a state, and the grand project of invading Andalusia was likely to be baulked by these embarrassments.

On the 30th Soult's advance from Cordova being decided, the fifth division was brought over the Guadiana as a reserve to the covering army; but Power's Portuguese brigade, with some cavalry, of the same nation, still maintained the investment on the right bank, the siege was urged forward very rapidly, forty-eight pieces of artillery were in constant play, and the sap against St. Roque advanced. The enemy was equally active, his fire was very destructive, and his progress in raising the ravelin and counter-guard of the front attacked was very visible.

The 1st of April the sap was pushed close to the San Roque, the Trinidad bastion crumbled under the stroke of the bullet, and the flank of the Santa

Maria, which was casemated and had hitherto resisted the batteries, also began to yield. The 2d the face of the Trinidad was very much broken, but at the Santa Maria the casemates being laid open, the bullets were lost in their cavities, and the garrison commenced a retrenchment to cut off the whole of the attacked front, from the town.

In the night a new battery against the San Roque was armed, and two officers with some sappers gliding behind that out-work, gagged the sentinel, placed powder barrels and a match against the dam of the inundation, and retired undiscovered, but the explosion did not destroy the dam, and the inundation remained. Nor did the sap make progress, because of the French musketeers; for though the marksmen set against them slew many they were reinforced by means of a raft with parapets, which crossed the inundation, and men also passed by the cloth communication from the Trinidad gate.

On the 3d some guns were turned against the curtain behind the San Roque, but the masonry proved hard, ammunition was scarce, and as a breach there would have been useless, while the inundation remained, the fire was soon discontinued. The two breaches in the bastion were now greatly enlarged and the besieged assiduously laboured at the retrenchments behind them, and converted the nearest houses and garden walls into a third line of defence. All the houses behind the front next the castle were also thrown down, and a battery of five guns, intended to flank the ditch and breach of the Trinidad, was commenced on the castle hill, but outside the wall; the besiegers therefore traced out a counter-battery,

BOOK XVI. of fourteen Shrapnel howitzers, to play upon that point during the assault.

1812. April. The crisis of the siege was now approaching rapidly. The breaches were nearly practicable, Soult, having effected a junction with Drouet and Daricau, was advancing; and as the allies were not in sufficient force to assault the place and give battle at the same time, it was resolved to leave two divisions in the trenches, and to fight at Albuera with the remainder. Graham therefore fell back towards that place, and Hill having destroyed the bridge at Merida, marched from the Upper Guadiana to Talavera Real.

Time being now, as in war it always is, a great object, the anxiety on both sides redoubled; but Soult was still at Llerena, when on the morning of the 5th the breaches were declared practicable, and the assault ordered for that evening. Leith's division was even recalled to the camp to assist, when a careful personal examination of the enemy's retrenchments caused some doubt in lord Wellington's mind, and he delayed the storm, until a third breach, as originally projected, should be formed in the curtain between the bastions of Trinidad and Maria. This could not, however, be commenced before morning, and during the night the enemy's workmen laboured assiduously at their retrenchments, regardless of the showers of grape with which the besiegers' batteries scoured the ditch and the breach. But the 6th, the besiegers' guns being all turned against the curtain, the bad masonry crumbled rapidly away, in two hours a yawning breach appeared, and Wellington, having again examined the points of attack in person, renewed the order for the assault. Then the soldiers eagerly made themselves ready for a combat, so fiercely fought, so terribly won, so dreadful in all its circumstances, that posterity can scarcely be expected to credit the tale; but many are still alive who know that it is true.

The British general was so sensible of Phillipon's firmness and of the courage of his garrison, that he spared them the affront of a summons, yet seeing the breach strongly entrenched, and the enemy's flank fire, still powerful, he would not in this dread crisis, trust his fortune to a single effort. Eighteen thousand daring soldiers burned for the signal of attack, and as he was unwilling to lose the service of any, to each division he gave a task such as few generals would have the hardihood even to contemplate.

On the right Picton's division was to file out of the trenches, to cross the Rivillas river, and to scale the castle walls, which were from eighteen to twenty-four feet in height, furnished with all means of destruction, and so narrow at top, that the defenders could easily reach and as easily overturn the ladders.

On the left, Leith's division was to make a false attack on the Pardaleras, and a real assault on the distant bastion of San Vincente, where the glacis was mined, the ditch deep, the scarp thirty feet high, and the parapet garnished with bold troops well provided; for Phillipon, following his old plan, had three loaded muskets placed beside each man, that the first fire might be quick and deadly.

In the centre, the fourth and light divisions under general Colville, and colonel Andrew Bar-

BOOK XVI. 1812. April.

nard, were to march against the breaches. They were furnished like the third and fifth divisions with ladders and axes, and were preceded by storming parties of five hundred men each with their respective forlorn hopes. The light division was to assault the bastion of Santa Maria; the fourth division to assault the Trinidad, and the curtain; and the columns were divided into storming and firing parties, the former to enter the ditch, the latter to keep the crest of the glacis.

Besides these attacks, major Wilson of the forty-eighth was to storm the San Roque with the guards of the trenches, and on the other side of the Guadiana, general Power was to make a feint on the bridge-head.

At first only one brigade, of the third division, was to have attacked the castle, but just before the hour fixed upon, a sergeant of sappers having deserted from the enemy, informed Wellington that there was but one communication from the castle to the town, whereupon he ordered the whole division to advance together.

This was the outline of the plan, but many nice arrangements filled it up, and some were followed, some disregarded, for it is seldom that all things are strictly attended to in a desperate fight. Nor were the enemy idle, for while it was yet twilight some French cavalry issued from the Pardaleras, escorting an officer who endeavoured to look into the trenches, with a view to ascertain if an assault was intended; but the picquet on that side jumped up, and firing as it run, drove him and his escort back into the works. Then the darkness fell and the troops only awaited the signal.

BREACHES

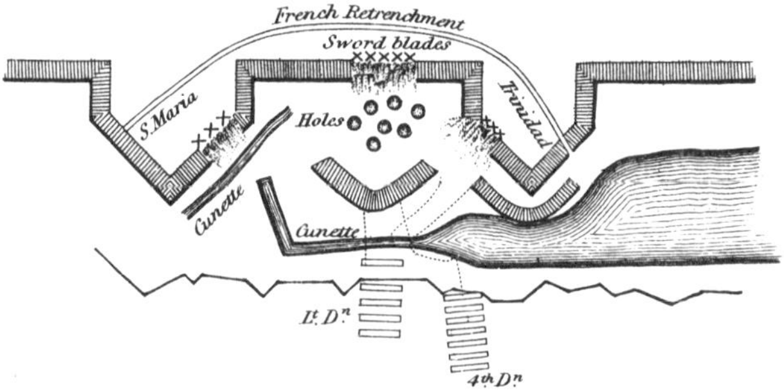

EXPLANATORY SKETCH
OF THE SIEGE OF
BADAJOS
1812.

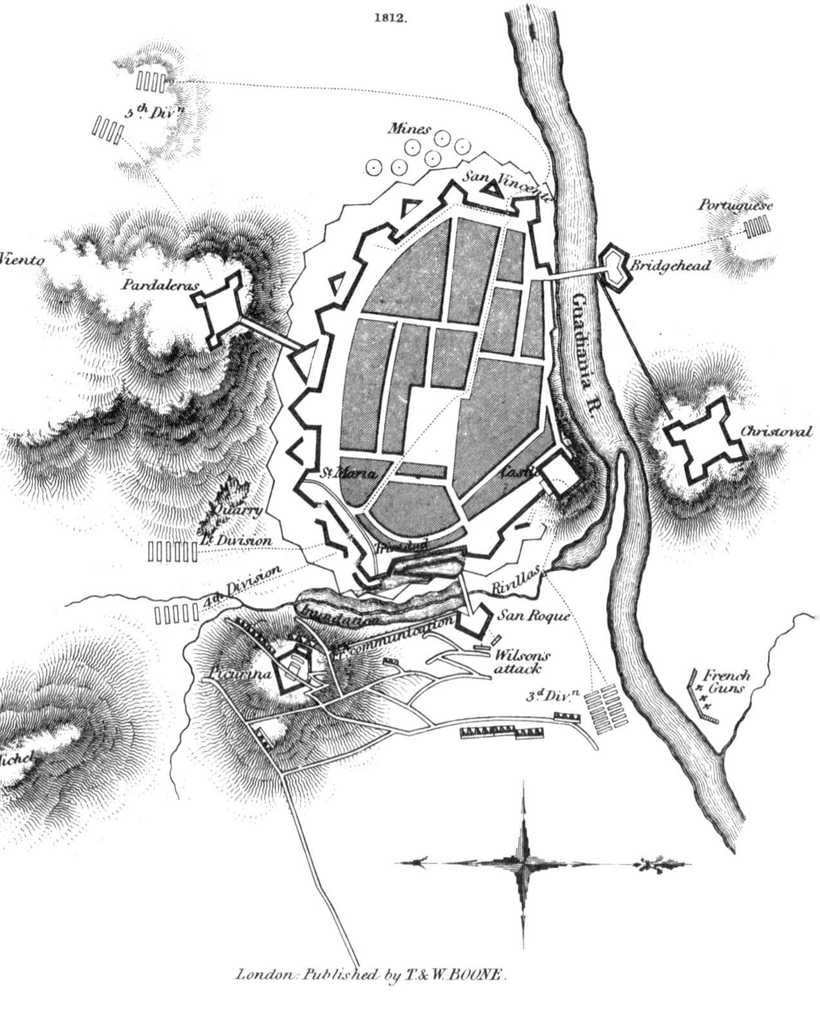

London: Published by T. & W. BOONE.

CHAP. V.

1812. April.

ASSAULT OF BADAJOS.

The night was dry but clouded, the air thick with watery exhalations from the rivers, the ramparts, and the trenches unususally still; yet a low murmur pervaded the latter, and in the former, lights were seen to flit here and there, while the deep voices of the sentinels at times proclaimed, that all was well in Badajos. The French, confiding in Phillipon's direful skill, watched, from their lofty station, the approach of enemies, whom they had twice before baffled, and now hoped to drive a third time blasted and ruined from the walls; the British, standing in deep columns, were as eager to meet that fiery destruction as the others were to pour it down; and both were alike terrible for their strength, their discipline, and the passions awakened in their resolute hearts.

Former failures there were to avenge, and on either side, such leaders as left no excuse for weakness in the hour of trial; and the possession of Badajos was become a point of honour, personal with the soldiers of each nation. But the strong desire for glory was, in the British, dashed with a hatred of the citizens on an old grudge, and recent toil and hardship, with much spilling of blood, had made many incredibly savage: for these things render the noble-minded indeed, averse to cruelty, but harden the vulgar spirit. Numbers also, like Cæsar's centurion who could not forget the plunder of Avaricum, were heated with the recollection of Ciudad Rodrigo, and thirsted for spoil. Thus every spirit found a cause of excitement, the wondrous power of discipline bound the whole together as

BOOK XVI.

1812. April.

with a band of iron, and, in the pride of arms, none doubted their might, to bear down every obstacle that man could oppose to their fury.

At ten o'clock, the castle, the San Roque, the breaches, the Pardaleras, the distant bastion of San Vincente, and the bridge-head on the other side of the Guadiana, were to have been simultaneously assailed, and it was hoped that the strength of the enemy would shrivel within that fiery girdle. But many are the disappointments of war. An unforeseen accident delayed the attack of the fifth division; and a lighted carcass, thrown from the castle, falling close to where the men of the third division were drawn up, discovered their array, and obliged them to anticipate the signal by half an hour. Then, every thing being suddenly disturbed, the double columns of the fourth and light divisions also moved silently and swiftly against the breaches, and the guard of the trenches, rushing forward with a shout, encompassed the San Roque with fire and broke in so violently that scarcely any resistance was made.

But a sudden blaze of light and the rattling of musketry indicated the commencement of a most vehement combat at the castle. There general Kempt, for Picton hurt by a fall, in the camp, and expecting no change in the hour, was not present, there general Kempt, I say, led the third division; he had passed the Rivillas, in single files by a narrow bridge, under a terrible musketry, and then reforming, and running up the rugged hill, had reached the foot of the castle when he fell severely wounded, and being carried back to the trenches met Picton who hastened forward to take the command. Meanwhile his troops spreading along the front reared their heavy ladders, some against the lofty castle, some against the adjoining front on the left, and with incredible courage ascended amidst showers of heavy stones, logs of wood, and bursting shells rolled off the parapet, while from the flanks the enemy plied his musketry with a fearful rapidity, and in front, with pikes and bayonets, stabbed the leading assailants or pushed the ladders from the walls; and all this attended with deafening shouts, and the crash of breaking ladders, and the shrieks of crushed soldiers answering to the sullen stroke of the falling weights.

Still, swarming round the remaining ladders, these undaunted veterans strove who should first climb, until all being overturned, the French shouted victory, and the British, baffled, but untamed, fell back a few paces, and took shelter under the rugged edge of the hill. Here when the broken ranks were somewhat re-formed the heroic colonel Ridge, springing forward, called, with a stentorian voice, on his men to follow, and, seizing a ladder, once more raised it against the castle, yet to the right of the former attack, where the wall was lower, and an embrasure offered some facility. A second ladder was soon placed alongside of the first, by the grenadier officer Canch, and the next instant he and Ridge were on the rampart, the shouting troops pressed after them, the garrison amazed, and in a manner surprised, were driven fighting through the double gate into the town, and the castle was won. A reinforcement, sent from the French reserve, then came up, a sharp action followed, both sides fired through the gate, and the enemy retired, but Ridge fell, and no man died that night with more glory—yet many died, and there was much glory.

During these events, the tumult at the breaches

BOOK XVI. 1812. April.

was such as if the very earth had been rent asunder and its central fires were bursting upwards uncontrolled. The two divisions had reached the glacis, just as the firing at the castle had commenced, and the flash of a single musket discharged from the covered way as a signal shewed them that the French were ready; yet no stir was heard, and darkness covered the breaches. Some hay-packs were then thrown, some ladders were placed, and the forlorn hopes and storming parties of the light division, about five hundred in all, had descended into the ditch without opposition, when a bright flame shooting upwards displayed all the terrors of the scene. The ramparts crowded with dark figures and glittering arms, were seen on the one side, and on the other, the red columns of the British, deep and broad, were coming on like streams of burning lava; it was the touch of the magician's wand, for a crash of thunder followed, and with incredible violence the storming parties were dashed to pieces by the explosion of hundreds of shells and powder-barrels.

For an instant the light division stood on the brink of the ditch, amazed at the terrific sight, then, with a shout that matched even the sound of the explosion, flew down the ladders, or disdaining their aid, leaped, reckless of the depth, into the gulf below; and nearly at the same moment, amidst a blaze of musketry that dazzled the eyes, the fourth division came running in and descended with a like fury. There were however only five ladders for both columns, which were close together, and a deep cut made in the bottom of the ditch, as far as the counter-guard of the Trinidad, was filled with water from the inundation; into this watery snare the head of the fourth division fell, and it is said that above a hundred of the fuzileers, the men

Appendix. No. VII. Section 2.

of Albuera, were there smothered. Those who followed, checked not, but as if such a disaster had been expected, turned to the left, and thus came upon the face of the unfinished ravelin, which, being rough and broken, was mistaken for the breach, and instantly covered with men; yet a wide and deep chasm was still between them and the ramparts from whence came a deadly fire wasting their ranks. Thus baffled, they also commenced a rapid discharge of musketry, and disorder ensued; for the men of the light division, whose conducting engineer had been disabled early, and whose flank was confined by an unfinished ditch intended to cut off the bastion of Santa Maria, rushed towards the breaches of the curtain and the Trinidad, which were indeed before them, but which the fourth division were destined to storm.

Great was the confusion, for now the ravelin was quite crowded with men of both divisions, and while some continued to fire, others jumped down and ran towards the breach, many also passed between the ravelin and the counterguard of the Trinidad, the two divisions got mixed, and the reserves, which should have remained at the quarries, also came pouring in, until the ditch was quite filled, the rear still crowding forward, and all cheering vehemently. The enemy's shouts also, were loud and terrible, and the bursting of shells and of grenades, the roaring of the guns from the flanks, answered by the iron howitzers from the battery of the parallel, the heavy roll and horrid explosion of the powder-barrels, the whizzing flight of the blazing splinters, the loud exhortations of the officers, and the continual clatter of the muskets, made a maddening din.

BOOK XVI. 1812. April.

Now a multitude bounded up the great breach as if driven by a whirlwind, but across the top glittered a range of sword-blades, sharp-pointed, keen-edged on both sides, and firmly fixed in ponderous beams, which were chained together and set deep in the ruins; and for ten feet in front, the ascent was covered with loose planks, studded with sharp iron points, on which the feet of the foremost being set the planks moved, and the unhappy soldiers, falling forward on the spikes, rolled down upon the ranks behind. Then the Frenchmen, shouting at the success of their stratagem, and leaping forward, plied their shot with terrible rapidity, for every man had several muskets; and each musket in addition to its ordinary charge contained a small cylinder of wood stuck full of leaden slugs, which scattered like hail when they were discharged.

Again the assailants rushed up the breaches, and again the sword-blades, immoveable and impassable, stopped their charge, and the hissing shells and thundering powder-barrels exploded unceasingly. Hundreds of men had fallen, and hundreds more were dropping, but still the heroic officers called aloud for new trials, and sometimes followed by many, sometimes by a few, ascended the ruins; and so furious were the men themselves, that in one of these charges, the rear strove to push the foremost on to the sword-blades, willing even to make a bridge of their writhing bodies, but the others frustrated the attempt by dropping down; and men fell so fast from the shot, that it was hard to know who went down voluntarily, who were stricken, and many stooped unhurt that never rose again. Vain also would it have been to break through the sword-blades, for the trench and parapet behind the breach were finished, and the assailants, crowded into even a narrower space than the ditch was, would still have been separated from their enemies, and the slaughter would have continued.

At the beginning of this dreadful conflict, colonel Andrew Barnard had with prodigious efforts separated his division from the other, and preserved some degree of military array; but now the tumult was such, that no command could be heard distinctly, except by those close at hand, and the mutilated carcasses heaped on each other, and the wounded, struggling to avoid being trampled upon, broke the formations; order was impossible! Yet officers of all stations, followed more or less numerously by the men, were seen to start out, as if struck by a sudden madness, and rush into the breach, which yawning and glittering with steel, semed like the mouth of some huge dragon belching forth smoke and flame. In one of these attempts, colonel Macleod of the forty-third, a young man, whose feeble body would have been quite unfit for war, if it had not been sustained by an unconquerable spirit, was killed. Wherever his voice was heard, there his soldiers gathered, and with such a strong resolution did he lead them up the fatal ruins, that when one behind him, in falling, plunged a bayonet into his back, he complained not, and continuing his course was shot dead within a yard of the sword-blades. But there was no want of gallant leaders, or desperate followers.

Two hours spent in these vain efforts convinced the soldiers that the breach of the Trinidad was impregnable; and as the opening in the curtain, although less strong, was retired, and the approach to

BOOK XVI. 1812. April.

it impeded by deep holes, and cuts made in the ditch, the troops did not much notice it after the partial failure of one attack which had been made early. Gathering in dark groups and leaning on their muskets, they looked up with sullen desperation at the Trinidad, while the enemy stepping out on the ramparts, and aiming their shots by the light of the fire-balls which they threw over, asked, as their victims fell, "*Why they did not come into Badajos?*"

In this dreadful situation, while the dead were lying in heaps and others continually falling, the wounded crawling about to get some shelter from the merciless fire above, and withal a sickening stench from the burnt flesh of the slain, captain Nicholas, of the engineers, was observed by Mr. Shaw, of the forty-third, making incredible efforts to force his way with a few men into the Santa Maria bastion. Shaw having collected about fifty soldiers of all regiments joined him, and although there was a deep cut along the foot of this breach also, it was instantly passed, and these two young officers at the head of their gallant band, rushed up the slope of the ruins; but when they had gained two-thirds of the ascent, a concentrated fire of musketry and grape, dashed nearly the whole dead to the earth! Nicholas was mortally wounded, and the intrepid Shaw stood alone! After this no further effort was made at any point, and the troops remained passive, but unflinching, beneath the enemy's shot, which streamed without intermission; for, of the riflemen on the glacis, many leaping early into the ditch had joined in the assault, and the rest, raked by a cross fire of grape from the distant bastions, baffled in their aim by

Now lieut.-col. Shaw Kennedy.

the smoke and flames from the explosions, and too few in number, had entirely failed to quell the French musketry.

About midnight, when two thousand brave men had fallen, Wellington, who was on a height close to the quarries, sent orders for the remainder to retire and re-form for a second assault; for he had just then heard that the castle was taken, and thinking the enemy would still hold out in the town, was resolved to assail the breaches again. This retreat from the ditch was, however, not effected without further carnage and confusion, for the French fire never slackened, and a cry arose that the enemy were making a sally from the distant flanks, which caused a rush towards the ladders; then the groans and lamentations of the wounded who could not move, and expected to be slain, increased, many officers who had not heard of the order, endeavoured to stop the soldiers from going back, and some would even have removed the ladders but were unable to break the crowd.

All this time the third division was lying close in the castle, and either from a fear of risking the loss of a point which ensured the capture of the place, or that the egress was too difficult, made no attempt to drive away the enemy from the breaches. On the other side however the fifth division had commenced the false attack on the Pardaleras, and on the right of the Guadiana, the Portuguese were sharply engaged at the bridge; thus the town was girdled with fire, for general Walker's brigade having passed on during the feint on the Pardaleras, was escalading the distant bastion of San Vincente. His troops had advanced along the banks of the river, and reached the French guard-

BOOK XVI. 1812. April.

house, at the barrier-gate, undiscovered, for the ripple of the waters smothered the sound of their footsteps; but just then the explosion at the breaches took place, the moon shone out, and the French sentinels, discovering the columns, fired. The British troops immediately springing forward under a sharp musketry began to hew down the wooden barrier at the covered way, while the Portuguese, being panic-stricken, threw down the scaling ladders. Nevertheless the others snatched them up again, and forcing the barrier, jumped into the ditch; but the guiding engineer officer was killed, and there was a *cunette*, which embarrassed the column, and when the foremost men succeeded in rearing the ladders, the latter were found too short, for the walls were generally above thirty feet high. Meanwhile the fire of the French was deadly, a small mine was sprung beneath the soldiers' feet, beams of wood and live shells were rolled over on their heads, showers of grape from the flank swept the ditch, and man after man dropped dead from the ladders.

Fortunately some of the defenders having been called away to aid in recovering the castle, the ramparts were not entirely manned, and the assailants, having discovered a corner of the bastion where the scarp was only twenty feet high, placed three ladders there under an embrasure which had no gun and was only stopped with a gabion. Some men got up, but with difficulty, for the ladders were still too short, and the first man who gained the top was pushed up by his comrades and then drew others after him, until many had gained the summit; and though the French shot heavily against them, from both flanks and from a house in front, they thick-

Appendix, No. VII. Section 2.

ened and could not be driven back; half the fourth regiment entered the town itself to dislodge the enemy from the houses, while the others pushed along the rampart towards the breach, and by dint of hard fighting successively won three bastions.

In the last of these combats general Walker leaping forward, sword in hand, at the moment when one of the enemy's cannoneers was discharging a gun, fell covered with so many wounds that it was wonderful how he could survive, and some of the soldiers immediately after, perceiving a lighted match on the ground, cried out a mine! At that word, such is the power of imagination, those troops whom neither the strong barrier, nor the deep ditch, nor the high walls, nor the deadly fire of the enemy could stop, staggered back appalled by a chimera of their own raising, and in this disorder a French reserve, under general Viellande, drove on them with a firm and rapid charge, and pitching some men over the walls, and killing others outright, again cleansed the ramparts even to the San Vincente. There however Leith had placed colonel Nugent with a battalion of the thirty-eighth as a reserve, and when the French came up, shouting and slaying all before them, this battalion, about two hundred strong, arose, and with one close volley destroyed them.

Then the panic ceased, the soldiers rallied, and in compact order once more charged along the walls towards the breaches, but the French, although turned on both flanks and abandoned by fortune, did not yet yield; and meanwhile the detachment of the fourth regiment which had entered the town when the San Vincente was first

BOOK XVI. 1812. April.

carried, was strangely situated, for the streets were empty and brilliantly illuminated, and no person was seen; yet a low buzz and whisper were heard around, lattices were now and then gently opened, and from time to time shots were fired from underneath the doors of the houses by the Spaniards. However, the troops with bugles sounding, advanced towards the great square of the town, and in their progress captured several mules going with ammunition to the breaches; but the square itself was as empty and silent as the streets, and the houses as bright with lamps; a terrible enchantment seemed to be in operation, for they saw nothing but light, and heard only the low whispers close around them, while the tumult at the breaches was like the crashing thunder.

There, indeed, the fight was still plainly raging, and hence, quitting the square, they attempted to take the garrison in reverse, by attacking the ramparts from the town-side, but they were received with a rolling musketry, driven back with loss, and resumed their movement through the streets. At last the breaches were abandoned by the French, other parties entered the place, desultory combats took place in various parts, and finally general Viellande, and Phillipon who was wounded, seeing all ruined, passed the bridge with a few hundred soldiers, and entered San Cristoval, where they all surrendered early the next morning upon summons to lord Fitzroy Somerset, who had with great readiness pushed through the town to the draw-bridge ere they had time to organize further resistance. But even in the moment of ruin the night before, the noble governor had sent some horsemen out from the fort to carry the news to Soult's army, and they reached him in time to prevent a greater misfortune.

Now commenced that wild and desperate wickedness, which tarnished the lustre of the soldier's heroism. All indeed were not alike, for hundreds risked and many lost their lives in striving to stop the violence, but the madness generally prevailed, and as the worst men were leaders here, all the dreadful passions of human nature were displayed. Shameless rapacity, brutal intemperance, savage lust, cruelty, and murder, shrieks and piteous lamentations, groans, shouts, imprecations, the hissing of fires bursting from the houses, the crashing of doors and windows, and the reports of muskets used in violence, resounded for two days and nights in the streets of Badajos! on the third, when the city was sacked, when the soldiers were exhausted by their own excesses, the tumult rather subsided than was quelled. The wounded men were then looked to, the dead disposed of!

Five thousand men and officers fell during this siege, and of these, including seven hundred Portuguese, three thousand five hundred had been stricken in the assault, sixty officers and more than seven hundred men being slain on the spot. The five generals, Kempt, Harvey, Bowes, Colville, and Picton were wounded, the first three severely; about six hundred men and officers fell in the escalade of San Vincente, as many at the castle, and more than two thousand at the breaches, each division there losing twelve hundred! And how deadly the strife was, at that point, may be gathered from this, the forty-third and fifty-second regiments, of the light division, alone lost more

BOOK XVI. — 1812. April.

men than the seven regiments of the third division engaged at the castle!

Let any man picture to himself this frightful carnage taking place in a space of less than a hundred square yards. Let him consider that the slain died not all suddenly, nor by one manner of death; that some perished by steel, some by shot, some by water, that some were crushed and mangled by heavy weights, some trampled upon, some dashed to atoms by the fiery explosions; that for hours this destruction was endured without shrinking, and that the town was won at last, let any man consider this and he must admit that a British army bears with it an awful power. And false would it be to say that the French were feeble men, for the garrison stood and fought manfully and with good discipline behaving worthily. Shame there was none on any side. Yet who shall do justice to the bravery of the soldiers? the noble emulation of the officers? Who shall measure out the glory of Ridge, of Macleod, of Nicholas, or of O'Hare, of the ninety-fifth, who perished on the breach, at the head of the stormers, and with him nearly all the volunteers for that desperate service? Who shall describe the springing valour of that Portuguese grenadier who was killed the foremost man at the Santa Maria? or the martial fury of that desperate soldier of the ninety-fifth, who, in his resolution to win, thrust himself beneath the chained sword-blades, and there suffered the enemy to dash his head to pieces with the ends of their muskets? Who can sufficiently honour the intrepidity of Walker, of Shaw, of Canch, or the resolution of Ferguson of the forty-third, who having in former assaults received

Appendix, No. VII. Section 2.

two deep wounds, was here, with his hurts still open, leading the stormers of his regiment, the third time a volunteer, and the third time wounded! Nor would I be understood to select these as pre-eminent, many and signal were the other examples of unbounded devotion, some known, some that will never be known; for in such a tumult much passed unobserved, and often the observers fell themselves ere they could bear testimony to what they saw; but no age, no nation ever sent forth braver troops to battle than those who stormed Badajos.

When the extent of the night's havoc was made known to lord Wellington, the firmness of his nature gave way for a moment, and the pride of conquest yielded to a passionate burst of grief for the loss of his gallant soldiers.

CHAPTER VI.

BOOK XVI.

1812. April.

The English general having now achieved the second part of his project, was desirous to fight a great battle in Andalusia, which would have been the crown of this extraordinary winter campaign; but the misconduct of others would not suffer him to do this. At Ciudad Rodrigo, the Spanish engineers had entirely ceased the repairs of the works; Carlos d'España besides neglecting to provision that place, had by his oppressive conduct alarmed all the people of the vicinity, and created a dangerous spirit of discontent in the garrison; Almeida was insecure, and Marmont's army was already between the Agueda and the Coa.

It was essential to place those fortresses in safety, ere the march into Andalusia could take place; but the English general knowing that the danger in Beira was not very imminent, lingered a few days, hoping that Soult, in his anger at the loss of Badajos, would risk a blow on this side of the Morena; and he was certain, that the French general could not stop more than a few days, because of the secondary armies whose operations were then in progress.

Soult was indeed deeply affected by the loss of Badajos, but he was surrounded by enemies and the contest was too unequal. He had quitted Seville the 1st of April with twelve regiments of infantry, two of cavalry, and one battery of artillery. His march was by Lora del Rio and Constantino upon Llerena; and, to impose upon the allies, general Gazan moved by the road of Monasterio with the remainder of the artillery and the baggage, escorted by Barois' division of infantry, and some cavalry. But this column turned into the cross roads, at Santa de Guillena, and so reached Constantino, whence they followed the main body, and thus the whole army was concentrated at Llerena on the 6th. This circuitous march had been determined by the situation of Drouet and Daricau, who having been before driven into the mountains by the Cordova roads, could not rally upon the side of Monasterio; now however they advanced to Fuentes de Ovejuña, and the allies fell back to Albuera and Talavera Real.

On the 7th the French reached Villafranca and their cavalry entered Villalba and Fuente del Maestro. The 8th they were in march to fight, when the horsemen sent by Phillipon from Badajos, during the assault, brought the news of its fall; at the same moment their general was apprized, by his spies, that Marmont by whom he expected to be joined was in the north and could not assist him. He immediately fell back to Llerena, for the allies could then bring forty-five thousand men into action, and the French army though strongly constituted and the best troops in Spain did not exceed twenty-four thousand.

Soult had now little time to deliberate, for Penne Villemur and Morillo, issuing out of Portugal with four thousand men, had crossed the Lower Guadiana, and seized San Lucar de Mayor on the 4th. This place was ten miles from Seville, which was only

BOOK XVI. 1812. April.

garrisoned by a Spanish Swiss battalion in Joseph's service, aided by "*Escopeteros*" and by the sick and convalescent men; the commandant Rignoux had therefore, after a skirmish, shut himself up in fortified convents. The 6th the Spaniards had occupied the heights in front of the Triana bridge, and the 7th attacked the French entrenchments, hoping to raise a popular commotion. But a worse danger was gathering on the other side, for Ballesteros, after the defeat of Maransin, at Cartama, had advanced with eleven thousand men intending to fall on Seville from the left of the Guadalquivir.

To distract the attention of the French, and to keep Laval from detaching troops to Seville, the Spanish general had sent Copons with four thousand men by Itar to Junquera, which is on the Malaga side of the Ronda; meanwhile he himself entered Los Barios with the rest of his army and thus threatened at once Grenada and the lines of Chiclana. At the same time all the smaller partidas of the Ronda were let loose in different directions, to cut the communications, to seize the small French magazines, and to collect the Spanish soldiers, who, at different periods, had quitted their colours and retired to their homes.

Copons remained at Junquera, but Ballesteros with three divisions commanded by Cruz Murgeon, the marquis de Las Cuevas, and the prince of Anglona, marched to Utrera as soon as Soult had departed from Seville; thus the communication of that city with Cadiz on one side, and with Malaga and Grenada on the other, was cut off. The situation of the French was very critical, and they wanted ammunition, because a large convoy, coming from Madrid, with an escort of twelve hundred men, was stopped in the Morena by the Partidas from the Ronda and from Murcia.

On the 6th the Spanish cavalry was within a few miles of Seville, when false information adroitly given by a Spaniard in the French interest, led Ballesteros to believe that Soult was close at hand, whereupon he immediately returned to the Ronda; the next day Penne Villemur having received notice from lord Wellington that the French would soon return, also retired to Gibraleon.

Ballesteros soon discovered the deceit, when, instead of returning to Seville, he on the 9th assaulted the small castle of Zahara in the hills, and being repulsed with considerable loss, made a circuit north of Ronda, by Albodonales, Alcala de Pruna, to Casarbonela, where he was rejoined by Copons. The division of Cuevas then marched against Ossuna, which being only garrisoned by "*Escopeteros*," was expected to fall at once; but after two days combat and the loss of two hundred killed and wounded, the three thousand patriots retired, baffled by a hundred and fifty of their own countrymen fighting for the invaders.

When Cuevas returned, Ballesteros marched in three columns, by roads leading from Casarbonela and Antequera, to attack general Rey, who was posted with eighteen hundred men near Allora, on the Guadaljore river. The centre column was first engaged without any advantage, but when Rey saw the flank columns coming on, he retired behind the Guadalmediña river, close to Malaga, having lost a colonel and two hundred men in passing the Guadaljore.

After this action Ballesteros returned to the

BOOK XVI. 1812. April.

Ronda, for Soult was now truly at hand, and his horsemen were already in the plains. He had sent Digeon's cavalry on the 9th to Cordoba, to chase the Partidas, and had ordered Drouet's division to take post at Fuentes Overjuña; then directing Peyreymont's cavalry upon Usagre, he had come himself by forced marches to Seville, which he reached the 11th, hoping to surprise the Spaniards; but the stratagem, which had saved Seville on the 6th also saved Ballesteros, for general Conroux was coming up on the other side from the Guadalete and the Spaniards would have been enclosed but for their timely retreat. And scarcely had Soult quitted Llerena when the French met with a disaster near Usagre, which though a strong position had always proved a very dangerous advanced post on both sides.

Sir Stapleton Cotton, while following the trail of the enemy, on the evening of the 10th, had received intelligence that Peyreymont's cavalry was between Villa Garcia and Usagre, and he immediately conceived hopes of cutting it off. To effect this Anson's brigade, then commanded by colonel Frederic Ponsonby, moved during the night from Villa Franca upon Usagre, and at the same time Le Marchant's brigade marched from Los Santos upon Benvenida to intercept the retreat on Llerena. Ponsonby's advanced guard having commenced the action too soon, the French fell back, before Le Marchant could intercept them, but as some heights, skirting the Llerena road, prevented them from seeing that general, they again drew up in order of battle behind the junction of the Benvenida road.

The hostile bodies were nearly equal in numbers, about nineteen hundred sabres on each side.

CHAP. VI.

1812. April.

but sir Stapleton soon decided the action; for ably seizing the accidental advantage of ground he kept the enemy's attention engaged by skirmishing with Ponsonby's squadrons, while Le Marchant secretly passing at the back of the heights, sent thè fifth dragoon guards against their flank, and the next moment Ponsonby charged their front. Thus assailed the French gave way in disorder, and being pursued for four miles left several officers and a hundred and twenty-eight men prisoners, and many were killed in the field. The loss of the British was only fifty-six men and officers, of which forty-five were of the fifth dragoon guards.

The beaten troops found refuge with Drouet's infantry which had not yet left Llerena; but after this action, that general fell back with all his troops behind the Guadalquivir, for Soult was then preparing to fight the allies at Seville.

The duke of Dalmatia was well aware of Wellington's intention to invade Andalusia. He knew exactly the amount and disposition of his forces, and was resolved to meet him coming out of the Morena, with all the French army united; neither did he doubt the final issue, although the failure of the last harvest and the non-arrival of convoys since February had lessened his resources. Wellington's plan was however deferred. He had levelled his trenches, and brought two Portuguese regiments of infantry from Abrantes and Elvas to form a temporary garrison of Badajos, until some Spaniards, who had been landed at Ayamonte in March, could arrive; then giving over the charge of the repairs to general Hill, who remained with two divisions of infantry and three brigades of cavalry in Estremadura, he marched himself upon

BOOK XVI.

Beira, which Marmont was now ravaging with great cruelty.

1812. April.

That marshal had been anxious to unite with Soult in Estremadura, but the emperor's orders were imperative, that he should make a diversion for Badajos by an irruption into Portugal. On the 14th of March he ascertained that none of Wellington's divisions were left on the Agueda, and on the 27th he was ready to move. Bonet, reinforced by Carier's brigade, was then on the Orbijo, in observation of the Gallicians; Ferrier's division was at Valladolid, and Foy's in the valley of the Tagus; but the other five divisions of infantry, and one of cavalry, had passed the mountains and concentrated on the Tormes, carrying with them fifteen days provisions, scaling ladders, and the materials for a bridge. Both Almeida and Ciudad Rodrigo were therefore in manifest peril, and Almeida which contained the allies' battering train was still very incompletely fortified. Hence on the first rumour of Marmont's movement, lord Wellington had thrown in two militia regiments, with a strong detachment of British artillery-men; the garrison was therefore three thousand six hundred strong, and the governor, colonel Le Mesurier, laboured hard to complete the defences.

Appendix, No. VIII. Section 1.

Of the northern militia, which had been called out before the allies quitted the Coa, six thousand infantry and three hundred cavalry were under Silveira, three thousand infantry under Trant, the same number under John Wilson, and two thousand five hundred under Lecor. But the law was, that persons liable to serve should be enrolled by classes in rotation, and therefore the present men, with the exception of

Silveira's, were raw peasants totally unskilled in the use of arms. All these officers save Lecor, whose post was at Castello Branco, had been for some time in movement, and Trant and Wilson were on the 22d at Lamego, where general Bacellar, who commanded the province, fixed his headquarters. Silveira had the same destination, but his march was slow, and his object rather to draw the wonder of his countrymen; for in his unquenchable vanity he always affected to act as an independent general.

When Trant was assured that Marmont's direction would be on Ciudad, and not Oporto, he advanced from Lamego followed by Wilson, intending to take post on the Lower Coa. While in march he received Le Mesurier's despatches, which induced him to make a forced march with one brigade to the Cabeça Negro mountain, behind the bridge of Almeida. His design was to break down the restored part of that structure, and so prevent the enemy from penetrating to Pinhel, where there was a magazine; and his march was well-timed, for two French divisions were then driving Carlos d'España over the plain beyond the Coa. It appeared that Marmont having come close to Ciudad Rodrigo on the 30th, the Spaniards and Victor Alten fell back from the Yeltes before him; and the latter, who had six hundred excellent German cavalry, immediately crossed the Agueda, and neither comprehending the spirit of lord Wellington's orders, nor the real situation of affairs, retreated at once to Castello Branco, four long marches from Ciudad, thus leaving all the country open to the enemy's marauding parties. Carlos d'España, who had eight

BOOK XVI.

1812. April.

hundred infantry, also retreated across the plain of the Cima de Coa to Fort Conception, but on the 3d the French, having laid their bridge at the ford of Caridad, passed the Agueda and drove him from thence, and he reached the Cabeça Negro in retreat with only two hundred men, at the very moment Trant arrived.

The latter seeing no French cavalry on the plain, and, being desirous of concerting his operations with Le Mesurier, immediately threw some skirmishers into the vineyards on the right of the road beyond the bridge, then escorted by some guides whom he had dressed in red uniform, he galloped to the glacis of the fortress, communicated with the governor, received from him a troop of English cavalry which happened to be in the place and returned at dusk. The Cabeça Negro was immediately covered with bivouac fires, and in the evening Le Mesurier sallied from the fortress, and drove back the enemy's light troops. Two divisions of infantry had come against Almeida, with orders to storm it, but these vigorous actions disturbed them; the attempt was not made, and the general commanding excused himself to Marmont, on the ground that the sudden appearance of Trant, indicated the vicinity of British troops. In this false notion he marched the next morning up the Coa towards Alfayates, where Marmont met him with two other divisions, and eight squadrons of cavalry, having left one division to blockade Ciudad.

Trant now sent back the horsemen to Le Mesurier and marched to Guarda to cover the magazines and hospital at Celerico. Here he was joined by Wilson, and here he ought also to have been joined by

Silveira; but that general instead of crossing the Douro on the 5th, and marching up to Guarda, only crossed it on the 14th, and then halted at Lamego. Thus, instead of twelve thousand infantry, and four hundred cavalry, who had seen some service, there were scarcely six thousand raw peasants, in a position, strong, if the occupying force had been numerous enough to hold the ridge of Porcas and other heights behind it, but a very dangerous post for a small force, because it could be turned by the right and left, and the line of retreat to the Mondego was not favourable. Neither had Trant any horsemen to scout, for Bacellar, a weak old man, who had never seen an enemy, was now at Celerico, and retained the only squadron of dragoons in the vicinity for his own guard.

This post Trant and Wilson held, with six thousand militia and six guns, from the 9th to the 14th, keeping the enemy's marauders in check; and they were also prepared to move by the high ridge of the Estrella to Abrantes, if the French should menace that fortress, which was not unlikely. For Marmont had pushed forward on Sabugal, and Victor Alten, abandoning Castello Branco, while the French were still at Memoa, fifty miles distant from him, had crossed the Tagus at Vilha Velha, and it is said had even some thoughts of burning the bridge. The French parties then traversed the Lower Beira in every direction, plundering and murdering in such a shameful manner, that the whole population fled before them. However, general Lecor, a good soldier, stood fast with the militia at Castello Branco; he checked the French cavalry detachments, removed the hospitals and some of the stores, and when menaced by a strong force of

BOOK XVI. 1812. April.

infantry on the 12th, destroyed the rest of the magazines, and fell back to Sarnadas, only one short march on the road to Villha Velha; and the next day when the French retired, he followed and harassed their rear.

Marmont's divisions being now spread over the country in search of supplies, Trant formed the very daring design of surprising the French marshal himself in his quarters at Sabugal. Bacellar's procrastinations fortunately delayed the execution of this project, which was undoubtedly too hazardous an enterprise to undertake with such troops; for the distance was twenty miles, and it was a keen observation of lord Wellington's, when Trant adverted to the magnitude of the object, to say that, "*In war nothing is so bad as failure and defeat.*" This would undoubtedly have been the case here; for in the night of the 13th, that on which Trant would have made the attempt, Marmont having formed the design of surprising Trant, had led two brigades of infantry and four hundred cavalry up the mountain. He cut off the outposts, and was actually entering the streets at day-break, with his horsemen, when the alarm was beaten at Trant's quarters by one drummer; this being taken up at hazard, by all the other drummers in different parts of the town, caused the French marshal to fall back at the moment, when a brisk charge would have placed every thing at his mercy, for the beating of the first drum was accidental, and no troops were under arms.

Marmont's Official Reports, MSS.

General Trant's papers, MSS.

The militia immediately took post outside Guarda, but they had only one day's provisions, and the French cavalry could turn their flank and gain Celerico in their rear, while the infantry attacked their front; the guns were therefore moved off under cover of the town, and the regiments, withdrawing in succession, retreated over three or four miles of open ground and in good order, although the enemy's cavalry hovered close on the flank, and the infantry followed at a short distance. Further on, however, there was a wooded declivity, leading to the Mondego, and here, while the head of the troops was passing the river below, forty dragoons, sent up by Bacellar, the evening before, were pressed by the French, and galloped through the rear-guard of eight hundred infantry; these last seeing the enemy dismount to fire their carabines, and finding that the wet had damaged their own powder, fled also, and the French followed with hue and cry.

All the officers behaved firmly, and the Mondego was finally passed, yet in confusion and with the loss of two hundred prisoners; and Marmont might now have crossed the river, on the flank of the militia, and galloped into Celerico where there was nothing to defend the magazines; instead of which he halted and permitted the disorderly rabble to gain that place. Such however was his compassion, that when he found they were really nothing but poor undisciplined peasants he would not suffer his cavalry to cut them down and no man was killed during the whole action. although the French horsemen were actually in the midst of the fugitives. Bacellar having destroyed a quantity of powder at Celerico retreated with Trant's people the next day towards Lamego; Wilson remained at Celerico, and when the enemy had driven in his outposts, he ordered the magazines to be destroyed, but the order was only partly executed when

BOOK XVI. 1812. April.

the French retired, and on the 17th the militia reoccupied Guarda.

This short campaign of the militia I have treated at length, because it produced an undue effect at the time, and because it shews how trifling accidents will mar the greatest combinations; for here the English general's extensive arrangements for the protection of Beira were utterly disconcerted by the slow advance of Silveira on the one side, and the rapid retreat of general Alten on the other. Again, the French deceived by some red uniforms and by some bivouac fires, on the Cabeça Negro, had relinquished the attack of Almeida to run after a few thousand undisciplined militia men, who were yet saved by the accidental beating of a drum; and it is curious to find a marshal of France personally acting as a partizan, and yet effecting nothing against these miserable troops.

The disaster on the Mondego spread consternation as far as Coimbra, and the most alarming reports reached lord Wellington, whose operations it is now time to notice. When Soult's retreat from Llerena was ascertained, the allied army had marched towards the Tagus, and on the 11th lord Wellington, hearing of Alten's retreat, sent him orders to recross that river without delay and return to Castello Branco. The 16th the advanced guard of the army also reached that town, and the same day a militia officer flying from Coimbra in the general panic, came to head-quarters and reported that the enemy was master of that town; but the next hour, brought general Wilson's report from Guarda, and the unfortunate wretch whose fears had led him to give the false information, was tried and shot by order of Beresford.

At this time the French army, in number about twenty-eight thousand, was concentrated, with the exception of Brennier's division which remained near Ciudad Rodrigo, between Sabugal and the ridge of hills overlooking Penamacor. Marmont was inclined to fight, for he had heard of a convoy of provisions which lord Wellington had some days before sent by the way of Almeida to Ciudad, and intended to cut it off; but the convoy having reached Almeida was safe, and the French general's own position was very critical. Almeida and the militia at Guarda were on his right flank, Ciudad Rodrigo was on his rear, and immediately behind him the Coa and the Agueda rivers were both swelled by heavy rains which fell from the 13th to the 19th, and the flood had broken the bridge near Caridad. There remained only the Puente de Villar on the Upper Agueda for retreat, and the roads leading to it were bad and narrow; the march from thence to Tamames was also circuitous and exposed to the attack of the allies, who could move on the chord through Ciudad Rodrigo. Marmont's retreat must therefore have been effected through the pass of Perales upon Coria, and the English general conceiving good hopes of falling on him before he could cross the Coa, moved forward to Pedrogoa; but the rear of the army was not yet across the Tagus, and a sufficient body of troops for the attack could not be collected before the 21st. On that day, however, the Agueda having subsided, the French restored their bridge, the last of their divisions crossed it on the 24th, and Marmont thus terminated his operations without loss. After this he again spread his troops over the plains of Leon, where some of

BOOK XVI. 1812. April.

his smaller posts had indeed been harassed by Julian Sanchez, but where the Gallician army had done nothing.

The Portuguese militia were immediately disbanded, and the English general made the greatest exertions to revictual Almeida and Ciudad Rodrigo, intending when that was effected to leave Picton with a corps upon the Agueda, and march himself against Andalusia, following his original design. The first division, which had only reached Castello Branco, returned to Castello de Vide, and as Foy's division had meanwhile reoccupied Truxillo, Hill advanced to observe him, and the fifth Spanish army returned to Estremadura. But the difficulty of supplying the fortresses was very great. The incursion of Marmont had destroyed all the intermediate magazines, and dispersed the means of transport on the lines of communication; the Portuguese government would not remedy the inconvenience either there, or on the other frontier, and Elvas and Badajos were suffering from the same cause as Ciudad and Almeida.

In this dilemma lord Wellington adopted, from necessity, a very unmilitary and dangerous remedy. For having declared to the members of the Portuguese government, that on their heads he would throw the responsibility of losing Badajos and Elvas, if they did not immediately victual both, a threat which had its due effect, he employed the whole of the carriages and mules attached to the army to bring up stores to Almeida and Ciudad Rodrigo; meanwhile he quartered his troops near the points of water-carriage, that is to say, on the Mondego, the Douro, and the Tagus. Thus the army was spread from the Morena to the Tagus, from the Tagus to the Douro, from the Douro to the Mondego, on a line little less than four hundred miles long, and in the face of three hostile armies, the farthest of which was but a few marches from the outposts. It was however scarcely possible for the French to assemble again in masses, before the ripening of the coming harvest; and on the other hand, even the above measure was insufficient to gain time; the expedition against Andalusia was therefore abandoned, and the fifth great epoch of the war terminated.

CHAPTER VII.

GENERAL OBSERVATIONS.

BOOK XVI.

1812.

In this campaign the French forces were too much scattered, and they occupied the countries bordering on Portugal rather as a conquered territory than as a field of operations. The movements of the armies of the north, of the centre, and of Portugal, might have been so combined as to present a hundred thousand men on a field of battle; yet Wellington captured two great fortresses within gun-shot as it were of them all, and was never disturbed by the approach of even thirty thousand men. This arose partly from want of union, partly from the orders of the Emperor, whose plans the generals either did not or would not understand in their true spirit, and therefore executed without vigour; and yet the French writers have generally endeavoured to fasten the failures on Napoleon, as if he only was mistaken about the war in Spain! It is easy to spurn the dead lion!

The expedition of Montbrun to Alicant has been fixed upon as the chief cause of the fall of Ciudad Rodrigo. Napoleon however did not desire that Montbrun's march should be held in abeyance for a week, upon the strength of some vague rumours relative to the allies' proceedings, and yet be finally sent at precisely the wrong period; neither did he contemplate that general's idle display at Alicant after the city of Valencia had fallen. But ill-executed and hurtful as this expedition doubtless was, in various ways, the loss of Ciudad Rodrigo cannot be directly traced to it. Montbrun was at Almanza the 9th of January and the 19th Ciudad was stormed; now, if he had not been at Almanza he would have been at Toledo or Talavera, that is, eight marches from Salamanca; and as the commencement of the siege was not known until the 15th, even at Valladolid, he could not have been on the Tormes before the 25th, which would have been five days too late. The emperor wished to strengthen Suchet at the crisis of the Valencian operations, and his intent was that Montbrun should have reached that city in December, but the latter did not arrive before the middle of January; had he been only a week earlier, that is, had he marched at once from Toledo, Mahy could not have escaped, Alicant would then have fallen, and if Blake had made an obstinate defence at Valencia the value of such a reinforcement would have been acknowledged.

At this period Valencia was the most important point in the Peninsula, and there was no apparent reason why Ciudad should be in any immediate danger; the emperor could not calculate upon the errors of his own generals. It is futile therefore to affirm that Montbrun's detachment was made on a false principle; it was on the contrary conceived in perfect accord with the maxim of concentrating on the important point at the decisive moment; errors, extraneous to the original design, alone brought it within the principle of dissemination.

The loss of Ciudad Rodrigo may be directly traced to the duke of Ragusa's want of vigilance,

BOOK XVI.

1812.

to the scanty garrison which he kept in the place, to the Russian war which obliged the emperor to weaken the army of the north; finally, to the extravagance of the army of the centre. Marmont expressly asserts that at Madrid three thousand men devoured and wasted daily the rations of twenty-two thousand, and the stores thus consumed would have enabled the army of Portugal to keep concentrated, in which case Wellington could not have taken Ciudad; and if the army of the centre had been efficient, Hill would have incurred great danger and Soult's power been vastly augmented.

It is not Napoleon's skill only, that has been assailed by these writers. Lord Wellington also is blamed for not crushing Souham's division at Tamames between the 23d and the 26th of January; although Souham, a good general, never entered Tamames, except with cavalry scouts, and kept his main body at Matilla, whence one forced march would have placed him behind the Tormes in safety! In such a shallow manner have the important operations of this period been treated. Nor will the causes commonly assigned for the fall of Badajos better bear examination.

"*Marmont instead of joining Soult in Estremadura, followed a phantom in Beira.*" "*It was his vanity and jealousy of the duke of Dalmatia that lost Badajos.*" Such are the assertions of both French and English writers; nevertheless the duke of Ragusa never anticipated any success from his movement into Beira, and far from avoiding Soult, earnestly desired to co-operate with him; moreover this invasion of Beira, which has been regarded as a folly, was the conception of Napoleon, the greatest of all captains! and it is not difficult to shew that the emperor's design was, notwithstanding the ill result, capacious and solid.

Let us suppose that Marmont had aided Soult, and that the army of the centre had also sent men. If they had made any error in their combinations the English general would have defeated them separately; if they had effected their junction, he would have retreated, and Badajos would have been succoured. But then eighty thousand French would have been assembled by long marches in the winter rains, to the great detriment of their affairs elsewhere, and unless they came prepared to take Elvas, without any adequate object; for lord Wellington could, after the fall of Ciudad Rodrigo, have repeated this operation as often as he pleased, which, besides the opening thus made for insurrection in Spain, would have stamped a character of weakness on the French arms, extremely injurious, since character is half the strength of an army.

The emperor judged better; he disliked such timid operations, he desired that his powerful armies should throw the allies on the defensive and he indicated the means of doing so. Wellington, he said, expecting an effort to retake Ciudad Rodrigo, had called Hill across the Tagus, and to prevent that movement Soult was directed to send twenty thousand men against the Alemtejo. The fall of Ciudad had thus by obliging the allies to defend it, given the French their choice of ground for a battle, and at a distance from the sea; it was for Marmont to avail himself of the occasion, not by marching to aid Soult, who had eighty thousand excellent troops, and at the worst could be only driven from Andalusia upon Valencia or Ma-

BOOK XVI. 1812.

drid; whereas if the army of Portugal or a part of it should be defeated on the Guadiana the blow would be felt in every part of Spain. Marmont's business was, he said, first to strengthen his own position at Salamanca, as a base of operations, and then to keep the allies constantly engaged on the Agueda until he was prepared to fight a general battle. Meanwhile Soult should either take the fortresses of the Alemtejo, or draw off Hill's corps from Wellington, who would then be very inferior to Marmont and yet Hill himself would be unequal to fight Soult.

"Fix your quarters," said the emperor, "at Salamanca, work day and night to fortify that place—organize a new battering train—form magazines—send strong advanced guards to menace Ciudad and Almeida—harass the allies' outposts, even daily—threaten the frontier of Portugal in all directions, and send parties to ravage the nearest villages—repair the ways to Almeida and Oporto, and keep the bulk of your army at Toro Zamora, Benevente, and Avila, which are fertile districts, and from whence, in four days, you can concentrate the whole upon Salamanca. You will thus keep the allies in check on the Agueda, and your troops will repose, while you prepare for great operations. You have nothing to do with the south. Announce the approach of your new battering train, and if Wellington marches to invest Badajos with a few divisions, Soult will be able to relieve it; but if Wellington goes with all his forces, unite your army, march straight upon Almeida, push parties to Coimbra, overrun the country in various directions, and be assured he will return. Twenty-four hours after the receipt of this letter you should be on your way to Salamanca, and your advanced guards should be in march towards Ciudad Rodrigo and Almeida." CHAP. VII. 1812.

Now, if Marmont had thus conceived the war himself, he could have commenced operations before the end of January; but this letter, written the 15th of February, reached him in the latter end of that month, and found him desponding and fearful even in defence. Vacillating between his own wishes and the emperor's orders, he did nothing; but had he, as his despatch recommended, commenced his operations in twenty-four hours, his advanced posts would have been near Ciudad early in March, that is at the moment when the allies were, as I have before shewn, disseminated all over Portugal, and when only the fifth division was upon the Coa to oppose him. The works of Almeida were then quite indefensible, and the movement upon Badajos must have necessarily been suspended. Thus the winter season would have passed away uselessly for the allies unless Wellington turned to attack Marmont, which was a difficult operation in itself, and would have been dangerous to the Alemtejo, while Soult held Badajos, for that marshal, as we have seen, had received orders to attack Hill with twenty thousand men. Here then the errors were of execution, not of design, and the first part of the emperor's combinations was evidently just and solid. It remains to test the second part which was to have been executed if lord Wellington invested Badajos.

Appendix, No. VIII. Section 2.

It must be remembered, that Marmont was so to hold his army, that he could concentrate in four days; that he was to make an incursion into Beira the moment Wellington crossed the Tagus; that

BOOK XVI. 1812.

Oporto was to be menaced, Almeida to be attacked, Coimbra to be occupied. These operations would undoubtedly have brought the allies back again at the commencement of the siege, because the fall of Badajos could not be expected under three weeks, which would have been too long to leave Beira and the fortresses at the mercy of the invader. Now Marmont did not reach the Agueda before the 31st March, when the siege of Badajos was approaching its conclusion; he did not storm Almeida, nor attack Ciudad Rodrigo, nor enter Coimbra, nor menace Oporto; and yet his operation, feebly as it was executed, obliged lord Wellington to relinquish his meditated attack on Andalusia, and return to the assistance of Beira. Again therefore the error was in the execution. And here we may observe how inferior in hardihood the French general was to his adversary. Wellington with eighteen thousand men had escaladed Badajos, a powerful fortress and defended by an excellent governor with five thousand French veterans; Marmont with twenty-eight thousand men would not attempt to storm Ciudad, although its breaches were scarcely healed, and its garrison disaffected. Nor did he even assail Almeida, which hardly meriting the name of a fortress, was only occupied by three thousand militia, scarcely able to handle their arms; and yet if he had captured Almeida, as he could scarcely have failed to do with due vigour, he would have found a battering train with which to take Ciudad Rodrigo, and thus have again balanced the campaign.

The duke of Ragusa was averse to serving in the Peninsula, he wished to be employed in the Russian expedition, and he had written to the emperor to desire his recal, or that the whole of the northern district, from Sebastian to Salamanca, including Madrid, should be placed under his orders. Unless that were done, he said he could only calculate the operations of his own troops. The other generals would make difficulties, would move slowly, and the king's court was in open hostility to the French interest. The army of the north had in retiring from Leon scrupulously carried away every thing that could be useful to him, in the way of bridge, or battering equipages, or of ammunition or provisions, although he was in want of all these things.

Then he painted all the jealousies and disputes in the French armies, and affirmed that his own force, care being had for the posts of communication, and the watching of the army of Gallicia, would not furnish more than thirty-four thousand men for the field; a calculation contradicted by the imperial muster-rolls, which on the 1st of March bore sixty thousand fighting men present with the eagles. He also rated the allies at sixty thousand, well provided with every thing and ready to attack him, whereas the returns of that army gave only fifty-two thousand men including Hill's corps; about thirty-five thousand only could have passed the Agueda, and their penury of means had, as we have seen, prevented them from even holding together, on the northern frontier. In like manner he assumed that two of the allied divisions were left upon the Agueda, when the army marched against Badajos, whereas no more than six hundred cavalry remained there. All these things prove that Marmont, either from dislike to the war, or natural want of vigour, was not equal to his task, and it is obvious that a diversion, begun so late, and followed up with so little energy, could have had little effect upon the siege of Badajos; it would have been far better to have followed his own first design of detaching three divisions to aid Soult, and retained the other two to menace Ciudad Rodrigo.

It is fitting now to test the operations of the armies of the south, and of the centre. The latter is easily disposed of. The secret of its inactivity is to be found in Marmont's letter. Every thing at Madrid was confusion and intrigue, waste and want of discipline; in fine, the union of a court and an army, had destroyed the latter. Not so at Seville. There the hand of an able general, an indefatigable administrator were visible, and the unravelling the intricate combinations, which produced such an apparent want of vigour in the operations of the duke of Dalmatia, will form at once the apology for that general, and the just eulogium of lord Wellington.

First it must be held in mind that the army of the south, so powerful in appearance, did not furnish a proportionate number of men for field-service, because the reinforcements, although borne on the rolls, were for the most part retained in the northern governments. Soult had sixty-seven thousand French and six thousand "Escopeteros" present under arms in September; but then followed the surprise of Girard at Aroyo de Molinos, the vigorous demonstrations of Hill in December, the failure of Godinot at Gibraltar, the check sustained by Semélé at Bornos, and the siege of Tarifa, which diminished the number of men, and occasioned fresh arrangements on the different points of the circle. The harvest of 1811 had failed in Andalusia, as in all other parts, and the inhabitants were reduced to feed on herbs; the soldiers had only half rations of bread, and neither reinforcements of men, nor convoys of money, nor ammunition, nor clothes, had come either from France or from Madrid for a long period.

It was under these circumstances that Soult received the order to send twenty thousand men against the Alemtejo. But the whole of the Polish troops, and the skeletons of regiments, and the picked men for the imperial guards, in all fifteen thousand, after being collected at the Despeñas Peros, while Suchet was before Valencia, had now marched to Talavera de la Reyna on the way to France; at that moment also Ballesteros appeared, with the fourth Spanish army, twelve thousand strong, in the Ronda, and his detachments defeated Maransin at Cartaña, which of necessity occasioned another change in the French dispositions. Moreover the very successes of Suchet had at this time increased Soult's difficulties, because all the fugitives from Valencia gathered on the remains of the Murcian army; and fifteen thousand men, including the garrisons of Carthagena and Alicant, were again assembled on the frontier of Grenada, where, during the expedition to Estremadura, the French had only three battalions and some cavalry.

Thus the army of the south was, if the garrison of Badajos be excluded, reduced to forty-eight thousand French sabres and bayonets present with the eagles, and this at the very moment when its enemies were augmented by twenty-five thousand fresh men. Soult had indeed besides this force five thousand artillery-men and other attendant

BOOK XVI.

1812.

troops, and six thousand "*Escopeteros*" were capable of taking the field, while thirty thousand civic guards held his fortified posts. Nevertheless he was forced to reduce all the garrisons, and even the camp before the Isla to the lowest numbers, consistent with safety, ere he could bring twenty-four thousand French into the field for the succour of Badajos, and even then as we have seen, he was upon the point of losing Seville. These things prevented him from coming against the Alemtejo in March, when his presence with an army would have delayed the commencement of the siege until a battle had been fought: but he was the less fearful for the fortress because Marmont on the 22d of February and Foy on the 28th had announced, that if Badajos should be menaced, three divisions of the army of Portugal, then in the valley of the Tagus, would enter Estremadura; and these divisions uniting with Daricau's and Drouet's troops would have formed an army of thirty thousand men, and consequently would have sufficed to delay the operations of the allies. But Marmont, having subsequently received the emperor's orders to move into Beira, passed the Gredos mountains instead of the Tagus river, and thus unintentionally deceived Soult; and whether his letters were intercepted, or carelessly delayed, it was not until the 8th of April, that the duke of Dalmatia was assured of his departure for Salamanca.

On the other hand Lord Wellington's operations were so rapidly pushed forward, that Soult cannot be censured for false calculations. No general could suspect that such an outwork as the Picurina, would be taken by storm without being first battered; still less that Badajos, with its lofty walls, its brave garrison, and its celebrated governor, would in like manner be carried before the counterscarp was blown in, and the fire of the defences ruined. In fine, no man accustomed to war could have divined the surpassing resolution and surpassing fortune also, of the British general and his troops; neither is it impertinent to observe here, that as the French never use iron ordnance in a siege, their calculations were necessarily formed upon the effect of brass artillery, which is comparatively weak and slow: with brass guns the breaches would have been made three days later.

The fall of Badajos may therefore be traced partly to the Russian war, which drew fifteen thousand men from the army of the south, partly to the irresolution of Marmont, who did neither execute the emperor's plan nor his own; finally, to the too great extent of country occupied, whereby time and numbers were swallowed. And here the question arises, if Soult, acting upon the principles laid down in his letter to Joseph, just before the battle of Talavera, should not have operated against the allies in great masses, relinquishing possession of Grenada, Malaga, in fine of every thing, save Seville and the camp before the Isla. If beaten, he would have lost Andalusia and fallen back on Suchet, but then the head of the French invasion, might have been more formidable at Valencia than at Seville, and Marmont could have renewed the battle. And such a chequered game, lord Wellington's political situation both in England and Portugal being considered, would have gone near to decide the question of the British troops remaining in the latter country. This however is a grave and difficult matter to resolve.

BOOK XVI.

1812.

In whatever light this campaign is viewed the talent of the English general is conspicuous. That fortune aided him is true, but it was in the manner she favours the pilot, who watching every changing wind, every shifting current, makes all subservient to his purpose. Ascertaining with great pains the exact situation of each adversary, he had sagaciously met their different modes of warfare, and with a nice hand had adapted his measures to the successive exigences of the moment. The army of the centre, where disorder was paramount, he disregarded; Marmont whose temperament was hasty he deceived by affected slowness; and Soult he forestalled by quickness. Twice he induced the duke of Ragusa to send his divisions into distant quarters, when they should have been concentrated, and each time he gained a great advantage; once when he took Ciudad Rodrigo, and again when, using a like opportunity, to obviate the difficulties presented by the conduct of the Portuguese government, he spread his own troops over the country, in an unmilitary manner, that he might feed and clothe them on their march to the Alemtejo. This he could not have done if the French had been concentrated; neither could he have so well concealed that march from the enemy.

In Estremadura, he kept his force compact and strong to meet Soult, from whose warfare he expected a powerful opposition, hard indeed to resist, yet not likely to abound in sudden strokes, and therefore furnishing more certain ground for calculation as to time; and then he used that time so wonderfully at the siege, that even his enemies declared it incomprehensible, and he who had hitherto been censured for over caution was now

CHAP. VII. 1812.

dreaded as over daring! This daring was, however, in no manner allied to rashness, his precautions multiplied as his enterprises augmented. The divisions of the army of Portugal, quartered in the valley of the Tagus, could by moving into Estremadura in March have delayed if not prevented the siege; lord Wellington had therefore with forecast of such an event, designed that Hill should, when the allies entered the Alemtejo, make a forced march to surprise the bridge and forts at Almaraz, which would have obliged the French divisions to make a long circuit by the bridges of Arzobispo and Talavera to reach the scene of action in Estremadura.

This bold and skilful stroke was baulked by the never-ceasing misconduct of the Portuguese government, with respect to means of transport; for the battering-guns intended for Hill's enterprise were thus prevented passing Evora. Nevertheless the siege was commenced, because it was ascertained that Marmont was still ignorant of the allies' march, and had made no change in his extended quarters, indicating a design to aid Soult; Hill also soon drove Drouet back towards the Morena, and by occupying Merida, intercepted the line of communication with Almaraz, which answered the same purpose. But the best testimony to the skill of the operation is to be found in the enemy's papers. "So calculated," said Soult, "was this affair (the siege of Badajos) that it is to be supposed lord Wellington had intercepted some despatches which explained to him the system of operations and the irresolution of Marmont."

Intercepted despatch of marshal Soult, 1812. MSS.

Nor when the duke of Ragusa was ravaging Beira, and both Almeida and Ciudad appeared in

BOOK XVI. 1812.

the utmost danger, did lord Wellington's delay in Estremadura arise from any imprudence; he had good grounds for believing, that the French would not attempt the latter place, and that the loss of a few days would not prove injurious. For when the first intelligence that the army of Portugal was concentrating on the Tormes reached him, he sent captain Colquhoun Grant, a celebrated scouting officer, to watch Marmont's proceedings. That gentleman, in whom the utmost daring was so mixed with subtlety of genius, and both so tempered by discretion, that it is hard to say which quality predominated, very rapidly executed his mission; and the interesting nature of his adventures on this occasion will perhaps excuse a digression concerning them.

Attended by Leon, a Spanish peasant of great fidelity and quickness of apprehension, who had been his companion on many former occasions of the same nature, Grant arrived in the Salamancan district, and passing the Tormes in the night, remained, in uniform, for he never assumed any disguise, three days in the midst of the French camp. He thus obtained exact information of Marmont's object, and more especially of his preparations of provisions and scaling ladders, notes of which he sent to lord Wellington from day to day by Spanish agents. However, on the third night, some peasants brought him a general order, addressed to the French regiments, and saying, that the notorious Grant being within the circle of their cantonments, the soldiers were to use their utmost exertions to secure him, for which purpose also guards were placed as it were in a circle round the army.

Nothing daunted by this news, Grant consulted

with the peasants, and the next morning, before daylight, entered the village of Huerta, which is close to a ford on the Tormes, and about six miles from Salamanca. Here there was a French battalion, and on the opposite side of the river cavalry videttes were posted, two of which constantly patrolled back and forward, for the space of three hundred yards, meeting always at the ford. When day broke the French battalion assembled on its alarm-post, and at that moment Grant was secretly brought with his horse behind the gable of a house, which hid him from the infantry, and was opposite to the ford. The peasants standing on some loose stones and spreading their large cloaks, covered him from the cavalry videttes, and thus he calmly waited until the latter were separated the full extent of their beat; then putting spurs to his horse he dashed through the ford between them, and receiving their fire without damage, reached a wood, not very distant, where the pursuit was baffled, and where he was soon rejoined by Leon, who in his native dress met with no interruption.

Grant had already ascertained that the means of storming Ciudad Rodrigo were prepared, and that the French officers openly talked of doing so, but he desired still further to test this project, and to discover if the march of the enemy might not finally be directed by the pass of Perales, towards the Tagus; he wished also to ascertain more correctly their real numbers, and therefore placed himself on a wooded hill, near Tamames, where the road branches off to the passes, and to Ciudad Rodrigo. Here lying perdue, until the whole French army had passed by in march, he noted every battalion and gun, and finding that all were directed towards Ciudad, entered Tamames after they had passed, and discovered that they had left the greatest part of their scaling-ladders behind, which clearly proved that the intention of storming Ciudad Rodrigo was not real. This it was which allayed Wellington's fears for that fortress.

When Marmont afterwards passed the Coa, in this expedition, Grant preceded him with intent to discover if his further march would be by Guarda upon Coimbra, or by Sabugal upon Castello Branco; for to reach the latter it was necessary to descend from a very high ridge, or rather succession of ridges, by a pass, at the lower mouth of which stands Penamacor. Upon one of the inferior ridges in the pass, this persevering officer placed himself, thinking that the dwarf oaks, with which the hills were covered, would effectually secure him from discovery; but from the higher ridge above, the French detected all his movements with their glasses, in a few moments Leon, whose lynx-eyes were always on the watch, called out "*the French! the French!*" and pointed to the rear, whence some dragoons came galloping up. Grant and his follower, instantly darted into the wood for a little space, and then suddenly wheeling, rode off in a different direction; yet at every turn new enemies appeared, and at last the hunted men dismounted and fled on foot through the thickest of the low oaks; but again they were met by infantry, who had been detached in small parties down the sides of the pass, and were directed in their chase by the waving of the French officers' hats on the ridge above. At last Leon fell exhausted, and the barbarians who first came up, killed him in despite of his companion's entreaties.

Grant himself they carried, without injury, to Marmont, who receiving him with apparent kindness, invited him to dinner. The conversation turned upon the prisoner's exploits, and the French marshal affirmed that he had been for a long time on the watch, that he knew all his haunts, and his disguises, and had discovered that, only the night before, he had slept in the French head-quarters, with other adventures, which had not happened, for this Grant never used any disguise; but there was another Grant, a man also very remarkable in his way, who used to remain for months in the French quarters, using all manner of disguises; hence the similarity of names caused the actions of both to be attributed to one, which is the only palliative for Marmont's subsequent conduct.

Treating his prisoner as I have said, with great apparent kindness, the French general exacted from him an especial parole, that he would not consent to be released by the Partidas, while on his journey through Spain to France, which secured his captive, although lord Wellington offered two thousand dollars to any guerilla chief who should rescue him. The exaction of such a parole, however harsh, was in itself a tacit compliment to the man; but Marmont, also, sent a letter, with the escort, to the governor of Bayonne, in which, still labouring under the error that there was only one Grant, he designated his captive as a dangerous spy, who had done infinite mischief to the French army, and whom he had only not executed on the spot, out of

BOOK XVI. 1812.

respect to something resembling an uniform which he wore at the time of his capture. He therefore desired, that at Bayonne, he should be placed in irons and sent up to Paris.

This proceeding was too little in accord with the honour of the French army to be supported, and before the Spanish frontier was passed, Grant, it matters not how, was made acquainted with the contents of the letter. Now the custom at Bayonne, in ordinary cases, was for the prisoner to wait on the authorities, and receive a passport to travel to Verdun, and all this was duly accomplished; meanwhile the delivering of the fatal letter being, by certain means, delayed, Grant, with a wonderful readiness and boldness, resolved not to escape towards the Pyrenees, thinking that he would naturally be pursued in that direction. He judged that if the governor of Bayonne could not recapture him at once, he would for his own security suppress the letter in hopes the matter would be no further thought of; judging, I say, in this acute manner, he on the instant inquired at the hotels, if any French officer was going to Paris, and finding that general Souham, then on his return from Spain, was so bent, he boldly introduced himself, and asked permission to join his party. The other readily assented; and while thus travelling, the general, unacquainted with Marmont's intentions, often rallied his companion about his adventures, little thinking that he was then himself an instrument in forwarding the most dangerous and skilful of them all.

In passing through Orleans, Grant, by a species of intuition, discovered an English agent, and from him received a recommendation to another secret agent in Paris, whose assistance would be necessary to his final escape; for he looked upon Marmont's double dealing, and the expressed design to take away his life, as equivalent to a discharge of his parole, which was moreover only given with respect to Spain. When he arrived at Paris he took leave of Souham, opened an intercourse with the Parisian agent, from whom he obtained money, and by his advice, avoided appearing before the police, to have his passport examined. He took a lodging in a very public street, frequented the coffee-houses, and even visited the theatres without fear, because the secret agent, who had been long established and was intimately connected with the police, had ascertained that no inquiry about his escape had been set on foot.

In this manner he passed several weeks, at the end of which, the agent informed him that a passport was ready for one Jonathan Buck, an American, who had died suddenly, on the very day it was to have been claimed. Seizing this occasion, Grant boldly demanded the passport, with which he instantly departed for the mouth of the Loire, because certain reasons, not necessary to mention, led him to expect more assistance there than at any other port. However, new difficulties awaited him and were overcome by fresh exertions of his surprising talents, which fortune seemed to delight in aiding.

He first took a passage for America in a ship of that nation, but its departure being unexpectedly delayed, he frankly explained his true situation to the captain, who desired him to assume the character of a discontented seaman, and giving him a sailor's dress and forty dollars, sent him to lodge the money in the American consul's hands as a pledge, that

BOOK XVI. 1812. he would prosecute the captain for ill usage when he reached the United States; this being the custom on such occasions the consul gave him a certificate which enabled him to pass from port to port as a discharged sailor seeking a ship.

Thus provided, after waiting some days, Grant prevailed upon a boatman, by a promise of ten Napoleons, to row him in the night towards a small island, where, by usage, the English vessels watered unmolested, and in return permitted the few inhabitants to fish and traffic without interruption. In the night the boat sailed, the masts of the British ships were dimly seen on the other side of the island, and the termination of his toils appeared at hand, when the boatman, either from fear or malice, suddenly put about and returned to port. In such a situation, some men would have striven in desperation to force fortune, and so have perished; the spirits of others would have sunk in despair, for the money which he had promised was all that remained of his stock, and the boatman, notwithstanding his breach of contract, demanded the whole; but with inexpressible coolness and resolution, Grant gave him one Napoleon instead of ten, and a rebuke for his misconduct. The other having threatened a reference to the police, soon found that he was no match in subtlety for his opponent, who told him plainly that he would then denounce him as aiding the escape of a prisoner of war, and would adduce the great price of his boat as a proof of his guilt!

This menace was too formidable to be resisted, and Grant in a few days engaged an old fisherman, who faithfully performed his bargain; but now there were no English vessels near the island; however the fisherman cast his nets and caught some fish, with which he sailed towards the southward, where he had heard there was an English ship of war. In a few hours they obtained a glimpse of her, and were steering that way, when a shot from a coast-battery brought them to, and a boat with soldiers put off to board them ; the fisherman was steadfast and true; he called Grant his son, and the soldiers by whom they expected to be arrested were only sent to warn them not to pass the battery, because the English vessel they were in search of was on the coast. The old man, who had expected this, bribed the soldiers with his fish, assuring them he must go with his son or they would starve, and that he was so well acquainted with the coast he could always escape the enemy. His prayers and presents prevailed, he was desired to wait under the battery till night, and then depart; but under pretence of arranging his escape from the English vessel, he made the soldiers point out her bearings so exactly, that when the darkness came, he ran her straight on board, and the intrepid officer stood in safety on the quarter-deck.

After this Grant reached England and obtained permission to choose a French officer of equal rank with himself, to send to France, that no doubt might remain about the propriety of his escape; and great was his astonishment to find, in the first prison he visited, the old fisherman and his real son, who had meanwhile been captured notwithstanding a protection given to them for their services. Grant, whose generosity and benevolence were as remarkable as the qualities of his understanding, soon obtained their release, and having sent them with a sum of money to France returned himself

BOOK XVI. 1812.

to the Peninsula, and within four months from the date of his first capture was again on the Tormes, watching Marmont's army! Other strange incidents of his life I could mention, were it not more fitting to quit a digression, already too wide; yet I was unwilling to pass an occasion of noticing one adventure of this generous and spirited, and yet gentle-minded man, who having served his country nobly and ably in every climate, died, not long since, exhausted by the continual hardships he had endured.

Having now shewn the prudence of lord Wellington with respect to the campaign generally, it remains to consider the siege of Badajos, which has so often been adduced in evidence, that not skill but fortune plumed his ambitious wing; a proceeding indeed most consonant to the nature of man; for it is hard to avow inferiority, by attributing an action so stupendous to superior genius alone. A critical scientific examination would be misplaced in a general history, but to notice some of the leading points which involve the general conception will not be irrelevent. The choice of the line of attack has been justified by the English engineers, as that requiring least expenditure of means and time; but this has by the French engineer been denied. Colonel Lamarre affirms that the front next the castle was the one least susceptible of defence; because it had neither ravelin nor ditch to protect it, had fewer flanks, and offered no facility of retrenching behind it; a view which is confirmed by Phillipon, who being the best judge of his own weak points, did for many days imagine that this front was the true object of the allies' approaches. But Lamarre advances a far more interesting question, when he affirms that the English general might have carried Badajos by escalade and storm, on the first night of the siege, with less difficulty than he experienced on the 7th of April. On that night, he says, the defences were not so complete, that the garrison was less prepared, and the surprise would have availed somewhat; whereas at the second period the breaches were the strongest part of the town, and as no other advantage had been gained by the besiegers, the chances were in favour of the first period.

This reasoning appears sound, yet the fact is one which belongs, not to the rules but the secrets of the art, and they are only in the keeping of great captains. That the breaches were impregnable has indeed been denied by the English engineers. Colonel Jones affirms that the centre breach had not the slightest interior retrenchment, and that the sword-blades in the Trinidad, might have been overturned by the rush of a dense mass of troops. This opinion is quite at variance with that of the officers and men engaged; it is certain also that all the breaches were protected by the sword-blades, and if the centre breach was not retrenched, it was rendered very difficult of approach by the deep holes digged in front, and it was more powerfully swept by flank-fire than the others were. It is also a mistake to suppose that no dense rush was made at the great breach. Engineers intent upon their own art sometimes calculate on men as they do on blocks of stone or timber, nevertheless where the bullet strikes the man will fall. The sword-blades were fitted into ponderous beams, and these last, chained together, were let deep into the ground; how then was it possible for men to

BOOK XVI. 1812. drag, or push them from their places, when behind them stood resolute men, whose fire swept the foremost ranks away? This fire could not be returned by the soldiers engaged in removing the obstacles, nor by those in rear, because, from the slope of the breach, they could only see their own comrades of the front ranks; and then the dead bodies, and the struggling wounded men, and still more the spiked planks, rendered a simultaneous exertion impossible. The breaches were impregnable!

And why was all this striving in blood against insurmountable difficulties? Why were men sent thus to slaughter, when the application of a just science would have rendered the operation comparatively easy? Because the English ministers, so ready to plunge into war, were quite ignorant of its exigencies; because the English people are warlike without being military, and under the pretence of maintaining a liberty which they do not possess, oppose in peace all useful martial establishments. Expatiating in their schools and colleges, upon Roman discipline and Roman valour, they are heedless of Roman institutions; they desire like that ancient republic, to be free at home and conquerors abroad, but start at perfecting their military system, as a thing incompatible with a constitution, which they yet suffer to be violated by every minister who trembles at the exposure of corruption. In the beginning of each war, England has to seek in blood for the knowledge necessary to insure success, and like the fiend's progress toward Eden, her conquering course is through chaos followed by death!

But it is not in the details of this siege we must

look for Wellington's merits. The apportioning of the number of guns, the quantity of ammunition, the amount of transport, the tracing of the works, and the choice of the points of attack, are matters within the province of the engineer; the value and importance of the place to be attacked in reference to other objects of the campaign, the time that can be spared to effect its reduction, the arrangements necessary to elude or to resist the succouring army, the calculation of the resources, from whence the means of attack are to be drawn, these are in the province of the general. With him also rests the choice of shortening the scientific process, and the judging of how much or how little ought to be risked, how much trusted to the valour and discipline of his army, how much to his own genius for seizing accidents, whether of ground, of time, or of conjunction to accelerate the gain of his object.

Now all armies come to the siege of a town with great advantages; for first the besieged cannot but be less confident than the assailants; they are a few against a many, and being on the defensive, are also an excised portion of their own army, and without news, which damps the fiery spirit. They are obliged to await their adversary's time and attack, their losses seem more numerous, in proportion to their forces, because they are more concentrated, and then the wounded are not safe even in the hospitals. No troops can hope to maintain a fortress eventually, without the aid of a succouring army; their ultimate prospect is death or captivity. The besiegers on the contrary have a certain retreat, know the real state of affairs, feel more assured of their object, have hope of profit, and a secure

BOOK XVI. 1812.

retreat if they fail, while the besieged faintly look for succour, and scarcely expect life. To this may be added that the inhabitants are generally secret enemies of the garrison as the cause of their own sufferings.

The number of guns and quantity of ammunition, in a fortress, are daily diminished; the besiegers' means, originally calculated to overpower the other, may be increased. Time and materials are therefore against the besieged, and the scientific foundation of the defence depends on the attack which may be varied, while the other is fixed. Finally the firmness and skill of the defence generally depends upon the governor, who may be killed, whereas many officers amongst the besiegers are capable of conducting the attack; and the general, besides being personally less exposed, is likely, as the chief of an army, to be a man of more spirit and capacity than a simple governor. It follows then that fortresses must fall if the besiegers sit down before them according to the rules of art; and when no succouring army is nigh, the time, necessary to reduce any place, may be calculated with great exactness. When these rules cannot be attended to, when every thing is irregular and doubtful, when the general is hurried on to the attempt, be it easy or difficult, by the force of circumstances, we must measure him by the greatness of the exigency, and the energy with which he acts.

This is the light in which to view the siege of Badajos. Wellington's object was great, his difficulties foreseen, his success complete. A few hours' delay, an accident, a turn of fortune, and he would again have been foiled! aye! but this is war, always dangerous and uncertain, an ever-rolling wheel and armed with scythes. Was the object worth the risk—did its gain compensate the loss of men—was it boldly, greatly acquired? These are the true questions and they may be answered thus. Suchet had subjugated Aragon by his mildness, Catalonia and Valencia by his vigour. In Andalusia, Soult had tranquillized the mass of the people, and his genius, solid and vast, was laying the deep foundation of a kingdom close to Portugal. He was forming such great establishments, and contriving such plans, as would, if permitted to become ripe, have enabled him to hold the Peninsula, alone, should the French armies fail in all other parts. In the centre of Spain the king, true to his plan of raising a Spanish party, was likely to rally round him all those of the patriots whom discontent, or weakness of mind, or corruption, might induce to seek a plausible excuse, for joining the invaders; and on the northern line the French armies, still powerful, were strengthening their hold of the country by fortifying all the important points of Leon and Old Castile. Meanwhile the great army, which the emperor was carrying to Russia, might or might not be successful, but in either case, it was the only moment when an offensive war, against his army in Spain, could have been carried on with success.

But how could any extensive offensive operation have been attempted while Badajos remained in the enemy's possession? If Wellington had advanced in the north, Soult making Badajos his base would have threatened Lisbon; if Wellington marched against the French centre, the same thing would have happened, and the army of the north would

BOOK XVI. 1812.

also have acted on the left flank of the allies or have retaken Ciudad Rodrigo. If an attempt had been made against Soult, it must have been by the Lower Guadiana, when the French army of Portugal coming down to Badajos, could have either operated against the rear of the allies, or against Lisbon.

Badajos was therefore the key to all offensive operations by the allies, and to take it was an indispensable preliminary. Yet how take it? By regular or by irreglar operations? For the first a certain time was required, which from the experience of former sieges it was not to be expected that the enemy would allow. What then would have been the result, if thus, year after year, the allies showed they were unable even to give battle to their enemies, much less to chase them from the Peninsula. How was it to be expected that England would bear the expense of a protracted warfare, affording no hope of final success. How were the opposition clamours to be replied to in Parliament? How were the secret hopes of the continental governments to be upheld if the military power of England, Portugal, and Spain united was unable to meet even a portion of the secondary armies of Napoleon, while with four hundred thousand men he stalked, a gigantic conqueror, over the wastes of Russia? To strike irregularly then was Wellington's only resource. To strike without regard to rules, trusting to the courage of his men and to fortune to bear him through the trial triumphant. Was such a crisis to be neglected by a general who had undertaken on his own judgement to fight the battle of the Peninsula. Was he to give force to the light declamation of the hour, when general officers in England were heard to say that every defeat of the French was a snare to decoy the British further into Spain! was he, at such a moment, to place the probable loss of a few thousand men, more or less, in opposition to such a conjuncture, and by declining the chance offered, shew that he despaired of success himself? What if he failed? he would not have been, save the loss of a few men, worse off than if he had not attacked. In either case, he would have been a baffled general with a sinking cause. But what if he succeeded? The horizon was bright with the coming glory of England!

APPENDIX.

APPENDIX.

JUSTIFICATORY PAPERS RELATIVE TO THE STATE OF SPAIN AT DIFFERENT PERIODS.

No. I.

SECTION 1.—NORTHERN PROVINCES.

Captain Irby to Mr. Croft.

"*H. M. S. Amelia,*
"*Coruña, May* 6, 1810.

"I have been cruizing for these two months past between Bayonne and Santona."

"In addition to the troops I have observed under arms, there has been a great proportion of armed peasantry at Baquio, a small place to the westward of Rachidaes; as our boats were returning from destroying some batteries, they were attacked by armed peasantry alone, who were dispersed by shot from the ship, and also since they have assisted the French troops, when we captured a vessel laden with military stores from St. Andero."

Mr. Stuart to general Walker.

"*Lisbon, February* 20, 1811.

"I own that from the various appointments which have lately taken place in their armies, I forbode little advantage in the course of the ensuing campaign; it is perhaps needful to tell you that my fears are grounded on the nomination of the duke of Albuquerque to Gallicia, Castaños to Estremadura, Mahi to Murcia, Coupigny to Valencia, and the brother of O'Donnel to Catalonia."

Sir Howard Douglas to lord Wellington.

"*Villafranca, January* 4, 1812.

"Each chief is allowed three servants, a captain two, a subaltern one; the number of soldiers employed in this way is certainly not *under* the regulation, and all officers resident in the interior likewise have this excessive indulgence. The officers' servants never do duty, or attend any drill or review. The cooks are in general changed weekly, and are never present at drill or review; one cook is allowed besides to every three serjeants. These two items certainly take 5000 choice men from the ranks of this army."

"Some very violent recriminations have been brought on by the imprudent reply of the military press, to some observations published in a Coruña paper extolling the Guerillas, and at the same time intended to convey a censure on the conduct of the army. I have had frequent conversations with general Abadia on the spirit of disunion which these two papers are sowing. He has at length prohibited the military press from publishing any thing but professional papers. I was present when he gave the order—he engaged me in the conversation, and I could not avoid observing, that what was lost could only be regained by the sword, not the pen. In this I alluded to the Asturias, where certainly reputation and public confidence were sacrificed."

"The truth is, the army is oppressive and expensive, as well as inefficient, from its disorganised state, particularly in the departments of supply; and it is a very unpleasant circumstance to hear it generally admitted, that a Spanish corps is much more destructive to the country than an equal French army. There are also violent dissentions between the juntas of Leon and Gallicia: inclosure No. 6 will shew this state of feeling."

Sir Howard Douglas to sir H. Wellesley.

"*Coruña, March* 1, 1812.

"On the 20th ultimo I had the honour to despatch to your excellency a copy of my letter of that date to lord Wellington, in which I acquainted his lordship that three battalions of the army of Gallicia are preparing for embarkation for America, and that I had positively declined making, and would not permit the delivery of any British arms or stores for that service. I have now discovered, that in addition to these troops it is intended to send a division of horse-artillery, to equip which, orders have been given to transfer appointments from the cavalry of the army, and a demand is made for funds to prepare the ordnance, and even to adapt to colonial service more of the field-artillery which I lately delivered for the use of the sixth Gallician army. This measure has never been openly avowed by the government of Cadiz, it has never been communicated to the junta of this province by the regency. It has, I imagine, been concealed from your excellency, and it has only come to my knowledge, by the arrangements no longer to be hidden, which general Abadia is making to carry it into effect."

SECTION 2.—CATALONIA.

Extract of a Letter from Don Antonio Rocca.

(Translated.)

" *Reus, January* 20, 1811.

" While we have venal men, ignorant men, and perfidious men in our government, no good can befal us. He must be mad who can expect our condition to ameliorate. The venal are those who, without being called, seemingly abandon their own affairs, and introduce themselves into the different branches of administration with no other view than to enrich themselves at the public expense. The ignorant are those who think themselves wise, and who either obtain by intrigue or accept without reluctance employments the duties of which they are not capable of discharging. The perfidious are all those who are indifferent spectators of this bloody struggle, and who care not for the issue, as they will equally submit to any master. Place no confidence, my friend, in these sort of persons, nothing can be expected from them, and yet by an inconceivable fatality which is attached to us, to the ruin of all parties, it would appear that the provinces employ none but these very people. Those who commend us are either venal or ignorant, or indifferent; at least the more we search for the remedy, the more our evil increases."

Captain Codrington to sir Charles Cotton.

" *April* 24, 1811.

...... " With respect to the proposed plan of admitting supplies of grain in neutral vessels from the ports of the enemy, &c., I have no hesitation in saying I do not see sufficient reason to justify it in the present circumstances of this part of the Peninsula, as I have always found bread for sale at the different places on the coast, at the rate of about *two pounds and three quarters for the quarter of a dollar*, at which price I yesterday bought it at Escala. And as there has been of late more corn at Taragona than money to purchase, I presume the latter has been the greater desideratum of the two."

...... "The difficulty of allowing a free passage of provisions from one part of the coast to the other would be lessened by being limited to vessels above the size of common fishing-boats, in which I have reason to believe considerable quantities have been carried to Barcelona; and captain Bullen, I understand, found even a mortar in a boat of this description."

General C. Doyle to captain Bullen.

"*Ripol, April*, 1811.

"Can you believe that in this town, *the only fabric of arms, six months* have passed without a firelock being made!!! They begin to-morrow, and give me two hundred and fifty every week, &c."

[Note. The italics and notes of admiration are in the original.]

Admiral Freemantle to captain Codrington.

"*Mahon, May* 19, 1811.

"The uncertainty of every thing connected with Spanish affairs is such, that I am tired of writing and explaining all that arises from their inconsistency and want of energy.

"Until eight o'clock I had understood that the intendant had procured one thousand quintals of biscuit for the army at Taragona, which number I find on inquiry has dwindled to fifty-seven bags. I have therefore been under the necessity of sending five hundred bags, which we can very ill spare, from our own stores, with a proportion of rice. I cannot tell you how much I have been worried and annoyed the last three days, particularly as I feel the very great importance Taragona is to the Spaniards, and how much this island is connected with the event of the fall of that fortress. The intendant here has wrote that he has sent two hundred and thirty-two bags of bread. You will have the goodness to explain that only fifty-seven were procured by him, which I have engaged to pay for, and that all the rest comes immediately from our own stores, and are consequently at the disposal of the British authorities at Taragona."

Extract of a Letter from Sir Edward Pellew to captain Codrington.

"*H. M. Ship Caledonia, July* 22, 1811.

"The indecision, inactivity, and apparent disunion amongst the Spanish leaders has been the great cause of failure throughout the whole of this arduous contest, and is especially observable in the late events in Catalonia; nor until the patriots are directed by pure military councils and more energy and decision, can I permit myself to think that any effectual stand can be made against the invaders."

Sir Edward Pellew to captain Codrington.

"*August* 2, 1811.

"I have to acknowledge the receipt of your letter, &c. The information therein conveyed affords me a very melancholy view of the affairs of the patriots, and gives me little reason to hope better things from their future exertions." .... "A despatch which reached me by the same opportunity from the superior junta of Catalonia contains a proposal for occupying a position on the coast as a naval depôt, and the selection of Palamos is presented to my choice. It does not appear to me that the junta possesses at present resources for defending any such position, and from the measures being submitted to my determination, it seems to be expected that I should provide means of defending them while employed in securing themselves in their new station." "Yet whilst the noble spirit of this ill-fated people remains unsubdued, it would not be just to expect a total failure, although the loss of all confidence between them and the privileged orders, and the want of leaders among themselves who possess either skill or competency to guide them, afford but a very precarious prospect of their doing anything effectual to stop the invaders."

Captain Codrington to sir E. Pellew.

"*November* 1, 1811.

"By a letter from captain Strong it seems the people of Cadagues in the early part of October openly refused assistance to the governor of the Medas islands, declaring that they only acknowledged the strongest party, and therefore paid their subscriptions to the French; and that upon the Bustard's going with a party of Spanish troops to enforce obedience, they rang the alarm-bell as the signal for the approach of an enemy, and sent to Rosas for assistance."

Extract of a Letter from captain Codrington to E. H. Locker, esq.

"*February* 7, 1812.

"Whilst the French pay the poor, who serve their purpose, at the expense of the rich, the Spaniards deal out severity to the lower classes, and oblige them to serve without pay and without clothes; and the debauched and profligate of higher life are in many instances rewarded, for imbecility, ignorance, and indifference to the fate of their country never yet exceeded, without one single example being made of the many traitors which have been discovered in the persons of priests, officers of rank, or what are termed gentlemen."

Captain Codrington to general Lacy.

"*February* 18, 1812.

"Being an eye-witness of the discontent of the people, which has arisen from their being partially disarmed, and knowing how fatal have been the consequences which have followed these practices on former occasions, I must own I cannot offer to the admiral my conviction of all that benefit arising from his good intentions in which I should otherwise have confided. The officers and men of the French army are walking about this part of the coast unarmed, because *the juntas and justices have concealed the muskets they had* at their disposal, and refused the people permission to attack the enemy. In the mean time the poor people, whose hearts are burning with patriotism, are starving for want of bread, and the richer citizens of this devoted country are supplying the enemy with corn and other species of provisions."

Captain Codrington to sir E. Pellew.

"*Villa Nueva, February* 22, 1812.

"I fear things are going on very ill in this principality from the sudden change in the system of general Lacy, and the consequent destruction of that confidence on the part of the people which was certainly the cause of his former successes. Nor can there be any doubt of the sound reason which guides the conduct of the Catalans on this occasion; for the mode in which general Lacy effected the dishonourable breach of faith of which they complain, bespeaks a mind practised in deception. He ordered the patriotic companies to be sent to particular points in subdivisions, at which points general Sarsfield was to take forcible possession of them, and attach them to different corps of the regular army. And the discovery of this treachery was made by the letter to general Sarsfield falling by mistake, into the hands of the officer who commanded the whole division of patriotic companies. In the meantime the discontent of the people gains ground with their sufferings, and instead of the Spanish army being increased by the late arbitrary mandate according to its avowed object, and not less probably in consequence of the late extraordinary conduct of general Sarsfield, many of the Catalan soldiers have actually passed over to the enemy."

"The letter of the baron de Eroles in the gazette No. 10, shews that he was again deceived in the promised support of general Sarsfield on the 24th, and I am told he says publicly it was part of a settled plan to sacrifice him and his whole division."

Captain Codrington to sir E. Pellew.

"*Villa Nueva de Sitjes, February* 22, 1812.

"Nothing but a total change can produce permanent good; for the villanies of the intendant and commissary departments are so thoroughly organized, that not one link of the chain can be left with safety. I have good reason to think that even the money furnished by England is so employed in the traffic of corn, by the individuals through whose hands it passes, as to be the direct means of supplying the enemy."

Captain Codrington to Mr. H. Wellesley.

"*March* 1, 1812.

"The change of the regency will I trust produce a radical change of that diabolical system by which plunder has been openly licensed, and despotism and injustice towards the people, and even treachery itself, in those of a higher class, have hitherto passed with impunity."

SECTION 3.—VALENCIA AND MURCIA.

The councillor of state, Mariano Orquijo, to king Joseph.

"*Madrid, Decembre* 4, 1810.

"Je viens de voir le proviseur et vicaire général qui fut arrêté à Logrogne par les insurgés. Son opinion prononcée en faveur de V. M. lui a attiré toutes sortes de mauvais traitemens et de disgraces, mais enfin il est parvenu à se sauver de Valence. Il m'a rapporté que l'esprit public de cette capitale a beaucoup changé depuis que le général Caro (frère de Romana) s'est livré aux vexations et aux dilapidations de toute espèce, et que son opinion est qu'on n'y éprouvera aucune résistance. L'Archevêque de Valence, qui jouit à présent d'une grande influence, lui a souvent parlé en secret d'une manière favorable de V. M. et de ses ministres. C'est à l'Archevêque qu'il est redevable de son evasion. Ce prélat m'ayant connu ainsi que à M. de Montarco dans d'autres tems le chargea de nous voir. Le général Bassecourt n'était nullement considéré. Le proviseur ajoute, qu'à Alicant d'où il est parti le 14 Novembre, tout était rempli, de réfugiés de Cadiz. D'après tout ce qu'il m'a dit, je conte qu' aussitôt la prise de Tortoze, Valence se rendra sans coup férir. J'ai renvoyé ce proviseur à Monsieur de Santa Fé qui l'a protégé en sa qualité de ministre des affaires ecclesiastiques et qui fut très sensible au malheur qui lui arriva à Logrogne."

General Doyle to Mr. Stuart.

"*March* 8, 1811.

"There is a strong French party in Valencia. It is a sad thing that we cannot *sacar Partido* of that kingdom, in which are more resources than in all the other provinces of Spain. With my head I answer for it that in one month two thousand cavalry and twenty thousand infantry, independent of the existing army, which is one thousand five hundred effective cavalry and eleven thousand infantry, could be raised, and there is money enough within the city to pay them for six months, and without looking elsewhere for assistance to clothe them. There is abundance of cloth, and provisions in abundance, yet Valencia is doing nothing! and this time so precious, while Massena draining all the rest of the Peninsula gives us time to organize. We want a Robespierre in the government, and another in every province ! !"

Colonel Roche to Mr. Stuart.

"*Carthagena, June* 20, 1811.

"After three years leaving them to themselves, this army (the Murcian) is everywhere in a worse state absolutely than it was in the commencement of the revolution."

"The fact is that the Spaniards have no confidence in their general, nor he in them, and thus Freire apprehends if he fights his people will disperse. Valencia, with an immense population and great resources, is doing little. Bassecour retired to Cuenca.

The same indolence, lassitude, and egotism prevails through the country, and I see little stimulus produced by the establishment of the cortes; that feeling of enthusiasm which existed is fast dying away. The thing in the world most agreeable to the Spaniards at this moment would be to be allowed to be neuter, and that England and France should fight the battle and pay all the expenses."

Captain Codrington to the honourable H. Wellesley.

"*September* 8, 1811.

"After ascertaining that much art was employed to disgust the army with general Blake, and at the same time to prejudice the people against their officers, I relied upon the purity of my motives, and opened the subject to the general with the candour and freedom it required. I had great satisfaction in finding him well aware of all that was passing, and upon his guard as to the consequences. Upon my mentioning that certain hand-bills were posted up, he produced and gave met he enclosed copies. He told me that upon obtaining them he went to the marquis of Palacios, who, necessarily agreeing in their evil tendency, consented to accompany the general to the palace of the archbishop, where I trust measures were adopted to prevent a repetition of the misconduct of the Padre Igual and his numerous bigoted coadjutors. I submitted to the general's attention the fatal effects of his quitting this part of the Peninsula, while the minds of the people were in such a state of fermentation, and allowing the supreme authority to revert to the marquis of Palacios. He assured me that he clearly saw the danger which would arise from it; he had determined on no account to do so until the marquis was removed by the government from his present situation."

Mr. Tupper's report to sir H. Wellesley.

(Extract.)

"*January* 27, 1812.

"The scandalous behaviour of the members of the junta will have more influence upon the public mind, will dishearten the people even more than the fall of Valencia and the dispersion of the army. For seeing their representatives return to their respective districts, it will give an example to follow that all is lost, and having no authority to protect them or to look to, the people have no other resource left than to submit to the yoke of the enemy."

Extracts from Mr. Tupper's report to sir Henry Wellesley from 22 to 27 January, 1812.

"Blake with his immense resources remained altogether inactive, and contented himself with observing the movements of the enemy, and his progress in fortifying himself under the walls of the city."

"With Blake's approbation I had raised a corps of about one hundred and eighty men to act as guerillas, and by beginning a plan of offensive operations I expected to see the example followed. I also demanded the direction of the chief battery, that of Santa Catalina, from whence the French camp might be much annoyed, and for the space of thirty successive days caused the French considerable damage in killed and wounded. Excepting this battery, that of St. Joseph contiguous to it, and that of the Puente del Mar, every thing else remained in a state of complete inactivity. Blake, lulled into a state of confidence that the enemy would not attack without reinforcements, had taken no measures whatever."

"The junta of Valencia was composed of members, as per list enclosed, of which only the first remained, the others having before retired and shamefully gone to their respective homes; but upon the fall of the capital where they had their property, those remaining sent in their resignation to Mahi, and without being competent to do so, gave up the only representative authority of the province which had been confided to them, and have thus thrown the whole country into a state of anarchy, abandoning it altogether to the will of the enemy; yet I am persuaded the spirit of the people is the same, great resources are left in the province, immense riches still remain in the churches, convents, diezmos, &c., &c."——

"I am however sorry to say that since the fall of the capital, nay, since the battle of the 26th ultimo, not a single step has been taken, and at this moment outside the walls of Alicant the province does not exist.—Mahi has objected to Padre Rico, the only man in my opinion, and in that of every body, capable of giving activity and soul to the resources of the country."

...... "I am sorry to inform your excellency that after repeated interviews with Mahi and the intendant Rivas, on the subject of the commission I had proposed, I am now clearly of the opinion from the repeated delays and studied objections that no authority will be established."—— "In short nothing has been done, and nothing will be done." ——

" I am firmly of opinion that the people now in authority are disposed, by leaving public affairs in their present abandoned state, to submit to the French yoke."——" On the 16th ultimo, when Montbrun made his appearance, the Ayuntamiento desired the Syndico Personeso to give a petition in the name of the people to enter into a capitulation ; he refused ; but I am informed there was some arrangement between the governor and the Ayuntamiento, the members whereof remain in office nothwithstanding their traitorous conduct on the 16th."

SECTION 4.—ANDALUSIA.

General Graham to Mr. Stuart.

9th May, 1810.

" Nothing new here ; the regency and the junta are as usual more asleep than awake, and I can augur nothing good from the government remaining in such hands—let their intentions be ever so good. Nothing but the assembly of the cortes, and from thence springing up a revolutionary system, overturning abuses and interesting the people in their own cause by solid and permanent, instead of contingent and prospective reforms, calling forth talents if to be found for the chief situations, and inforcing vigour and rousing enthusiasm. Nothing but some great change (such as we might in the beginning have assisted in bringing about) can carry on this war to any good result. The people are obstinate in their hatred of the French, and from that alone spring the fits of patriotism and loyalty which keep alive the flame in some place or another. That it is so one cannot doubt from the effects, but it is never to be met with where one is, at least I have never yet seen enthusiasm though I have heard of it. Hence the bulk of the people seem to be completely indifferent to what is going on, and all seem most unwilling to submit to the deprivation of any comfort, and to the sacrifices which a state of siege requires. They would be very well pleased to have any thing done for them, and to see the enemy driven away, that they might go to eat strawberries at Chiclana, and they are much disposed to blame our inactivity, especially that of the navy, in permitting the enemy to have advanced so near on the point of Trocadero. The destruction of these two forts at first was certainly a great error in admiral Purvis ; had they been kept up and well garrisoned, as they support one another, it would have been a very tedious operation to have reduced them. Meanwhile you will hear that the improvidence of the junta, and their denial of any such risk to Mr. Wellesley, placed the bread provision of the town in much too precarious a situation; in short, they completely deceived him by their assurances of the most ample means of subsistence, and both flour and wheat have been sent away since he came."

Mr. Wellesley to Mr. Stuart.

" *Isla de Leon, February* 5, 1811.

" Blake is becoming very unpopular, and I think his reign will be short. He is supposed to be by no means partial to the English. I know not whether you will approve of the appointments to Estremadura and Gallicia, but I am sure you will be surprised to hear that general Mahi is appointed to command the army of the centre. I communicated confidentially to general Blake the copy of the letter which you forwarded to me from general Walker, taking care to conceal general Walker's name, so that Blake was fully apprised of our opinion of general Mahi previously to his appointment of him to the command in Murcia."

Mr. Vaughan to Mr. Stuart.

" *Cadiz, February* 27, 1811.

" It grieves me to see from day to day how little is done by the Spaniards, and how little is likely to be done. The cortes have not given a new impulse to the war as was expected. They look to their regency for plans of reform for their armies, and their regency is worse than any former government. Blake, of whom I know that you as well as the world in general have a good opinion, does nothing. He refuses to reform abuses that are pointed out to him, passes his days in deliberation upon questions of no moment, and is in my opinion decidedly adverse to the English. Whittingham's plan, (disciplining a separate corps,) which was approved of before his arrival, he has endeavoured by every kind of trick to reject or render useless."

" The cortes is full of priests, who, united with the Catalans, are for preserving the old routine of business, and adverse to every thing that can give energy and vigour to the operations of government. Fanaticism and personal interest direct their opinions; Arguelles and his party are anxious that something should be done to remedy the disgraceful state of their armies.

I have no doubt but that they would remove the present government, though the friends of Blake, if there was any chance of the Catalan party permitting them to elect a better."

" Be assured, my dear Stuart, that the cortes is, as at present constituted, any thing but revolutionary or jacobinical. They love their monarchy, and are anxious to maintain the inquisition in all its forms, the only branch of government to which they seem disposed to communicate any energy. If there is not soon some new spirit infused into the cortes, it will become an overgrown junta, meddling with every paltry detail of police, and neglecting the safety of their country—and the regency will be content to reign (very badly) over Cadiz and the Isla."

Mr. Vaughan to Mr. Stuart.

" *Cadiz, August* 5, 1811.

" The temper of the public mind at Cadiz is very bad, the press has lately teemed with publications filled with reproaches of the English."

" The regency and cortes have lost all influence every where, and the distress for money added to the general depression here after the campaign in Estremadura may possibly throw us into a state of anarchy."

" I am somewhat alarmed by the state of the Serranos de Ronda; the Spanish generals have been quarrelling, and the peasants declare they are tired of the abuses committed there, and that it is reported they mean to capitulate with the French."

General Graham to Mr. Stuart.

" *Isla de Leon, April* 24, 1811.

" The Spanish government has published an official narrative of the expedition (Barosa) full of misrepresentations and blinking the question of the cause of failure entirely—this has obliged me to add something to what I wrote before to Mr. Wellesley. There are some instances of impudence supporting falsehood beyond example. The *proud* Spaniard is no less *vain* I think."

General Graham to Mr. Stuart.

" *Isla, May* 6, 1811.

" The government here supported by the cortes seemed to be determined to adhere with blind obstinacy and pride to a system that has nearly brought the cause to ruin, and notwithstanding

Lord Wellington's great efforts they are playing Buonaparte's game so positively that I despair of any great good."

Colonel Austin to Mr. Stuart.

" *Faro, March* 24, 1811.

" Whether Ballesteros is authorized by his government to pursue the steps he has taken, I know not, but I certainly cannot but consider them as just and necessary. The junta de Seville is a mere farce supported at an immense expense without the least utility or benefit, and preserving in its train a number of idle characters who ought to be employed in the defence of the nation, but who now only add to its burthens. I have had many negotiations with the junta, and though I have always kept up appearances through policy, yet I have found, in the room of the honour and candour which ought to characterize it, nothing but chicanery and dissimulation."

General Carrol to Mr. Stuart.

" *Olivenza, April* 29, 1811.

" Would to Heaven that the Spanish armies, or, more properly speaking, the skeletons of the Spanish armies were under his lordship's (Wellington's) command; we might in that case do great things, but alas! our pride seems to increase with our misfortunes, and is only equalled by our ignorance!"

Mr. Stuart to Lord Wellesley.

" *July* 13, 1811.

" I have endeavoured to throw together the numbers, &c. of the different guerillas, &c., which clearly demonstrate the false exaggerations circulated respecting that description of force; though their appearance in different parts has most unreasonably encreased the alarm of the enemy and proportionable confidence of the Spaniards, they cannot be calculated to exceed in the aggregate twenty-five or thirty thousand men at the utmost."

Note. Here follows a list of the Partidas with their numbers and stations too long to insert.

Mr. Wellesley to Mr. Stuart.

" *Cadiz, July* 31, 1811.

" Nothing can be more wretched than the state of affairs here; the regents are held in universal contempt, and such is the want of talent, I can hardly hope that a change will make any improvement: the treasury is empty, and no probability of the arrival of any money from America, so that affairs are really in a worse state than they have been at any time since the commencement of the war."

Extract from the manifesto of the Spanish regency.

"*January* 23, 1812.

"There have reached the government the cries of the armies which defend us, depicting their painful privations; the groans of the inhabitants of districts, ready to fall under the yoke of the barbarous invaders; the complaints of the provinces already occupied, always loyal though oppressed and laid waste."

"Cease now, and henceforward, all personal pretensions; the ill-understood feelings of interest dictated by provincial spirit; exemptions unjustly demanded at this period of desolation, writings which, while they ought to create the most ardent patriotism, to unite and enlighten the nation, appear inspired by the enemy for the purpose of enslaving it."

SECTION 5.

PRIVATEERS.

Captain Codrington to sir E. Pellew.

"*Arens de Mar, August* 23, 1811.

"I have numberless complaints of the Spanish privateers that come upon the coast, and I am sure it would be a benefit to the country if they were all deprived of their commission. They do nothing but plunder the inhabitants of those places which are occasionally overrun by the French armies, and who embrace the opportunity of their absence to carry on a little trade with other parts of the Peninsula."

Ditto to sir H. Wellesley.

"*Valencia, September* 8, 1811.

"I trust some decisive measures will be taken to abolish altogether a system of privateering nothing short of piracy; and in which the vessels from Gibraltar seem to take the lead. I have great reason to believe that they plunder the unfortunate vessels of all countries by hoisting whatever colours may answer their purposes of assumed national hostility; and as we never hear of their attacking each other, I have no doubt that the British and French flags are often united in furtherance of this predatory warfare. The numberless complaints which I receive from all parts of the coast, and the difficulty of trading betwixt Catalonia and Valencia, on account of the privateers which swarm in these seas, drive many into an intercourse with Barcelona and other places in the occupation of the enemy, in order to get a livelihood."

Ditto to admiral Penrose, Valencia.

" The depredations of the Gibraltar privateers have been carried on to such an extent, in all parts of the Mediterranean, as to bring serious reflections upon the British flag."

SECTION 6.

FRENCH PRISONERS AT CABRERA.

Captain Codrington to E. Locker, Esq.

" *September* 18, 1811.

" I cannot at all events think it a wise measure to receive into colonel Whittingham's corps the prisoners at Cabrera, who have long ago withstood the offers of general Roche, *when naked as they were born, and fighting for each other's miserable rations to prolong an existence inconceivably wretched,* in hopes of rejoining the French."

Sir H. Wellesley to captain Codrington.

" *October* 10, 1811.

" With regard to the French prisoners at Cabrera, I procured from the Spanish government long since an order to the governor of the Balearic Islands to suspend all negotiations with the French on that subject, and not on any account to consent to exchange them."

No. II.

SECTION 1.

SIEGE OF TARAGONA.

Captain Codrington to sir C. Cotton.

" *Taragona, May* 15, 1811.

" During the panic which seems to have prevailed upon the unexpected arrival of the French army, the greatest exertions and the most extensive sacrifices appear to have been readily submitted to. But from the present apathy and indifference in those who should set an example of activity, and from the general deficiency of ordnance stores, I by no means consider the place in that state of security which the strength of its works and position would otherwise lead me to expect."

" A well planned sortie was made yesterday, but failed through the backwardness of some of the officers employed in it."—" I had the satisfaction of being assured by an officer, who conspicuously did his duty on this occasion, and who was outflanked by the enemy, from the backwardness of the column directed to support him, that he attributes the salvation of his troops entirely to the fire from the shipping."

Ditto to ditto.

" *Blake, off Villa Nueva, June* 15, 1811.

" Leaving Taragona on the 16th (May), we reached Peniscola in the forenoon of the 17th."—" From thence general Doyle wrote to general O'Donnel an account of the situation of Taragona and of my detaining captain Adam at Peniscola, in readiness to receive any reinforcement which he might be pleased to send to that garrison. Upon our arrival off Murviedro, we found general O Donnel had already ordered the embarkation of two thousand three hundred infantry and two hundred and eleven artillery-men."—" Delivering to general O'Donnel two thousand stand of arms, accoutrements, and clothing to enable him to bring into the field as many recruits already trained as would supply the place of the regular soldiers ; thus detached from his army, we proceeded to Valencia and landed the remainder of our cargo, by which means the troops of general Villa Campa, then dispersed as peasantry for want of arms, were enabled again to take the field, and the corps of Mina and the Empecinado completed in all the requisites of active warfare."

" At Alicant we proceeded to take in as many necessary materials for Taragona as the ship would actually stow, besides eighty artillery-men and a considerable quantity of powder, ball-cartridge, &c. sent in the Paloma Spanish corvette from Carthagena in company with a Spanish transport from Cadiz deeply laden with similar supplies."

" After returning to Valencia, where we landed the additional arms, &c. for the Aragonese army, we moved on to Murviedro, where the conde of Bispal proceeded from Valencia to join us in a consultation with his brother, although, on account of his wound, he was very unfit for such a journey. The result of this conference was a determination on the part of general O'Donnel to commit to my protection, for the succour of Taragona, another division of his best troops under general Miranda, consisting of four thousand men, whilst he himself would move forward with the remainder of his army to the banks of the Ebro."

"The frequent disappointments which the brave Catalonian army had heretofore met with from Valencian promises, made the sight of so extensive and disinterested a reinforcement the more truly welcome, because the less expected, and the admiration which was thus created in the besieged appeared to produce proportionate anxiety on the part of the enemy."

"I shall direct the whole of my attention to the neighbourhood of Taragona, in readiness for harassing the retreat of the French, if general Suchet should unfortunately be obliged to raise the siege, and for reembarking and restoring to general O'Donnel whatever may remain of the Valencian troops, according to the solemn pledge he exacted from me before he would consent thus to part with the flower and strength of his army. He even went so far as to declare, in the presence of general Miranda, the principal officer of his staff, general Doyle, captain Adam, captain White, and myself, that he considered me as entirely answerable for the safety of the kingdom of Valencia, and that if I failed in redeeming my pledge he would resign his command for that particular account."

"It is but justice to myself, however, that I should tell you that I did most distinctly warn general O'Donnel, that I would in no case answer for his army if placed under the immediate command of Campo Verde, for any distant inland operation, more particularly as I knew that, in addition to his own deficiency in ability, he was surrounded by people whose advice and whose conduct was in no case to be relied on."

Ditto to ditto.

"*Blake, Taragona, June* 22, 1811.

"I found upon my last return here an arrangement made, that in case of the enemy gaining the Puerto, general Sarsfield should retire to the Mole with part of his division, from whence I had only to assist, but was much astonished to find, by a message, through colonel Green, from general Contreras, that although he had heard of such a disposition being made by general Sarsfield, and assented to by the English squadron, it had not his official knowledge or approbation."—"I understand that an order had arrived in the morning from the marquis of Campo Verde for general Velasco to take the command of the Puerto, and for general Sarsfield to join his army, that the latter had given up his command to some colonel at about three o'clock, who was, by his own confession, totally unfit for it, and that general Velasco only arrived in time to find the Spanish troops flying in confusion from the want of being properly commanded and the French assaulting the place."

Captain Codrington to sir E. Pellew.

"*Mattaro, November* 1, 1811.

"Having stated in a letter to sir Charles Cotton, on the 22d June last, that I understand general Sarsfield had quitted the Puerto and embarked without the knowledge of general Contreras, (which indeed was the substance of a message sent me by general Contreras himself,) I owe it to an officer of general Sarsfield's high military character to declare my conviction that the statement there made by general Contreras is absolutely false and unfounded, and I beg leave to enclose in justification of my present opinion; 1st, a passport sent by general Contreras to general Sarsfield in consequence as he alleged of an order from the marquis of Campo Verde. 2d. An extract from the manifesto of the marquis, in which he disavows having any knowledge of the passports. 3d. A letter from general Contreras to general Sarsfield in answer to one written by the latter requesting to see the order by which he was directed to quit the Puerto at such a critical moment, in which he says 'that he cannot send him a copy of that letter, because it is confidential, but that his presence is necessary at the head-quarters to assist in the operations about to take place for the relief of the garrison, and that he has not a moment to lose.' 4th. The copy of another letter written on the same day by general Contreras to the superior junta, in which he says that general Sarsfield quitted the Puerto without his knowledge!!!"

General Doyle to colonel Roche.

"*June* 23, 1811.

"Is it possible to conceive any thing so absurd, and I could almost say *wicked*, as the conduct of the junta or captain-general of Cartagena in taking away the firelocks from the regiments *they sent with such a parade of their patriotism to relieve*

Taragona. Two thousand men are already in this city without firelocks, such is the daily destruction of arms by the enemy's fire and the getting out of repair from constant use."

Captain Codrington to sir Charles Cotton.

"*Off Taragona, June* 23, 1811.

"Another regiment arrived from Carthagena yesterday under convoy of the Cossack, but, as on a former occasion, their arms were taken from them by colonel Roche, upon their going to embark, and therefore, as being of no use to the garrison, I have by desire of the general sent them to Villa Nueva, and as there are already 2000 men in the place without arms, I have sent the Termagant to Carthagena, to endeavour to procure those which have been thus inconsiderately taken from the troops belonging to that place."

Captain Codrington to sir C. Cotton.

(Extract.)

"*June* 29, 1811.

"The Regulus with five transports including a victualler arrived with colonel Skerrett and his detachments on the 26th. The surf was so great on that day that we had no other communication in the forenoon than by a man swimming on shore with a letter, and upon colonel Skerrett putting questions to general Doyle and myself upon the conduct he should pursue according to his orders, we agreed in our opinion that although the arrival of the troops before the Puerto (lower town) was taken would probably have saved the garrison, it was now too late, and that their being landed, if practicable, would only serve to prolong the fate of the place for a very short time at the certain sacrifice of the whole eventually. This opinion was grounded on a number of different circnmstances, and was in perfect coincidence with that of captains Adam and White. In the evening the surf abated sufficiently for general Doyle, colonel Skerrett, and some of his officers, as well as the captains of the squadron and myself, to wait upon general Contreras, who repeated his determination to cut his way out and join the marquis of Campo Verde *the instant the enemy's breaching battery should open*, and which he expected would take place the following morning, and who agreed the English ought not to land with any view of defending the town, although he wished them to join in his meditated sortie."

Extracts from general Contreras' report.

(Translated.)

" I saw myself reduced to my own garrison." " I considered if my force was capable of this effort (defending the breach), one of the most heroic that war furnishes, and to which few men can bring themselves. I recollected however that I *had still eight thousand of the best and most experienced troops in Spain.*" " All conspired against this poor garrison. Campo Verde in quitting the place promised to come back quickly to its succour, but he did not, although he daily renewed his promises. The kingdom of Valencia sent Miranda with a division which disembarked, and the day following re-embarked and went to join Campo Verde.

" An English division came on the 26th, colonel Skerrett, who commanded them, came in the evening to confer with me and to demand what I wished him to do. *I replied that if he would disembark and enter the place, he should be received with joy and treated as he merited; that he had only to choose the point that he wished to defend and I would give it to him, but that all was at his choice, since I would neither command nor counsel him.* The 27th the English commandants of artillery and engineers came to examine the front attacked, and being convinced that the place was not in a state to resist, returned to their vessels, and then all went away from the place they came to succour.

" *This abandonment on the part of those who came to save was the worst of all;* it made such an impression on the soldiers, that they began to see that they were lost, became low-spirited and only resisted from my continual exhortations, and because they saw my coolness and the confidence I had, that if they executed my orders the French would fail. But this only lasted a few hours, the notion of being abandoned again seized them and overcame all other ideas."

Captain Codrington to sir C. Cotton.

" *12th July*, 1811.

" The vacillating conduct of general Contreras regarding the defence of Taragona is a principal feature in the loss of that important fortress."

Captain Codrington to sir E. Pellew.

" 12*th July*, 1811.

" The marquis blames generals Caro and Miranda, whilst the latter retort the accusation; and I am inclined to think that in giving full credit to what each says of the other, neither will suffer ignominy beyond that to which his conduct has entitled him."

Ditto to Mr. Wellesley.

(Extract.)

" 20*th July*, 1811.

" The disasters which have befallen the principality will produce material accusations against the generals who lately commanded in it, without, I fear, any of them meeting the punishment which is their due. Some of the enclosed papers may help you to form a just opinion of their conduct and that of the Spanish marine; and those respecting the arms for which I sent to Carthagena will show how far colonel Roche is entitled to the merit which he so largely assumes on that occasion."

" To enable you to form a correct opinion of general Contreras I must refer you to general Doyle, as from his ignorance of our service, the various requests and proposals which arose from the vacillations in what he called his determinations, were signified to me through him. It does not appear to me that he ever visited the works himself, or it would not have fallen to the lot of captain Adams and myself to remove two boats, two large stages, sixteen gun-carriages, and a mortar from the mole, long after the French were advanced beyond the Francoli battery, and two nights previous to their gaining the Puerto; an accidental visit to the mole one night, just after placing the gun-boats and launches, discovered to me this mortar with no less than twelve guns in readiness for forming a battery; and upon general Doyle, by my request, representing this to the general of artillery, he talked of *inquiring into it to-morrow.*"

" It would be a waste of words to describe further the conduct of the general of artillery, or I might find sufficient subject in the events of every passing day from the first investment of the place."—" I shall be very ready to come forward personally in aid of that justice which is due to the numberless brave men who fell a sacrifice to the criminality of the persons alluded to who have so grossly misconducted themselves."

SECTION 2.

Captain Codrington to sir E. Pellew.

" *29th July,* 1811.

" Had colonel Green, the military agent appointed to succeed general Doyle, adopted the plan of his predecessor of continuing at the head-quarters of the army and in personal communication with the captain-general instead of retiring to Peniscola with the money and arms remaining, we should not be left as we are to the precarious source of mere accidental communications for receiving intelligence."

Ditto to Don F. Savartes, vocal of the Junta.

" *28th July,* 1811.

" ——Colonal Green, the British military agent, being at Peniscola, I have opened the letter from the junta to him."—" Had I not in this instance opened the letters to the admiral and the military agent, the junta would have received no answer to them until it would have been too late to execute their object."

Captain Thomas to captain Codrington.

(Extract.)

" *H. M. S. Undaunted, off Arens, 7th Oct.* 1811.

" Having observed, in the Catalonia Gazette of the 24th of September, the copy of a letter said to be written by colonel Green to his excellency general Lacy, relative to our operations on the Medas Islands, from the surrender of the castle to the period of our quitting them, I beg leave to state to you my surprise and astonishment at seeing facts so grossly misrepresented, and request you will be pleased to contradict in the most positive manner the assertions there made use of. To prove how inconsistent this letter is with real facts, it may be necessary for me only to say that colonel Green, in the presence and hearing of all the English officers, on my asking him a question relative to the practicability of keeping the island, did declare that he had nothing to do with the expedition; that my instructions pointed him out as a volunteer only. But immediately after, in the hearing of all, did declare it to be his opinion that the island was not tenable.

" As I understood it was intended to form an establishment on the larger island, I judged it proper to retire from it for a short time and destroy the remains of the castle, which might induce the enemy to withdraw from the works he had thrown up, and thereby afford our ally an opportunity whenever he chose to occupy them again, to fortify himself without molestation; and this supposition it has appeared was well grounded. But while the ruins of the castle stood, it was an object of jealousy to the French; nor would they in my opinion have quitted the ground they occupied, nor the Spaniards have been enabled to settle themselves, had this measure not been adopted. I therefore gave orders for embarking the guns and stores.

"If necessary, I could say much more on the subject of this most extraordinary letter; the few remarks I have made will, I think, be sufficient. As an act of courtesy to colonel Green, on landing the marines I directed the marine officers to receive their orders from him; but military aid was not necessary, for you may recollect before the expedition sailed, on your informing me that general Lacy had offered some Spanish troops, and asking how many I thought would be necessary, my answer was 'about forty;' and I have no hesitation in declaring that without the assistance of even a single soldier the castle would have fallen into our hands as speedily as it did on this occasion.

SECTION 3.

Captain Codrington's orders to captain Adam of the Invincible.

"*July* 1*st*, 1811.

"You are hereby directed, in consequence of a representation made to me by general Doyle, to proceed towards Majorca in search of the Spanish frigates Prueba, Diana, and Astrea, which the general reports to be going to that island (contrary to orders) with the treasure, archives of the province, and the vessels laden with stores and ammunition destined for the inland fortresses of Catalonia, together with the officers and soldiers which were saved from Taragona, and which are required to join the army immediately. Upon meeting them you are to deliver the accompanying order for them to return here, and you are, if necessary, to enforce obedience."

Captain Codrington to sir Charles Cotton.

" *Villa Nueva, 3d July*, 1811.

" I should feel the more hurt by being driven to adopt such a measure had not the whole conduct both of the Prueba and Diana made their captains a disgrace to the situation they hold. These two frigates remained quiet spectators of the British squadron engaging the batteries of the enemy on the 22d of last month, and never attempted to give any assistance to the garrison, except by now and then sending a gun-boat to join those manned by the English. They did not assist in the embarkation of the numberless women, children, and wounded soldiers, until goaded into it by the orders of general Contreras, after I had already sent above two thousand to this place; and even when I had no longer any transports for their reception, the captain of the Prueba refused to receive some wounded officers."

Ditto to ditto.

" *18th July*, 1811.

" I cannot describe to you the difficulties which I have been put to by the misconduct of all the Spanish ships and vessels of war which I have had to communicate with upon the coast, with exception of the Astrea frigate and the Paloma corvette. In the others I have seen neither courage to oppose the enemy nor humanity to alleviate the distresses of their countrymen."—" I have heard also that the Algesiras, which lately arrived at Arens, has landed the stores and ammunition, with which she was charged, at the risk of their falling into the hands of the enemy, and has quitted the station!"

SECTION 4.

Captain Codrington to sir E. Pellew.

" *12th July*, 1811.

" General Milans is collecting a mixture of troops, consisting of those who have escaped the enemy."

" He speaks loudly of his indifference to a command, while he boasts that if he were captain-general he would raise forty thousand men and clear the country of the enemy! But in the midst of this disgusting rhodomontade it is not difficult to see that self-interest is the main spring of all his actions, and that instead of raising an army he is more likely, by the system he has adopted, to shake the stability of that which is still left for the defence of the principality."

Captain Codrington to sir H. Wellesley.

" *September* 1, 1811.

" The affair of general Milans" (namely, the sending of corn to Barcelona under his passport) " which I mentioned to you in my last private letter, is still involved in mystery, which I hope however to penetrate upon my return to Arens de Mar. The Mataro papers reported that two soldiers were shot and a serjeant flogged at Arena for suffering corn to pass their guard at Mongat on its way to Barcelona. The *fact* of the punishment is I believe truly stated, but the *cause* no less falsely, enterely as I suspect with the view of terminating my investigation into this nefarious traffic. General Lacy, instead of answering my letter, refers me by word of mouth to the junta, and the deputation from the junta, who went to Mataro (as they assured me) purposely to investigate the business, now tell me that it is an affair purely military, and refer me to general Milans himself.

SECTION 5.

Extract from a minute made by captain Codrington.

" *Mattaro, July* 6, 1811.

" Colonel O'Ronan, aid-du-camp to the marquis of Campo Verde, arrived, and informed me that he came from the marquis, who was on his march to this town or Arens, for the purpose of embarking all the infantry not Catalans, and the whole of the remaining cavalry, leaving the horses on the beach. Colonel O'Ronan said this determination was the result of a junta, composed of the marquis, general St. Juan, general Caro, general Miranda, the general of artillery, brigadier Santa Cruz, Velasco, and Sarsfield; that after the thing had been proposed and discussed a long time, Sarsfield was the first to give his vote, that he rose from his seat and said, ' any officer who could give such an opinion must be a traitor to his country, and that he and his division would stand or fall with the principality." Every other officer was of a contrary opinion, except the marquis (it afterwards appeared that Santa Cruz also supported Sarsfield), who thought with Sarsfield, and yet it seems he allowed himself to be led on by the other generals. *In short, it appears he was resolved to abandon the principality.*

"I told him, without hesitation, that to embark the Valencians I felt a duty to general O'Donnel, to the kingdom of Valencia, and to the whole nation, but that I felt it equally my duty upon no account to embark the army of Catalonia, and thus become a party concerned in the abandonment of a province I had been sent to protect."—"The colonel, who could not venture on shore again lest he should be murdered by the inhabitants of Mattaro, for having been the bearer of a commission to arrest brigadier Milans about a month ago, sent to the marquis my answer."

Extract from a minute of information given by the baron d'Eroles.

"*July* 9, 1811.

"The baron d'Eroles was appointed captain-general of Catalonia by the junta of general officers, of which the marquis of Campo Verde was president, and by the voice of the people. His reply was, that so long as the army continued in the principality, and that there was a senior general officer, he would not admit it, but that the moment the army passed the frontier (it was then at Agramunt, in full march to Aragon), he would accept the command, unmindful of the dreadful situation in which he should place himself, but he would do so in order to continue the struggle, and to prevent anarchy and confusion. In this state things were when general Lacy arrived. The baron instantly sought him, could not find, but met one of his aid-du-camps, by whom he wrote to him to say what had occurred, but that he was resolved to support general Lacy in his command, not only with all his local influence, but by his personal exertions, and that he would immediately join him to put this resolution in practice."

Extract from general Doyle's Letter after seeing the above.

"The Valencian division, that is to say, two thousand four hundred of the four thousand three hundred soldiers who disembarked in this province, are now on board to return to Valencia. General Miranda says the desertion took place in consequence of the marquis's determination to proceed to Aragon, which made them believe they would not be embarked. In short, most disgraceful has been the conduct of this division, and the marquis, as you will see by this letter to me, attaches to it no small portion of blame."

Captain Codrington to the marquis of Campo Verde.

"*Blake, July* 5, 1811.

"I have to remind you that by ordering the Valencian division out of Taragona, in breach of the terms by which I bound myself when I brought them, you yourself broke the pledge given by me, and dissolved the contract."

Extracted from captain Codrington's papers.

"Minute of a conference betwixt generals Caro and Miranda with general Doyle and myself this day.

"*July* 9, 1811.

"About eight o'clock generals Caro and Miranda came on board the Blake. After being seated in the cabin with general Doyle and myself, general Caro begged general Doyle would explain to me, that they were come in consequence of my promise, to request I would embark the division of Valencian troops which I had brought from Peniscola. I desired to know what promise general Caro understood me to have made? He answered, that I would take the above troops back to Valencia. I denied positively that I had made any promise to re-embark them if they should ever join the marquis of Campo Verde, although I had deeply pledged myself to restore them to general O'Donnel if they joined in a sortie from the garrison, which I was very confident would be decisive of its success. I then referred general Miranda to a similar explanation, which I gave to him, through general Doyle, on the day after our quitting Peniscola, when he had said he was ordered, both by his written instructions and by verbal explanation from general O'Donnel, not to land within the garrison. General Miranda instantly repeated that so he was; upon which general Doyle, to whom he had shewn those instructions jointly with myself, after leaving Taragona for Villa Nueva, when under a difficulty as to how he should proceed, referred him to them again, when it appearing that he was therein positively ordered 'desembarear en la plaza de Tarragona," general Doyle stopped.

"*General Miranda.* 'Ah! but read on.'

"*General Doyle.* 'No, sir, there is the positive proof of your receiving such an order.'

"*General Miranda.* 'Well, but read on.'

"*General Doyle.* 'No, sir. This (*pointing to the paper*) is the positive proof of your receiving such an order, which we wanted to establish, because you positively denied it.'

"Upon this general Caro, shrugging up his shoulders, said, 'he was not aware of there being any such order.' And general Miranda again requested general Doyle would read on.

"*General Doyle.* 'For what purpose?'

"*General Miranda.* 'To prove that I was not to shut myself up with the division in the plaza de Taragona.'

"*General Doyle.* 'There is no occasion, sir, for any proof of that, for it was a part of the very stipulation made by captain Codrington when he strongly pledged himself to general O'Donnel.'

"General Doyle continued,—'And now, general Caro, that we have proved to you that general Miranda *had* orders to land in Taragona, and that captain Codrington is bound by no such promise as you had imagined, I must inform you that he has been eight days upon the coast with all the ships of war and transports which are wanted for other services, for the sole purpose of embarking these troops; and he desires me to add that in consideration of what is due to the liberal and exemplary assistance afforded by general O'Donnel and Valencia in aid of Taragona, but not at all on account of any pledge he has been said to have given, that he will use the same exertion in re-embarking and restoring the troops which he would have done if so bound by his word of honour.'"

Mr. Wellesley to lord Wellesley.

"*July* 28.

"The morning of 30th of June, a few hours after the arrival of the British squadron and Spanish vessels in the roadstead of Villa Nueva, five thousand French infantry and five hundred cavalry surprised the place by a night-march, and seized all the property of Taragona, which had been sent there before the siege. Twenty-five thousand dollars for each of the next three months was demanded, but no violence or plunder allowed. Eroles narrowly escaped. Lacy, appointed to command in Catalonia, arrived 1st July at Villa Nueva, the 6th went to Igualada to join Campo Verde."

"Desertion in the army at Mataro has been carried to a most alarming extent since the fall of Taragona; the first night fifteen hundred men disappeared, nearly three hundred cavalry had likewise set off towards Aragon; and these desertions are to be attributed to the gross neglect and want of activity on the part of the officers."—— "The only division that keeps together in any tolerable order is that of general Sarsfield, of about two thousand men." —— "He had however disputes with Eroles, and the people called for the latter to lead them."

No. III.

SECTION 1.

POLITICAL STATE OF KING JOSEPH.

SPANISH MINISTER'S COMPLAINTS OF THE FRENCH GENERALS.

From the councillor of state, Mariano Luis Orquijo, to king Joseph.

"*Madrid*, 22 *Juillet*, 1810.

"SIRE,—Le commissaire royal de Cordoue me mande, que le duc de Dalmatie lui a fait écrire officiellement de ne remettre aucune somme d'argent à la capitale lors même que le ministre des finances le demanderait, jusqu'à ce que les dépenses de l'armée des regimens qu'on lève et des employés de la province, &c., furent pleinement couverts, et que le duc prendrait les mesures convenables, dans le cas que cette détermination ne fut pas suivie."

"*Madrid*, 3 *Agosto de* 1810.

"Le général Sebastiani a fait voir au commissaire royale à Grenade, un ordre du duc de Dalmatie, qui lui enjoint de la manière la plus expresse, de le mettre en état d'arrestation si pour le 1 er Août lui et le préfet de Malaga ne mettent au pouvoir de Sebastiani quatre millions de réaux. L'exorbitance de cette somme, pour une province qui a déjà payé son contingent, et le court terme de huit jours designé pour le payement, donnent à croire que cette somme une fois livrée on en demandera une plus forte. Selon toutes les apparences, et d'après les conversations particulières, il s'agit de profiter de l'absence du roi pour mettre les Andalousies sur le même pied que les provinces de Biscaye, Burgos, &c. Il se peut néanmoins qu'on ait voulu inspirer ces craintes dans des idées tout-à-fait différentes. Quoiqu'il en soit il serait scandaleux de voir un commissaire qui représente la personne du roi arrêté dans une de ses provinces."

From Mariano Luis Orquijo to king Joseph.

"*Madrid*, 7 *Août*, 1810.

"Monsieur d'Aranza m'écrit en dâte du 22 Août dans une lettre particulière les paroles suivantes, en les soulignant pour mieux fixer l'attention: '*Le maréchal Soult est très content, mais il ne fera usage de son autorité que pour le bien: il aime le roi et la nation: ce pays lui plait beaucoup.*'"

Ditto to ditto.

"*Madrid*, 13 *Août*, 1810.

"Parmi les lettres que m'a porté le courrier d'Andalousie arrivé hier, j'en remarque une de monsieur Aranza écrite dans un stile étudié et que je soupçonne redigée d'accord avec le duc de Dalmatie. C'est un panégyrique à la louange de ce maréchal dans léquel monsieur d'Aranza porte aux nues l'intelligence et la zêle du duc de Dalmatie dans la partie administrative; la considération qu'il donne aux autorités espagnoles; son extrême adresse à manier les esprits, et l'habilité de ses dispositions militaires, dans un pays couvert d'insurgés. M. d'Aranza termine en formant le vœu que le maréchal ne soit aucunement troublé dans l'exécution de ses plans, et que le sort de l'Andalousie soit mis entièrement a sa discretion."

Ditto to ditto.

"*Madrid, le* 23 *Août*, 1810.

"Par ma correspondance avec l'Andalousie j'ai appris; de Cordone: que M. Angulo a reçu les lettres qui l'appellent à Madrid, et qu'il se dispose à suivre le grand convoi sorti de Seville le 11 du courant. De Seville: qu'un corsaire Française s'étant emparé d'un paquebot qui allait de Cadiz à Alicante, on y avait trouvé entr'autres depêches une lettre de Campmany, grand partisan des Anglais, et un des Coryphées de la revolution. Il avouait à son ami, don Anselmo Rodriguez de Ribas, intendant de l'armée du centre, qui s'était plaint à lui des excès que commettaient certaines juntes, que Cadiz n'offrait pas un spectacle moins digne de pitié: que les Anglais qu'il avait appris à connaître s'arrogaient peu à peu toute l'autorité: que le commerce libre accordé aux ports d'Amerique excitait à Cadiz un mécontentement général, et que Venegas allait au Mexique en qualité de viceroi:

il parle en outre de l'arrestation de plusieurs personnes connues, et de la de considération dans laquelle est tombée la regence."

Ditto to ditto.

" *Madrid*, 27 *Septembre*, 1810.

" Le maréchal Victor permet le passage à beaucoup de femmes qui veulent se réunir à leurs maris, les femmes en contant les choses telles qu'elles sont, detruisent bien des erreurs dans lesquelles on a généralement été entrainé par le gouvernement actuel. L'ennemi permit ces jours derniers l'entrée dans l'île à plusieurs femmes qui voulaient passer par Chiclanes pour se réunir à leurs parents, mais dernièrement elles furent contenus à coups de canon, et un boulet emporta la tête de celui qui les accompagnait. Le gouvernement Anglais preside à toutes les opérations, et crainte cette espèce des communications."

" *Valladolid, le* 11 *Août*, 1810.

" Sire,—Je suis arrivé à Valladolid, où je n'ai pas trouvé le général Kellermann. Il parait que les Espagnols ont cerné un détachement de Français qui se trouve à la Puebla de Sanabria, et que ce général y eu allé pour le débloquer. Les guerrilles ont été hier aux portes de Valladolid, et il y a cinq à six jours que soixante dix Français ont été détruits à Villalon ; la terreur s'est emparée de tous les esprits, et l'on croit que trois cent hommes ne suffisent pas pour faire paner un courrier: malgré cela, je parterai demain, escorté par deux cent hommes avec un convoi de prisonniers de Ciudad Rodrigo, donc le nombre n'est pas considérable, parcequ'ici on leur accorde la liberté moyennant une somme qu'on règle avec le général Kellermann pour les frais de la guerre.

" Toutes les autorités du pays sont venues me visiter, et me consulter sur la conduite qu'elles doivent tenir depuis les derniers ordres du général Kellermann pour qu'elles n'obeinent ni ne correspondent avec d'autre autorité que la sienne. C'est la chancellerie qui se trouve plus embarrassée que toute autre, parcequ'elle ne peut concilier l'administrat de la justice au nom de votre majesté avec l'impossibilité de correspondre avec son ministre.

" Je n'ai pas reçu le moindre égard du général Dufrene qui est à la place du général Kellermann. Il ne m'a pas visité, ni même accordé un factionnaire ; tout le monde s'en est apperçu, et cette conduite a confirmé l'opinion que l'on a conçue que votre majesté ne règne point dans ce pays. J'ai tâché de detruire une idée qui décourage les véritables sujets de votre majesté, et soutient les espérances de ses ennemis. Les généraux ne s'apperçoivent pas du mal qu'ils produisent en ferant croire que le service de l'empereur, et ses intérêts peuvent être en contradiction avec ceux de votre majesté.

"Si le général Dufrene s'était borné à ne rien faire pour faciliter mon voyage, j'aurai moins de motifs de plainte contre lui, mais il a retenu l'escorte de cavalerie que le général Tilly m'avait donnée. De toutes les manières, Sire, je ferai tout ce qui sera en mon pouvoir pour accélérer mon voyage, et répondre à la confiance avec laquelle votre majesté a daigné me distinguer.

'Le marquis Almenara."

Orquijo to Joseph, relating his conference with the French ambassador.

(Extract.)

"*Madrid, Août* 22, 1810.

"Je lui dis de s'adresser sur ces deux points au ministre des relations extérieures, il me répondit qu'un désagrément qu'on éprouvait avec lui était l'obligation de lui donner à tout bout de champ des notes écrites, qu'à Vittoria il l'avait compromis en présentant à votre majesté ces notes comme officielles, que le bon vieux duc (ce sont ses propres expressions) étourdissait dans l'instant, qu'il n'entendait point, ou ne voulait point entendre ce qu'on lui disait, et qu'il demandait qu'on lui donnat par écrit ce qui n'était pas nécessaire d'écrire. Je lui répétais toujours qu'il devait s'adresser au duc puisque c'était le seul canal par lequel il devait diriger ses demandes, que je ne me mélais point de ces affaires, et que je n'en entretiendrais votre majesté à moins que votre majesté ne m'en parlat la première, mais comme simple particulier je l'assurai de l'inviolabilité des promesses de votre majesté et de ses idées liberales. L'ambassadeur ajouta que dans la matinée du jour de St. Napoleon, et les jours suivants, le général Belliard, Borelli, et leurs alentours avaient parlé fort mal des expressions de votre majesté sur ses premiers devoirs, et qu'il ne doutait pas qu'ils n'en eussent écrit à Paris; qu'il n'avait pas pu se dispenser de transmettre à sa cour ces paroles; mais qu'il les avait présentés comme une conséquence du premier discours tenu par votre majesté et une nuance nécessaire pour adoucir le mauvais effet qu'avait produit ici l'article du Moniteur sur les mots de l'empereur au duc de Berg. Je le lui avais présenté de cette manière en sortant de l'appartement de votre majesté, et je lui montrai en même temps un rapport venu de la Navarre dans lequel on dépeignait le facheux étât de ce royaume en proie aux excès des bandes de brigands et aux dilapidations des gouvernemens militaires. Si l'ambassadeur a écrit dans ces termes comme il me l'a dit, autant par honneur que par attachement à votre majesté, à son pays et au notre, il a bien rempli ses devoirs. Quoiqu'il en soit, je me lui cru obligé de donner connaissance à votre majesté de ces faits ainsi que de la surprise que, selon l'ambassadeur, a causé à l'empereur et au ministère Français le silence du duc de Santa Fé qui ne s'explique sur rien. L'ambassadeur se plaint d'avoir été compromis par lui, car à sa demande et en consequence des conversations fréquentes qu'il eut avec lui pendant les trois jours qu'il passa à Madrid, il écrivit à sa cour que le duc de Santa Fé était chargé de négocier sur la situation de votre majesté et celle de notre pays, que l'ambassadeur lui-même disait ne pouvoir pas durer. C'est à la lettre ce que c'est dit entre l'ambassadeur et moi." &c. &c.

Ditto to ditto.

"*Madrid, le* 13 *Novembre*, 1810.

"Monsieur Pereyra a reçu du maréchal Soult une réponse extrêmement aigre. Ce commissaire royal persiste dans son opinion que les mesures indiquées par le duc de Dalmatie pour l'approvisionnement de l'armée ne rempliront pas le but qu'il se propose; mais le maréchal veut être obéi. D'un autre côté le général Sebastiani l'a contraint à lui donner onze cent mille réaux. Placé entre ces deux écueils, Monsieur Pereyra a perdu courage et demande à votre majesté de le rappeller à Madrid. Le général Dufour a pris le commandement de Grenade.

"MARIANO LUIS DE ORQUIJO."

Ditto to ditto.

"*Madrid*, 19 *de Decembre*, 1810.

"Monsieur le comte de Montarco était le 11 courant à Manzanares, il m'écrit que les habitans de la Manche se plaignent de ce que les troupes qui retrouvent dans la province ne les protégent pas autant que leur nombre le leur permet, que les brigands viennent leur enlever leurs grains pour les transporter dans les royaumes de Valence et de Murcie, ou dans l'Estremadoure. Ils craignent une disette et désirent ardemmement qu'il se forme de grands dépôts de grains dans des places à l'abri des incursions des partis d'insurgés. Les commandants des troupes Françaises sont d'une exigence et d'une hauteur insupportables, et les rapports faits au comte de Montarco par toutes les autorités légales du pays confirment complettement ceux que l'intendant de la Manche necesse de faire aux divers ministères depuis plusieurs mois."

"*Madrid, le* 15 *Février*, 1811.

"SIRE,—Le préfet de Santander me remêt, en dâte du 16 Janvier, copie des offices qu'il a reçus pour la réunion de cette province au gouvernement militaire de Biscaye. J'ai l'honneur de les mettre sous les yeux de votre majesté en lui observant que cette mesure a été prise sur la proposition du général Caffarelli.

"On a demandé au préfet de Santander un état des employés civils et militaires, des moines, du clergé, et des appointemens dont ils jouissent. Il croit en conséquence que des attributions ainsi que celles des employés seront nulles des que la province sera gouvernée à l'instar de celle de Biscaye. Il ajoute que lui et les chefs principaux de l'administration sont décidés à ne travailler que sous les ordres de votre majesté et demandent avec instance que votre majesté ne les abandonne pas.

"Le sous-préfet de Logrogne me dit en dâte du 22 Janvier que l'opinion publique s'est améliorée depuis qu'on y a appris les nouvelles du Portugal, et qu'on y connait le peu de moyens de defense qu'offre Valence dans le désordre extrême qui y règne. La Riofa ne renferme plus de bandes complettes d'insurgés, mais on y trouve encore quelques brigands épars et des voleurs de grands chemins.

"MARIANO LUIS DE ORQUIJO."

SECTION 2.

(Relating to Joseph's abdication.)

Vindication of the King.

Le ministre secretaire d'état à monsieur le duc de Santa Fé, et en son absence à monsieur le marquis d'Almenara.

Palais de Madrid, le 12 *Septembre*, 1810, *Pars.*

EXCELLENCE,—Le courrier de cabinet, Don Martin Estenoz, qui partit de Paris le 22 Juillet, a remis les lettres écrites par V. E. le même jour et les copies de celles que vous envoyâtes le 19 Juin par le courrier Alvarez, qui furent interceptées. Le roi les a lues avec la plus grande attention, et après s'être bien pénétré des communications faites à V. E. au nom de l'empereur, par monsieur le duc de Cadore, et les observations particulières de ce ministre, S. M. desirant détruire d'un seul trait, les craintes et la défiance que des personnes, tout au moins mal instruites, se sont efforcées d'inspirer, m'a ordonné d'entrer en explication sur tous les points dont elles traitent. Mais je dois avant tout faire connaître à V. E. que le roi s'est montré satisfait de la juste interprétation donnée à ses idées, et à ses sentimens dans la réponse que V. E. a faite au duc de Cadore, relativement à la protection dont S. M. I. désire que le commerce Français jouisse dans les réglemens des douanes, en offrant d'assurer une faveur réciproque dans ses états aux productions d'Espagne. L'empereur ne peut ignorer les vues liberales de son auguste frère, et si S. M. I. a été exactement informée sur ce point, elle saura que, dès son avénement au trône, le roi a écarté bien des obstacles opposés à l'industrie française qu'il s'agit de favoriser encore par de nouvelles dispositions.

Il est bien douloureux pour le roi d'avoir à se justifier de plusieurs imputations auxquelles on a dû croire puisqu'on les a communiquées a V. E. L'une d'elles est que le roi a rendu à leurs propriétaires, ou disposé à son gré, d'une partie des biens confisqués par l'empereur. Cela supposerait de la part de S. M. un oubli de la parole donnée à l'empereur de ne se mêler en aucune manière de ces confiscations: mais c'est un infame imposture, et son auteur mérite un chatiment exemplaire. Qu'on cite une propriété un pouce de terrain confisqué par l'empereur, et dont on ait disposé: on ne le pourra point si dans une pure question de fait on en impose ainsi à l'empereur, que sera ce lorsqu'on ne parle que par conjectures et présomption? Le roi porte à un si haut degré son respect pour les décrets de confiscations de S. M. I. qu'ayant besoin d'un des édifices qui y sont compris pour y placer des établissemens publics, il n'a même pas voulu s'en servir provisoirement. S. M. n'a-t-elle pas, en conséquence, le droit de réclamer, pour son honneur, la punition de ses detracteurs? S. M. I. s'est expliquée sur la direction donnée à la guerre et la manière dont elle a été faite.

L'empereur écrivit au roi pour lui représenter la lenteur des opérations, et l'inaction des armées. Aussitôt S. M. entreprit la conquête de l'Andalousie. Le duc de Cadore a dit à V. E. que la soumission de cette province était illusoire, puisqu'elle se trouve inondée de partis d'insurgés et de bandes de brigands. Qu'on considère la vaste étendue de l'Andalusie; le petit nombre de troupes françaises que l'obstination de Cadiz permêt d'y repandre;

les pièges de toute espèce que tendent les Anglais et leurs continuelles attaques: qu'on parcoure l'histoire de toutes les guerres contre l'Angleterre et l'on verra qu'indépendamment des vingt mille Espagnols constamment stationés à St. Rocq, il était encore nécessaire d'entretenir sur cette côté un nombre considérable de troupes pour les opposer aux entreprises partielles de l'ennemi. Si ces précautions étaient indispensables dans un tems de calme et de tranquillité, qu'elles doivent être les espérances et les moyens de l'Angleterre dans l'agitation actuelle de l'Espagne et la nature de la guerre dont elle est le théâtre? Le roi peut dire avec verité que la conquête militaire et morale de l'Andalousie est son ouvrage, et que ses paroles, sa conduite, et les sages mesures qu'il a prises, ont preparé la tranquillité dont elle jouit. S. M. y a organisé des gardes civiques chargées de défendre leurs foyers, et malgré le voisinage de cette province avec l'Estremadure et les instigations continuelles de la junte de Cadiz et des Anglais, l'Andalousie renferme beaucoups moins de partis ou de bandes d'insurges que la Castille, la Biscaye, et la Navarre, qui ont été placés sous le régime militaire. Enfin l'on trouve en Andalousie une organisation complette de compagnies de Miguelettes, qui veillent à la tranquillité des villes et à la sûreté des chemins. Leurs services sont tellement utiles que le maréchal duc de Dalmatie a donné le plus de développement possible à cette institution.

Si l'Andalousie n'est pas entièrement pacifiée, si la junte de Cadiz existe encore, et si les Anglais y exercent leur fatale influence, on doit l'attribuer en grande partie aux machinations et aux traines ourdies par la junte et l'Angleterre au moment où parvint à leur connaissance le décret du 8 Février qui établit des gouvernemens militaires dans la Navarre, la Biscaye, l'Aragon, et la Catalogne. Quelques gouverneurs français ayant traité ces provinces comme si elles étaient absolument détachées de la monarchie, les membres de la junte de Cadiz et les Anglais en profitèrent pour souffler de nouveau le feu de la discorde et refuter les expressions du roi qui répétait sans cesse, 'Que la nation conserverait son intégrité et son indépendance: que ses institutions s'amélioreraient sous la protection d'un trône soutenu par les relations intimes du roi avec l'empereur; qu'elle n'aurait à combattre que l'ennemi qui voulait s'arroger l'empire exclusif des mers.' Voila le sens qu'on a toujours donné en Espagne aux mots indépendance et intégrité. Ce langage est celui dont s'est servi S. M. I. non seulement avec les Espagnols, mais à la face de l'univers: il ne peut donc être odieux ni criminel dans la bouche du roi. Mais combien n'est-il pas démenti par la conduite de certains gouverneurs qui paraissent s'obstiner à prolonger l'insurrection d'Espagne à l'annihiler ou la détruire plutôt qu'à la soumettre! car dans plusieurs endroits on ne se contente pas d'exclure toute idée de l'autorité du roi en faisant administrer la justice au nom de l'empereur, mais ce qui est pire, on a exigé que les tribunaux civils de Valladolid et de Valencia prêtassent serment de fidélité et d'obéissance à S. M. I. comme si la nation Espagnole n'avait pas de roi.

Monsieur le duc de Cadore se plaint de l'indulgence dont on en a usé en Andalousie; S. M. a montré contre ses ennemis, dans les champs de Talavera et Ocana, toute la fermeté de son caractère; mais serait-il juste, conviendrait-il à ses intérêts et aux vues de l'empereur, que S. M. deployât de la rigueur contre des vaincus, des prisonniers qui doivent être ses sujets? Si le maréchal Ney eut suivi ce généreux exemple dans les villes de Galice où il fut reçu à bras ouverts, et n'eut pas au contraire opprimé et saccagé cette province, elle serait heureuse et soumise, et non livrée aux maux de l'insurrection comme tant d'autres à qui l'on a fait éprouver le même sort. Cette conduite de S. M. dans des pays soumis est vraisemblablement ce que le duc de Cadore appelle des graces accordées aux insurgés de préférence aux personnes attachées à la cause du roi. Les insurgés n'ont obtenu d'autres graces que elles qui leur fûrent offertes dans les proclamations pour dissiper l'erreur dans laquelle les Anglais les avaient induits. Si le sequestre mis sur les biens invendus de quelques habitans ou réfugiés, a été levé posterieurement, cet exemple d'indulgence a eu d'heureux résultats, puisqu'il a attiré un grand nombre de personnes á l'obéissance du roi: et qu'on ne croye pas que ces individus n'aient point subi le chatiment qui leur était dû pour le retard qu'ils ont mis à se soumettre, car s'ils possedaient des billets royaux, il les ont perdues pour ne les avoir pas présenté à tems au timbre sec; et s'ils sont porteurs d'autres titres de créances sur l'état, ils doivent, pour les valider, solliciter un décret particulier.

Les avantages de la formation des corps Espagnols sont à la portée de tout le monde: leur présence a influé plus qu'on ne pense sur l'heureuse issue de la bataille d'Ocaña et de l'expédition d'Andalousie. En y admettant un grand nombre d'officiers, on est parvenu à éloigner de l'insurrection des hommes inquiets qui seraient devenus chefs de brigands, et tout en avouant que la désertion a eu lieu parmi les soldats, et qu'il en est resulté quelques maux, on peut hardiment affirmer que la somme des biens est infiniment plus grande, et qu'il n'y a pas de moyens qu'on ne doive employer pour faire revenir de son égarement une nation de douze millions d'âmes qu'il n'est pas facile d'assujettir par la force des bayonnettes, et dont on veut d'ailleurs faire une amie et une alliée.

On a parlé du mauvais emploi des ressources de l'Espagne, et du dénuement dans lequel ont été laissées les troupes françaises. Les soldats ont eu en Espagne des vivres en abondance: les hôpitaux français ont été les mieux pourvus, il a fallu pour cela exiger des contributions extraordinaires et des emprunts forcés, et vaincre le grand obstacle de l'interceptation des communications de province à province, et souvent de ville à ville. L'Espagne se trouve divisé en gouvernemens militaires de sorte que S. M. est à peine maître de la capitale et de sa banlieue: n'est ce donc point par une espèce de miracle qu'elle y fait subsister des troupes, et qu'elle y soutient des hôpitaux. Les gouverneurs français imposent, il est vrai, des contributions extraordinaires sur leurs provinces, mais ils les vexent et les ruinent, et certes ce n'est pas là le moyen de les maintenir dans l'obéissance, ni un exemple bien attrayant pour les provinces soulevées: cette ressource est d'ailleurs précaire et insuffisante comme le prouvera bientôt l'expérience. S. M. se flatte de ce que les intentions de l'empereur en faveur de la nation seraient mieux remplies et ses troupes mieux dirigées, si toutes celles qui sont en Espagne étaient sous ses ordres, et si les propositions qu'il a faites à son auguste frère étaient acceptées. Le duc de Cadore a évalué à plusieurs millions les confiscations de marchandises anglaises, et l'enlévement de l'argenterie des églises et des couvents qu'on aurait dû faire en Andalousie. Les confiscations eurent lieu par ordre des généraux français à leur entrée dans chaque ville, et si leur valeur fut exagerée, dans le principe, pour donner plus d'éclat aux entreprises militaires, on reconnut dès qu'on en vint à l'examen l'erreur dans laquelle on était tombé; et dans le fait comment ne pas apperçevoir qu'après la bataille d'Ocaña l'invasion d'Andalousie devant être prévue, chacun avait grand soin de faire refluer les marchandises confiscables sur les points les plus capables de resistance, afin de les mettre hors de la portée du vainqueur. L'argenterie d'église a beaucoup d'apparence et fort peu de valeur. On a pris dans les couvents, où il en restait très peu, ainsi que dans les églises toute celle qui n'a pas été jugée nécessaire pour la decence du culte, et comme le roi ne voulait ni ravager ni détruire, mais bien pacifier et conserver, il a dû régler sa conduite sur ce principe.

Monsieur le duc de Cadore parle de dépenses, c'est vraiment

une fatalité qu'il soit si mal informé de faits généralement connus. Le trésor public est ouvert à quiconque voudra s'assurer de la vérité. On y verra que S. M. a reçu à peine chaque mois le cinquième de l'assignation de la liste civile : qu'il a dû se reduire à la plus stricte économie, et que non seulement il s'est vu faute de pouvoir donner aux acteurs une légère avance, dans l'obligation de supprimer le théâtre Italien qui était son unique délassement, mais encore de vendre sa vaisselle platte, et de se défaire des choses les plus nécessaires à l'ornement de sa cour. Aussi dans le répas que S. M. donna, à l'occasion de la fête de l'empereur, à ses ministres, aux grands officiers de la couronne, et à l'ambassadeur de France, la table fut elle servie en fayence semblable à celle qu' avait S. M. au camp de Boulogne. Certainement l'embarras et la confusion que cette excessive simplicité causait au roi n'aura pas échappé à l'ambassadeur. Au milieu de tant de privations, et dans une situation aussi contraire à sa dignité S. M. a la douleur de voir que ses ministres, le conseil d'état, les tribunaux de la capitale, et les employés civils, qui sont en petit nombre, ne perçoivent pas leur traitement depuis plus de sept mois. Ce sont là les faveurs que S. M. a dispensés avec tant de prodigalité. Le roi a donné, il est vrai, quelques cédules aux officiers de sa maison, et à quelques individus attachés à sa personne, pour les aider à acheter des biens nationaux : on donne à ces bienfaits le nom de prodigalité, et d'un autre côté l'on se plaint de l'abandon dans lequel S. M. laisse d'autres individus, ce qui serait incompatible avec la façon de penser du roi et la connaissances de ses devoirs comme homme et comme monarque. C'est l'unique chose dont le roi puisse disposer dans la situation où il se trouve et outre le but politique de ces donations, S. M. a cru que c'était le seul moyen d'assurer à ces individus une médiocre existence, et encore sa prévoyance à cet égard a-t-elle été trompée, car les revenues des terres et des biens qui se trouvent dans les personnes soumises au gouvernement militaire dont les limites s'étendent jusqu'aux portes de Madrid, où ne se payent pas, tant est grande la misère des fermiers, où les biens ne s'affermentpas de crainte d'extorsions de la part des gouverneurs, où, enfin, les revenus se trouvent absorbés par les contributions extraordinaires. Les faits sont evidens, ils parlent d'eux-mêmes, et toute personne impartiale peut en faire l'examen.

Mais il faut qu'elle soit de meilleure foi que celle qui a voulu imputer à S. M. l'aliénation des biens confisqués par l'empereur, et les griefs auxquels on vient de répondre. S. M. pourrait, à bien plus juste titre, se plaindre de la conduite des gouverneurs Français: de celle du général Dufour, par exemple, qui a exigé des dix membres dont il composa à sa manière ce conseil de Navarre qu'on s'est vu bientôt obligé de dissoudre, qu'ils rédigeassent une adresse à l'empereur dans laquelle ils demandaient à S. M. I. un code des lois, et se mettaient à sa discrétion. Trois de ces membres réfusèrent de signer, les autres cédèrent à la violence. S. M. pourrait citer encore une foule d'actes qui ont exaspéré les esprits, fourni des armes à l'insurrection, et donné aux Anglais des prétextes pour supposer des projets qui n'existent pas, et rendre la guerre interminable. Qu'on compte le nombre des bandes de brigands et d'insurgés en Espagne, et l'on verra combien il s'est accru depuis l'institution des gouvernemens militaires. S. M. ne peut elle se plaindre avec autant de justice de la situation équivoque dans laquelle elle se trouve? qu'on en juge par le fait suivant. Le nouveau ministre de finances venait d'entrer en fonction, et il s'agissait déjà de réunir les plus forts capitalistes de la place pour les engager à avancer une bonne somme d'argent, lorsque le payeur de l'armée, monsieur Crouchart, et l'intendant-général, monsieur Denniers, assurèrent au ministre que des employés venaient de Paris avec des lettres cachetées qu'ils avaient l'ordre de n'ouvrir qu'à Madrid. On prétendit aussitôt qu'ils devaient se charger de l'administration civile, que les rentrées seraient invariablement affectées à l'entretien et à la solde de l'armée, et le surplus seulement, à la liste civile. C'était annoncer la dissolution de l'état. Des bruits de cette nature répandus dans toute la ville par les employés français parvenus à la connaissance de l'ambassadeur de S. M. I. et appuyés par des malveillans qui abondent toujours dans les capitales surtout à la suite des guerres d'opinions, ne pouvait produire que de malheureux effets. La confiance de ce petit nombre d'hommes qui aurait pu faire des avances s'eteignit à l'instant, et toutes les portes furent fermées. S. M. ignorait l'arrivée des nouveaux employés du trésor de France, et il n'a connu comme le dernier de ses sujets, le contenu des lettres dont ils étaient porteurs qu'à leurs ouvertures.

Dans cet état de choses il est facile de se faire l'idée de la confiance que peut inspirer le roi, et lorsque S. M. se trouve hors d'état de faire le bonheur du pays qu'il doit gouverner et de concourir à la réalisation des vues de son auguste frère: qu'il voit enfin sa dignité avilée, doit on s'étonner qu'il ait manifesté l'impossibilité de vivre plus long temps dans une situation aussi précaire? Monsieur le duc de Cadore tout en reconnaissant les hautes qualités du roi, a prétendu, que les personnes qui approchent S. M. lui ont conseillé et lui conseillent sans cesse de se maintenir dans l'indépendance de la France, et que ce principe se suivait avec trop de rigueur. Monsieur le duc de Cadore sait que S. M. dans aucune époque de sa longue et glorieuse carrière n'a eu besoin de conseils et ne s'est soumis à aucune influence, surtout s'il s'est agi de détruire 'son système inaltérable d'amitié sincère et éternelle avec son auguste frère l'empereur; d'alliance et de bienveillance affectueuse envers la nation Espagnole à la tête de laquelle il est placé, et dont il s'efforcera de conserver la splendeur et le bien-être, avec l'indépendance et l'integrité de territoire. Les vœux les plus constants de son cœur sont que les deux nations unies entr'elles par les mêmes liens que leur monarques concourent d'une manière uniforme à la félicité commune en forçant leur ennemie à abandonner le sceptre des mers.'

Le prince don Fernando, ajoute le duc de Cadore, se prêterait à céder les provinces qui conviennent à l'empereur et à toutes les conditions qu'il voudrait lui imposer. Le roi ne veut entrer en comparaison avec personne; mais il observera que ce ne fut pas dans ces sentimens ni dans cette croyance qu'il accepta la couronne d'Espagne en déposant celle de Naples: que l'empereur ni la France ne devraient avoir confiances en des offres que la nation repousserait, et qui ne pourrait avoir d'ailleurs qu'une exécution passagère; car comme le sait très bien monsieur le duc de Cadore, les nations humiliées dissimulent leur haine en attendant le moment favorable de venger leurs outrages. Une semblable conduite serait incompatible avec le façon de penser du roi, avec son noble caractère et celui de la nation que S. M. gouverne. Elle est diamétralement en opposition avec les assurances données par S. M. I. à la nation Espagnole 'qu'il était nécessaire pour son bonheur qu'elle se régénérat sous sa dynastie, et sous le prince qu'elle lui donnait égal en tout à son auguste personne.' A cette occasion le duc de Cadore parle du peu d'avantages que rapporte à la France la guerre d'Espagne en proportion des sacrifices immenses qu'elle a faits. Certes le roi ne les ignore pas, et sa reconnaissance éclatera quand S. M. se trouvera en état de les récompenser. Dans ce moment cela lui est impossible; mais S. M. I. pourrait mettre le comble à ses bons offices en s'offrant pour garant de l'emprunt ouvert en Hollande sous les mêmes conditions que celui de Prusse, ou du moins en lui donnant son assentiment comme à celui d'Autriche. S. M. I. se convaincra facilement que les liens du sang, les rélations les plus intimes et les plus sûres d'une étroite amitié entre les deux nations, et enfin la position même de ces armées seront les meilleurs garants de l'exactitude des remboursements quelques sacrifices qu'ils exigent.

Quant aux avantages futurs que promettent les sacrifices actuels de la France, ce serait faire injure aux lumières du duc de Cadore que de la fatiguer en les lui developpant. Lorsque S. M. I. crut nécessaire l'établissement en Espagne de sa dynastie, l'expérience lui avait démontré que survenant des troubles dans le nord, il ne pouvait jamais compter sans ce changement, sur la sûreté d'une des plus importantes frontières de son empire. Un siècle d'amitié presque non interrompue depuis le regne en Espagne et en France de la maison de Bourbon, le pacte de famille et la tournure différente que prirent les relations entre les deux pays après l'exclusion de la maison d'Autriche, sont les témoignages les plus authentiques de l'utilité des efforts et des sacrifices de la France pendant six ans, au commencement du siècle dernier. La résistance opiniâtre de presque toute l'Europe et surtout celle de l'Angleterre, qu'elle renouvelle dans cette guerre avec un plus grand developpement de moyens démontrent l'importance de cet événement pour la France. Ses meilleurs écrivains politiques ont indiqué avec la plus grande clarté les avantages qui en ont resulté pour le commerce Français et les richesses qu'il a procurées à la nation. Que ne doit elle pas attendre aujourd'hui de la réunion des deux couronnes dans la même famille, de l'analogie de leurs codes politiques et de leurs institutions, des qualités d'un roi sage et éclairé qui aime tendrement son auguste frère et la France, et qui est pénétré de la nécessité d'abattre l'orgueil de l'Angleterre! n'est ce pas le plus grand fruit qu'elle puisse retirer de cette resolution et de tels résultats ne valent ils pas les sacrifices momentanées qu'elle s'impose?

Il a été bien sensible pour S. M. que les rapports mensongers de personnes peu interessées à l'union et à l'amitié des deux frères et des deux pays, ayant pu inspirer à S. M. I. un seul instant de doutes. Quoique le roi a déjà écrit à l'empereur son auguste frère, S. M. veut que V. E. ou en votre absence le marquis d'Almenara, remette une copie de cette lettre à monsieur le duc de Cadore, dans l'espérance que V. E. developpera à S. M. I. avec sa sagacité ordinaire les causes qui ont influé sur la conduite du roi dans les affaires d'Espagne, que S. E. lui depeindra l'état véritable de la nation, et qu'elle contribuera de cette manière à l'éxécution des intentions des deux monarques qui n'ont été, et qui ne peuvent être que les mêmes.

Le ministre secrétaire d'état,
(Signé) MARIANO LUIS D'ORQUIJO.

Letters from king Joseph to his ministers.

10 *Février*, 1811.

Je suis peiné que l'empereur ait cru nécessaire d'employer des formes diplomatiques avec moi et même avec la reine. Qu'il me fasse clairement connoître sa volonté et je n'aurai rien de plus agréable que de m'y conformer puisqu'elle ne peut être ni compatible avec mon honneur qui me paroit inséparable du sien, comme mon intérêt. Le fait est que je désire complaire, à la fois, à l'empereur et à mon frère; il m'a fait reconnoître roi de Naples, roi d'Espagne, et a garanti mon existence politique sans que je l'aie demandé. Je n'ai pas sollicité le trône j'y suis monté parcequ'il l'a voulu, aujourd'hui l'empereur désire-t-il que je rentrois dans la retraite. Je suis d'autant plus prêt à le faire que les événemens de trois années ont levé bien des scrupules et empêcher venir bien des regrets.

J'ai dû croire que l'empereur vouloit que je quittâsse l'Espagne dès que j'ai vu graduellement mon existence y devenir humiliant, impossible, et qu'il doit savoir que je ne puis pas supporter longtemps de me voir degradé: dans ce cas je désire partir pour France. L'ordre publique sera assuré ici, je m'entendrai avec mon frère, ou pour mieux dire je lui porterai moi-même mon blanc-seing.

Je m'abandonne entièrement à sa justice et à ses sentimens paternels pour ma famille, aussi point de négociations particulières; je rétourne dès ce moment à l'empereur tous les droits qu'il m'a transmis sur l'Espagne si son ambassadeur juge que je puisse partir demain pour Morfontaine, et s'il eu autorisé à croire que l'empereur verra ce parti sans déplaisir.

L'empereur veut-il réellement que je reste au trône d'Espagne? Je reste quelques qui soient les désagrémens indépendant de la volonté qui m'y attendent. Mais il faut que je n'éprouve que ceux qu'il ne peut m'éviter; je le répéte jamais les intérêts politiques ne me diviseront avec lui, qu'il me fasse connoître sa volonté. Si l'empereur venir ici, tout s'arrangera entre nous; s'il ne vient pas en Espagne, qu'il me laisse aller le voir à Paris. S'il juge ce voyage inopportun, qu'il rende mon existence tolerable pendant la guerre: il sait mieux que personne ce qu'il doit faire pour cela.

Il faut un changement marqué dans tout, avancer ou reculer, vous connoissez l'état actuel; j'ignore comment je pourrai gagner le mois nécessaire pour connoître la determination de l'empereur.

(The following abdication, by Joseph, was drawn up but never made public.)

L'expérience de trois années nous ayant convaincu que l'ordre social ne peut être recomposé en Espagne qu'en cumulant dans les mêmes mains les droits de souveraintè dont nous sommes investés, et les moyens de force et de puissance militaire dont dispose notre august frère l'empereur des Français, de qui nous tenons les droits que nous exerçons aujourd'hui sur la monarchie Espagnole, nous avons résolu de notre pleine et libre volonté de rétrocéder à notre frère l'empereur des Français les droits qu'il nous a remis et en vertu des quels nous sommes entré dans ce royaume en 1808 à la suite de la constitution que nous avons signée à Bayonne dans la même année.

C'est pourquoi par les presents signées de notre main nous declarons céder, transporter, et remettre à notre dit frère l'empereur des Français, tous les droits qu'il nous transmis en 1808 sur la monarchie d'Espagne et des Indes dans toute leur integrité et tels qu'il les reçut lui-même du roi Charles Quatre.

Nous entendons que la présente rétrocession n'ait de force et valeur que ce l'epoque ou nous aurons pleine et entière connoissance de l'acceptation de la présente rétrocession de la part de notre frère l'empereur des Français : et comme nous ne sommes portés à cet acte par aucune considération particulière, mais par l'unique considération que nous avons exprimée plus haut et qu'en quittant le trône d'Espagne nous n'avons en vue que le plus grand bien du peuple Espagnol que nous ne pourrons pas rendre aussi heureux que nous voudrions, et que nous n'avons d'autre ambition que celle de rentrer dans la vie privée et dans la retraite la plus absolue. Nous nous abandonnons entièrement à la justice de notre frère l'empereur des Français pour le sort des personnes qui nous sont attachées au sentimens de la gloire qui garantit ses efforts pour le bonheur de l'Espagne et à ses sentimens paternels pour nos enfans, pour la reine, notre épouse, et pour nous.

Nous nous engagerons à faire revêtir de toutes les formes qui pourroient paroître plus authentiques le présent acte écrit, rédigé, et signé de notre propre main. Ayant jugé que le plus grand secret était indispensable jusqu'à ce que nous ayons connoissance de l'acceptation de S. M. l'empereur des Français, roi d'Italie.

Fait à Madrid, etc. etc.

Paris, 1811.

Depuis la conversation que j'ai eu avec vous sur ma position, elle ne s'est pas améliorée; elle est telle aujourd'hui que je me voir forcé d'embrasser le seul pratique qui me reste à prendre, celui de la rétraite la plus absolue en France. Je serois déjà parti si je ne venois d'être instruit que S. M. l'empereur qui a sû que j'avois donné ordre d'acheter ou de louer une terre a cent lieues de Paris, avoit disapprouvé cette demarche, et qu'il trouvait plus convenable, si je persistois dans ma resolution, qui je me rendisse à ma terre de Morfontaine après vous avoir prévenu de ma détermination, et avoir assuré ici l'ordre publique après mon départ. Je dirai en partant que je vais m'entendre avec l'empereur pour les affaires d'Espagne, et je ferois les mêmes dispositions par rapport aux provinces qui entourent Madrid que je fit lorsqu'il y a un an je partis pour l'expedition d'Andalousie; cet état dura six mois sans nul désordre, et je ne doute pas que les choses n'aillent de la même manière et ne donnent le tems à l'empereur de prendre les dispositions définitives.

Je suis prêt à rendre l'empereur les droits qu'il me rémit à Bayonne sur la monarchie d'Espagne et des Indes si ma position ici ne change pas; parceque je dois croire que c'est le désir de l'empereur puisqu'il est impossible qu'il veuille que je reste roi d'Espagne, et qu'il m'ôte tous les moyens d'existence. Il en peut être malheureux que l'empereur ait voulu me reconnoître roi de Naples, il y a six ans lorsqu'à la tête de ses troupes je fis la conquête de ce royaume; ce fut malgré moi, et mes instances pour rester au commandement de son armée avec la simple qualité de son lieutenant furent le sujet d'une lettre dont je me rappelle très-bien.

Lorsqu'en 1808 je fus proclamé roi d'Espagne, je l'ignorois encore; cependant arrivé à Bayonne je fis tout ce que voulus l'empereur, je signerais une constitution, je le signai appuyée par sa garantie. Les événemens n'ayant pas répondu à nos espérances est ce ma faute? Est celui qui en est le plus victim qui doit en porterla peine? Cependant tant que la guerre dure je me suis soumis a tout ce que l'on a voulu, mais je ne puis pas l'impossible; je ne puis pas rester ici plus longtems si l'empereur ne vient à mon secours. En ordonnant qu'il soit versé dans mon trésor à Madrid un million de francs par mois, les autres provinces doivent contribuer aux besoins de la capitale. Les troupes françoises qui sont dans les provinces du centre (elles sont peu nombreuses) doivent être soldées par le trésor de France.

A la pacification générale l'empereur exigera des indemnités; s'entendrer alors il posséde de fait presque toutes les provinces aujourd'hui, il sera bien le maître de ne les évacuer qu'à mesure qu'il croira que l'Espagne aura satisfait aux obligations qu'il lui aura imposées. En résume je suis prêt à faire la volonte de l'empereur pourvu que je la connoîsse.

1°. Veut-il que je reste roi d'Espagne, je reste dès qu'il m'en donne la possibilité, et je supporte tous les gouvernemens militaires qu'il a établis puisqu'il les croit indispensables pendant la guerre.

2°. Préféreroit-il que je rentrasse dans la sein de ma famille à Morfontaine d'abord et l'hiver dans le midi. Je suis prêt à partir dès que je connoîtrai sa volonté. J'ajoute de plus que le parti de la retraite me conviendra beaucoup plus que l'autre dès que je saurai qu'il lui convient. Je suis sur alors qu'il aura quelques bontés pour les Français qui se sont attachés à mon soit, et que je ne serai pas à même de rendre aussi heureux qu'ils le méritent. Quant à moi, à la reine, et à mes enfans, l'empereur me faisant payer mon traitement de prince Français, nous en aurons assez, mon intention étant de vivre dans la retraite en m'occupant de l'education des mes enfans, laissant a l'empereur le soin de leur établissemens, car je ne doute pas si ce projet se verifie que je ne retrouve le cœur de mon frère, et que dans les intervalles où il se rappellera qu'il est homme, il ne trouve encore quelque consolation en retrouvant mon cœur pour lui aussi jeune qu'il y a trente ans.

Enfin j'aime mieux vivre sujet de l'empereur en France que de rester en Espagne roi nominal, parceque je serai bon sujet en France, et mauvais roi en Espagne, et que je veux rester digne de l'empereur, de la France, et de moi-même.

Marquis of Almenara to the minister secretary of state. Translated from a deciphered Spanish letter.

Fontainebleau, Novembre 4, 1810.

" This government is very uneasy about the military operations in Portugal, from whence they receive no accounts except through England, described therefore factitiously and with the strongest hopes of resisting the French forces that oppose their army. This problem will probably be already solved and its conclusion will decide what is interesting to Spain. It is therefore very important that our government should write all it knows, and what will prove that it takes part in what belongs to both countries, because here I am often asked what is said in Madrid on this subject, and people are surprised that we limit ourselves entirely to the urgent points of our negotiation. This explains the proofs of affection which the prince royal of Sweden desired that the king should give to the emperor, being convinced that the letters of his majesty, written in his own familiar style when he explains his sentiments, produce a great sensation with the emperor."

SECTION 3.

Letters from the prince de Neufchatel to king Joseph.

Paris, 28 *Janvier*, 1811.

SIRE,—J'ai l'honneur de prévenir votre majesté que l'empereur par sa décision du 21 Janvier a fixé les traitemens extraordinaires qui pourront être payés en Espagne à date du 1er de l'année 1811, dans l'arrondissement des armées du midi, du nord, de l'Arragon, &c. Ces traitemens sont déterminés ainsi qu'il suit.

Savoir :

	Fr. par mois.
Les généraux gouverneurs dans les quatre gouvernemens comprises dans l'arrondissement de l'armée du nord ..	4000
Le général chef de l'état major général de l'armée	3000
Généraux de division	1800
Généraux de brigade, inspecteurs aux revues et commissaires ordonnateurs	1200
Adjudans commandans, colonels, et sous-inspecteurs aux revues	750
Officiers de santé principaux	500
Chefs de bataillons, d'escadrons, commissaires de guerre, et chefs d'administration des différens services	400
Commandans de place occupant dans l'armée un grade inférieur à ceux ci-dessus désignées, savoir .... capitaines	400
Commandans de place ... lieutenans et sous-lieuts.	300

Au moyen de ces indemnités il ne sera rien alloué au-dessus des sommes fixées ni pour dépenses de bureaux ou de table, ni pour frais extraordinaires de quelque nature qu'ils soient et sous quelque prétexte que ce puisse être, et cette décision n'a aucun effet rétroactif. J'écris à MM. les maréchaux et généraux commandant en Espagne, pour leur faire connoître que, d'après les intentions de l'empereur, tout militaire Français qui à l'avenir aurait exigé ou reçu des traitemens extraordinaires plus forts que ceux fixés par la décision du 21 Janvier, et qui s'en serait fait payer sans une ordonnance régulière des intendans généraux ou commissaires ordonnateurs, sera suspendu de ses fonctions et qu'il en sera rendu compte dans les vingt-quatre heures pour prendre les ordres de l'empereur. Votre majesté jugera sans doute convenable de donner ses ordres au général Belliard pour que cette disposition soit suivie dans l'arrondissement de l'armée du centre. Je prie votre majesté d'agréer l'hommage de mon respect.

Paris, 14 *Février*, 1811.

Sire,—L'empereur ne m'a encore donné aucun ordre relatif à l'objet de la lettre apportée par votre aide-de-camp le colonel Clermont Tonnere. On pense que Valence ne se soumettra que par l'approche d'une armée, et après la prise de Tarragone le corps du général Suchet sera disponible.—Les affaires paroissent s'améliorer en Portugal, le duc d'Istrie va établir l'ordre dans le nord de l'Espagne. J'envoye mon aide-de-camp le colonel Le Jeune voir l'état des choses à Grénade, Malaga, Cadiz et Badajos. Je prie votre majesté d'avoir des bontés pour lui. L'empereur est en bonne santé, l'imperatrice est bientôt à terme, et nous esperons un roi des Romains. L'empereur affermit de plus en plus le grand empire. Votre majesté le seconde mais nous apprécions ses peines et ses privations. Une nouvelle armée de deux-cent-milles hommes se forme dans le nord de la France, et l'empereur est en position d'en imposer à qui tenteroit de contrarier ses grandes conceptions, tout est bien et va bien en France.

Paris, le 11 *Avril*, 1811.

Sire,—J'ai eu l'honneur de mander votre majesté, que l'empereur avoit donné des ordres pour qu'il lui fut envoyé chaque mois cent mille francs, et je lui ai fait connoître combien il étoit important que les troupes destinées pour l'Andalusie y arrivassent sans retard.

L'empereur pense qu'il seroit utile de chercher à tirer parti de bons Espagnole pour réunir de vrais cortez qui pourroient avoir de l'influence sur les esprits: l'intégrité de l'Espagne peut encore être maintenue si les cortez operoient une réaction dans l'opinion: le Perou et le Méxique se sont déjà declarés independant, et toutes les autres colonies sont échapper à l'Espagne: les vrais Espagnols doivent savoir combien les Anglais les maltraitent. On voit par les gazettes Anglaises que les cortez rassemblés dans l'île de Leon ne furent qu'une miserable canaille et des gens obscures qui n'ont autre projet que d'aller végéter dans les tavernes de Londres il ne peut y avoir rien à faire avec de pareils hommes. Sa majesté trouve qu'il y auroit un grand avantage à former des cortez tirer de toutes les provinces de l'Espagne occupées par les armées françaises. Une discussion éclairée qui s'établiroit auroit beaucoup d'influence sur les esprits. L'empereur est obligé d'abandonner le projet qu'il avoit de s'entendre avec les cortez de l'île de Leon, puisque ce n'est qu'un composé de gens sans aveu: ce ne seroit donc qu'avec des cortez formé d'hommes tirés de toutes les parties de l'Espagne qu'on pourroit éclairer l'opinion des Espagnols qui aiment leur pays.

L'ambassadeur de l'empereur a transmis des plaintes sur votre major-général. Votre majesté commande l'armée du centre. Par consequent la hiérarchie militaire ne peut pas permettre qu'il s'écarte de ses devoirs. Si je correspond souvent avec le général Belliard, c'est que votre majesté est un général roi, et que je dois lui éviter des details qu'un major-général lui soumet.

Aucun village d'Espagne n'a été réuni à la France, et l'empereur tient à ce que votre majesté ait en Espagne toute la considération qui lui est due. Tout depend encore du parti qu'on peut tirer de la nation. Ce qu'il y a de certain, c'est que les Anglais n'ont qu'un but; celui de ruiner la peninsule, de la détruire, parcequ'ils sentent bien qu'elle doit finir par appartenir à la France ou à un prince de la maison de l'empereur, et qu'ils trouvent un grand avantage à diviser un pays qu'il savent ne pouvoir gardes.

Je presente à votre majesté l'hommage avec mon respect.

Le Prince Neufchatel, Major-Général,

ALEXANDRE.

Paris, ce 6 *Mai,* 1811.

SIRE,—J'ai montré à l'empereur la lettre de votre majesté, en date du 21 Avril par laqu'elle elle fait connoître qu'elle se met en route pour Paris: l'empereur ne s'attendoit pas à cette resolution; votre majesté lui ayant promis de ne pas quitter l'Espagne sans être convenu à l'avance des mesures à prendre et qu'exige une pareille détermination. L'empereur trouve que dans ces circonstances le départ de votre majesté devoit être précédé de l'évacuation de l'Andalousie afin de concentrer les armées. Car dans la position des choses, le départ de votre majesté va donner une secousse défavorable à la situation des armées de l'empereur. Si votre majesté avoit quitté l'Espagne au mois de Janvier, où les armées étoient en position sans agir, cela auroit eu moins d'inconvenient. Dans ce moment votre arrivée met l'empereur dans de grandes inquiétudes, en vous considerant comme roi d'Espagne, et comme général-en-chef, l'empereur voit que votre rétour sera interpreté selon l'esprit et la tournure que les Anglais voudront y donner, et fera un mauvais effet; qu'il est pénible que votre majesté se soit portée à cette démarche dont il ne peut resulter aucun avantage, et qui peut avoir beaucoup d'inconvenients, car dans ce moment d'agitation, l'Espagne va se trouver sans chef. Votre majesté ne voulant pas rester à Madrid, l'empereur trouve qu'il auroit été très utile qu'elle allât passer la revue de l'armée de Portugal ou de l'armée d'Andalousie; l'influence de votre majesté auroit surtout été bien utile pour procurer à l'armée de Portugal tout ce qui lui est nécessaire. L'empereur, sire, est dans une grande anxieté de savoir à qui vous avez donné le commandement de l'armée du centre; si vous avez prévenu le duc de Dalmatie de votre départ, et qui étant aux mains avec l'ennemi trouvera ses embarras augmentés, n'ayant aucune direction sur ses derrières. S'il étoit possible que votre majesté reçut cette lettre encore en Espagne, l'empereur m'ordonne d'engager votre majesté à sentir les inconvéniens de son rétour si contraire aux circonstances. L'empereur n'a aucune nouvelle ni de l'armée d'Andalousie ni de l'armée du centre. J'expédie à votre majesté un de mes aides-de-camp. Etc. etc.

ALEXANDRE.

Paris, le 1 *Juin*, 1811.

SIRE,—L'empereur a examiné attentivement les observations que votre majesté lui a adressées, et me prescrit de me rendre auprès d'elle pour avoir l'honneur de lui donner connoissance de ce qu'il juge le plus convenable sur les divers points qui en sont l'objet. L'empereur pense, sire, que votre majesté peut partir de Paris quand elle le jugera à-propos, et même sans attendre son rétour, si cela entrait dans les intentions de votre majesté. L'armée du centre en Espagne est pleinement entièrement sous les ordres de votre majesté, le général Belliard ne doit point prendre le titre de major général, mais celui que lui ont toujours attribué les ordres émanées de l'empereur, *de chef d'état major de l'armée du centre*. Si votre majesté n'est pas content de ce général, je vous engage, sire, à en proposer un autre qui ait votre confiance. C'est à votre majesté, sire, qu'il appartient de suspendre, de renvoyer, de traduire même à des commissions militaires quand il y a lieu, les généraux et officiers de l'armée du centre; d'administrer les provinces comprises dans l'arrondissement de cette armée comme votre majesté le jugera le plus convenable au bien du service. A l'armée du nord de l'Espagne, l'empereur a besoin d'un maréchal qui soit chargé du commandement des troupes stationées dans les provinces formant l'arrondissement de cette armée. Le maréchal duc d'Istrie exerce maintenant ce commandement; dans le cas, sire, ou ce maréchal ne conviendroit pas à V. M. l'empereur ne serait pas eloigné de le remplacer par le maréchal Jourdan, si cette disposition étoit agréable à votre majesté et à ce maréchal. Mais l'empereur ne juge pas qu'on puisse rien changer à l'organisation de l'armée du nord; il est essentiel que cette organisation reste telle qu'elle est, si ce n'est de mettre cette armée sous les ordres d'un maréchal français qui posséde d'avantage la confiance de votre majesté. Dans les gouvernemens qui forment l'arrondissement de cette armée, c'est au nom de votre majesté, sire, que la justice doit se rendre; le commandant doit envoyer des rapports journaliers à V. M. l'intendant général M. Dudon doit envoyer à V. M. l'état de la perception des contributions et de leur emploi. L'empereur pense que V. M. doit avoir auprès du général-en-chef de l'armée du nord un commissaire Espagnol pour veiller à ce que le quart du revenu des provinces de l'arrondissement de cette armée, soit versé à Madrid pour le service de votre majesté et pour sécourir l'armée du centre. L'empereur consent à ce que toutes les fois que les provinces auraient les moyens nécessaires pour se garder et se garantir des incursions des guerillas, elles puissent rentrer entièrement sous l'administration Espagnole en ne fournissant que ce qui sera convenu. Quant à l'armée du midi de l'Espagne, l'empereur approuve qu' ainsi qu' à l'armée du nord, le maréchal qui commande envoie des rapports à V. M. et l'instruire de tout ce qui se passe; les budgets en recettes et en dépenses des différentes provinces de l'armée du midi, doivent aussi être envoyés à votre majesté, qui y tiendra un commissaire pour percevoir le quart des revenues.

La même méthode sera pareillement appliquée à l'armée d'Arragon. L'empereur, sire, satisfait aussi aux désirs exprimés par V. M. Quant à ce qui concerne le commandement général de ses armées en Espagne, sa majesté ne croit pas pouvoir donner un tel commandement qui doit être simple et un; votre M. sentira qu'il est dans la nature des choses qu'un maréchal résident à Madrid et dirigeant les opérations voudrait en avoir la gloire avec la responsibilité, et que dans ce cas, les commandans des armées du midi et de Portugal se croyant moins réellement sous les ordres de votre M. que sous de son chef d'état major, pourraient ne pas obéir, ou exécuter ce qui leur serait prescrit. Mais indépendamment du commandement de l'armée du centre, V. M.

sire, aurait le commandement des troupes qui entreraient dans l'arrondissement de cette armée. Si l'armée du Midi se repliait sur l'armée du centre, elle serait dès-lors sous les ordres de V. M. et il en serait de même pour l'armée de centre.

Dans celles des armées ou V. M. se rendrait, elle aurait les honneurs du commandement; mais, sire, l'empereur juge très important de ne rien changer au commandement militaire ni à l'armée du nord, ni à l'armée d'Arragon, ni aux armées du midi et de Portugal, excepté ce qu'il est nécessaire d'établir pour que V. M. ait des rapports de tout ce qui se passe, connaisse tout et puisse se servir de ces relations, dans sa position centrale, pour instruire les autres généraux : sa majesté pense que cette communication de renseignemens, d'observations, de conseils, peut même avoir lieu par le canal du ministre de la guerre de V. M. L'empereur désire, sire, que V. M. veuille bien correspondre directement avec moi par des lettres signés de sa main ; j'aurai l'honneur d'adresser directement les miennes à V. M. l'empereur désire également qu'elle s'en reserve l'ouverture et fasse connaître ensuite à son chef d'état-major ce qu'elle jugera convenable. Je prie votre M. de vouloir bien donner ses ordres pour que tous les comptes rendus en états de situation me soient adressés, que les rapports soient très exacts et que je sois instruit de tout ce qui peut intéresser le service de l'empereur comme cela est d'usage dans une armée. D'après les ordres de l'empereur une somme de cinq cent mille francs par mois sera envoyée à V. M. jusqu'au 1er Juillet, et à compter du 1er Juillet, cet envoi sera d'un million par mois pendant le reste de l'année.

L'empereur, sire, me prescrit d'avoir l'honneur de concerter avec votre majesté les mesures qu'elle jugera convenables à l'organization de l'armée du centre ainsi que pour en retirer les généraux qui ne conviendraient pas à votre majesté, faire des examples de ceux qui auroient commis des dilapidations, leur faire restituer les sommes qu'ils auraient dilapidées ; enfin, sire, l'empereur se repose essentiellement sur votre majesté du soin de maintenir les officiers de son armée dans la discipline convenable et de faire des examples, et il désire que V. M. envoie journellement des rapports détaillés sur tout ce qui est important. Votre majesté, sire, reconnaîtra dans ces dispositions que le désir de l'empereur est de faire tout ce qui peut donner un nouvel éclat à l'entrée de V. M. en Espagne, en maintenant d'ailleurs dans leur intégrité, ainsi que sa majesté le gage indispensable, l'organisation de l'armée d'Andalousie et des autres armées de l'Espagne. &c.

Observations faites par le roi d'Espagne sur la lettre du major général, de la 1ère *Juin*, 1811.

Le roi demande.

1°. Que messrs. les maréchaux commandant-en-chef les armées de l'empereur, à l'armée du nord, du Portugal, de midi, et de l'Arragon, ne puissent augmenter les impôts existant à ce jour, ni lever aucune contribution extraordinaire sans l'autorization du roi, ou de l'empereur.

2°. Le roi désire que le maréchal Jourdan remplace le maréchal duc d'Istrie dans le commandement de l'armée du nord.

3°. Que les maréchaux commandant les armées de l'empereur et les intendans général ne puissent vendre aucune bien national ou communal sans l'autorization du roi; qu'il en soit de même pour les plombs et vif argent appartenant à l'état.

4°. Que les administrations Espagnoles dans l'arrondissement des armées du nord, du midi, de l'Arragon, resteront telles qu'elles sont, et que si des changemens paroissent utiles, ils seront demandés au roi.

5°. Qu'il soit specifié que le quart des revenues des provinces occupées par les armées de l'empereur, en Espagne, sera versé net dans le trésor du roi à Madrid, et que les trois autre quartes seront employés aux besoin de l'armée dans les dites provinces, et en payement des traitemens des administrations Espagnoles.

6°. Le roi se trouvant avoir l'honneur du commandement près des armées ou il se trouve, pense qu'il est dans les intentions de votre majesté qu'il puisse voir et réunir les autorités Espagnoles comme bon lui semblera pour leur parler dans l'intérêt des affaires d'Espagne: ce que le roi trouve utile de faire dans les lieux où il l'arrêtera pour se rendre à Madrid.

7°. Il paroit entendu que le maréchal commandant l'armée de Portugal rendra compte au roi des toutes les opérations, aussi que doivent le faire les autres maréchaux.

8°. Le roi trouve utile pour les intérêts des affaires d'Espagne de pouvoir s'attacher des officiers Espagnols ou autres qui se trouveroient parmi les prisonniers, et qui par des motifs particuliers il jugeroit convenable d'employer.

9°. Le roi de Westphalie qui ne peut pas recruter les regimens qu'il a en Espagne est disposé à mettre le petit nombre d'hommes qui restent aux drapeaux à la disposition du roi d'Espagne pour être à la solde et à son service; le roi d'Espagne les placeroit utilement dans la guarde.

10°. Le roi désire que le général Maurice Mathieu remplace le général Lorge.

11°. Qu'il ne reste à Madrid que l'administration nécessaire pour l'armée du centre, et que cette grande quantité d'administrateurs appartenant à l'administration générale qui n'existe plus à Madrid soit envoyée à Burgos ou en France.

12°. Que la solde des troupes françaises faisant partie de l'armée du centre continue n'être payée par le trésor de France.

13°. Sa majesté conservera le général Belliard comme chef de son état major.

14°. Le roi désire pouvoir prendre toutes les mesures politiques qu'il jugera convenable, et faire toutes autres dispositions à l'egard de cortez en se conformant aux vues contenues dans la lettre que j'ai écrite d'après l'ordre de V. M. pour cet objet.

15°. Sur les 500,000 francs que V. M. met à la disposition du roi à Madrid on en retient 100,000 francs pour l'arrière. Le roi demande que cette somme soit pour le service courant.

Paris, le 17 *Juin,* 1811.

Sire,—L'empereur m'ordonne de vous envoyer la copie de la lettre que j'adresse au duc d'Istrie: j'écris à-peu-près dans les mêmes termes aux autres commandants. Je n'ai pas encore vu le maréchal Jourdan; je le verrai demain et immediatement après il partira pour Madrid, où l'empereur apprendra avec plaisir qu'il est employé comme gouverneur.

Le duc de Raguse mande qu'il est en marche sur le Tage. L'empereur désire que V. M. donne ses ordres pour qu'on lui procure tous les secours dont il peut avoir besoin: il a avec lui vingt-huit mille bayonnettes, trois mille hommes de cavalerie, et trent-six pièces de canon. L'empereur désire que V. M. puisse l'appuyer avec dixhuit cent chevaux, quinze à dixhuit pièces de canon et deux à trois mille hommes d'infanterie: ce corps pourroit être placé à proximité afin de pouvoir rejoindre et aider le duc de Raguse, s'il devoit donner bataille aux Anglais. L'empereur verroit avec plaisir, Sire, qu'après votre arrivée à Madrid vous vous rendissiez à l'armée de Portugal, pour la passer en revue, l'animer, et prendre dans vôtre revue l'état des emplois vacans.

J'écris au duc de Raguse que si l'on pouvoit retrancher Alcantara et faire une tête de pont sur la rive droite, ce seroit une bonne opération. Si l'armée de Portugal arrivoit à tems pour secourir l'armée du midi devant Badajoz, le petit corps de reserve dont je viens de parler ci-dessus à votre majesté ne pourroit être que de la plus grande utilité.

Le siège de Tarragone a déjà attiré une partie des bandes qui étoient dans l'arrondissement de l'armée du centre. Deux divisions de l'armée de reserve que forme l'empereur arriveront l'une à Pampelune, l'autre à Vittoria vers le 14 Juillet: cela mettra à même d'envoyer encore aux armées du midi et de Portugal environ douze milles hommes qui sont en Navarre, et qui passeront par Madrid.

L'Empereur ne peut qu'engager votre majesté à envoyer à l'armée du midi tout ce qui lui appartient, car c'est là que se portent les grands coups et qu'ont lieu les opérations les plus importantes.

&c. &c.

ALEXANDRE.

To the duke of Istria.

Paris, Juin 1811.

J'ai prevénu, monsieur le maréchal, le général Monthion, les généraux Caffarelli et Dorsenne directement les dispositions dont je vais vous entretenir, et qui ont rapport aux intentions de l'empereur rélativement au rétour de roi d'Espagne dans ses états.

Le roi commande en chef l'armée du centre, mais l'intention de l'empereur est que vous correspondiez avec S. M. C. en lui faissant le rapport de ce qui se passe afin de la mettre à même de connoître l'ensemble des événemens en Espagne comme les autres généraux en chef ont l'ordre d'en agir de même, le roi sera dans le cas de pouvoir comme point central vous faire faire des communications qui contribueront au succès des armes de l'empereur.

S. M. I. m'ordonne aussi de vous faire connaître, M. le duc, que son intention est que pendant le voyage du roi dans son rétour à Madrid, tous les honneurs lui soient rendus dans les gouvernemens et dans l'arrondissement de l'armée du nord comme si S. M. commandait cette armée. Le roi donnera l'ordre et recevra les honneurs du commandement. Les gouverneurs l'accompagneront dans leur gouvernement et lui feront fournir toutes les escortes qui lui seront nécessaires. Il est à présumer que le roi séjournera quelque tems à Vittoria et à Burgos, et qu'il profitera de son séjour pour rassembler les notables du pays les éclairer sur la situation des affaires,et améliorer l'esprit public. Vous seconderez, mons. le maréchal, les mesures que le roi pourra prendre pour rendre les villes et les villages responsibles des abus qui se commettent sur leur territoire. Vous agirez de même si le roi accorde le pardon à quelques bandes de guerillas qui se rendraient. Vous devez aider de tous vos moyens les mesures que S. M. prendra pour le rétablissement de l'ordre et de la tranquillité publique. Du reste les troupes composant l'armée du nord doivent rester sous le commandement respectif de leurs chefs et vos ordres doivent continuer à être exécutés sans qu'aucun ordre de qui que ce soit puisse les changer. Quant à l'administration du pays, elle doit continuer à marcher dans la direction donnée par les instructions et les ordres de l'empereur; les fonds doivent être destinées aux besoins de l'armée, à l'entretien des hôpitaux, et vous devez défendre et empêcher toute espèce d'abus. Le roi ayant plus particulièrement encore que vous, les moyens de connaître les abus qu'ont lieu, l'empereur ordonne que vous profiteriez des lumières que le roi pourra vous donner à cet égard pour les réprimer. Il est nécessaire, monsieur le duc, que vous me fassiez connaître le budjet des ressources et des dépenses afin de savoir la partie des revenues qui pourront être versés à Madrid, dans la caisse du gouvernement pour le service du roi et pour l'armée du centre.

Je n'ai pas besoin de vous répéter que la justice doit se rendre au nom du roi; cela a toujours dû avoir lieu; le droit de faire grace ne vous appartient pas pour les individus condamnés par les tribunaux; vous n'êtes autorisé qu'à suspendre l'exécution dans les cas que vous jugerez graciables. Le droit de faire grace n'appartient qu'au roi. Vous n'avez pas non plus le droit de nommer à aucune place du clergé; le roi y nomme dans toutes les parties de son royaume.

Si le roi juge à-propos de tenir près de vous et des gouverneurs un commissaire Espagnol pour connaître les recettes et les dépenses, vous devez donner à ce commissaire les renseignemens dont il aura besoin pour remplir sa mission. Vous aurez soin, monsieur le maréchal, de me rendre compte journellement de ce qui se sera fait pendant le séjour du roi afin que j'en informe l'empereur."

&c. &c.

Paris, le 24 *Août*, 1811.

Sire,—J'ai l'honneur d'informer votre majesté que d'après les ordres de l'empereur, je viens de faire connaître à M. le maréchal duc de Raguse que l'armée de Portugal doit prendre désormais sa ligne de communication sur Madrid; je lui mande que c'est là que doit être son centre de dépôt, et que toute opération que l'ennemi ferait sur la Coa ne peut déranger cette ligne; que si l'ennemi veut prendre l'offensive il ne peut la prendre que dans l'Andalousie parceque de ce côté il a un objet à remplir, qui est de faire lever le siège de Cadiz, tandis que ses efforts dans le nord s'avença-t-il même jusqu'à Valladolid, n'aboutiraient à rien puisque les troupes que nous avons dans ces provinces en se repliant lui opposeraient une armée considérable et qu' alors l'armée de Portugal devrait faire pour l'armée du nord ce qu'elle ferait pour l'armée du midi. Je le préviens que l'objet important est que sa ligne d'opérations soit sur Talavera et Madrid parceque son armée est spécialement destinée à protéger celle du midi. Je lui fais observer que l'armée de Portugal étant attaquée de front, son mouvement de retraite est encore sur Madrid parceque dans tous les cas possibles ce doit être sa ligne d'opérations, qu'il faut donc que tous les dépôts quelconques appartinant à l'armée de Portugal soient dirigés sur Talavera et Madrid. Je donne l'ordre impératif au général Dorsenne de faire partir dans les 24 heures tous les dépôts et détachemens qu'il a appartenant à l'armée de Portugal; tout ce qui est en état de servir sera dirigé en gros détachemens par Avila sur Placentia, et quant aux hommes qui ne sont pas pour le moment en état de servir, le général Dorsenne les fera diriger sur Madrid, et aura soin d'en informer à l'avance votre majesté, de manière qu'il ne lui restera plus un seul homme appartenant à l'armée de Portugal, sauf la garnison de Ciudad Rodrigo qu'il fera relever et rejoindre aussitôt après l'arrivée des renforts qui vont se rendre à l'armée du nord."

&c. &c.

Boulogne, le 20 *Sept.* 1811.

Sire,—L'empereur m'a demandé si j'avois reponse à la lettre que j'ai eu l'honneur d'adresser à V. M. en lui rendant compte de la reddition de Figueras. L'empereur m'ordonne d'annoncer à V. M. que son intention est d'étendre à toute la rive gauche de l'Ebre la mesure qu'elle à jugé devoir adopter pour la Catalogne. L'empereur pense que V. M. temoin de la resistance qui éprouvent les armées et des sacrifices des toutes espèces que la France est obligé de faire, est trop juste pour ne point apprecier les motifs de la conduite de l'Empereur, et je suis autorisé à assurer V. M. des sentimens d'intérêt et d'amitié qui continuent à animer l'empereur pour V. M. mais il ne pouvent pas faire negliger à S. M. I. et R. ce qu'elle doit à la sureté de son empire et à la gloire de son règne.

&c. &c.

No. IV.

SECTION 1.

CONDUCT OF THE ENGLISH GOVERNMENT.

EXTRACT FROM MR. CANNING'S INSTRUCTIONS TO MR. STUART AND MR. DUFF, 1808.

To Mr. Stuart.

" You are to enter into no political engagements."

To James Duff, Esq.

" *July* 26, 1808.

" You will embark on board his majesty's ship, Stately; on board of that ship are embarked to the amount of one million of Spanish dollars, three fourths in dollars and one fourth in bars, which sum is consigned to your care and is destined by his majesty for the use of the kingdom of Andalusia and the provinces of Spain connected with them.

" His majesty has no desire to annex any conditions to the pecuniary assistance which he furnishes to Spain."

" Military stores to a considerable amount are now actually shipping for Cadiz, and the articles required for the clothing of the Andalusian army will follow."

" It was only by a direct but secret understanding with the government of Spain, under the connivance of France, that any considerable amount of dollars has been collected in England."

" Each province of Spain made its own application with reference to the full amount of its own immediate necessities, and to the full measure of its own intended exertions, but without taking into consideration that similar necessities and similar exertions lead to similar demands from other parts, and that though each separate demand might in itself be reasonably supposed to come within the limits of the means of Great Britain, yet that the whole together occasion a call for *specie*, such as never before was made upon this country at any period of its existence."

" In the course of the present year it is publicly notorious that a subsidy is paid by Great Britain to Sweden of one million two hundred thousand pounds, the whole of which, or nearly the whole, must be remitted in specie, amounting to at least seven million dollars. One million of dollars has already been sent to Gihon, another to Coruña *in part* of the respective demands of the principality of Asturias and the kingdom of Gallicia, and the remainder of these demands as already brought forward would require not less than eight million dollars more to satisfy them."—" An application from Portugal has also been received for an aid, which will amount to about twelve or thirteen hundred thousand dollars, one million as has been stated goes in the ship with you to Cadiz, and the remainder of the Andalusian demand would require between three and four millions of dollars more. Here, therefore, there are not less than three-and-twenty millions of dollars, of which near sixteen millions for Spain and Portugal required to be suddenly drawn from the British treasury."

" In addition to this drain it is also to be considered that the British armies are at the same moment sent forth in aid of the same cause, and that every article of expence to be incurred by them on foreign service in whatever country they may be employed, must be defrayed by remittances in silver."*—" You will be particularly careful in entering upon the explanation with the junta of Seville, to avoid any appearance of a desire to overrate the merit and value of the exertions now making by Great Britain in favour of the Spanish nation, or to lay the ground for restraining or limiting those exertions within any other bounds than those which are prescribed by the limits of the actual means of the country."

Mr. Canning to Mr. Stuart.

July 27, 1808.

" Already the deputy from Coruna has added to his original

* Note by Editor.—Nevertheless sir John Moore had only £25,000 in his military chest, and sir David Baird only £8,000 which were given him by sir John Moore.

Admiral De Courcy to Mr. Stuart, October 21, 1808.

" Mr. Frere will have told you that the Semiramis has brought a million of dollars in order to lie at his disposal, besides £50,000 in dollars, which are to be presented to the army of the marquis of Romana."—" In the meantime the British troops remain in their transports at Coruna, uncertain whether they shall be invited to the war, and without a shilling to defray their expences."

demand for two millions of dollars, a further demand for three millions on learning from the Asturian deputies that the demand from Asturias had amounted to five millions in the first instance. Both profess in conversation to include a provision for the interests of Leon and of Old Castile in the demand. But this has not prevented a direct application from Leon."

"It is besides of no small disadvantage that the deputies from the Asturias and Gallicia having left Spain at so early a period are really not competent to furnish information or advice upon the more advanced state of things in that country."—"I have already stated to you that in applications for succours, there is an underground appearance of rivalry, which with every disposition to do every thing that can be done for Spain, imposes a necessity of perpetual caution with respect to the particular demands of each province. The Asturians having been rebuked by their constituents for not having applied for pecuniary aid as quickly as the Gallicians are bent upon repairing this fault, and the Gallician having been commended for promptitude, is ambitious of acquiring new credit by increasing the amount of his demand. Whatever the ulterior demands, these several provinces have to make, will be made with infinitely more effect through you and Mr. Hunter respectively, as they will then come accompanied with some detailed and intelligible exposition of the grounds and objects of each particular application."

Mr. Stuart's despatches to Mr. Canning.

Coruna, July 22, 1808.

"Accounts of advantages in the quarters, which from the present state of things can have little or no communication with this place, appear to be numerous in proportion as the north of Spain is barren of events agreeable to the existing government; and I am disposed to consider unauthenticated reports of success in Catalonia, Valencia, Murcia, and Andalusia, to be a mode of concealing or palliating disasters in Leon, Castile, and the Montana."

July 24, 1808.

"One thousand men, under de Ponte, is the utmost force the Asturias have yet organized or sent into the field, and the contingents of Leon are very trifling.

"Thirty thousand men, of which twenty thousand are regular troops under Blake, were united to ten thousand Castilian recruits under Cuesta. They went to Rio Seco to march against Burgos, and cut off Bessieres' retreat to France, but they lost seven thousand men at Rio Seco."

"The Estremadura army under Gallegos is at Almaraz, consisting of twenty-four thousand infantry and four thousand cavalry, but the battle of Rio Seco has cut the communication which had been before kept up to Andalusia.

Abstract of information sent to Mr. Canning by Mr. Stuart.

July 26, 1808.

"The 29th of May the inhabitants of Coruna appointed a provisional junta of forty members taken from the notables of the place, and this junta despatched circulars to the seven provinces of St. Jago, Betanços, Coruna, Mondonedo, Orense, Lugo, and Tuy, desiring that deputies from each should come to Coruña to form a junta for Gallicia entire. Seven persons came and immediately seized the government and dissolved the local junta; the troops marched to the frontier, deputies went to England, and all seemed to proceed well until contributions were demanded. Then the provinces demurred saying, their deputies were empowered only to signify their approbation of what had past, but not to seize the government, and St. Jago insisted upon sending more deputies, and having additional votes as being of more consequence. It was then arranged that two deputies from each province should be sent to Coruña with more power. The archbishop and a Mr. Friere came from St. Jago, and others were arriving when the first deputation resolved not to submit, and declared the second to be an ordinary junta, chosen for the mere purpose of raising money, and subordinate to themselves. The archbishop and the bishop of Orense refused to act in such a capacity; but a letter from the latter painting the true state of things being intercepted, he was arrested and confined in the citadel. A body of troops was sent to St. Jago, it was uncertain whether to seize the archbishop or to awe the people; but Mr. Stuart was secretly assured it was for the former purpose. The archbishop thought so also and came immediately to Coruña. This transaction was studiously concealed from the English envoy but he penetrated the secret. The people were discontented at this usurpation of the junta of seven, but the lavish succours sent to them by Mr. Canning and the presence of Mr. Stuart induced them to submit, as thinking the junta were supported by England.

" This junta of seven adopted no measures in common with any neighbouring province, but willingly entered into close alliance with the insurgents of Portugal as one independent state with another; and they withheld any share of the English supplies for the armies of Asturias and Leon.

" The archbishop was an intriguing dangerous man, and secretly wrote to Blake to march with the army against the junta, his letter being intercepted six voted to arrest him, but the seventh with the assistance of Mr. Stuart persuaded them to avoid so violent a measure as tending towards a civil commotion. Tumults however did take place, and the English naval officers were requested and consented to quell a riot, and it proved that they had more influence over the people than the junta.

" In August the archbishop was commanded to leave Coruña, he obeyed, and the bishop of Orense was after some resistance made a member of the junta."

Mr. Stuart to Mr. Canning.

" *August 7.*

" There is no common plan, and consequently no concert in their proceedings. No province shares the succour granted by Great Britain with its neighbour, although that advantage may not be useful to themselves. No gun-boats have been sent from Ferrol to protect St. Andero on the coast of Biscay, and the Asturians have in vain asked for artillery from the depots of Gallicia.

" The stores landed at Gihon, and not used by the Asturians have remained in that port and in Oviedo, although they would have afforded a reasonable relief to the army of Blake.

" The money brought by the Pluto for the province of Leon which has not raised a man and was till this moment in the hands of the French, remains unemployed in the port where it was landed. Estremadura is said to have nine thousand cavalry, which are of little service since the French quitted that province. Yet they have not sent a man to Blake who cannot prudently stir from his present position without cavalry. General Cuesta also has deprived him of six hundred horse and his flying artillery with which he has actually quitted Salamanca on his way to join the Estremadura army."

Ditto to Ditto.

(Abstract.)

" *August* 12.

" The duke of Infantado reached Blake's quarters, after escaping from France. Blake gave him his confidence and sent him to Madrid to form a council of war, and to persuade Cuesta to send two thousand cavalry to the army of Gallicia. The junta did not approve of this; they suspected Infantado as a double dealer and in the French interest.

" After Baylen, the juntas of Seville and Murcia wished to establish a despotism, differing in nothing from that of Charles III. and Charles IV. save that Florida Blanca was to be the head of a regency. But in the north they were all for liberty, and put forward the British constitution as a model. The army spoke of Infantado as regent, but the civilians disliked him. All the English guns sent out for Gallicia went by mistake to the Asturias, the succours were absurdly distributed and every thing was in confusion."

Mr. Stuart to Mr. Canning.

" *Coruna, August* 9.

" I am placed at the very extremity of the kingdom where I cannot possibly obtain any sort of information respecting other provinces, and my presence has very materially contributed to cherish the project of separation from the rest of the peninsula in the minds of the Gallicians.

" Besides the constant communication of the navy with the junta, a military mission is placed here consisting of several persons who communicate regularly with the government and the admiralty, and whose correspondence with England being a mere duplicate of my own renders the one or the other perfectly useless. The packet instead of coming weekly only arrived every fortnight, being sent to Gihon to carry home Mr. Hunter's letters, who I understand has no order to report to me!

" The admiral having no official notice of my situation here on the part of government, cannot be expected to detach vessels for the purpose of sending my despatches at a time when he is occupied in sending his own accounts of the events taking place in Spain to the admiralty.

SECTION 2.

LORD WELLESLEY'S INSTRUCTIONS TO MR. STUART.

(Extracts.)

"*January* 5, 1810.

"In return for these liberal supplies, his majesty is entitled to claim from the Portuguese government every assistance which can be afforded to the British commander and troops, a faithful and judicious application of the funds granted for the support of so large a portion of the Portuguese force, which must otherwise be supplied from the exclusive resources of Portugal."

"I am commanded to signify to you the expectation that the extraordinary efforts of his majesty's government for the aid of Portugal, and the consequent pressure upon the British resources, will be met with corresponding exertions on the part of the regency, and that all local and temporary prejudices will be submitted to the urgent necessity of placing the finances of the kingdom in that state which may render them available for its defence in the approaching danger. You will direct your immediate and vigilant attention to this most important object, nor will you refrain from offering, or even from urging, your advice on any occasion which may open the prospect of effecting any useful reduction in the civil charges, or augmentation in the revenues or military resources of the country."

"In addition to these arrangements his majesty will expect to receive regular monthly accounts of the expenditure of the sums applicable to the military charges of Portugal, under the orders issued to lord Wellington, as well as accurate returns of the state and condition of the several corps receiving British pay."——"It is also desirable that his majesty should be acquainted with the state and condition of that part of the Portuguese force which is to be maintained from the revenues of Portugal."——"The crisis demands the most unreserved confidence and communication between his majesty's ministers and the local government of the prince regent. No jealousy or suspicion should be harboured under such a pressure of common danger; the great sacrifices which we have made for the interests of our ally must not be frustrated by any consideration inferior to the main purpose of our mutual security, nor must we now hesitate to take the lead in any measures necessary to enable Portugal to contribute a just share of their own efforts and resources for the accomplishment of their own safety."

"The governing power in Spain does not derive its authority from the appointment of the sovereign, the disposition of some of its leading members is at least equivocal, and its conduct has not satisfied any expectations either of the Spanish nation or of the allies."——"In Spain, the assembly of the cortes is the only remedy to which that country can resort for the purpose of investing the government with a regular force or a national spirit, nor can any hope be entertained of a sufficient exertion of the military resources of Spain, until a governing power shall be so framed as to unite a due representation of the crown with a just security for the interests and welfare of all the estates of the realm."——

SECTION 3.

CONDUCT OF THE ENGLISH GOVERNMENT.

Lord Wellington to Mr. Stuart.

"*Viseu*, *March* 30, 1810.

"I don't understand the arrangements which government have made of the command of the troops there. I have hitherto considered them as part of this army, and from the arrangements which I made with the Spanish government they cost us nothing but their pay, and all the money procured at Cadiz for bills was applicable to the service in this country. Their instructions to general Graham alter this entirely, and they have even gone so far as to desire him to take measures to supply the Spaniards with provisions from the Mediterranean, whereas I had insisted that they should feed our troops. The first consequence of this arrangement will be, that we shall have no more money from Cadiz. I had considered the troops at Cadiz so much part of my army, that I had written to my brother to desire to have his opinion whether, if the French withdrew from Cadiz when they should attack Portugal, he thought I might bring into Portugal at least the troops which I had sent there. But I consider this now to be out of the question."

General Graham to Mr. Stuart.

" *Isla, May* 22, 1810.

" I add this note merely as a postscript to my last, to tell you that lord Liverpool has decided the doubt, by declaring this a part of lord Wellington's army, but saying it is the wish of government that though I am second in command to him I should be left here for the present. This is odd enough. I mean that it should not have been left to his judgement to decide where I was to be employed; one would think he could judge fully better according to circumstances than people in England."

No. V.

SECTION 1.

MARMONT AND DORSENNE'S OPERATIONS.

Intercepted letter from Foy to Girard, translated from the cypher.

" *Truxillo*, 20 *Août*, 1811.

" MONSIEUR LE GÉNÉRAL,—Wellington bloque Rodrigo avec quarante mille hommes; son avant garde occupe la Sierra de Francia. On assure que l'artillerie du train arrive de Porto pour faire le siège de cette place. C'est approvisionnée pour trois mois. Marmont va se porter vers le nord pour se réunir avec l'armée commandée par le général Dorsenne et attaquer l'ennemi. Ma division partira le vingt six pour passer le Tage et suivre le mouvement de Marmont. Huit mille hommes de l'armée du centre nous remplaceront à Placentia et au Pont d'Almaraz.

" Monsieur le maréchal duc de Raguse me charge de vous écrire que c'est à vous à contenir quatre mille Espagnols qui sont en ce moment réunis devant Truxillo." &c. &c.

" FOY."

Intercepted letter from general Wattier to the general commanding at Ciudad Rodrigo.

(Extract.)

" *Salamanca, September* 1, 1811.

" L'armée Espagnol de Galice, honteusement chassée de ses

positions de la Baneza et de Puente de Orvigo et poursuivie par l'avant garde au delà de Villa Franca, s'est retirée en grande hâte sur la Coruñe. Le général-en-chef après avoir nettoyé ces parages, vient ici sous six jours avec vingt-cinq mille hommes de la garde, et nous irons tous ensemble voir s'il plait à ces illustres Anglais de nous attendre, et de nous permettre de rompre quelques lances avec eux. Le duc de Raguse à qui j'envoie de vos nouvelles est autour de vous à Baños, Val de Fuentes, Placentia, &c., et nous agirons de concert avec lui."

Intercepted letter from Marmont to Girard.

" *Placencia, 7embre*, 1811.

" GÉNÉRAL,—Je vous ai écrit pour vous prier de faire passer une lettre que j'addressai au maréchal duc de Dalmatie. Les Anglais ont réuni toutes leurs forces auprès de Rodrigo, les corps Espagnols même qui étoient sur la rive gauche du Tage passent en ce moment cette rivière ; vous n'avez presque personne devant vous. Il serait extrêmement important que pendant que la presque totalité de l'armée va se porter sur Rodrigo vous puissiez faire un mouvement pour opérer une diversion utile et rapeller un portion de la force ennemie de votre côté. J'ignore quelles sont vos instructions, mais je ne doute pas que ce mouvement n'entre dans les intentions du duc de Dalmatie."

Du maréchal Marmont au général de division Foy.

" *Talavera, Octobre* 21, 1811.

" GÉNÉRAL,—Je reçois seulement dans ce moment votre lettre du 18me avec la copie de celle du général d'Aultanne. Pour instruction générale vous ne devez obéir à aucun ordre qui vous serait donné au nom du roi lorsqu'elles sont contraires à mes intentions particulières. Ne vous départez jamais de ces dispositions. L'armée de Portugal ne doit point servir aux escortes, ni à la communication de l'armée du midi,—nos troupes auront bien assez de courses à faire pour assurer la rentré de nos approvisionnemens. Le roi a paru désirer que je n'occupe point Illescas, à cause de son voisinage de Madrid ; par ce motif et plus encore en raison de l'éloignement et du service pénible des troupes, je ne veux point l'occuper. Mon intention était de ne point occuper Aranjuez ; mais puisque les ministres du roi ont pris la mésure inconsiderée d'ordonner la vente des magazins, ne perdez pas un seul instant pour envoyer un détachement occuper Aranjuez, où le préfet de Toledo fera faire le plus de biscuit possible. Prenez la même mesure pour tous les points où il y a des magazins.—Emparez vous en,—et que personne n'y touche. —L'empereur a indiqué la province de Toledo et non la préfecture ; ainsi ce sont les réssources de toute la province qui nous sont affectés.—Emparez vous en,—et que le préfet administre tous le pays. Dites bien au préfet qu'à quelque titre que ce soit aucun des réssources en blé, argent de quelque source qu'elles prévien-nent ne doit être distraits pour Madrid, et qu'elles doivent toutes être conservés pour l'armée de Portugal. À la fin du mois la division de dragons arrivera dans les environs de Tolede.—J'espère qu'elle éloignera les guerillas. Dans le cas ou ils resteroient dans le voisinage on leur donnera la chasse. Voyez à obtenir du préfet de Tolede qu'il fasse un effort extraordinaire pour envoyer à Talavera le blé et l'orge qui lui ont été demandés, attendu que comme ici on est obligé de faire des expéditions en avant, nous sommes dans un besoin très pressant. Je désirerois rentrer dans la possession de tout le blé qui a été vendu. On renverroit les acheteurs par devant le gouvernement Espagnol pour être in-demnisées,—s'il y a possibilité engagez le préfet à prendre des mesures conservatoires en attendant que je prenne un arrête à cet égard sur le rapport que vous me ferez. Je me rends à Madrid où je passerai deux jours dans l'espérance d'éclairer le roi sur la conduite que ses véritables intérêts lui commandent de tenir envers l'armée française. De là je me rends à Tolede. Je n'ai pas besoin de vous recommander, général, d'envoyer à Aranjuez un officier sage et ferme, qui exécute ponctuellement les ordres qui lui seroient donnés, qui se fasse obéir et qui mette le plus grand soin à faire respecter l'habitation du roi."

Intercepted letter in cypher from general Montbrun to the governor of Ciudad Rodrigo.

Val de Fuentes, Septembre, 1811.

Je reçu le — du courant, mon cher général votre réponse du — à la lettre que je vous écrivis le —, et je m'empressai d'en commu-niquer le continue à S. E. le maréchal duc de Ragusa, qui me charge de me mettre en communication avec vous. Je m'en acquitterai avec plaisir puisque c'en est toujours un nouveau pour moi de récevoir de vos nouvelles. Je vous annonce qu'un appro-visionnement très considérable se prépare à Salamanque par les soins du général-en-chef Dorsenne, le maréchal, sur lequel vous pouvez compter aussi fait des preparatifs pour vous envoyer des vivres. Tous les convois partiront sous bonne escorte, et se mettront en marche d'après ce que je presume du — au — du courant au plus tard. Dans tous les cas ne vous impatientez pas. Nous sommes prêts à venir à votre sécours de toutes les manières. Vous ne sauriez trop de votre côté nous mettre au courant de la force de la position et enfin vous ne pourriez nous donner trop de détails sur l'armée Anglo-Portugaise.

Je reçois à l'instant le billet que vouz avez écrit hier au général Boyer, par lequel vous nous faites connoître que d'après tous les renseignemens que vouz avez obtenus, vouz croyez que les sept divisions Anglaises sont dans vos parages. Il importe de s'en assurer positivement de connoître leur position, et, s'il est possible, leur composition. Il parait que vous n'avez pas beaucoup de monde dans votre place sur qui vous puissiez compter. Proposez à l'homme que je vous envoie d'aller reconnoître les Anglais à Gallegos et Fuente Guinaldo, et de révenir par El Bodon, et vous me le renverriez ensuite. Dites lui que je le paierai bien s'il veut faire cette tournée, mais s'il s'y refuse je vous prie de ne pas l'y contraindre. &c., &c.

General Walker to lord Wellington.

"*Coruna, September* 4, 1811.

"I saw the whole of the troops with him (general Abadia) in and about a league in front of Astorga, having their advanced posts on the Esla, the whole not amounting to above seven thousand men, independent of a reserve of about fifteen hundred near Foncebadon and Bembibre or on the road from Lugo. The force of the enemy in his front when collected being estimated at about thirteen thousand men. The wretched situation of the Gallician troops, in want almost of every thing, one third part at least without shoes, and dependent on the precarious subsistence that can day by day be collected, certainly does credit to their patience and good inclination."

——"In consequence of this movement, (Abadia's retreat,) the great road by Manzanal and Bembibre being left open or nearly so, the French pushed forward on it so rapidly that shortly after my arrival here (Coruña) intelligence was received of their having got possession of the important pass of Villa Franca, and that the Gallician troops thus cut off from it, had been obliged to make their retreat by the Valdes Orres. Without any correct information of the force of the enemy, and the entrance of Gallicia thus left entirely in his hands, a very considerable alarm was for some time occasioned here, of which I took every advantage to urge upon the junta the necessity of a full compliance with the recommendation and wishes of the general to enable him to put the troops in such a state of equipment as might render them, either for defence or attack, in every way disposable in his hands; and at the same time to put Coruña into temporary security by withdrawing to it all the guns (amounting to no less than fifteen hundred) of the indefensible arsenal of Ferrol, which would otherwise become a sure depôt for the enemy in any attack he might contemplate on this place, and who might not otherwise venture to bring with him heavy artillery on so distant an excursion."

SECTION 2.

Official letters from the prince of Neufchatel to marshal Marmont, extracted from the duke of Rovigo's Memoirs.

" *Paris, le* 21 *Novembre*, 1811.

" L'empereur me charge de vous faire connaître, monsieur le maréchal, que l'objet le plus important en ce moment est la prise de Valence. L'empereur ordonne que vous fassiez partir un corps de troupes qui, réuni aux forces que le roi détachera de l'armée du centre, se dirige sur Valence pour appuyer l'armée du maréchal Suchet jusqu'à ce qu'on soit maître de cette place.

" Faites exécuter sans délai cette disposition de concert avec S. M. le roi d'Espagne, et instruisez-moi de ce que vous aurez fait a cet égard. Nous sommes instruits que les Anglais ont vingt mille malades, et qu'ils n'ont pas vingt mille hommes sous les armes, en sorte qu'ils ne peuvent rien entreprendre; l'intention de l'empereur est donc que douze mille hommes, infanterie, cavalerie et sapeurs, marchent de suite sur Valence, que vous détachiez même trois à quatre mille hommes sur les derrières, et que vous, monsieur le maréchal, soyez en mesure de soutenir la prise de Valence. Cette place prise, le Portugal sera près de sa chute, parcequ'alors, dans la bonne saison, l'armée de Portugal sera augmentée de vingt cinq mille hommes de l'armée du midi et de quinze mille du corps du général Reille, de manière à réunir plus de quatre-vingt mille hommes. Dans cette situation, vous recevriez l'ordre de vous porter sur Elvas, et de vous emparer de tout l'Alemtejo dans le même temps que l'armée du nord se porterait sur la Coa avec une armée de quarantre mille hommes. L'équipage de pont qui existe à Badajoz servirait à jeter des ponts sur le Tage; l'ennemi serait hors d'état de rien opposer à une pareille force, qui offre toutes les chances de succès sans presenter aucun danger. C'est donc Valence qu'il faut prendre. Le 6 Novembre nous étions maîtres d'un faubourg; il y a lien d'espérer que la place prise en Décembre, ce qui vous mettrait, monsieur le duc, à portée de vous trouver devant Elvas dans le courant de Janvier. Envoyez moi votre avis sur ce plan d'opérations, afin qu'après avoir reçu l'avis de la prise de Valence, l'empereur puisse vous donner des ordres positifs.

"Le prince de Wagram et de Neuchâtel, major-général."

(Signé) "ALEXANDRE."

"*Paris, le* 15 *Février*, 1812.

"Sa majesté n'est pas satisfaite de la direction que vous donnez à la guerre. Vouz avez la supériorité sur l'ennemi, et au lieu de prendre l'initiative, vous ne cessez de la reçevoir. Quand le général Hill marche snr l'armée du midi avec quinze mille hommes c'est ce qui peut vous arriver de plus heureux; cette armée est assez forte et assez bien organisée pour ne rien craindre d'armée Anglaise, aurait-elle quatre ou cinq divisions réunies.

"Aujourd'-hui l'ennemi suppose que vous allez faire le siège de Rodrigo; il approche le général Hill de sa droite afin de pouvoir le faire venir à lui à grandes marches, et vous livrer bataille réunis, si vous voulez reprendre Rodrigo. C'est donc au duc de Dalmatie à tenir vingt mille hommes pour le contenir et l'empêcher de faire ce mouvement, et si général Hill passe le Tage, de se porter à sa suite, ou dans l'Alemtejo. Vous avez le double de la lettre que l'empereur m'a ordonné d'écrire au duc de Dalmatie le 10 de ce mois, en réponse à la demande qu'il vous avait faite de porter des troupes dans le midi; c'est vous, monsieur le maréchal, qui deviez lui écrire pour lui demander de porter un grand corps de troupes vers la Guadiana, pour maintenir le général Hill dans le midi et l'empêcher de se réunir à lord Wellington.... Les Anglais connaîssent assez l'honneur français pour comprendre que ce succès (la prise de Rodrigo) peut devenir un affront pour eux, et qu'au lieu d'améliorer leur position, l'occupation de Ciudad-Rodrigo les met dans l'obligation de défendre cette place. Ils nous rendent maîtres du choix du champ de bataille, puisque vous les forcez à venir au sécours de cette place et à combattre dans une position si loin de la mer....Je ne puis que vous répéter les ordres de l'empereur. Prenez votre quartier-général à Salamanque, travaillez avec activité à fortifier cette ville, réunissez-y un nouvel équipage du siège pour servir à armer la ville, formez-y des approvisionnemens, faites faire tous les jours le coup de fusil avec les Anglais, placez deux fortes avant gardes qui menacent, l'une Rodrigo, et l'autre Almeida; menacez les autres directions sur la frontière de Portugal, envoyez des partis qui ravagent quelques villages, enfin employez tout ce qui peut tenir l'ennemie sur le qui-vive. Faites réparer les routes de Porto et d'Almeida. Tenez votre armée vers Toro, Benavente. La province d'Avila a même de bonnes parties où l'on trouverait des ressources. Dans cette situation qui est aussi simple que formidable, vous reposez vos troupes, vous formez des magasins, et avec de simples démonstrations bien combinées, qui mettent vos avant-postes à même de tirer journellement des coups de fusil avec l'ennemi, vous aurez barre sur les Anglais, qui ne pourront vous observer.... Ce n'est donc pas à vous, monsieur le duc, à vous disséminer en faveur de l'armée du midi. Lorsque vous avez été prendre le commandement de votre armée elle venait d'éprouver un échec par sa retraite de Portugal; ce pays était ravagé, les hôpitaux et les magasins de l'ennemi étaient à Lisbonne; vos troupes étaient fatiguées, dégoutées par les marches forcées, sans artillerie, sans train d'equipages. Badajoz était attaqué depuis long temps; une bataille dans le midi n'avait pu faire lever le siège de cette place. Que deviez vous faire alors? Vous portez sur Almeida pour menacer Lisbonne? Non, parceque votre armée n'avait pas d'artillerie, pas de train d'équipages, et qu'elle était fatiguée. L'ennemi à cette position, n'aurait pas cru à cette menace; il aurait laissé approcher jusqu'à Coimbre, aurait près Badajos, et ensuite serait venu sur vous. Vous avez donc fait à cette époque ce qu'il fallait faire; vous avez marché rapidement au secours de Badajoz; l'ennemi avait barre sur vous, et l'art de la guerre était de vous y commettre. Le siège a été levé, et l'ennemi est rentré en Portugal; c'est ce qu'il y avait à faire. .... Dans ce moment, monsieur le duc, votre position est simple et claire, et ne demande pas de combinaisons d'esprit. Placez vos troupes de manière qu'en quatre marches elles puissent se réunir et se grouper sur Salamanque; ayez-y votre quartier-général; que vos ordres, vos dispositions annoncent à l'ennemi que la grosse artillerie arrive à Salamanque, que vous y former des magasins.....Si Wellington se dirige sur Badajoz, laissez le aller; réunissez aussitôt votre armée, et marcher droit sur Almeida; poussez des partis sur Coïmbre, et soyez persuadé que Wellington reviendra bien vîte sur vous.

Ecrivez au duc de Dalmatie et sollicitez le roi de lui écrire également, pour qu'il exécute les ordres impératifs que je lui donne, de porter un corps de vingt mille hommes pour forcer le général Hill à rester sur la rive gauche du Tage. Ne pensez donc plus, monsieur le maréchal, à aller dans le midi et marchez droit sur le Portugal, si lord Wellington fait la faute de se porter sur la rive gauche du Tage······ Profitez du moment où vos troupes se réunissent pour bien organiser et mettre de l'ordre dans le nord. Qu'on travaille jour et nuit à fortifier Salamanque qu'on y fasse venir de grosses pièces, qu'on fasse l'équipage de siège; enfin qu'on forme des magasins de subsistances. Vous sentirez, monsieur le maréchal, qu'en suivant ces directions et en mettant pour les exécuter toute l'activité convenable, vous tiendrez l'ennemi en échec······ En recevant l'initiative au lieu de la donner, en ne songeant qu' à l'armée du midi qui n'a pas besoin de vous, puisqu'elle est forte de quatre-vingt mille hommes des meilleures troupes de l'Europe, en ayant des sollicitudes pour les pays qui ne sont pas sous votre commandement et abandonnant les Asturies et les provinces qui vous regardent, un combat que vous éprouveriez serait une calamité qui se ferait sentir dans toute l'Espagne. Un échec de l'armée du midi la conduirait sur Madrid ou sur Valence et ne serait pas de même nature.

" Je vous le répète, vous êtes le maître de conserver barre sur lord Wellington, en placant votre quartier-général à Salamanque, en occupant en force cette position, et poussant de fortes reconnaissances sur les débouches. Je ne pourrais que vous rédire ce que je vous ai déjà expliqué ci-dessus. Si Badajoz était cerné seulement par deux ou trois divisions Anglaises, le duc de Dalmatie le débloquerait; mais alors lord Wellington, affaibli, vous mettrait à même de vous porter dans l'intérieur du Portugal, ce qui secourrait plus efficacement Badajoz que toute autre opération······ Je donne l'ordre que tout ce qu'il sera possible de fournir vous soit fourni pour completer votre artillerie et pour armer Salamanque. Vingt-quatre heures après la réception de cette lettre l'empereur pense que vous partirez pour Salamanque, à moins d'événemens inattendus; que vous changerez une avant-garde d'occuper les débouches sur Rodrigo, et une autre sur Almeida; que vous aurez dans la main au moins la valeur d'une division; que vous ferez revenir la cavalerie et artillerie qui sont à la division du Tage······Réunissez surtout votre cavalerie, dont vous n'avez pas de trop et donc vous avez tant de besoin····"

Valladolid, le 23 *Février*, 1812.

Au Prince de Neuchâtel.

Monseigneur,—J'ignore si sa majesté aura daigné accueillir d'une manière favorable la demande que j'ai eu l'honneur d'adresser à votre altesse pour supplier l'empereur de me permettre de faire sous ses yeux la campagne qui va s'ouvrir; mais qu'elle que soit sa décision, je regarde comme mon devoir de lui faire connaître, au moment où il semble prêt à s'éloigner, la situation des choses dans cette partie de l'Espagne.

" D'après les derniers arrangemens arrêtés par sa majesté, l'armée de Portugal n'a plus le moyen de remplir la tâche qui lui est imposée, et je serais coupable, si, en ce moment, je cachais la verité. " La frontière se trouve très affaiblie par le départ des troupes qui ont été rappelées par la prise de Rodrigo, qui met l'ennemi à même d'entrer dans le cœur de la Castille en commençant un mouvement offensif; ensuite par l'immense étendue de pays que l'armée est dans le devoir d'occuper, ce qui rend toujours son rassemblement lent et difficile, tandis qu'il y a peu de temps elle était toute réunie et disponible.

" Les sept divisions qui la composent s'éleveront, lorsqu'elles auront reçu les régimens de marche annoncés, à quarante-quatre mille hommes d'infanterie environ; il faut au moins cinq mille hommes pour occuper les points fortifiés et les communications qui ne peuvent être abandonnés; il faut à peu près pareille force pour observer l'Esla et la couvrir contre l'armée de Galice, qui évidemment, dans le cas d'un mouvement offensif des Anglais, se porterait à Bénavente et à Astorga. Ainsi, à supposer que toute l'armée soit réunie entre le Duero et la Tormes, sa force ne peut s'élever qu'à trente-trois ou trente-quatre mille hommes, tandis que l'ennemi peut présenter aujourd'hui une masse de plus de soixante mille hommes, dont plus de moitié Anglais, bien outillés et bien pourvus de toutes choses: et cependant que de chances pour que les divisions du Tage se trouvent en arrière! Qu'elles n'aient pu être ralliées promptement, et soient separées de l'armée pendant les momens les plus importans de la campagne; alors la masse de nos forces réunies ne s'éleverait pas à plus de vingt-cinq mille hommes. Sa majesté suppose, il est vrai, que, dans ce pas l'armée du nord soutiendrait celle de Portugal par deux divisions; mais l'empereur peut-il être persuadé que, dans l'ordre de chose actuel, ces troupes arriveront promptement et à temps?

" L'ennemi parait en offensive: celui qui doit le combattre prépare ses moyens; celui qui doit agir hypothétiquement attend sans inquiétude, et laisse écouler en pure perte un temps precieux; l'ennemi marche à moi, je réunis mes troupes d'une manière méthodique et précise, je sais à un jour près le moment où le plus grand nombre au moins sera en ligne, à qu'elle époque les autres seront en liaison avec moi, et, d'après cet état de choses, je me détermine à agir ou à temporiser; mais ces calculs, je ne puis les faire que pour des troupes qui sont purement et simplement à mes ordes. Pour celles qui n'y sont pas, que de lenteurs! que d'incertitudes et de temps perdu. J'annonce la marche de l'ennemi et je demande des sécours, on me répond par des observations; ma lettre n'est parvenue que lentement parceque les communications sont difficiles dans ce pays; la réponse et ma réplique vient de même, et l'ennemi sera sur moi. Mais comment pourrai-je même d'avance faire des calculs raisonnables sur les mouvemens de troupes dont je ne connais ni la force ni l'emplacement? Lorsque je ne sais rien de la situation du pays ni des besoins de troupes qu'on y éprouve. Je ne puis raisonner que sur ce qui est à mes ordres, et puisque les troupes qui n'y sont pas me sont cependant nécessaires pour combattre, et sont comptées comme partie de la force que je dois opposer à l'ennemi, je puis en fausse position, et je n'ai les moyens de rien faire méthodiquement et avec connaissance de cause.

Si l'on considère combien il faut de prévoyance pour exécuter le plus petit mouvement en Espagne, on doit se convaincre de la nécessité qu'il y a de donner d'avance mille ordres préparatoires sans lesquels les mouvemens rapides sont impossibles. Ainsi les troupes du nord m'étant étrangères habituellement, et m'étant cependant indispensables pour combattre, le succès de toutes mes opérations est dépendant du plus ou du moins de prévoyance et d'activité d'un autre chef: je ne puis donc pas être responsable des événemens.

Mais il ne faut pas seulement considérer l'ètat des choses pour la défensive du nord, il faut la considérer pour celle du midi. Si lord Wellington porte six divisions sur la rive gauche du Tage le duc de Dalmatie a besoin d'un puissant secours; si dans ce cas, l'armée du nord ne fournit pas de troupes pour rélever une partie d'armée de Portugal dans quelques-uns des postes qu'elle doit évacuer alors momentanement, mais qu'il est important de tenir, et pour la sûreté du pays et pour maintenir la Galice et observer les deux divisions ennemies qui seraient sur l'Agueda, et qui feraient sans doute quelques demonstrations offensives; si dis-je l'armée du nord ne vient pas à son aide, l'armée de Portugal, trop faible, ne pourra pas faire un détachement d'une force convenable, et Badajoz tombera. Certes, il faut des ordres pour obtenir de l'armée du nord un mouvement dans cette hypothèse, et le temps utile pour agir; si on s'en tenait à des propositions et à des négociations, ce temps, qu'on ne pourrait remplacer, serait perdu en vaines discussions. Je suis autorisé à croire ce résultat.

L'armée de Portugal est en ce moment la principale armée d'Espagne; c'est à elle à couvrir l'Espagne contre les entreprises des Anglais; pour pouvoir manœuvrer, il faut qu'elle ait des points d'appui, des places, des forts, des têtes-de-pont, etc.

Il faut pour cela du matériel d'artillerie, et je n'ai ni canons ni munitions à y appliquer, tandis que les établissemens de l'armée du nord en sont tout remplis; j'en demanderai, on m'en promettra, mais en résultat je n'obtiendrai rien.

Après avoir discuté la question militaire, je dirai un mot de l'administration. Le pays donné à l'armée de Portugal a des products présumés le tiers de ceux des cinq gouvernemens.

L'armée de Portugal est beaucoup plus nombreuse que l'armée du nord; le pays qu'elle occupe est insoumis; on n'arrache rien qu'avec la force, et les troupes de l'armée du nord ont semblé prendre à tâche, en l'évacuant, d'en enlever toutes les ressources. Les autres gouvernemens, malgré les guérillas, sont encore dans la soumission, et acquittent les contributions sans qu'il soit besoin de contrainte. D'après cela il y a une immense différence dans le sort de l'une et de l'autre et comme tout doit tendre au même but, que partout ce sont les soldats de l'empereur, que tous les efforts doivent avoir pour objet le succès des opérations, ne serait-il pas juste que les ressources de tous ces pays fussent partagées proportionnellement aux besoins de chacun; et comment y parvenir sans une autorité unique?

Je crois avoir demontré que, pour une bonne défensive du nord, le général de l'armée de Portugal doit avoir toujours à ses ordres les troupes et le territoire de l'armée du nord, puisque ces troupes sont appelées à combattre avec les siennes, et que les ressources de ce territoire doivent être en partie consacrées à les entretenir.

Je passe maintenant à ce qui regarde le midi de l'Espagne. Une des tâches de l'armée de Portugal est de soutenir l'armée du midi, d'avoir l'œil sur Badajoz et de couvrir Madrid; et pour cela, il faut qu'un corps assez nombreux occupe la vallée du Tage; mais ce corps ne pourra subsister et ne pourra préparer des ressources pour d'autres troupes qui s'y rendraient pour le soutenir, s'il n'a pas un territoire productif, et ce territoire, quel autre peut-il être que l'arrondissement de l'armée du centre?

Quelle ville peut offrir des ressources et des moyens dans la vallée du Tage si ce n'est Madrid? Cependant aujourd'hui l'armée de Portugal ne possède sur le nord du Tage, qu'un désert qui ne lui offre aucune espèce de moyens, ni pour les hommes ni pour les chevaux, et elle ne rencontre de la part des autorités de Madrid, que haine, qu'animosité. L'armée du centre, qui n'est rien, possède à elle seule un territoire plus fertile, plus étendu que celui qui est accordé pour toute l'armée de Portugal; cette vallée ne peut s'exploiter faute de troupes, et tout le monde s'oppose à ce que nous en tirions des ressources. Cependant si les bords du Tage étaient évacués par suite de la disette, personne à Madrid ne voudrait en apprécier la veritable raison, et tout le monde accuserait l'armée de Portugal de découvrir cette ville.

Il existe, il faut le dire, une haine, une animosité envers les Français, qu'il est impossible d'exprimer, dans le gouvernement espagnol. Il existe un desordre à Madrid qui présente le spectacle le plus révoltant. Si les subsistances employées en de fausses consommations dans cette ville eussent été consacrées à former un magasin de ressources pour l'armée de Portugal, les troupes qui sont sur le Tage seraient dans l'abondance et pourvues pour long-temps; on consomme 22 mille rations par jour à Madrid, et il n'y a pas 3,000 hommes: c'est qu'on donne et laisse prendre à tout le monde, excepté à ceux qui servent. Mais bien plus, je le répète, c'est un crime que d'aller prendre ce que l'armée du centre ne peut elle-même ramasser. Il est vrai qu'il parait assez conséquent que ceux qui, depuis deux ans, trompent le roi, habillent et arment chaque jour des soldats qui, au bout de deux jours, vont se joindre à nos ennemis, et semblent en vérité avoir ainsi consacré un mode régulier decrutement des bandes que nous avons sur les bras, s'occupent de leur réserver des moyens de subsistances à nos dépens.

La seule communication carrossable entre la gauche et le reste de l'armée de Portugal est par la province de Ségovie, et le mouvement des troupes et des convois ne peut avoir lieu avec facilité, parceque, quoique ce pays soit excellent et plein de ressources, les autorités de l'armée du centre refusent de prendre aucune disposition pour assurer leurs subsistances.

Si l'armée de Portugal peut être affranchie du devoir de sécourir le midi, de couvrir Madrid, elle peut se concentrer dans la Vieille-Castille, et elle s'en trouvera bien; alors tout lui devient facile; mais si elle doit au contraire remplir cette double tâche, elle ne le peut qu'en occupant la vallée du Tage, et dans cette vallée elle ne peut avoir les ressources nécessaires pour y vivre, pour y manœuvrer, pour y préparer des moyens suffisans pour toutes les troupes qu'il faudra y envoyer, qu'en possédant tout l'arrondissement de l'armée du centre et Madrid. Ce territoire doit conserver les troupes qui l'occupent à présent, afin qu'en marchant à l'ennemi, l'armée ne soit obligée de laisser personne en arrière mais qu'au contraire elle en tire quelque secours pour sa communication. Elle a besoin surtout d'être délivrée des obstacles que fait naître sans cesse un gouvernement veritablement ennemi des armes françaises; quelles que soient les bonnes intentions du roi, il parait qu'il ne peut rien contre l'intérêt et les passions de ceux qui l'environnent; il semble également que jusqu'à présent il n'a rien pu contre les désordres qui ont lieu à Madrid, contre l'anarchie qui règne à l'armée du centre. Il peut y avoir de grandes raisons en politique pour que le roi réside à Madrid, mais il y a mille raisons positives et de sûreté pour les armes françaises, qui sembleraient devoir lui faire choisir un autre séjour. Et en effet, ou le roi est général et commandant des armées, et dans ce cas il doit être au milieu des troupes, voir leurs besoins, pourvoir à tout, et être responsable; ou il est étranger à toutes les opérations, et alors, autant pour sa tranquillité personnelle que pour laisser plus de liberté dans les opérations, il doit s'éloigner du pays qui en est le théâtre et des lieux qui servent de points d'appui aux mouvemens de l'armée.

"La guerre d'Espagne est difficile dans son essence, mais cette difficulté est augmentée de beaucoup par la division des commandemens et par le grande dimunition des troupes que cette division rend encore plus funeste. Si cette division a déjà fait tant de mal, lorsque l'empereur, étant à Paris, s'occupant sans cesse de ses armées de la péninsule, pouvait en partie remédier à tout, on doit fremir du résultat infallible de ce système, suivi avec diminution de moyens, lorsque l'empereur s'eloigne de trois cents lieues.

"Monseigneur, je vous ai exposé toutes les raisons qui me semblent démontrer jusqu'à l'evidence la nécessité de réunir sous la même autorité toutes les troupes et tout le pays, depuis Bayonne jusques et y compris Madrid et la Manche; en cela, je n'ai été guidé que par mon amour ardent pour la gloire de nos armes et par ma conscience. Si l'empereur ne trouvait pas convenable d'adopter ce système j'ose le supplier de me donner un successeur dans le commandement qu'il m'avait confié. J'ai la confiance et le sentiment de pouvoir faire autant qu'un autre, mais tout restant dans la situation actuelle la charge est au-dessus de mes forces. De quelques difficultés que soit le commandement général, quelqu'imposante que soit la responsabilité qui l'accompagne, elles me paraissent beaucoup moindres que celles que ma position entraine en ce moment.

"Quelque flatteur que soit un grand commandement, il n'a de prix à mes yeux que lorsqu'il est accompagné des moyens de bienfaire: lorsque ceux-ci me sont enlevés, alors tout me paraît préférable, et mon ambition se réduit à servir en soldat. Je donnerai ma vie sans regret, mais je ne puis rester dans la cruelle position de n'avoir pour résultat de mes efforts et de mes soins de tous les momens, que la triste perspective d'attacher mon nom à des evénémens facheux et peu dignes de la gloire de nos armes.

"(Signé) Le Marechal Duc de Raguse."

Joseph to Napoleon.

Madrid, May 18, 1812.

Sire,—Il y a aujourd'hui un mois et demi que j'ai reçu la lettre du prince de Neufchatel en dâte du 16 Mars dernier, qui m'annonce que votre majesté imperiale et royale me confiait le commandement de ses armées en Espagne, et me prevenait que les généraux-en-chef des armées du Nord, de Portugal, du midi, et de l'Arragon recevaient les ordres convenables.

Depuis cette époque il m'a été impossible de remplir les intentions de V. M. imperiale et royale. Le général-en-chef de l'armée du nord s'est refusé à m'envoyer aucune rapport disant et écrivant qu'il n'avait aucun ordre à cet égard. M. le maréchal commandant en chef l'armée du midi n'a encore répondu à aucune des lettres que je lui ai écrites ou fait écrire depuis cette époque. M. le maréchal commandant en chef l'armée d'Arragon ne m'envoye aucune rapport, et reste entièrement isolé de moi. M. le maréchal commandant en chef l'armée de Portugal m'a fait beaucoup de demandes auxquelles il savait parfaitement que je ne pouvais satisfaire, comme celles des troupes de l'armée du nord, des vivres, &c. Sa conduite est tellement indécente qu'elle n'est pas concevable. V. M. I. et R. pourra en juger par mes dépêches au prince de Neufchatel.——Sire, en acceptant le commandement des armées françaises à l'époque ou je l'ai reçu, j'ai cru remplir un devoir que tous les liens qui m'attachent à V. M. I. et R. et à la France m'imposaient parceque j'ai pensé pouvoir être utile, mais j'étais persuadé que V. M. I. et R. me confiant un dépôt si precieux les généraux-en-chef s'empresseraient d'obeir à la volonté de V. M. Il n'en est pas ainsi, je m'adresse donc à elle pour qu'elle veuille bien écrire ou faire écrire aux généraux-en-chef qu'elle est sa volonté pour qu'elle leur fasse déclarer que leur désobeissance à mes ordres les mettrait dans le cas d'être renvoyés en France où ils trouveraient un juge juste mais sévère dans V. M. I. et R. Si V. majesté ne trouve pas le moyen de persuader à ces messieurs que sa volonté est que je sois obéi, je la supplie de considérer que le role auquel je suis exposé est indigne de mon caractère et du nom de V. M. Si la guerre du nord a lieu, je ne puis être utile ici qu'autant que je suis obéi, et je ne puis être obéi qu'autant que ces messieurs sauront que j'ai le droit de les remplacer; je ne puis infliger, moi, d'autre punition que celle là à un général-en-chef. Si je ne suis pas obéi, et que V. M. aille au nord, l'Espagne sera évacué honteusement par les troupes imperiales, et le nom que je porte aura présidé inutilement à cette époque désastreuse.

Le mal est grand, mais il n'est au-dessus ni de mon devouement ni de mon courage. C'est à votre majesté à les rendre efficaces par la force dont il est indispensable qu'elle m'entoure; le salut des armées impériales et de l'Espagne independent.

No. VI.

TARIFA.

[The anonymous extracts are from the memoirs and letters of different officers engaged in the siege. The Roman characters mark different sources of information.]

SECTION 1.

Number and conduct of the French.

A.

" As to the numbers of the French; the prisoners, the intercepted letters, the secret information from Chiclana, all accounts, in fact, concurred in stating that the troops employed *exceeded nine thousand men!*"

Extracts from colonel Skerrett's despatch.

" The enemy's force employed in the siege is stated at *ten thousand, probably this is in some degree exaggerated.*"

B.

" The fact of the enemy, with *eleven thousand experienced soldiers*, not having made another effort after his assault of the 31st, &c."

Lord Wellington's despatch.

" *January* 19, 1812.

" By accounts which I have from Cadiz to the 27th December, I learn that the enemy invested Tarifa with a force of *about five thousand men* on the 20th December, covering their operation against that place by another corps at Vejer."

Conduct of the French.

A.

" There was not, on the part of the leading French officer (an old lieutenant of the 94th) or of his followers, any appearance of panic or perturbation. Their advance was serene, steady, and silent, worthy of the 5th corps, of their Austrian laurels, of their '*vielles moustaches.*' "

SECTION 2.

Conduct of the Spanish soldiers.

B.

" At the assault general Copons himself was the only person who shewed his head above the parapet. The precaution of outflanking him by three companies of the 47th regiment remedied the chance of evil, which so lamentable a want of chivalry might have occasioned, but the knights of older times were probably better fed than were our poor distressed friends."

SECTION 3.

Conduct of colonel Skerrett.

A.

" It is necessary to advert to the 18-pounder mounted on the Gusmans' tower, as Southey's History contains some strange misrepresentation on the subject." " The French made the 18-pounder an early object of attack, but they did not succeed in crushing it. Unfortunately one of the spherical case shot, not precisely fitting its old and worn calibre, burst in passing over the town, and killed or wounded a person in the street. This produced some alarm and complaint amongst the inhabitants for a moment, and in the first feeling of that moment, Skerrett, with characteristic impetuosity, directed the gun to be placed '*hors de service*.' There was no ambiguity in his command, '*Let it be spiked*.'" "Had he referred the case to the commanding officer of artillery, the order would not have been executed, means would have been found to remove the first impression and tranquillize the people, without the sacrifice of the gun which might have added materially to the offensive powers of the garrison, particularly if the siege had been prolonged."

B.

"On the 29th of December, colonel Skerrett with a rare activity, dismounted a 32-pound carronade, that looked into the enemy's batteries at the distance of about four hundred yards, and he succeeded in spiking and knocking off the trunnion of an 18-pounder, borrowed from the Stately. This gun was mounted on the tower of the Gusmans."

General Campbell to lord Liverpool.

"*January* 3, 1812.

"Annexed is a letter received last night from colonel Skerrett; and, notwithstanding the despondency therein expressed, which has been equally so in other letters that I have received from him, my opinion remains the same as formerly."

A.

"At the crisis produced by Skerrett's desire to retire from the town, and desire to leave the island also, general Campbell sent express instructions that the town should not be abandoned without the concurrence of the commanding officers of artillery and engineers; and accompanied these instructions with a positive command that every officer and soldier belonging to Gibraltar should, in future, be stationed in the island, to insure at all events the preservation of that port."

SECTION 4.

Sir C. Smith's conduct.

"Smith never tolerated the idea of surrender—never admitted the possibility of defeat."

"Comprehending from the first the resources and capabilities of his post, and with a sort of intuition anticipating his assailant, he covered the weak points while he concealed its strength; and so conducted the skirmish which preceded the investment, that he, as it were, dictated the whole plan of attack, and in reality pointed out with his finger the position of the breaching battery."

"Had the dictates of his vigorous mind and enterprising spirit been duly listened to within, the defence would have been more active and more brilliant."

SECTION 5.

(Extracts.)

Lord Wellington to lord Liverpool.

"*January* 9, 1812.

"From the accounts which I have received of the place (Tarifa) it appears to me quite impossible to defend it, when the enemy will be equipped to attack it. The utmost that can be done is to hold the island contiguous to Tarifa; for which object colonel Skerrett's detachment does not appear to be necessary. I don't believe that the enemy will be able to obtain possession of the island, without which the town will be entirely useless to them, and, indeed, if they had the island as well as the town, I doubt their being able to retain these possessions, adverting to the means of attacking them with which general Ballesteros might be supplied by the garrison of Gibraltar, unless they should keep a force in the field in their neighbourhood to protect them."

Lord Wellington to major-general Cooke.

"*February* 1, 1812.

"SIR,—I have omitted to answer your letters of the 27th December and of the 7th January, relating to the correspondence which you had had, with the governor of Gibraltar, upon the conditional orders, which you had given colonel Skerrett to withdraw from Tarifa, because I conclude that you referred that correspondence to the secretary of state with whom alone it rests to decide whether it was your duty to recal colonel Skerrett, and whether you performed that duty at a proper period, and under circumstances which rendered it expedient that you should give colonel Skerrett the orders in question. From the report of colonel Skerrett and Lord Proby, and other information which I had received respecting Tarifa, I concurred in the orders that you gave to colonel Skerrett, and my opinion on that subject is not at all changed by what has occurred since. We have a right to expect that his majesty's officers and troops will perform their duty upon every occasion; but we have no right to expect that comparatively a small number would be able to hold the town of Tarifa, commanded as it is at short distances, and enfiladed in every direction, and unprovided with artillery and the walls scarcely cannon proof. The enemy, however, retired with disgrace infinitely to the honour of the brave troops who defended Tarifa, and it is useless to renew the discussion. It is necessary, however, that you should now come to an understanding with general Campbell regarding the troops which have been detached from Cadiz and this army under colonel Skerrett."

Ditto to Ditto.

" *February* 25, 1812.

" I have already, in my letter of the 1st instant, stated to you my opinion regarding Tarifa, I do not think that captain Smith's letter throws new light upon the subject. The island appears still to be the principal point to defend, and the easiest to be defended at a small expense and risk of loss. Whether the town and the hill of Santa Catalina can be made subservient to the defence of the island depends upon circumstances upon which it would be possible to decide only by having a local knowledge of the place. It is very clear to me, however, that the enemy will not attack Tarifa in this spring, and that you will not be called upon to furnish troops to garrison that place so soon as you expect. If you should be called upon either by the Spanish government or by the governor of Gibraltar you must decide the question according to the suggestions which I made to you in my despatch of the 15th instant. If you should send a detachment from Cadiz at the desire of the Spanish government for purposes connected with the operations of general Ballesteros, I conceive that the governor of Gibraltar has nothing to say to such detachments, if you should send one to Tarifa at the desire of the governor of Gibraltar, or of the Spanish government, it is better not to discuss the question whether the detachment shall or shall not obey the orders of the governor of Gibraltar. He has occupied Tarifa permanently, and he is about to improve the defences of the place which he conceives to be under his orders; but, according to all the rules of his majesty's service, the senior officer should command the whole. I have nothing to say to the division of the command of the island and town of Tarifa, which I conclude has been settled by the governor of Gibraltar."

Extract from the notes of an officer engaged in the siege.

"Though the duke of Wellington yielded to the opinions and wishes of general Cooke, colonel Skerrett, and lord Proby, yet his characteristic and never failing sagacity seems to have suggested to him a fear or a fancy, that part of the case was kept concealed. A local knowledge was necessary, not only to judge of the relation and reciprocal defences and capabilities of the town and island, but to estimate the vast importance of the post, the necessity in fact of its possession. It was my impression then, and it amounts to conviction now, that the island, particularly during the winter, half fortified as it was, and totally destitute of shelter from bombardment or from weather, could not have been maintained against an enemy in possession of the town, the suburb, and the neighbouring heights. But even if it had, by means of British bravery, resolution, and resource, been provisioned and defended, still the original and principal objects of its occupation would have been altogether frustrated, namely, the command and embarkation of supplies for Cadiz and the fostering of the patriotic flame. It is demonstrable that, had the duke of Dalmatia once become possessor of the old walls of Tarifa, every city, village, fort, and watch-tower on the Andalusian coast, would soon have displayed the banner of king Joseph, and the struggle in the south of Spain was over."

General Campbell to lord Liverpool.

"*Gibraltar, April* 2, 1812.

"My Lord,—I have the honour to acknowledge the receipt of your lordship's letter of the 8th of February last, and I beg leave to refer your lordship to the documents herewith, particularly to the report of captain Smith, royal engineers, which I trust will prove that the defence of the town of Tarifa was not taken up on slight grounds, and that the detachment from Cadiz under the orders of colonel Skerrett, together with the troops from hence which formed the garrison of the town, were never in any danger of being cut off, as their retreat would have been covered by the castle of the Guzmans, the redoubt of Santa Catalina, and the island; the two first of these points being connected by a field-work, and the whole mounting twenty-nine pieces of cannon and mortars exclusively of what remained in the town: the enemy's batteries being completely kept in check during such an operation by the island and the castle of the Guzmans. My lord, colonel Skerrett stood alone in his opinion respecting this post, and in direct opposition to my own and that of captain Smith, royal engineers, who is considered by his corps as an officer of first-rate professional abilities. Major-general Cooke must therefore have acted on the reports of the colonel when he authorised him to abandon his post, for the major-general was unacquainted with its resources: besides, my lord, I had a right to expect that troops sent to that point to assist in its defence should not be withdrawn without my consent. Had the place been lost, my lord, by such misrepresentation, it would have been attributed to any other than the real cause, and the odium would have been fixed upon me, as having taken up the position; I am happy, however, that its capability has been proved whilst it remained under my orders, and that by interposing my authority the valuable possession of Tarifa has been saved from the grasp of the enemy. I was besides deeply concerned in the fate of the place; a great quantity of military stores and provision having been embarked on that service by my authority, from a conviction that they were fully protected by this additional force.

"After the execution of a service, my lord, from which I concluded I was entitled to some consideration, it is no small mortification for me to find that my conduct should be deemed questionable; but I flatter myself that if the government of his royal highness the prince regent will do me the justice to read the annexed papers, they will perceive that if I had done less his majesty's arms must have been dishonoured. In regard to the assumption of command on that occasion, I have only to observe that, considering the post of Tarifa as a dependency of Gibraltar, having occupied it exclusively for these two years past, and that a commandant and staff were appointed from my recommendation, with salaries annexed, and this with the approbation of both governments, these circumstances, added to what I have seen on similar occasions, put it past a doubt in my mind, and colonel Skerrett having applied to me for 'precise orders,' shows that he was aware that such was the case. If, my lord, I ever had a right to exercise an authority over the post of Tarifa from what I have stated, the entry of troops from another quarter, unless actually commanded by an officer senior to myself, could not, according to the custom of our service, deprive me of it; and I have heard that the case has been referred to lord Wellington, who was of the same opinion. This, however, I only take the liberty to advance in justification of my conduct, and not in opposition to the opinion formed by the government of his royal highness the prince regent. I trust, therefore, I shall be excused in the eyes of government in declaring, without reserve, that if I had not retained the command the place would not now be in our possession, and the wants of our enemies would have been completely supplied by its affording a free communication with the states of Barbary. I have the honour to report that I have made the necessary communication with major-general Cooke, in consequence of its being the wish of government that Tarifa shall be occupied by troops from Cadiz. The major-general informs me, in answer thereto, that he has communicated with lord Wellington, as he has not received orders to that effect, nor has he the means at present to make the detachment required, and your lordship is aware that I have it not in my power to reinforce that post in case of need." &c. &c.——P. S. "Should your lordship wish any further information with respect to that post, it will be found on referring to my report made after I had visited Tarifa, where commodore Penrose and colonel sir Charles Holloway, royal engineers, accompanied me."

Extract from captain C. F. Smith's report.

"*Tarifa, December* 14, 1811.

"I do not hesitate to declare that I place the utmost reliance on the resources of the place, and consider them as such as ought to make a good and ultimately successful defence."

Ditto ditto.

"*December* 24, 1811.

"My opinion respecting the defences of this post is unalterable, and must ever remain so,—that till the island is more independent in itself, there is a necessity of fairly defending the town as an outwork."

No. VII.

STORMING OF CIUDAD RODRIGO AND BADAJOS.

[The anonymous extracts are taken from the memoirs and journals of officers engaged in, or eye-witnesses of the action described. The Roman characters mark different sources of information.]

SECTION I.—CIUDAD RODRIGO.

A.

"The duke of Wellington, standing on the top of some ruins of the convent of Francisco, pointed out to colonel Colborne and to major Napier,* commanding the storming-party of the light division, the spot where the small breach was. Having done this, he said, '*Now do you understand exactly the way you are to take so as to arrive at the breach without noise or confusion?*' He was answered, '*Yes, perfectly.*' Some one of the staff then said to major Napier, 'Why don't you load?' He answered, 'No, if we can't do the business without loading we shall not do it at all.' The duke of Wellington immediately said, 'Leave him alone.'

—— "The caçadores under colonel Elder were to carry hay-bags to throw into the ditch, but the signal of attack having been given, and the fire commencing at the great breach, the stormers would not wait for the hay-bags, which, from some confusion in the orders delivered, had not yet arrived; but from no fault of colonel Elder or his gallant regiment; they were always ready for and equal to any thing they were ordered to do.

"The troops jumped into the ditch; the '*fausse braye*' was faced with stone, so as to form a perpendicular wall about the centre of the ditch; it was scaled, and the foot of the breach was attained. Lieutenant Gurwood had gone too far to his left with the forlorn hope, and missed the entrance of the breach; he was struck down with a wound on the head, but sprang up again, and joined major Napier, captain Jones 52d regt., Mitchell 95th, Ferguson 43d, and some other officers, who at the head of the stormers were all going up the breach together."

—— "Colonel Colborne, although very badly wounded in the shoulder, formed the fifty-second on the top of the rampart, and led them against the enemy."

"The great breach was so strongly barricaded, so fiercely

* Brother to the author of this work.

defended, that the third division had not carried it, and were still bravely exerting every effort to force their way through the obstacles when colonel M'Leod of the forty-third poured a heavy flank fire upon the enemy defending it."

B.

" The third division having commenced firing, we were obliged to hurry to the attack. The forlorn hope led, we advanced rapidly across the glacis and descended into the ditch near the ravelin, under a heavy fire. We found the forlorn hope placing ladders against the face of the work, and our party turned towards them, when the engineer officer called out, ' *You are wrong, this is the way to the breach, or the fausse braye which leads to the breach you are to attack.*' "

—— " We ascended the breach of the fausse braye, and then the breach of the body of the place, without the aid of ladders."

—— " We were for a short time on the breach before we forced the entrance. A gun was stretched across the entrance, but did not impede our march. Near it some of the enemy were bayonetted, amongst the number some deserters, who were found in arms defending the breach."

—— " Major Napier was wounded at the moment when the men were checked by the heavy fire and determined resistance of the enemy about two-thirds up the ascent. It was then that the soldiers, forgetting they were not loaded, as the major had not permitted them, snapped all their firelocks."

—— " No individual could claim being the first that entered the breach; it was a simultaneous rush of about twenty or thirty. The forlorn hope was thrown in some degree behind, being engaged in fixing ladders against the face of the work, which they mistook for the point of attack.

" Upon carrying the breach, the parties moved as before directed by major Napier; that is, the fifty-second to the left, the forty-third to the right. The forty-third cleared the ramparts to the right, and drove the enemy from the places they attempted to defend, until it arrived near the great breach at a spot where the enemy's defences were overlooked. At this time the great breach had not been carried, and was powerfully defended by the enemy. The houses being on it were loop-holded, and a deep trench lined with musketry bearing directly upon it; the flanks of the breach were cut off, and the descent into the town from the ramparts at the top of it appeared considerable, so as to render it exceedingly difficult, if not impossible, to force it without some other aid than a front attack."

—— "The moment the light division storming-party arrived at the spot described, they opened a heavy enfilading fire of musketry upon the trench, which was the main defence of the great breach, and drove the enemy from it with the aid of the storming-party of the third division that now entered. I was wounded at this time, and retired a short way back on the rampart, when I saw the first explosion on the rampart near the great breach. It was in my opinion next to impossible, as I have said before, to force the great breach by a front attack as long as the enemy held their defences, but the moment the light division turned their defences the breach was instantly carried."

Abstract of the journal of general Harvey, Portuguese service.

"I stood on rising ground and watched the progress of the attack. The great breach was attacked first. At the top of it the third division opened their fire heavily, and it was returned heavily, but there was a distressing pause. The small breach was carried first, and there was one considerable explosion and two or three smaller ones on the ramparts."

SECTION 2.

BADAJOS.—ASSAULT OF PICURINA.

C.

"An engineer officer, who led the attack, told me, two days after, 'that the place never would have been taken had it not been for the intelligence of these men (a detachment from the light division) in absolutely walking round the fort, and finding out the gate, which was literally beaten down by them, and they entered at the point of the bayonet. Lieutenant Nixon of the fifty-second was shot through the body by a Frenchman a yard or two inside the gate."

D.

ASSAULT OF BADAJOS.

"For the descent of the light and fourth division into the ditch only *five ladders* were placed, and those five ladders were close to each other. The *advance* (or storming party) of the eighth division preceded that of the fourth division, and I believe that no part of the fourth division was up in time to suffer from the first great explosion, and the storming-party only had entered when that explosion took place; but observe that although the *advance* of the light division preceded the *advance* of the fourth division, I only mean by that, that the head of the light division entered the ditch sooner than the *head* of the fourth division, for the main bodies of the two divisions joined at the ladders, and were descending into the ditch at the same time.

"I consider that the centre breach at Badajos was never seriously attacked. I was not at the centre breach on the night of the assault, therefore I cannot positively assert what took place there. But there were not bodies of dead and wounded at the centre or curtain breach in the morning to indicate such an attack having been made upon it, and being in the curtain it was far retired from the troops, and the approach to it was made extremely difficult by *deep cuts*, and I think it passed unobserved except by a straggling few."

—— "I consider that '*chevaux de frise*' were placed upon the summit of the centre breach during the assault. I was there at day-break. The approach to it was extremely difficult, both from the difficulty of finding it, and from the deep holes that were before it, which to my recollection resembled the holes you see in a clay-field, where they make bricks. Another great obstruction was the fire from the faces and flanks of the two bastions, which crossed before the curtain."

Extract from a memoir by captain Barney, Chasseurs Britanniques, acting engineer at the siege.

"The explosion of the '*Bariques foudroyantes*' resembled '*fougasses*,' and I expected the bastion would have crumbled to pieces. At this moment I perceived one person in the midst of fire, who had gained the top of the breach in the face of the bastion, he seemed impelling himself forward towards the enemy in an offensive position when he sank down, apparently destroyed by the fire. On examining this breach at day-light I found a Portuguese grenadier, whom I suppose to be the person, as he lay dead the foremost on this breach."

—— "Twice the bugles sounded to retire from the breaches. The fire diminished, and passing along the glacis of the ravelin I hastened to the attack of general Picton, and found but *two ladders*, one only just long enough to reach the embrasure, and the other with several of the upper rounds destroyed. The castle was full of men, and had the enemy thrown shells among them, I do not think it could have been kept possession of. Major Burgh came to ascertain the result of the attack, and the reserves were ordered up. On coming down from the castle I met general Picton, and told him the castle was full of men, but they had not advanced into the town. He immediately ordered sorties to be made to clear the breach, and a good look-out to be kept towards Christoval."——"Passing in front of the battery where lord Wellington was, I went on the right bank of the inundation till I could cross, and going towards the breach, I was overtaken by the prince of Orange, carrying an order for colonel Barnard to occupy the breach. The enemy's fire had ceased, yet none of the storming-party knew whether we were successful or not. I told the prince I was just come from the castle, which was occupied in force. As we approached the breach the stench of burnt hair and scorched flesh was horrible, and on the crest of the glacis the dead and wounded lay in such numbers it was impossible to pass without treading on them."

"Here I also found but *three ladders*, one broken so as to render it useless. On arriving at the *curtain-breach*, some men of the light division assisted me in removing from the top *the chevaux de frise of sword-blades and pikes.*

Extract from a memoir on the escalade of St. Vincent, by captain Edward P. Hopkins, fourth regiment.

"The column halted a few yards from a breast-work surmounted with a stockade and a '*chevaux de frise*' concealing a guard-house on the covered way, and at this moment a most awful explosion took place, followed by the most tremendous peals of musketry. 'That is at the breaches,' was the whisper amongst our soldiers, and their anxiety to be led forward was intense, but their firmness and obedience were equally conspicuous. The moon now appeared. We could hear the French soldiers talking in the guard-house, and their officers were visiting the sentries. The engineer officer who preceded the column, said, '*now is the time*;' the column instantly moved to the face of the gateway. It was only at this moment that the sentry observed us, and fired his alarm-shot, which was followed by musketry. The two companies of Portuguese carrying the scaling-ladders threw them down, and deaf to the voices of their officers, made off. This occurrence did not in the least shake the zeal and steadiness of our men, who occupied immediately the space left, and shouldering the ladders moved on. We could not force the gate open, but the breast-work was instantly crowded, and the impediments cut away sufficiently to allow of two men entering abreast."——" The engineer officer was by this time killed. We had no other assistance from that corps, and the loss was most severely felt at this early period of the attack."

——" The troops were now fast filling the ditch; they had several ladders, and I shall never forget the momentary disappointment amongst the men when they found that the ladders were too short."——" The enemy took advantage of this to annoy us in every way, rolling down beams of wood, fire-balls, &c. together with an *enfilading* fire.

" We observed near us an embrasure unfurnished of artillery, its place being occupied by a gabion filled with earth. A ladder was instantly placed under its mouth, and also one at each side. This allowed three persons to ascend at once, but only one at a time could enter in at the embrasure. The first several attempts were met with instant death. The ladders were even now too short, and it was necessary for one person to assist the other by hoisting him up the embrasure." " Some shots were fired from a building in the town, and colonel Piper was sent with a party to dislodge the enemy, while general Walker, at the head of his brigade, attempted to clear the rampart to the right," &c. &c.

" The enemy retired from the building on our approach, and colonel Piper did not return to the ramparts, but moved into the body of the town. Could we have divested our minds of the real situation of the town it might have been imagined that the inhabitants were preparing for some grand fête, as all the houses in the streets and squares were brilliantly illuminated, from the top to the first floor, with numerous lamps. This illumination scene was truly remarkable, not a living creature to be seen, but a continual low buz and whisper around us, and we now and then perceived a small lattice gently open and re-shut, as if more closely to observe the singular scene of a small English party perambulating the town in good order, the bugleman at the head blowing his instrument. Some of our men and officers now fell wounded; at first we did not know where the shots came from, but soon observed they were from the sills of the doors. We soon arrived at a large church facing some grand houses, in a sort of square. The party here drew up, and it was at first proposed to take possession of this church, but that idea was abandoned. We made several prisoners leading some mules laden with loose ball-cartridges in large wicker baskets, which they stated they were conveying from the magazines to the breaches. After securing the prisoners, ammunition, &c., we moved from the square with the intention of forcing our way upon the ramparts. We went up a small street towards them, but met with such opposition as obliged us to retire with loss. We again found ourselves in the square. There an English soldier came up to us who had been confined in the jail, probably a deserter. He said our troops had attacked the castle, and had failed, but that the French troops had afterwards evacuated it. At this period rapid changes took place. Several French officers came into the square; the town belonged to the English; the great Wellington was victorious. A scene of sad confusion now took place; several French officers of rank, their wives, and children, ran into the square in a state of frenzy, holding little caskets containing their jewels and valuables, and their children in their arms. The situation of these females was dreadful; they implored our protection, and I believe this party escaped the plunder and pillage which was now unfortunately in progress. The scene that now commenced surpassed all that can be imagined; drunkenness, cruelty, and debauchery, the loss of many lives, and great destruction of property, was one boon for our victory. The officers had lost all command of their men in the town; those who had got drunk and had satisfied themselves with plunder congregated in small parties and fired down the streets. I saw an English soldier pass through the middle of the street with a French knapsack on his back; he received a shot through his hand from some of the drunkards at the top of the street; he merely turned round and said, damn them, I suppose they took me for a Frenchman. An officer of the Brunswickers, who was contending with a soldier for the possession of a canary bird, was shot dead by one of these insane drunkards. Groups of soldiers were seen in all places, and could we have forgotten the distressing part of the scene, never was there a more complete masquerade. Some dressed as monks, some as friars, some in court-dresses, many carrying furniture, cloth, provisions, money, plate from the churches; the military chest was even got at by the soldiers."

No. VIII.

SECTION 1.

ENGLISH PAPERS RELATING TO SOULT'S AND MARMONT'S OPERATIONS.

Colonel Le Mesurier, commandant of Almeida, to brigadier-general Trant.

" *Almeida, March* 28, 1812.

" When I took possession of the fortress ten days since, I found not a single gun in a state for working; either owing to the want of side-arms or the ill assortment of shot and ammunition, not a single platform was laid down, and scarcely a single embrasure opened in any part of the newly repaired fronts. My powder was partly in an outwork, partly in two buildings scarcely weather-proof, only one front of my covered way pallisaded, and the face of one of my ravelins without any revêtement whatever; the revêtement throughout the whole of the nearly repaired fronts not being more than one-third or one-fourth of its former height. Many of these defects have been remedied; we have platforms and embrasures throughout the new fronts, the guns posted with their proper side-arms and shot-piles, and with a proper assortment of ammunition in the caissons; the bulk of our powder and ordnance-cartridge being distributed in bomb proofs; we have formed a respectable entrenchment on the top of the breach of the mined ravelin, which it is proposed to arm with pallisades, but the almost total want of transport has prevented our being able to complete more than two fronts and a half of our covert way with those essential defences. From this sketch you will collect that, though the fortress is not to be walked into, it is yet far from being secure from the consequences of a resolute assault, particularly if the garrison be composed of raw and unsteady troops."

Extract from a memoir of general Trant.

" Now it so happened that on this same night Marmont had marched from Sabugal in order to attack me in Guarda; he had at the least five thousand infantry, some reports made his force seven thousand, and he had five or six hundred cavalry. My distrust of the militia with regard to the execution of precautions such as I had now adopted, had induced me at all times to have a drummer at my bed-room-door, in readiness to beat to arms; and this was most fortunately the case on the night of the 13th April, 1812, for the very first intimation I received of the enemy being near at hand was given me by my own servant, on bringing me my coffee at daybreak of the 14th. He said such was the report in the street, and that the soldiers were assembling at the alarm rendezvous in the town. I instantly beat to arms, and the beat being as instantly taken up by every drummer who heard it, Marmont, who at that very moment was with his cavalry at the very entrance of the town (quite open on the Sabugal side more than elsewhere), retired. He had cut off the outposts without their firing a shot, and, had he only dashed headlong into the town, must have captured Wilson's and my militia divisions without losing probably a single man. I was myself the first out of the town, and he was not then four hundred yards from it, retiring at a slow pace. I lost no time in forming my troops in position, and sent my few dragoons in observation. When at a couple of miles distant Marmont drew up fronting Guarda, and it turned out, as I inferred, that he expected infantry."

Lord Wellington to sir N. Trant.

"*Castello Branco, April* 17, 1812.

"Dear Sir,—I arrived here about two hours ago. Marshal Beresford received your letter of the 13th upon the road, and I received that of the 12th from general Bacellar this morning. We shall move on as soon as the troops come up: it would appear that the French are collecting more force upon the Agueda and Coa. You should take care of yourselves on Guarda if they should collect two divisions at or in the neighbourhood of Sabugal: Guarda is the most treacherous position in the country, although very necessary to hold. I should prefer to see an advanced guard upon it, and the main body on the Mondego behind. Have you saved my magazines at Celerico? I enclose a letter for the commissary there and one for don Carlos d'Espagna. Pray forward both; the former is to order forward fresh supplies to Celerico. Shew this letter to general Bacellar: I don't write to him as I have no Portuguese with me." &c. &c.

"Wellington."

Ditto to ditto.

" *Pedrogao, April* 21, 1812.

" DEAR SIR,—I have received your letter of the 15th, and you will see by mine of the 17th, written as soon as I knew that your division and that of general Wilson were on Guarda, that I expected what happened, and that I wished you to withdraw from that position. In fact, troops ought not to be put in a strong position in which they can be turned if they have not an easy retreat from it; and if you advert to that principle in war, and look at the position of Guarda, you will agree with me that it is the most treacherous position in Portugal. I can only say that, as Marmont attacked you, I am delighted that you have got off so well; which circumstance I attribute to your early decision not to hold the position, and to the good dispositions which you made for the retreat from it.

" As to your plan to surprise Marmont at Sabugal, you did not attempt to put it in execution, and it is useless to say any thing about it. I would observe, however, upon one of your principles, viz. that the magnitude of the object would justify the attempt, that in war, particularly in our situation and with such troops as we, and you in particular, command, nothing is so bad as failure and defeat. You could not have succeeded in that attempt, and you would have lost your division and that of general Wilson. I give you my opinion very freely upon your plans and operations as you have written me upon them, begging you at the same time to believe that I feel for the difficulty of your situation, and that I am perfectly satisfied that both you and general Wilson did every thing that officers should do with such circumstances, and that I attribute to you the safety of the two divisions. I shall be at Sabugal to-morrow or the next day; and I hope to see you before we shall again be more distant from each other." &c. &c.

" WELLINGTON."

SECTION 2.

FRENCH PAPERS RELATING TO SOULT'S AND MARMONT'S OPERATIONS.

Translated. Extracts from Soult's intercepted despatches.

" *Seville, April* 14, 1812.

" I enclose copies of a letter from the duke of Ragusa, dated

22d February, and another from general Foy, dated Velvis de Jara, 28th February, which announced positively that three divisions of infantry and one division of cavalry of the army of Portugal would join me if Badajos was attacked; but those divisions, fifteen days afterwards, marched into Old Castile at the moment when they knew that all the English army was moving upon Badajos, and at the instant when I, in virtue of your highness's (Berthier's) orders, had sent five regiments of infantry and two of cavalry, and my skeleton regiments to Talavera. It is certain that if those three divisions had remained in the valley of the Tagus the enemy would not have attacked Badajos, where they could have been fought to advantage.

"The contrary has arrived. I have been left to my own forces, which have been reduced by fifteen thousand men, as I have stated above, and not even a military demonstration has been made, much less succour, because the attack on Beira could not influence the siege, and did not."—"Badajos fell by a '*coup de fortune*,' because it was not in human foresight to think that five thousand men defending the breach successfully, would suffer a surprise on a point where no attack was directed, and when I was within a few marches with twenty-four thousand men strongly organized.

"If I had received your highness's letter when I was before the English, I might, although unaided by M. Marmont and numerically inferior, have given battle to save Badajos; but I should probably have been wrong, and I should have lost the force I left in Andalusia, where not only Seville was invested and my communications cut, but a general insurrection was commencing. Happily I heard in time of the fall of Badajos; but I have not even yet opened my communications with New Castile, Grenada, or Malaga. I have, however, prepared in time to deliver a great battle on my own ground—Andalusia.

"The emperor, of course, cannot foresee all things, and in his orders naturally meant that his generals should act with discretion on such occasions; hence if Marmont had only made demonstrations on Beira with a part of his army, and had crossed the Tagus to unite with my troops, the siege would have been raised before the breach was practicable. Marmont had nothing before him, and he knew Wellington had passed the Guadiana and commenced the siege: I say that all the English army had passed the Guadiana, and this was its disposition.

"General Graham commanding the first corps of observation

had the sixth and seventh divisions of infantry and Cotton's cavalry two thousand five hundred strong, with thirty guns. This corps pushed my right wing to Granja and Azagua at the '*debouche*' of Fuente Ovejuna, while Hill, with the second and third divisions, twelve hundred cavalry under Erskine, and twelve guns, moved on my extreme right in the direction of La Lerena from Belendenzer.

"Wellington carried on the siege in person, having the fourth division, part of the third division, a Portuguese corps; and I am assured he has also two or three thousand Spaniards, which made round the place eighteen thousand men.

"The fifth division remained at first on the right bank of the Tagus with a brigade of cavalry; but they were also called up and came to Elvas on the 4th or 5th of April. The best accounts gave Wellington thirty thousand men, and some make him as high as forty thousand, at the moment when I was before him at Villalba; and if the army of Portugal had joined me with twenty-five thousand men, Badajos would have been saved or retaken: and a great victory would throw the English back into their lines. I was not strong enough alone; and besides the loss I should have suffered, I could not have got back in time to save my troops in Andalusia.

"The English did not hide their knowledge that Marmont was gathering in Leon; but they knew he had no battering-train, and that the wasted state of the country would not permit him to penetrate far into Portugal. So measured, indeed, were their operations, that it is to be supposed they had intercepted some despatch which explained the system of operation and the irresolution of Marmont."

"Your highness tells me I 'should not have left Hill after his last movement in December on Estremadura, nor have permitted him to take my magazines:' I say he has taken nothing from me. The advanced guard at Merida lived from day to day on what was sent to them from La Lerena. I know not if some of this has fallen into his hands; but it can be but little. But at this period Wellington wished to besiege Badajos, and only suspended it because of the rain, which would not let him move his artillery, and because three divisions of the army of Portugal were in the valley of the Tagus. If they had remained the siege would not have been undertaken, and Marmont knew this; for on the 22d February he wrote to me to say that, independent of those three divisions under Foy, which he destined to send to the aid of Badajos, he himself would act so as to surmount the difficulties which the state of his munitions opposed to his resolution to defeat the enemy's projects."

" If your highness looks at the states of the 14th April, you will see that I had not, as you suppose by your letter of 19th February, forty thousand men; I had only thirty-five thousand, including the garrison of Badajos, out of which I had brought with me twenty-four thousand, the rest being employed before Cadiz at Seville, in Grenada and Murcia, and against Ballesteros. You must consider that fifteen days before the English passed the Guadiana I had sent five regiments of infantry, two of cavalry, and many skeletons upon Talavera, in all fifteen thousand men; and since two years I have sent many other skeleton regiments to France, being more than fifteen thousand men changing their destination or worn out, without having yet received the troops from the interior destined for my army, although these are borne on the states: besides which, I have four thousand men unfit for the field, who ought to go to France, but I am forced to employ them in the posts. Ballesteros has, besides the army of Murcia, ten thousand men; and in Murcia the Spaniards are strong, because the fugitives from Valencia had joined two divisions which had not been engaged there, and thus, including the garrisons of Alicant and Carthagena, they had fifteen thousand men. Suchet's operations have certainly produced great results, but for *the moment* have hurt me, because all who fly from him come back upon my left flank at a moment when I have only three battalions and four hundred cavalry to oppose them at Grenada only. I have sent my brother there in haste to support them. The English, Portuguese, and Spanish at Cadiz, Gibraltar, and on the ocean could also at any time descend with ten or twelve thousand men on any part of my line, and I want at least as many to oppose them and guard my posts. I may therefore be accused of having carried too many men to the relief of Badajos; and that army was not strong enough, though excellent in quality.

I cannot hold twenty thousand men, as your highness desires, on the Guadiana, unless I am reinforced, especially since the fall of Badajos; but as soon as I know the English have repassed that river, all my right under d'Erlon, *i. e.* nine regiments of infantry and four of cavalry, and twelve guns, shall march into the interior of Estremadura, and occupy Medellin, Villafranca, and even Merida, and, if possible, hold in check the garrison of

Badajos and the English corps left in Alemtejo, and so prevent any grand movement up the valley of the Tagus against Madrid.

"Since my return here the demonstrations of the English appear directed to invade Andalusia so far as to have obliged me to unfurnish many points, and even in a manner raise the siege of Cadiz, Graham has come to Llerena, and Cotton to Berlanga, where we had an affair and lost sixty men." "I have ordered d'Erlon to repass the Guadalquivir and come to me to fight the English if they advance; if not, he shall go on again, and I think the English general will not commit the fault of entering the mountains, though he says he will!"

No. IX.

SECTION 1.

SUMMARY OF THE FORCE OF THE ANGLO-PORTUGUESE ARMY AT DIFFERENT PERIODS, EXCLUSIVE OF DRUMMERS AND ARTILLERY-MEN.

October 1, 1811.—Cavalry.

	Present.	Sick.	Command.	Prisoners.	Total.
British	3571	1114	947	298	5930
Portuguese	1373	256	1140	—	2769
Total Cavalry	4944	1370	2087	298	8699

Infantry.

	Present.	Sick.	Command.	Prisoners.	Total.
British	29530	17974	2663	1684	51851
Portuguese	23689	6009	1707	75	31480
Total Infantry	53219	23983	4370	1759	83331

General Total, including serjeants, 58263 sabres and bayonets in the field.

January 8, 1812.—Cavalry.

	Present.	Sick.	Command.	Prisoners.	Total.
British	4949	841	741	—	6531
Portuguese	613	43	275	—	391
Total Cavalry	5562	884	1016	—	7462

Infantry.

	Present.	Sick.	Command.	Prisoners.	Total.
British	30222	11414	2827	—	14463
Portuguese	20455	4849	2360	51	27715
Total Infantry	50677	16263	5187	51	72178

General Total, including sergeants, 56239 sabres and bayonets in the field.

Note. The abuses and desertions in the Portuguese cavalry had been so great that one division was suppressed.

April 5, 1812.—Cavalry.

	Present.		Sick.		Command.		Prisoners.		Total.
British	4299	....	564	....	755	....	3	....	6048
Portuguese ..	347	....	9	....	492	....	—	....	808
Total Cavalry	4646	....	573	....	1247	....	3	....	6896

Infantry.

British	26897	....	11452	....	2779	....	2	....	40703
Portuguese ..	20224	....	5532	....	1507	....	18	....	27281
Total Infantry	47121	....	16984	....	4286	....	20	....	67984

Sabres and bayonets	51767
Field artillery-men	1980
Gunners in the batteries	900
General Total	54647

Note. The heavy German cavalry were in the rear at Estremos, and two Portuguese regiments were in Abrantes.

TROOPS EMPLOYED AT THE SIEGE OF BADAJOS, APRIL, 1812.

British.

Light division	2679	
Third division	2882	
Fourth division........................	2579	
Fifth division	2896	
		11036

Portuguese.

Hamilton's division	4685	
Light division	858	
Third division	976	
Fourth division........................	2384	
Fifth division	1845	
		10748
Total		21,784

ALLIED COVERING CORPS IN APRIL, 1812.

Cavalry under general Hill.—Left Wing.

British	783	
Portuguese	347	
		1130

Infantry ditto.

British	6156	
Portuguese	2385	
		8541
Total under general Hill............		9671

Cavalry under general Graham.—Right Wing.

British	3517	
Portuguese	—	
		3517

Infantry ditto.

British	10154	
Portuguese	5896	
		16050
Total under general Graham		19567

General Total of the covering army, exclusive of the artillerymen and the heavy German cavalry, who remained in the rear at Estremos, 29238 sabres and bayonets.

SECTION 2.

SUMMARY OF THE ANGLO-PORTUGUESE LOSSES AT BADAJOS, 1812.

ASSAULT.

British Loss.

	Killed.	Wounded.
Generals	—	5
Staff	1	11
	Officers.	Soldiers.
Artillery	2	20
Engineers	5	5
Total	7	25

Light division.—*Line.*

	Officers.	Soldiers.	Total.	
43d	18	329	347	670
52d	18	305	323	
95th, 1st bat.	14	179	193	
95th, 3d bat.	8	56	64	
Total	58	849	927	

Third division.

5th	4	41	45	490
45th	14	83	97	
74th	7	47	54	
77th	3	10	13	
83d	8	62	70	
88th	10	135	145	
94th	2	154	173	
	48	442	490	

Fourth division.

	Officers.	Soldiers.	Total.
7th	17	163	180
23d	17	134	151
27th	15	170	185
40th	16	124	140
48th	19	154	173
	84	745	829

Fifth division.

1st	2	—	2
4th	17	213	230
9th	—	—	—
30th	6	126	132
38th	5	37	42
44th	9	95	104
	39	471	510
60th *	4	30	34
Brunswick Oels *	2	33	35

Total British loss at the assault.

	Officers.	Sergeants.	Soldiers.		Total.
	51	40	560	killed	3022
	213	153	1983	wounded	
	—	1	21	missing	
Total Portuguese loss at the assault.					
	8	6	141	killed	730
	45	32	468	wounded	
	—	—	30	missing	
Grand Total	317	232	3203		3752

* These regiments were attached by companies to the third, fourth, and fifth divisions.

British loss during the whole siege.

	Officers.		Sergeants.		Soldiers.		Total.
	60	......	45	......	715	killed	3860
	251	......	178	......	2578	wounded	
	—	......	1	......	32	missing	

Portuguese loss during the whole siege.

	12	......	6	......	137	killed	965
	55	......	38	......	687	wounded	
	—	......	—	......	30	missing	
General Total	378		268		4179		4825

SECTION 3.—SUMMARY OF THE FRENCH FORCE IN SPAIN AT DIFFERENT PERIODS, EXTRACTED FROM THE IMPERIAL MUSTER-ROLLS.

	Under arms.		Detached.		Absent.		Effective.	
	Men.	Horses.	Men.	Horses.	Hospital.	Pris.	Men.	Horses.
August 1811	262,276	37,669	50,502	10,869	41,452	00	354,418	35,348 13,190 train
Reinforcements in March.....	17,361	3,929	81	,,	981	00	18,423	3,929
Total	279,637	41,598	50,583	10,869	42,433	00	372,841	52,467
January 1812 ..	258,156	41,049	22,805	5,434	42,056	00	324,933	42,348
April 1812	240,654	36,590	12,224	3,814	33,504	,,	286,440	40,461
Reserve at Bayonne	4,038	157	36	35	865	,,	4,939	192
Total	244,692	36,747	12,260	3,849	34,369	,,	291,379	40,653

Observation.—In September 1811 an army of reserve, consisting of two divisions of infantry and one of cavalry, with artillery, in all 20,287 under arms, was formed for the armée du midi.

1st August, 1811.

	Under arms.		Detached.			Effective.		
	Men.	Horses.	Men.	Horses.	Hospital.	Men.	Horses.	
Armee du Midi....	50,597	10,008	32,043	5,359	11,836	94,508	1,195 / 3,413	4,608
du centre	16,540	3,729	391	64	1,781	18,712	3,236 / 557	3,793
de Portugal......	38,392	5,826	7,901	3,100	10,424	56,733	6,692 / 2,234	8,926
d'Aragon	45,102	5,718	1,397	388	5,458	51,957	3,667 / 2,439	6,106
du Nord	88,092	11,020	7,617	1,805	6,654	102,413	3,531 / 4,294	12,825
de Catalogne	23,553	1,368	1,153	153	5,305	30,095	1,268 / 253	1,521
Total...........	262,276	37,669	50,502	10,869	41,452	354,418	35,348 / 13,190	48,538
Reinforcements ...	17,361	3,929	81	,,	981	18,423	3,929	
General total..	279,637	41,598	50,583	10,869	42,433	372,841	39,277 / 13,190	52,467

STATE OF THE IMPERIAL GUARDS.

15th August, 1811.

Under arms.		Detached.			Effective.	
Men.	Horses.	Men.	Horses.	Hospital.	Men.	Horses.
12,797	3,193	3,944	14	1,189	17,613	3,179

STATE OF THE GARRISON OF BADAJOS.

16th May, 1811.—Fifth battalion.

2,887	239	361	,,	380	3,725	239

1st March, 1812.

4,393	44	,,	,,	478	5,034	44

STATE OF THE GARRISON OF CIUDAD RODRIGO.

15th December, 1811.

1,764	19	,,	,,	130	1,956	19

Return of numbers, by armies, 1st October, 1811.

	Under arms.		Detached.		Absent.		Effective.		
	Men.	Horses.	Men.	Horses.	Hospital.	Pris.	Men.	Horses.	
Armee du Midi	66,912	11,757	7,539	2,232	13,398	,,	88,033	9,251 / train 3,393	12,644
du centre......	19,125	6,262	511	84	1,685	,,	21,321	5,196 / 553	5,749
de Portugal ..	50,167	11,662	1,283	858	10,012	,,	61,462	6,909 / 4,706	11,615
d'Aragon	28,966	5,303	6,583	308	4,424	,,	39,953	3,322 / 1,960	5,282
du Nord........	87,913	10,821	6,201	1,069	9,414	,,	10,528	6,769 / 4,186	10,955
de Catalogne..	26,954	1,365	993	168	11,186	,,	39,241	1,150 / 289	1,439
Total........	280,017	47,270	23,110	4,717	50,119	,,	353,538		37,684
Reinforcements.	9,232	689			1,226		10,458		516
General Total.	289,249	47,959	23,110	4,717	51,345	,,	363,996		38,200

15th April, 1812.

	Under arms.		! Detached.			Effective.	
	Men.	Horses.	Men.	Horses.	Hospital.	Men.	Horses.
Armee du Midi......	55,797	11,014	2,498	70	6,065	64,360	11,714
du centre	19,148	3,293	144	51	624	19,916	4,044
de Portugal........	56,937	8,108	4,394	2,278	7,706	69,037	10,386
d'Aragon	14,786	3,269	2,695	658	1,467	18,948	3,927
de l'Ebre............	16,830	1,873	21	6	3,425	20,276	1,879
de Catalogne	28,924	1,259	1,163	49	5,540	35,627	1,308
du Nord	48,232	7,074	1,309	72	8,677	58,276	7,213
Total..............	240,654	36,590	12,224	3,814	33,534	286,440	40,461
Reserve a Bayonne..	4,038	157	36	35	865	4,939	192
Grand total......	244,692	36,747	12,260	3,849	34,369	291,379	40,653

END OF VOL. IV.